ILLINOIS CENTRAL COLLEGE 2

A12901 349497

WITHDRAWN

W9-BSA-398

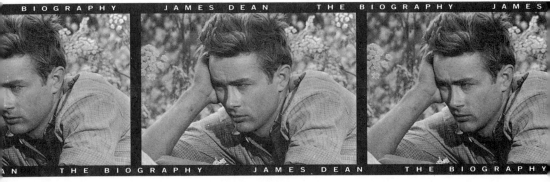

VAL HOLLEY

JAMES DEAN

The Biography

St. Martin's Griffin ✦ New York

I.C.C. LIBRARY

JAMES DEAN: THE BIOGRAPHY. Copyright © 1995 by Val Holley. All rights reserved.
Printed in the United States of America. No part of this book may be used or repro-
duced in any manner whatsoever without written permission except in the case of brief
quotations embodied in critical articles or reviews. For information, address St. Martin's
Press, 175 Fifth Avenue, New York, N.Y. 10010.

Design by Junie Lee

Library of Congress Cataloging-in-Publication Data

Holley, Val.
    James Dean : the biography / Val Holley.
      p. cm.
    ISBN 0-312-15156-X
    1. Dean, James, 1931–1955.   2. Motion picture actors and
actresses—United States—Biography.   I. Title.
PN2287.D33H55   1995
791.43'028'92—dc20   95-20000
                                                                  CIP

First St. Martin's Griffin Edition: January 1997

10 9 8 7 6 5 4 3 2 1

For Pete

Contents

Author's Note

In this biography the names of persons are given as James Dean knew them and, for this reason, many women are referred to by their maiden names. However, Adeline Nall, Dean's legendary high school speech teacher, was known as Mrs. Brookshire during the bulk of the years he knew her, and is referred to as such. Jonathan Gilmore decided to become John in later life, and he signed his book on Dean as John Gilmore.

No effort has been made to reconcile the conflicting views of Dean's masculinity or sexuality expressed by different sources. Although some acknowledged that Dean had sexual relations with both men and women, others were categorical in their insistence that he was either heterosexual or homosexual. These assertions have been allowed to stand as examples of the great variance in the images that different persons projected onto Dean.

The author was unable to verify certain stories that have circulated about Dean in recent years, and so they have been omitted from this biography. Among these was the tale of a one-night stand between Dean and Woolworth heiress Barbara Hutton, which surfaced in *Poor Little Rich Girl,* C. David Heymann's 1983 biography of Hutton (subsequently recalled by its publisher, Random House). Heymann said the biography was based on Hutton's private notebooks, although two close friends and one former husband (Cary Grant) said they never knew Hutton to keep notebooks.

Another omitted story materialized in a September 1992 *Entertainment Tonight* segment and was then elaborated in the 1992 book *James Dean: Little Boy Lost,* by Joe Hyams: that Dean spent a whopping four months in 1954 on a Salinas, California, ranch to prepare for his role in *East of Eden.* Although it is possible that Dean spent a few days at the ranch, he did not arrive in California until April 8, 1954, then spent a few days in Borrego Springs and San Francisco, and was back in Hollywood no later than May 4, the day Julie Harris arrived in California and was taken for a ride in Dean's new MG.

A number of potentially important sources were unavailable during the researching and writing of this book. The papers of Jerry Fairbanks Studios lie uncatalogued in the basement of the UCLA research library. A diary kept by the actress Pier Angeli, alleged to contain her account of her summer romance with Dean, was reported in 1993 by *Daily Variety* to have been discovered and to be the basis for a potential book-movie deal. Letters from Dean to his father have been held back by the family. A few kinescopes of Dean's live television shows remain in the hands of private collectors who were unwilling to let them be viewed. All of these could be points of departure for a future Dean biographer.

A James Dean Primer

The CBS studio at Sunset Boulevard and Gower Street in Hollywood was in a state of flux in 1951. That summer, network television shows, winding up only their second season in Hollywood, were rapidly pushing radio out the studio door. Several top programs had not been renewed for the fall, and radio actors who had enjoyed steady casting for years were advised to seek other livelihood. The confusion and nervousness in the network's radio division were proportionate to the excitement and adventure in TV production. TV's future, one successful agent was saying, would depend on the grooming of young talent coming up through the ranks, since motion picture people were too set in their ways to learn from TV.

Hot tips and gossip inevitably spilled over from the CBS studio into Ted's Auto Park next door. In those days, Ted's was not only temporary employment for struggling would-be actors; it was a lower-class version of the Beverly Hills Hotel pool, a place to be noticed and discovered. "Several boys worked there," recalled one of the parking lot's alumni. "We were all literally starving actors, ready and willing to take almost anything that came along." The wages at Ted's were a dollar an hour, before taxes. But the owner was sympathetic to his employees' situation and maintained a liberal leave policy to accommodate their casting appointments. The directors and producers who used the lot were good tippers. And they could hire you. It could be a godsend to a young nobody.

One of the boys at Ted's in the summer of 1951 was a restless twenty-year-old UCLA dropout who had lost patience with academic theater arts and was now hanging around Hollywood casting offices. Often he would ask a UCLA friend to work for him on the lot so he could go out on appointments. He would say he'd be gone four hours and then be gone all day. "And sometimes, for several days," recalled the friend. "It got so I never expected him to show up until I did see him. There were times when he didn't even have a place to sleep and slept in his car, an old jalopy he used to love to barrel around in. He would drive the hell out of it . . . and how he loved it when he had a chance to drive a real car."

One of the customers at Ted's that summer was a multitalented man in his mid-thirties who was directing *Alias Jane Doe,* a CBS summer radio show starring Lurene Tuttle. He was refined, devastatingly witty, and well-connected in performing arts circles on both coasts. "The man had dark hair, glasses, was effeminate—not obnoxiously so but obviously so," recalled another lot attendant. And he liked beautiful young men—the younger, the better.

The UCLA dropout had met many directors and producers at Ted's, but none had ever done anything for him. Then one day he parked the *Alias Jane Doe* director's car, and a spark was struck. The two went out for coffee, and the director, ever watchful for talent in combination with good looks, saw possibilities. He told the dropout he might be able to use him in *Alias Jane Doe.* Soon he did call the young man, who auditioned and was cast in a few of the episodes.

Thus the simple canonic scenario, one that was and is repeated time after time, with minor variations, in all facets of the show business industry. Simple as it was, though, it precipitated the rise to stardom of one of Hollywood's greatest legends, James Dean. Thanks to his serendipitous encounter with director Rogers Brackett, James Dean would find, many times in the year ahead, that he was in the right place at the right time when career opportunities came his way.

Rogers Brackett spent much effort introducing Dean to people who mattered in Hollywood. Soon, when Dean found himself in need of a new place to live, Brackett invited him to move into his well-appointed apartment in the Sunset Plaza, just off Sunset Boulevard. Dean's agent, Isabel Draesemer, says, "Jimmy came to me and asked whether marrying Beverly Wills [the young woman he was dating then] or moving in with Rogers Brackett would be better for his career." She knew Hollywood well enough to guess Brackett's proclivity and asked Dean if he knew what he might be in for. "I can have my own room," he explained. "But, Jimmy," Draesemer countered, "what will you do on the nights you're drunk? Fight him off?" "I can handle it," he insisted. Draesemer was not the only one to raise eyebrows at this new arrangement. "At the parking lot," said Dean's occasional substitute, "we didn't know what the relationship was, but we worried about Jimmy. He took chances—any chance that might pay off."

After Dean moved in with Brackett, he invited James Bellah, a fraternity friend from UCLA, to drop by the lavish apartment. Brackett, Bellah later reported, "flew" into the living room and offered to make Bellah a drink. "Hey, that guy's queer!" whispered a startled Bellah to Dean while the drink was being mixed. "Yeah, I know," Dean deadpanned, showing no sign of shock at Bellah's deduction.

Why would Dean accept the amenities and charms Rogers Brackett could offer? "Jimmy was an opportunist," says Isabel Draesemer. "He would latch onto anyone who could do something for him." But Brackett, beyond his usefulness, was an immensely appealing and entertaining fellow. "Dean must have been impressed with Rogers's great flair and style and, above all, by Rogers's abundant store of movie history, lore, and gossip from D. W. Griffith to Thelma Todd to Paul Bern to whoever might be the centerpiece of this morning's *scandale,*" says a close friend of Brackett. "The Rogers that Dean first encountered must have been charming and full of droll fun: the sophisticated sprite who could make you laugh at and embrace Hollywood's dream factory at the same moment. And he may have been quite as ardent in his private life as he was witty publicly."

Together, Brackett and Dean sunned themselves by the Sunset Plaza's pool, or they motored down to Tijuana, accompanied by Brackett's friends, to attend the bullfights. Brackett would coach him in readings, including *Hamlet.* Sundays they often drove to the Malibu beach cottage of costume designer Miles White, where Brackett, White, and other cronies would volley risqué epigrams and the latest intrigue from

New York, while Dean sat silently in a corner, nursing a beer. "Rogers and I were such good friends that it didn't bother me that he brought along a trick," says White. "It wasn't an imposition." White knew Dean only by Brackett's nickname for him, "Hamlet"; it was not until years later that White realized his taciturn guest had been James Dean. "I just figured he was another one of Rogers's beauties," White admits. "He was Rogers's type."

Brackett was an advertising man at Foote, Cone & Belding and directed *Alias Jane Doe* for one of its clients. All too soon after Dean had settled into life at the Sunset Plaza, the show ended, and Foote, Cone & Belding offered Brackett a television producing assignment in Chicago. Radio in Hollywood was in a shaky state that fall: "If you think the movie moguls are worried about the possible disastrous effects of TV, you ought to hold the head of a radio exec for a while," a columnist noted tactlessly. Brackett saw the writing on the wall and accepted the Chicago television job. Dean tried to act stoic in the face of this news, but since he had recently suffered other sudden bouts of homelessness, the pose was too difficult to maintain. Brackett's mother discovered him sobbing in the bathroom soon after he was told of the transfer. In spite of himself, Dean had grown attached to Brackett's kindnesses and feared being abandoned.

Dean jumped at the chance to accompany Brackett to Chicago but became fidgety soon after arriving. So Brackett, who expected an assignment in New York in the near future, bought him a ticket on the Twentieth Century Limited and sent him there. New York offered unlimited opportunities for young actors, but Dean arrived without any plan of attack. He initially found the city so intimidating that he spent most of his time at the movies, nearly depleting the money Brackett and other friends had given him. Eventually he got a grip and in the next two-and-a-half years racked up an impressive list of acting credits.

But when he returned to California to embark on his brief but dynamic movie career, he went to great lengths to expunge the facts of his earliest Hollywood days from the record. The publicity pumped out by his studio and the interviews he fed to Hollywood columnists gave no clue that he had been rescued from a parking lot and sent to New York because he found favor with an adoring older man. Instead, one read that Dean's Professor Higgins had been James Whitmore, a stage and screen actor whose acting workshop Dean had attended after dropping out of UCLA.

Gossip columnist Hedda Hopper asked Dean who had helped him the most on his way to success in Hollywood. He replied, "There's always someone in your life who opens your eyes, makes you see your mistakes, and stimulates you to the point of trying to find your way. In my life that somebody was James Whitmore. He encouraged me to go to New York and with the fortification of his knowledge of theater and the right way of working, I went. When I came back to Warner Brothers, Whitmore was on the lot. I wanted to thank him for his kindness and patience."

Whitmore, according to Dean, said thanks were not necessary and that Dean would surely do something for someone else. "I've tried to pass it on. I feel I've been of some benefit to young actors. It's the only way to repay James Whitmore," he declared. Similar statements were made to columnist Louella Parsons. Meeting Whitmore was the turning point in his nascent career, Dean told her, and a young actor "could do no better than study Whitmore's work."

Whitmore *had* advised Dean to go to New York, but so had Isabel Draesemer and others who were eager for his career to develop in the best possible way. "I insisted that he go to New York so he could do some stage productions, which would give him recognition," says Draesemer. In Whitmore's case, Dean had asked him for advice on what to do with his life. "It was really no more than a two-hour talk over coffee one day," Whitmore recalled. "He asked me to see a television program he had done, and at that time Jimmy didn't know whether the idea was to become a motion picture star, ideally, or what. As I told Jimmy, go back and find out whether you're an actor first. And I feel that New York was the place to find that out."

Dean convinced the columnists that he had fled to New York as soon as the summons left Whitmore's lips, but such was not the case. The television program he wanted Whitmore to see was *Hill Number One,* an Easter special. It was broadcast seven months before Dean relocated to New York. Good as Whitmore's advice turned out to be, it was not a proximate cause of the move.

Two other considerations make Dean's case for Whitmore even weaker. Immediately before the move, he was finally enjoying the good fortune of regular work; in just the week before he abandoned Hollywood he had worked in two movies. "The guy we thought was just a rank amateur was getting walk-on parts," recalled a UCLA friend, "while the 'better' campus actors were turned away by the studio folk." He would not have uprooted himself at such an auspicious time if not for his sense of dependence on Brackett.

Then there was the poorly prepared state in which he stumbled into New York, an indication of a swift and sudden displacement. If he had been planning to act on Whitmore's advice, he might have started making the rounds of contacts and casting calls sooner than he did. As it turned out, the contacts he eventually made were referrals from Brackett and Brackett's friends, not from Whitmore.

Rogers Brackett was the key to Dean's career. He took him in when almost no one else believed in him; fed, clothed, and employed him; and planned and financed his move to New York. Eventually he introduced Dean to the producer who would put him on Broadway for the first time. No one would deny, of course, that the biggest break in Dean's short career was to be tapped by director Elia Kazan to star in *East of Eden.* But during 1951 and 1952, Brackett was unquestionably the most influential person in Dean's life.

Why then would Dean later fixate on James Whitmore without giving Brackett any credit? Composer Alec Wilder, Brackett's best friend and a mentor to Dean, offered an explanation. "It's my belief," Wilder wrote, "that when Jimmy became a star, he was terrified that his homosexual background might be revealed. It was long before the 'let it all hang out' era. Besides, Jimmy wasn't very bright and he *was* very young." Wilder lamented the public's ignorance of Dean's true beginnings: "They swallowed hook, line, and sinker the publicity Jimmy had allowed to be spread about him, and this, in turn, was further distorted by the flagrant lies he himself told about his background."

The debate over who and what James Dean really was, which still rages four decades after his death, is rooted in Dean's own efforts to throw the press and public off the trail of his private life. Vastly different interpretations have been advanced by his fans, his friends and lovers, his colleagues in theater and film, and his family and neighbors in Fairmount, Indiana.

In September 1956, Evelyn Washburn Nielsen, an Indianan and friend of Dean's family, boldly rose to defend him against posthumous allegations that he had been ill-adjusted, irresponsible, and speed-crazy. "The stories Hollywood inspired about him made good reading for many, but they sickened those closest to him," wrote Nielsen. "If people could know how Jimmy grew up, there would be no mystery." Then she inadvertently made her key observation: "The folks who knew him best in Fairmount will never believe that he was anything but the fine, sensitive, quiet lad they remember, both before and after he became the rage of Hollywood."

Nielsen's comments were far more revealing of Fairmount than of the actor. The town that gave the world James Dean has always refused to acknowledge things about him that, in spite of being "un-Indianan," were true. Some of its residents condition their cooperation with biographers on a promise not to write about any of his homosexual experiences. Willful blindness to Dean's bohemian life in New York and Hollywood—the surly moodiness, promiscuity, and noteworthy ability to mislead—became a hallmark of Fairmount life. This was due in part to another of Dean's cover-ups: his letters home avoided references to Rogers Brackett, Alec Wilder, girlfriends, and boyfriends, leading his family to believe he remained untainted by the tents of wickedness. "Hell, I've said it until I'm sick of sayin' it," droned Dean's uncle, Marcus Winslow, to a reporter in 1973. "Jim Dean was just like any other kid who grew up in this town. But Hollywood and the rest of the world refuse to believe any of that." In brief, for Fairmount, the authentic Dean remained in stasis after he left town in May 1949 for southern California.

In stark contrast to this beatific, American Gothic depiction, a portrait of bellicosity and selfishness emerges from some of the professionals who worked with him. Soon after Dean's death, Elia Kazan spoke publicly of problems they had had on *East of Eden:* "The late Jimmy Dean was a very difficult and most times a thoroughly impossible character. He fought with fellow artists and the crew and tried to ruin Julie Harris's good scenes." Daniel Mann, who directed *The Immoralist* on Broadway, recalled that "Jimmy had no graciousness, or politeness, or concern on stage."

Dean himself would be of little help in cutting through the confusion; as he occasionally admitted in letters to friends, *he* had no idea who he was. This absence of self-knowledge helped make him a universal icon: fans from the most diverse walks of life imaginable have all identified with the image he projected in his three major film roles: Cal Trask in *East of Eden,* Jim Stark in *Rebel Without a Cause,* and Jett Rink in *Giant.* So strong has this identification with the movie image been that fans typically adopt Dean's on-screen accouterments and ignore his perfectly obvious real-life trappings. Classic-car enthusiasts, for example, tend to show up at commemorative events driving a 1949 Mercury, the car from *Rebel Without a Cause,* rather than the Porsche or MG models that he owned as a private citizen.

Nowadays, the first question asked about James Dean is often "Was he gay?" Recent biographical efforts declared that Dean was in fact gay, but the very source whose homosexual experiences with Dean formed the basis for such an "outing" disputes that conclusion. As Jonathan Gilmore said recently, "I am as opposed to the conclusion that Jimmy was 'homosexual' and 'a gay man' as I am to the assertions of his being 'true-blue heterosexual.'

"I was there," Gilmore continues. "I was involved in it in New York and Hollywood. I knew the people he slept with and I knew who he was not with. Both Jimmy and I had relations with girls. While Jimmy was making *Rebel Without a Cause,* I introduced him to a Hollywood High School boy, an actor and dancer whom I was quite taken with. Jimmy also found him very attractive, and I know something happened between them that summer.

"That's how it was, neither black nor white. Jimmy thought of himself as an explorer, making discoveries in life, things, and sex. He had no conclusions about anything. For Jimmy, a conclusion would've conflicted with an almost uncontrollable need he had to try to go beyond the limitations set by others. Positioning himself as a 'gay man' would have created great stress, though in fact he could play it delightedly. But he would have been the first to scoff at the notion of labeling himself anything other than an explorer. His words to me were, 'If you aren't willing to take the risks, then you can't make the discoveries.' "

Dean was conflicted, to say the least, on the issue of homosexuality. In some ways his attitude toward it was remarkably liberated for the

Fifties. He seemed to have no discomfort over playing Bachir, a homosexual Arab procurer (and a rather sleazy one at that), in *The Immoralist.* Nor did he mind, in many cases, that his roommate was homosexual, which was the rule rather than the exception whenever he was living with a man.

Nonetheless, when it came to his family, or women with whom he was at least periodically romantic, Dean was squeamish about association with homosexuals, and he became adept at hiding or lying about it. While in high school, he kept frequent company with James DeWeerd, a prominent Wesleyan Methodist minister, knowing full well that De-Weerd was gay. But he did not want to give the impression that he was of the same stripe. Once Deweerd invited him and Bette McPherson, an art teacher Dean was seeing, to dinner. McPherson recalled that De-Weerd was "flutterin' around" as he cooked and set the table, and that while he was out of earshot Dean would mimic him and call him "De-Queerd."

No sooner had McPherson related this than a formidable frown distorted her attractive face. "But I can tell you one thing," she admonished, "Jimmy wasn't 'like that'—unless he could change from night to day, he wasn't." Dean may have convinced McPherson that he disdained DeWeerd's sexuality, but on his own volition he remained closer to the minister for the rest of his life than he did to her. Dean's pattern of belittling male homosexual friends for the benefit of his women was consistent throughout his life. He would mislead his girlfriend Dizzy Sheridan about Rogers Brackett, and Barbara Glenn, another girlfriend, about Jonathan Bates, a roommate. While living in Bates's apartment in the summer of 1953, Dean cracked in a letter to Glenn that Bates was flying to London, not on his own power, but in a plane.

Some of Dean's female contemporaries have come forward to say he and they were lovers: Dizzy Sheridan, Betsy Palmer, Arlene Sachs (now known as Tasha Martel), and others. But even in these more liberated times, it's a rare male who will own up to having been Dean's sexual partner. Only Gilmore and Rogers Brackett have said so on the record.

Producer Terese Hayden, who knew Dean from *The Scarecrow* and *The Immoralist,* cautions against emphasizing Dean's sexuality at the expense of his talent. "What if he was one of 'the boys'?" she asked.

"That's not important. What's important about Jimmy is that in spite of his short life, he had really lived—and with his beauty, he acted in ways that other actors only dream about."

How he became the captivating actor we know is the important question in any study of James Dean. Even in childhood, he charmed his relatives with mimickings and flights of fancy, and won medals for recitations at Woman's Christian Temperance Union speech meets. As an adolescent he was the kingpin in all plays presented at his small high school, and made town history by winning a statewide declamation contest. However, in college, the majority of his fellow thespians had grave doubts about his aptitude for an acting career. It was not until his training with James Whitmore that he found within himself his singular mechanisms of becoming a character.

Certainly the public came to identify Method acting with him, a perception that grew out of his making *East of Eden* under Elia Kazan, cofounder of the Actors Studio. Dean's particular talent was perfect for what the Studio was trying to accomplish, but the reverse was not true. He was too thin-skinned to accept or tolerate the harsh and often devastating critiques of the artistic director, Lee Strasberg.

To be sure, Dean was naturally endowed with gifts the Studio could not give him. Sadly, he could not be malleable enough to receive what it *could* give him. The Actors Studio's current artistic director, Frank Corsaro, knew Dean and easily discerned that "his talent was instinctual; his technique: zero." Kazan agreed. "Dean had no technique to speak of," he wrote in his autobiography. "When he tried to play an older man in the last reels of *Giant,* he looked like what he was: a beginner."

There was about Dean a sense of urgency, a desire to get to the top of the acting profession as rapidly as possible. He didn't want to be bothered with such details as technique. Fellow students at UCLA were struck by his lack of concern with becoming well-rounded—studying costuming, makeup, scenery, for example—as the Theater Arts Department required.

Nonetheless, the signals and messages that emanated from him on the screen enthralled his own generation and each one after it. His strength as an actor was his ability to move into the life of a character. With this ability came excellent instincts for stage business and for creating "the illusion of the first time," wherein his reactions seemed to flow spontaneously from what had just been spoken or done. "Jimmy was *organic,* in that the character and his being were one," says Terese Hayden. "He had the same gift with language as with movement—he released sound and motion with the same felicity."

Two innate characteristics further enhanced Dean's acting, one genetic and one environmental. The former was a mild reading disability. "If Jimmy read with someone," notes Jonathan Gilmore, "then either that other person read or Jimmy mumbled so you couldn't tell what he was saying. Because if he read it out loud, he'd already mostly memorized what he was holding. He had bad trouble reading and couldn't deal with a page, so it took him ages to finish a few paragraphs."

Dean covered the flaw adeptly, asking to be briefed orally—rather than handed a script—when auditioning or, when he couldn't avoid reading, blaming any slipups on cracked or misplaced eyeglasses. But the reading disability was in some respects a blessing, in the same way that jazz musicians are often poor sight-readers or don't read music at all. It liberated him from the printed page and allowed him to soar in his improvisations.

As a son of Indiana, with its heritage of traveling ministers, medicine shows, and temperance lecturers, Dean was an inveterate teller of tall tales. Playwright N. Richard Nash remembers joining him and Geraldine Page to drink beer after performances of *The Immoralist* and listening to him carry on. "Gerry and I used to scream with laughter at him," Nash reminisces. "She would say, 'Jimmy, that's *not true!*' His stories were not lies but tall tales."

The roster of colleagues taken in at one time or another by Dean's whoppers is endless. Meeting Dean for the first time, Alec Wilder remembered, "Jimmy started to fabricate his own sources, immediately started to tell me some silly story to throw me off. I was a stranger and he was going to show me that he was the wild young man. It was some nutty story about a fire in Chicago, something like that." In New York, Dean once horrified director Jack Garfein with a distressing tale of family skeletons, as they were walking along together—only to lose character and break into a smile as he saw that Garfein had fallen for the prank.

Among the criticisms of Dean's acting, one voiced most consistently was that he often had no perspective on the time and place of the character he was playing. He was taken to task for this even on his first television appearance, a role as John the Beloved in *Hill Number One.* Nina Skolsky, a UCLA classmate, remembers arguing with him when he told her he knew nothing about the apostle he was portraying. "How can you play a role and not do any history on it?" she asked in exasperation. Later, when Dean was in *The Immoralist* (set in Algeria at the turn of the century), his friend Madison Musser[1] complained, "Jimmy played Bachir like a Third Avenue faggot.[2] He had no sense of the period. He played it like an American prostitute."

Not even in *East of Eden,* his first major film, did Dean feel it was necessary to research his character's world—the Salinas, California, of 1917. "No, I didn't read the novel," he told an interviewer. "The way I work, I'd much rather justify myself with the adaptation than the source. . . . I knew that if I had any problems over the boy's background, I could straighten it out with Kazan." To be fair, Kazan did not assign him to study the character; he felt Dean's obvious alienation from authority figures made him a perfect match for it. But while costar Julie Harris on her own initiative kept the Warner Brothers research department busy with her questions—Had cotton candy and crazy mirrors really been invented by 1917? Could she get copies of popular magazines of the era?—Dean simply brooded and complained about California while waiting for shooting to begin. To him, it was still the same hostile, predatory place it had been when he was parking cars in 1951.

Item in the *Hollywood Reporter* of February 15, 1955: "Jimmy Murphy, parking lad at Ciro's, tests at Warners this week as James Dean's backstop in *Rebel Without a Cause.*"

After four years, Hollywood had forgotten that the now-hot Dean

---

1. Not his real name.
2. At midcentury, there were many antique shops in the East Fifties along New York's Third Avenue, as well as the gay bars of the "bird circuit"—the Blue Parrot, the Golden Pheasant, and the Swan. "It was known as a cruisy area," says Miles White, "and advertising men who worked on Madison wouldn't even walk on that part of Third."

had once been just another anxious parking lad, desperately stalking that one magic chance to be a face in the chorus; to play the backstop or the bellhop or the butler. Although his talent and photogenic face ensured that he would have been discovered eventually, it was Rogers Brackett who delivered him from the obscurity of Ted's Auto Park. The rest of Dean's life would be constrained and ultimately destroyed by the steps he took to suppress his secret.

The Recovering Hoosier

The remarkable thing about James Dean's Indiana background is that he rose above it. He threw off aspects that were limiting—racist and homophobic bigotry, small-mindedness—and retained only those that were charming and natural.

While living in New York, Dean wrote a poem to express his feelings about his Fairmount, Indiana, heritage. The poem catalogued Fairmount's external virtues: pervasive worship of God, daily perusal of newspapers, and sweetness. But, wrote Dean, its superficial morals masked profound defects beneath its surface; he accused Fairmount of industrial impotence, idolatry, and "dangerous" bigotry (including hatred of Catholics and Jews). He concluded by proclaiming that Fairmount was "not what I am"—precisely the reason he was not there but in New York.

Indiana, with its great scenic beauty, long-standing tradition of excellence in education, and many native literary and political stars, certainly has its points. But it also has a dark past. Due to geographical factors, Indiana's principal settlement was not from the east, as with other midwestern states, but from the south, so its attitudes were largely southern. Although Indianapolis had a bigger automobile industry than Detroit at the end of the nineteenth century, Detroit would soon steal its thunder by welcoming Eastern Europeans and southern blacks as auto plant workers—a step Indianapolis prohibited through commercial zoning restrictions.

During the widespread resurgence of the Ku Klux Klan in the 1920s, it was not Georgia or Mississippi but Indiana that was the organization's banner state. It permeated every county and most of its small towns; Fairmount was no exception. Issues of the *Fairmount News* from the early 1920s are replete with accounts of surprise appearances by hooded Klan representatives at local church services. Usually these visitors delivered a monetary contribution and a letter to the minister commending the church's efforts to keep America white, and signed "Knights of the Ku Klux Klan, Fairmount, Indiana."[1]

James Dean refused to limit himself with strictures imposed by others. As an adult he was happy to count African-Americans among his friends; he was particularly interested in what they could teach him. Thus he would study dance with Katherine Dunham and bongos with Cyril Jackson, and enjoy the company of Eartha Kitt, Bill Gunn, Sammy Davis, Jr., Marietta Canty, and others.

Nor was James Dean an anti-Semite; he could claim that most of his best friends were Jewish: Dizzy Sheridan, Barbara Glenn, Roy Schatt, David Diamond, Leonard Rosenman, James Sheldon, Norma Crane, Arlene Sachs, Bob Heller, Martin Landau. Race, creed, or sexual preference had no bearing on Dean's estimation of others; he judged them on the basis of what he could learn from them.

Another of Dean's virtues was his feeling for the underdog. Various experiences made him aware of his own separateness: being a de facto orphan and particularly his suspension from high school. Nicholas Ray, his director in *Rebel Without a Cause,* said Dean "would extend sudden affection to lonely and struggling people; he 'adopted' several." One such adoptee in Fairmount was Larry Lee Smith, who regarded Dean as a hero for being nice to him while his older brother, one of Dean's basketball teammates, always bullied him.

---

1. According to the *Fairmount News* of January 9, 1923, one of these letters stated, "We are convinced that the white race is the race chosen by God to accomplish His purposes and fulfill the destinies of this nation."

Dean's separateness was not invisible to other people in Fairmount; he was not quite the "regular guy" that his uncle insisted he was. "We watched Jimmy with a little awe, but felt he was explosive and not part of the community," remembers Sue Hill, three years younger than Dean. "We were aware he marched to a different drummer than ninety-nine percent of Fairmount. Some people in town were glad to see him go to California." Hill's twin sister, Shirley, adds, "His dramatic ability awed us, but his artistic capability in oils and his basketball and baseball talents gave him peer acceptance and popularity in spite of his individuality."

Among the younger female students at Fairmount High, Dean was viewed as "a little off-limits—almost juvenile delinquent status," says Sue Hill. Once he pulled a girl's bra strap and let it snap in Raymond Elliott's study hall, which was "just about the most daring thing you could think of to do under a strict disciplinarian like Mr. Elliott." Hill telephoned her friends that evening to ask, "Do you know what Jim Dean did today?"

In the summer of 1948, the local Veterans of Foreign Wars sponsored weekend dances in a hall above Fairmount's dime store to give the local teens an alternative to driving into Marion, the county seat. "Once, Jim came with an out-of-town girl," says Hill, "and they proceeded to make out like bandits. Well, the chaperones sent everyone home early and that was the last of those weekend dances."

Another classmate, Barbara Leach, felt that "audacious" would be the single best word to describe Dean. "He was a little more daring" than her other peers, she said. Her earliest memory of Dean (she moved to Fairmount just in time for their senior year) was at a Halloween party in a barn. From up in the loft, Dean tried to pour cider into the open mouths of the kids below.

James Byron Dean was born in a house at Fourth and McClure streets in Marion, Indiana, on February 8, 1931. His parents, Winton and Mildred Wilson Dean, had married a little more than six months earlier, on July 26, 1930. Winton Dean was a dental technician at the local veterans' hospital, and Mildred Dean worked in a drugstore. The small family would soon move to Fairmount, Winton Dean's hometown, and live at a variety of addresses there and in Marion over the next five years. James Byron would be his parents' only child.

Virtually all descriptions of his childhood involve his mother's nurturing. She had dreams of his being a performer and enrolled him in tap dance lessons at the Marion College of Dance and Theatrical Arts when he was three. Zina Gladys Pitsor, who ran the dance school, described a revue given by her troupe when Dean was five. "Jimmy did an intricate tap dance routine," said Pitsor, "and his cousin Joan Winslow did a waltz clog. Joan was older and very talented, but little Jimmy upstaged her with his bright smile and quick legs. The audience loved him."

There was a troubling side to Dean's early childhood. Mildred Dean's cousin, Lottie Wilson Patterson, recalled that Mildred told her the boy was bleeding to death under his skin and she often stood by his bed crying because she thought he would die. Sources close to the family reported that the boy suffered from frequent nosebleeds, which sometimes caused him to faint. "His arms and legs were usually covered with ugly black-and-blue marks the size and shape of a silver dollar," wrote one reporter after interviewing Dean's grandmother. A trip to the doctor yielded no diagnosis and the pessimistic opinion that if the boy survived, he would outgrow it. Nowadays, of course, a child brought to an emergency room in such condition would likely trigger a social services department's intervention.

In 1936, Winton Dean accepted a transfer to the Sawtelle Veterans' Administration Hospital in Santa Monica, California. In the summer of 1937, when he was six, Dean entered kindergarten at McKinley Elementary School and then completed grades one through three there. The family first made its home at 1215-A Twenty-sixth Street, moving two years later to 1422 Twenty-third Street.

Mildred Dean had lost her mother before she married, which may have contributed to her unusually close bonding with her son. Dean would later talk at length about his mother to a friend, Jonathan Gilmore, who reports that Mildred sensed her son's difficulties in making friends with the other Santa Monica children and so gave him a sense of refuge and even isolation at home—teaching him to play the violin, reading him stories, playing games of make-believe. They would make up adventure stories and act out the parts, or invent words whose secret meaning only they knew. Mildred was said to be a gifted mimic, often goaded by others to imitate this or that person. According to Gilmore, she understood the limitations of her modest station in life and grasped the possibility of transcending it through her son.

There are no surviving accounts of any influence Winton Dean had on his son. (The only thing Dean said publicly about his father was that he had a "remarkable adeptness with his hands.") Gilmore was told that Winton took a dim view of this special bond between Mildred and their son, feeling that spending so much time with his mother instead of playmates was not typical of a boy and certainly not any son of his. "When Jimmy was older," Gilmore wrote, "he would make great pretenses to others about the closeness and the warmth he shared with his distant father. But he was never able to keep the truth from himself."

A friend from Fairmount who visited the Deans in 1938 reported that Mildred said, "I don't want Jimmy to grow up out here. I've even been thinking about going back home to Indiana. Everything's so artificial here. I want my Jimmy to grow up where things are real and simple." Her prayer would be answered tragically. In September 1939, when her son was eight, an operation revealed that Mildred had uterine cancer.

Watching helplessly throughout the next year as his mother's health deteriorated must have made third grade a hellish experience for Dean. Mildred finally died on July 14, 1940, when he was nine. As a high school senior, he would write that he had never reached an understanding of Mildred's death and that it still haunted him.

When Mildred died, Winton's sister Ortense and her husband, Marcus Winslow, asked him to send his son back to Indiana and let them rear him. No member of the Dean family has ever elaborated on the Winslows' reasoning that the boy would be better off with them than with his father, or on the emotions underlying Winton's decision to say yes. Still, the offer was accepted with little or no debate, and there is no record of a competing offer from Mildred's family, though her two sisters were with her throughout her illness. Winton's mother, Emma Dean, grandson in tow, accompanied Mildred's body back to Indiana on the train.

Dean would never get over his mother's death. Barbara Glenn, a very special person in his adult life, said that where Mildred was concerned, Dean forever remained a nine-year-old; he could not talk about her on any other level. Marietta Canty, an actress in *Rebel Without a*

Cause, said Dean once blurted out to her on the set that God couldn't possibly care about him: "Just look at the dirty trick He played on me with my mother and father." Although only one parent died, he felt that he had lost both.

Ortense and Marcus Winslow had a daughter, but no son of their own. So nine-year-old James Dean was treated as if he were theirs, and fourteen-year-old Joan Winslow was shown no favoritism. "Jimmy was never one to sit still," she said, "always having to be the best at everything. He kept pestering everyone to teach him how to drive the tractor. Once he learned, he forgot about the tractor and wanted to raise chickens instead."

Although Dean's natural curiosity made him want to learn how a farm was run, he only tolerated farm work, never coming to love it, according to his friend Bob Middleton, who as a boy worked for Marcus Winslow. "Jimmy and I traded off on the tractor," Middleton said. "I would do the night plowing because he didn't like it."

One thing Dean did like about farm life was its seemingly unlimited opportunities for recreation. A large pond on his uncle's property accommodated swimming in summer and ice-skating in winter. The Winslow barn, said his friend Rex Couch, was known as the county's basketball center. "Every Sunday, there were anywhere from ten to thirty-five guys playing there," he recounts. "At an early age, Jimmy was playing with guys much older than he was." The barn was also perfect for trapeze stunts. Dean lost his two front teeth while essaying one stunt that his uncle had shown him, and he would have to wear false teeth for the rest of his life.

Middleton remembered Dean as "a kid you'd teach something to, and the next week he'd do it better than you." Once Middleton's father asked Dean if he wanted to try firing his .38 revolver. "Jimmy was a good shot with a rifle, but he had never fired a revolver," said Middleton. "They went outside and my dad started shooting. For a few minutes Jimmy just stood there and watched. Then he took the .38 and duplicated nearly every shot my dad had made. It was an almost impossible thing for anybody to do the first time they picked up a revolver."

Ortense Winslow would later reflect, "When Jimmy was set to do something, nobody could stop him. He was tough-minded when he felt he had to be. And when he laughed, the whole world laughed, and when he cried, it rained. He was always able to get people into his moods. It was a wonderful gift."

The late Ralph Riley, Fairmount's "senior statesman" for many years, had many vivid memories of the young James Dean. Riley had a car dealership, and Dean loved to come in and talk about cars. "He knew hot rods and what it took to build 'em," recalled Riley. "He'd be talkin' about 'four-barrel carburetors' and 'cut the camshaft,' which was way over my head because I only knew the automobiles I sold."

Riley also ran a newspaper delivery service and employed local youngsters. Dean never worked for him but would come in to talk to the other kids, start arguments, and be ordered to leave. Once when Dean was a sophomore basketball player on the second team, the entire Fairmount squad was on the road and stopped for something to eat. "Ed Johnson, the coach, said, 'All right, first team in here, second team over there,' " Riley recalled. "But Jimmy sat with the first team. Coach Johnson said, 'Dean, sit with the second team.' Jimmy got mad and went back and sat in the bus. He refused to eat. Usually the coach would drive the kids home after they got back to town, but Jimmy was still mad at him and walked home in the rain."

Bearing in mind that Dean attended a small school, he had an outstanding senior year (1948–49), filled with achievement. A benefactor had established a series of awards at Fairmount High, given at the end of each school year to the outstanding senior student in fourteen different categories. Dean captured two of the awards (in athletics and forensics).

Early in the school year the student newspaper carried a short profile of him, noting his early childhood in California and return to Fairmount but avoiding any mention of his mother's death. Banana salad was listed as his favorite food; women and the "new look" his pet peeves; and motorcycles, ice-skating, art, and dramatics his hobbies.

Asked to name the highlight of his basketball career, Dean cited the previous season's game against Jefferson Township. At first blush it seems an odd choice; he scored eight points, respectable but by no means the game's highest total, and less flashy than his efforts in the same season's sectional game against St. Paul's, in which he was high scorer with seventeen points. But there was a world of difference in the emotional impact of each game: St. Paul's was an effortless win, but Jefferson

Township, having been undefeated and favored, was a major upset of the season.

Dean's propensity to break his glasses during basketball games is well known, as is the local optometrist's remark, "About every other week I had to mend Jim Dean's glasses or get him a new pair because he was always breaking them." However, it wasn't because he was playing a contact sport. "He often broke them," reports Sue Hill, "after being called for a personal foul in basketball. He threw them; that's why they broke. He wore a rubber strap to hold them on his head, and they wouldn't have fallen off so easily. You got the sense that he would push as far as he could with someone, not just in basketball with the referees but in everything with everyone."

An article on the Fairmount team at the beginning of Dean's senior season listed his height as five feet, seven-and-a-half inches and his weight as one hundred forty-six pounds—hardly the raw material for a phenomenal player. Yet Dean was a top scorer all season, averaging eight points per game, which he managed by virtue of his skill at hitting long shots. During a home game played on his eighteenth birthday, the fans sang "Happy Birthday" to him. Having attained this age, he was required under the Selective Service Act of 1948 to register for the draft, which he did on February 14. His registration card listed his height as five feet, eight inches, and his weight at one hundred fifty.

A magical transformation seemed to come over Dean in the sectional tournament at season's end. He had been good before, but he would now enjoy his biggest success. Fairmount went into the sectional a definite underdog, but the team went much further than it was expected to. In their first round they beat Van Buren High, and in the semifinal round they beat Mississinewa; both games were startling upsets because those teams had each defeated Fairmount twice in regular season play. And Dean, as Fairmount's top scorer in each game, was the biggest factor in the victories. "Dean did his damage through the middle portion of the game," reported the *Marion Chronicle-Tribune* on the Mississinewa game. "He hit four baskets in the second period and two more in the third."

In the final round, Fairmount faced Marion, a kind of Goliath in Grant County because its size and talent pool far exceeded any other school's. Although they lost, Dean was the game's star with fifteen points, high for both teams. A local sports reporter, summing up the tournament, wrote, "There were stars galore in the sectional meet, but Bob Shugart of Swayzee and Jim Dean of Fairmount are the lads we would select as the outstanding players. . . . Dean was a constant threat, both from long range and from close in. He accumulated forty points in the three games [the highest individual total of the tournament]."

Dean's athleticism extended to track and field, although he was less gifted in it. As a junior he was an undistinguished high and low hurdler. In his senior year he turned to pole vaulting, but he came nowhere near winning the state championship as he later told Hedda Hopper.[2] During the regular track season he usually vaulted at nine feet, nine inches. As with the basketball season, he rose to the occasion in the sectional meet with a vault of ten feet, three inches. Still, this earned him only a three-way tie for third place, which he lost after a coin was flipped.

Dean tried his hand at debate as a senior, with moderate success. His partner was Barbara Leach. "She was the only one who was his intellectual equal in putting things together," Sue Hill says. "When we all would check into the Marion Library to do research, Jim and Barbara would go off together for long periods of time." On February 13, 1949, Dean and Leach represented Fairmount in an hourlong debate against Marion High that was broadcast on local radio. They argued the affirmative side of the proposition, "The election of United States presidents should be by the direct vote of the people." At the program's conclusion, the judges declared Fairmount the winner.

Decades later, Leach revealed what she thought had been her secret about Dean: if he couldn't find documentation to back up a particular point, he faked it. "I lived in dread that he would be found out and the good name of Fairmount High ruined," she confessed. But a couple of times Sue Hill substituted as Dean's debate partner when Leach was ill. "I remember him fabricating sources, pretending to read them off

---

2. Another persistent athletic myth about Dean is that as a senior basketball player he hit a last-second field goal from midcourt, enabling Fairmount to defeat Gas City by two points. But Gas City had been incorporated into another school that year and no longer existed. Newspaper reports of the Gas City game of Dean's junior year show no such feat.

his cards, and we still won," Hill confesses. "Then he tried to get away with it again the next time, but that judge was too knowledgeable and we lost."

Don Martin, music teacher and band director at Fairmount during Dean's senior year, remembers, "On the drums, Jimmy had a tremendous sense of rhythm. He had to prove it to the world and he wanted to be heard. He was a difficult individual at that time. He was an introvert. He had a terrible complex. He was always asking questions.

"The home I was boarding at had a swing on the porch. The boys would come by, and we would sit on the swing and talk. I had an antique clock in the form of a man playing a lute. Once Jimmy came into my room and looked at the clock. 'What do you want that for?' he asked. I tried to explain—he was always questioning in this manner.

"Once I remarked to him, 'You never talk about anyone.' His reply was startling: 'The unspoken word we control. Once spoken, it controls us.' Such a profound statement impressed me."

Despite his local renown for athletic prowess or relatively outrageous behavior, Dean's real forte was acting and emoting. He had been a standout in class plays since his freshman year, and he might have been expected to have the lead in the senior play, George S. Kaufman and Moss Hart's great *You Can't Take It With You.* However, Adeline Brookshire, the drama teacher, realized that of all her students, only Dean could bring off the eccentric Russian ballet instructor, Boris Kolenkhov. "Heavily bearded and caked with his own makeup job, he reveled in the role," she remembers.

"Jim was very good in that part, once he made up his mind to put himself into it," adds Joyce John. "Quite often he was late for practice and sometimes didn't show up at all. The thing I remember most about him in that play, or any play, is that he could upset Mrs. Brookshire, and that always made me angry. He had quite a temper and would walk out of practice if things didn't suit him. He was disruptive—but he was good!"

The high-water mark of Dean's high school years was his winning first place in dramatic declamation in the statewide National Forensic League meet on April 9, 1949. His selection was "A Madman's Manuscript" from Charles Dickens's *Pickwick Papers,* a monologue of (as he later told the *New York Times*) "this real gone cat who knocks off several people." Under Adeline Brookshire's coaching, Dean spent several months rehearsing the reading.

Just before Christmas break, Dean recited "Madman" before his peers in advanced speech class and was heckled by David Fox, one of his basketball teammates. The two young men got into a brawl, for which Dean, but not Fox, was suspended from school for three days.[3] Dean was not allowed to play in the basketball game against Sweetser High, which his team barely won without him, forty-three to forty-two. Adding insult to injury, when he tried to buy a student ticket to watch, the ticket taker happened to be Raymond Elliott, the study hall disciplinarian, who told him he was not a student. And that was not the end of it. At season's end, the two teammates who edged Dean out as top season scorer had played eighteen games, while Dean, without the Sweetser game to his credit, had played only seventeen.

But Dean continued to perfect his reading. "From the start," Brookshire relates, "he had a natural feeling for the piece's mood contrasts, the almost imperceptible drifting from sanity to madness and back again." When the statewide competition arrived, the judges were struck by the eerie, glassy look in his eyes. After four rounds over two days of competition, Dean was declared the winner. The meet was open only to schools with National Forensic League charters, and none of the big high schools of Indianapolis had been represented. Still, many of Dean's competitors were from schools with long-standing traditions of forensic excellence, and his victory was a solid achievement. He would now represent Indiana in the national meet in Longmont, Colorado.

On the morning of April 27, the Fairmount High student body gave Dean a send-off on the school grounds, planned by the principal, who had forgiven him for punching David Fox. The band played, the cheerleaders led a yell, and Dean choked up. "He bawled," said Joyce John, "In fact, we all got rather dewy-eyed." From the school, a caravan of cars trailing streamers took Dean to the Marion depot, where he and Adeline Brookshire, chaperone as well as coach, boarded a train to Chi-

---

3. Brookshire speculates that the principal, who was new that year, hoped to establish his authority by suspending Dean.

cago. Dean cried for the second time that morning as he recounted the send-off for Brookshire.

In Chicago, Brookshire, Dean, and the other Indiana winners and coaches boarded the Denver Zephyr. Brookshire was a closet smoker and, while ostensibly in the powder room, would slip out to the car's rear platform for an unobserved cigarette. Forty years later she learned from the Fort Wayne contestant that Dean was resorting to the same subterfuge so Brookshire would not observe *his* smoking. When it came time to sleep, a porter brought pillows, but Dean thrashed about restlessly, keeping Brookshire awake in the adjacent seat. Finally he repaired with Lester Tucker, coach of the Howe Military Academy contestants, to the glass-domed observation coach on the upper deck, leaving Brookshire in peace.

In Longmont, Dean placed sixth out of twenty-two contestants. He was eliminated after four rounds and just missed being one of five finalists. Brookshire says, "I can still remember seeing him huddled in his seat during the finals, heartsick that he was out of the running." She notes that he could have been penalized for exceeding the ten-minute time limit or for using a selection that was not the standard cutting from a play with two or more different characters. She also denies that he opened with a bloodcurdling scream or ripped his shirt, as later press accounts alleged. "I would never have a student begin so shockingly," she insists. "It was foreign to my training."

Although Dean usually got along well with his peers, he could find no comparable vision among them of the potential of life outside Fairmount. For this he turned to select adult friends. The Reverend James DeWeerd, fifteen years older than Dean, was essentially an outsider, and though he lived in Fairmount, he had seen the world.

There are different schools of thought on DeWeerd. The traditional view was that he was a great guy whose influence on young James Dean was wholesome and constructive. His reputation as an exemplary Christian was established early on; attending Fairmount High in 1931, he wrote the constitution of the Hi-Y Club, which existed "to create, maintain, and extend throughout the school and community high standards of Christian character" through "clean speech, clean sports, clean scholarship, and clean living." As a chaplain in World War II, he was wounded twice while trying to rescue his men and was awarded the

Silver Star and the Purple Heart. He was on the Fairmount School Board and often charmed the other members by having them to his home for dinner before meetings or inviting them for dessert and coffee afterward. Much later an Indiana governor appointed him chairman of the state Juvenile Delinquency Study Commission.

This view of DeWeerd was reinforced by Evelyn Washburn Nielsen, the self-anointed Fairmount apologist, who in 1956 wrote a series of articles to set forth what she saw as the correct interpretation of James Dean. "To really understand [Dean], as his hometown understands him, you must know about the man after whom he patterned his life," Nielsen insisted. "To know this cultured, tolerant man [DeWeerd] with his flair for living, his fire and humor, his dazzling intelligence, is to know Jimmy Dean."

Quoting Marcus Winslow, Nielsen said DeWeerd's "heroic war record" was what initially drew Dean's admiration. She and a variety of sources report that Dean felt comfortable pouring out his heart to DeWeerd about the unrelenting reverberations of his mother's death. Eventually DeWeerd became Dean's "closest friend in Fairmount" and "the center of his life."

"Jimmy was usually happiest stretched out on my library floor reading Shakespeare or other books of his choosing," DeWeerd told Nielsen. "He loved good music playing softly in the background; Tchaikovsky was his favorite." Nielsen concluded that "these brilliant, considering minds met in a flawless companionship . . . in this truly great man Jimmy found his strength and courage to follow his rugged path to success."

DeWeerd later explained to a reporter, "All of us are lonely and searching. But, because he was so sensitive, Jimmy was lonelier and he searched harder. He wanted final answers, and I think that I taught him to believe in personal immortality." DeWeerd realized that Dean was a "moocher" and "tried to get as much from you as possible. If he didn't consider you worth anything, he dropped you." But DeWeerd had plenty to give. He had taken up yoga to ease the nagging pain of his war injuries, and taught some of the techniques to Dean. He had home movies of bullfights in Mexico, where his speaking engagements had taken him, which fascinated Dean. He loved big and expensive cars and is said to have taught Dean how to drive a car and taken him to the Indy 500 once.

A different view of DeWeerd was held by Fairmount folk whose religious inclinations stopped short of fundamentalism. Sue Hill recalls DeWeerd coming into the Dairy Bar after speaking at a revival meeting in Fairmount. "DeWeerd was talking about how much money he had taken in the previous night and how much of it was his take. I was disillusioned," she said. "My father knew DeWeerd right after the war and encouraged him to write about his experiences. However, when DeWeerd became an evangelist and embraced the sin-devil concepts, it was too far from our Quaker concepts, and my father spoke of him as more involved in the money than the help to others."

"As kids working in the Dairy Bar," Hill said, they would see people from the revivals come in, and "we were shocked at their pious conversations—'Are you saved by our Lord, Jesus Christ?'—but *very* sexually involved behavior *in* the shop. My folks would say, 'They're in heat.'"

One of DeWeerd's forms of community service was to take small groups of Fairmount boys to the YMCA pool twenty miles south in Anderson. Nude swimming was the accepted practice in those days, and it was a splendid occasion for DeWeerd to show off his war wounds and invite his young friends to feel what was left of his rib cage. "I saw scars all over his naked body," says one Fairmount man, "and he looked terrible. It was a wonder he survived."

DeWeerd would then take the boys to his home, call their parents to say where they were, and fix sloppy joes for everybody. "Then he would get out letters women had sent him, either to propose or ask for a date," the Fairmount man recalls, "and read them to us. He'd say, 'This ol' gal thinks she's gonna hook me, but I'll tell her where to get off' or 'I'll fix her.'" This same man always enjoyed DeWeerd's sermons. "I dearly loved that man," he says.

The income from DeWeerd's road show enabled him to indulge a lifelong passion for flashy cars. The late Xen Harvey, a local Quaker minister who shared the sacred desk with DeWeerd at Dean's funeral, said, "He was active about town, riding around in a high-powered car." Fairmount resident Marge Kientz recalls DeWeerd speaking at her Bible college in Fort Wayne in the late Forties. "But I was more impressed," she said, "with his convertible car and can remember seeing him with a carload of young men."

By all accounts, DeWeerd cast a spell of enchantment over his spiritual customers. Don Martin, the high school music teacher, said the minister "had a tremendous sense of humor and kept his congregations in stitches. But he could be very caustic." Xen Harvey said DeWeerd "had memorized a great deal of poetry and could just pull it out at will, which made him very popular. Whether he was talking to you personally or from the pulpit, he was a showman."

According to Harvey, DeWeerd loved to make light of marriage in his sermons. "He would say, 'The only reason to get married is to get a woman to keep you warm, and I've got an electric blanket to do that.' " DeWeerd finally married at the age of forty-seven.

To this day, DeWeerd remains a touchy subject among those residents of Fairmount who remember him, and there is considerable reluctance to discuss him. Ralph Riley talked loquaciously about James Dean's early life, but when asked about DeWeerd simply stared stone-faced at his interviewer. Harvey declared, "I'm not free to speak about him. It'd stir up a hornet's nest in Fairmount. But I don't care about anyone's sexual preference."

Biographer Joe Hyams wrote that DeWeerd had carried on a sexual relationship with young James Dean during his high school years. When DeWeerd allegedly confessed the liaison to Hyams, who was a complete stranger, he was a highly visible public figure: pastor at the historic Cadle Tabernacle in Indianapolis, daily speaker on the "Nation's Family Prayer Period" radio broadcast, and host of a weekly religious television program. It strains credibility to imagine that DeWeerd would jeopardize his career at its height and risk vigilante reprisals were such revelations to leak out and become public. Hyams did not substantiate the story, and although DeWeerd may have liked boys more than a clergyman should, irrefutable proof of a sexual connection with Dean has never turned up.[4]

---

4. Hyams's September 1956 article on Dean in *Redbook* included a profile of DeWeerd rife with errors. Although DeWeerd corrected these errors in a subsequent letter to *Redbook,* Hyams kept the profile substantially intact, including some of the errors, in his 1992 Dean biography *Little Boy Lost.* DeWeerd died in 1972, but Hyams failed to include these sexual allegations in the chapter on Dean in his 1973 *Mislaid in Hollywood.*

Hyams wrote in *Redbook* that DeWeerd was "openly critical of Fairmount and its limited way of life," a statement that ruffled feathers in the town. DeWeerd's apology

The other adult to whom Dean was close in Fairmount was his art teacher, Bette McPherson. "My homeroom in the 1948–49 school year consisted of seniors," said McPherson, "and Jim was in that group. He was very good as an artist. Since I drove from Marion to school every day, Jim asked to ride with me. My route went by where he lived anyway, so I would pick him up. He was always joking, so it made the days. When I moved to Fairmount, my landlady would get annoyed when he roared up on his motorcycle."

McPherson, who died after a 1990 automobile accident, maintained she was eight years older than Dean, but her family genealogy shows that she was actually eleven years his senior. She and her husband, who had infantile paralysis and used crutches, lived in an apartment over a bar in Marion; they separated sometime during the 1948–49 school year. In the evenings McPherson worked for Joe Payne, an interior decorator of churches and public buildings, in Payne's warehouse near the center of Fairmount. "After basketball practices, Jim would come by and spend time with me there," she said. "We had a lot of good times together. He didn't seem that different to me then, although he was very dramatic about things." She was aware, she said, that Marcus Winslow did not approve of her, but he never tried to dissuade Dean from seeing her.

During Dean's brief suspension from school for punching David Fox, he turned to McPherson for consolation. "He was unhappy about people talking about him," she said. "One night he came in with three watercolors he had painted. The first painting depicted people running him down. The second one was eyeballs that are crushing him, and the third represents his wanting to get back at everybody and show them, but he can't because his foot is tied down."

One day at school a student was taking pictures on the front lawn. "Jim came up to me and put his arm around my neck for the pictures," McPherson said. "That's the first time I knew he liked me. Later on he

---

appeared in the *Fairmount News* of September 6, 1956: "I understood what I said to the reporter and it is regrettable that he misunderstood," said the minister. "We live and learn . . . apparently, instead of painting the unknown or little-known phases of Jim's inner life in its true light, I have only added to the confusion, for which I am heartily sorry."

fell in love with me. For a long time after his death I didn't talk about him or see his movies. I had phone calls asking for information, but I did not want my personal experiences in print. I wouldn't mind now—some of them."

As a senior class sponsor, McPherson chaperoned the class trip to Washington, D.C., at the end of the school year. Denying a persistent Fairmount legend of her involvement in a boys' beer bust in Washington's Roosevelt Hotel, she said, "I did not get beer for any of the kids, nor did I drink beer on the D.C. trip. I was accused of a lot of things in Fairmount; it was a real Peyton Place." Partying aside, Dean made a special pilgrimage to Ford's Theater during some free time, which Adeline Brookshire had urged him to do. On the bus back to Indiana, some of the young women snipped locks of hair off Dean and another male student while they were snoozing.

Graduation came the week after the D.C. trip, and Dean was asked to give a prayer at the baccalaureate service. Wondering how to pray publicly, he turned to James DeWeerd. The preacher loaned him some prayer books, from which Dean chose a supplication by John Henry Newman invoking "safe lodging and a holy rest and peace at last."

By the end of the school year Dean had decided to join his father in Santa Monica and go to college there. At a farewell party hosted by Joyce Wigner, whom Dean had dated, and Bob Middleton's sister Barbara, music teacher Don Martin was at the piano, playing "California, Here I Come" and "Back Home in Indiana." Martin, with two other newly graduated seniors, drove Dean to Chicago on the first leg of his journey. "It was just a fun thing to do," recalled Martin. "On the way to Chicago, Jimmy was a little arrogant, making caustic remarks, disagreeing with everybody."

Martin asked him, "What'll you do if you don't make it out there?" Dean acted as if he had given no thought to that possibility. He replied, "When you go hunting for two rabbits, you don't get either. You hunt for one." Martin was impressed at such a profound statement, but he remarked to others at the time, "He thinks he's going to crash the gates out there, but he'll be surprised." Decades later, Martin says, he is still embarrassed to have been so wrong.

Byron James

In Santa Monica, Dean made his home with his father, Winton, and stepmother, Ethel Case Dean, at 814-B Sixth Street. According to his friend Jonathan Gilmore, Dean knew "within five minutes" of being back with his father that it had been a "miserable, rotten mistake. . . . Jimmy said his stepmother told him his father felt it was 'a shame' that Jimmy 'had been duped' into thinking he could earn a living in the movies. Winton said being an actor wasn't a 'manly profession' and 'the movies were full of pantywaists.' " Complicating things further, Dean did not like his stepmother and spent little time at home. But he said nothing about these matters in his letters to the Winslows and his grandparents, mentioning only that he and his father had gone bowling and golfing.

Halfway through June 1949, Dean discovered a welcome diversion to life at his father's apartment. He joined the experimental wing of the Santa Monica Theater Guild, which was presenting a series of four one-act plays at the Miles Playhouse. Writing to his grandparents, he called himself "a full-fledged member of the troop [*sic*]." Although he hadn't joined soon enough to be cast in any of the plays, he wrote that his high school experience in designing and painting sets qualified him to become head stage manager as of Thursday, June 23. What he didn't tell his grandparents was that, at least for the duration of the one-act festival, he had dropped his, and their, surname and was billing himself on the program as Byron James.

Beginning with his teens and intermittently thereafter, Dean toyed with the idea of changing his name to sound more like a celebrity. In high school he had "rushed" into Adeline Brookshire's classroom one day and said, "I have a brilliant idea. I'm going to change my name to Marcus Dean. My aunt and uncle will like that." The Winslows were flattered, but they dissuaded him. Later an agent talked him out of a similar scheme. His first summer in Santa Monica was the only time he used a stage name.

What really made Dean's summer was the arrival in Los Angeles of Bette McPherson, whose teaching contract at Fairmount High had not been renewed. "I had been told that an apartment over a cocktail lounge was not a good place for a teacher to live," she explained. "Then on weekends I would go with my boss, Joe Payne—who also happened to be president of the school board—to paint churches. Rumors started about him and me, and the superintendent called me in about it. I said, 'Do you think I'm that hard up?' and that sounded worse than it was. This was my undoing. I was fired by the end of the 1949 school year."

To recuperate from her dismissal, she decided to spend the summer in Los Angeles with two other young women, Julia Barron and Donna Jean Morris, friends from her hometown who were also schoolteachers. Her cousin, Marjorie Armstrong, already lived there. "Bette loved to go to bars," Armstrong related. "She just wanted to have a beer and talk. She wasn't promiscuous. I can assure you she wasn't an alcoholic."

McPherson said when she notified Dean she was coming, he was happy "because he would know someone with a car. When I arrived, my cousin was away for the weekend. So I called Jim and he found a place for us to stay that Sunday night. He took Julia and me to the place, drove my car on home, and came back for us the next morning.

"Jim didn't have anything to do that summer, so he went around with us. He showed us a lot—Alvarado Drive, Forest Lawn Cemetery, with lots of famous people buried there. I remember admiring the stained glass. I don't know how on earth he knew so many places. He hadn't been in L.A. too much longer than I, and Winton certainly hadn't shown him.

"My friend Julia met the actor Don Ameche's mother, Babe, at Catholic fellowship one Sunday and was invited to go over to the family home in the San Fernando Valley. Jim and all of us went with her. He was thrilled to see Don Ameche's house.

"He had a job making signs for someone. Once when he got paid, we got beer, drove to the beach, and had a beer party. Then there was a friend of mine, originally from Indiana but living in L.A., who would have parties, and Jim and I would go. We went to dances; I taught him to dance. Once we got stopped by the police on the way to Lake Arrowhead, early in the morning, for running a stop sign. Another time, we got stopped for having the lights on bright."

Marjorie Armstrong had a cabin on Lake Arrowhead's Emerald Bay. Dean and McPherson went there to water ski a few times. "Bette said he scared her spitless as he drove up to Arrowhead, and Bette didn't scare easily," Armstrong remembered. "My husband didn't mind the girls, but he didn't like the boys. There was more than one—Jimmy Dean brought his friends along. In fact, I don't remember which one of them he was. Since they hadn't been invited and didn't strike us as high-classed, they slept on the lawn or in the car. They didn't look respectable. They looked sloppy—hippie, before hippies were in style."

For most of the summer, McPherson, Julia Barron, and Donna Jean Morris lived in the front half of a UCLA professor's home on the Hollywood–Beverly Hills line. "Jimmy had a motorcycle," Morris remembers. "He came to our place because he seemed very lonesome, and was always in blue jeans. He talked little. It was hard to carry on a conversation with him. I would only say hi."

With his foot already in the door of the Santa Monica Theater Guild, Dean was a prime candidate for its annual production of *The Romance of Scarlet Gulch,* a melodrama with a California gold rush motif. Once again billing himself as Byron James, he played Charlie Smooch, a habitual drunk. Other stock characters included a hero, a handsome sheriff, a Spanish villainess, a gambler, and a judge. The melodrama opened on August 11 and ran until September 17.

Extolling Dean's contributions to the production, the florid program notes said, "The management has procured all the elegant scenic designs from the hand of the director, lavishly decorated by Mr. Byron James (who did the outdoor scene), and Mr. Byron James, ably assisted by all the actors, who also assisted in the construction." Dean had recruited Bette McPherson to help him paint scenery for the melodrama. "He wanted me to be in the play," she said. "I took him to rehearsals a lot. He didn't have a car, so we used mine. By this time, we were arguing a lot—all day."

Dean's feelings for McPherson had grown intense. In spite of their eleven-year age difference, he asked her to marry him. "I said no," she recalled. "So he said we could just live together. He was hurt." In 1989, McPherson said she had lingering mixed emotions about discussing Dean. "It still makes me sad," she confessed. "Maybe if I would have stayed in L.A., he would still be alive, but not famous. Who knows?"

After *Scarlet Gulch* began its run, Dean wrote to the Winslows to inform them that the melodrama's first three performances had been a success. He said he was enjoying the experience and was trying to view it as an inexpensive stage education, even if in reality he disliked melodrama-style acting.

He complained about the behavior of his fellow thespians, saying they were usually bickering with each other unless someone outside their group criticized them, which made them forget their quarrels and unite. It made him nostalgic for the simpler life he had left behind. He reminisced about his small motorcycle that had remained behind in Indiana, saying he thought of it as a friend or even a blood relative, and that he couldn't imagine ever selling it.

Dean was also doing some sort of work that summer in an unidentified television studio. He wrote that it was simple and the opportunities for promotion were great, even if the remuneration was marginal or nil. Realizing that breaking into the film and television world was an arduous process, he was trying to be patient while actors and actresses such as David Bruce, Barbara Brown, Hal Price, and Joan Leslie gave him pointers about their craft.[1] Some of them, he noted, hadn't got their breaks until they were middle-aged.

Significantly, Dean said nothing in his letter about Bette McPher-

---

1. In March 1951, Joan Leslie would be featured in Dean's television debut, *Hill Number One*. Four decades later, Miss Leslie said she had no idea she had acted with James Dean.

son. Despite his wounded feelings at her rejection of his marriage proposal, the two of them parted as friends when she returned to Indiana. "We kept in touch. He wrote—I didn't keep the letters," she later said. "I was supposed to meet him when he was back in Indiana the following summer, but couldn't make it. Actually, I never saw him again. But we stayed in contact, because I called him in Texas, during the filming of *Giant,* because I happened to be in Albuquerque. Unfortunately, it was a weekend and the cast was on a break. We were planning to get together at my cousin's place in the summer of 1956."

Over the years there had been enough migration from Fairmount to southern California to justify an annual "Fairmount Picnic." The 1949 festivities were held on September 25 in Whittier, another Quaker stronghold, and as usual was written up in the *Fairmount News.* Pains were taken to list every guest, and Winton and James Dean were not among them—in 1949 or any succeeding year. Perhaps they felt no strong connection to the other expatriates.

On many occasions Dean had told the folks in Indiana that he was bound for UCLA. He even wrote to his grandparents in June that he would be taking an English exam there and was already registered for summer and fall classes. But at summer's end, whatever tentative inquiries he had made to UCLA were moot. Somehow it was decided that he would attend Santa Monica City College, a two-year institution. Perhaps UCLA's out-of-state tuition rates were beyond Winton Dean's ability to pay. Larry Swindell, Dean's pal at SMCC, recalled, "More than once Jimmy told me that he went to Santa Monica to get residency to qualify for UCLA's in-state fees."

In some ways, Dean's freshman year was simply an extension of high school; once again he would have a nurturing drama teacher and go out for basketball and field events. He was still thoroughly Indianan that fall but would continue the process of social and intellectual climbing that had started with his emulation of James DeWeerd. He would pursue and date the homecoming queen, campaign for and win membership in the Opheleos (an elite male service organization), and fraternize with students whose sophistication he hoped would rub off. "The Jim Dean we knew at Santa Monica," said Larry Swindell, "was entirely different from the Dean of legend, suggesting a personal evolution that has never really been tracked."

The Santa Monica City College of Dean's day was not at all like today's attractive campus on Pico Boulevard. Located at Seventh Street and Michigan Avenue, the old campus was a series of World War I barracks—Splinterville was one of its nicknames—intended only as temporary quarters until the anticipated 1941 construction of a new campus. But World War II forced the indefinite postponement of those plans. When Dean arrived, the college was still adjacent to Santa Monica High School; the two institutions shared many facilities, including the athletic field and theater.

Larry Swindell first met Dean through the Schenk brothers, Herb and Dick, at their home at 2619 Fifth Street in Ocean Park. "Jimmy was writing a radio script with Herb Schenk," Swindell remembers. "He was fresh from Indiana, and it was immediately clear that he was never going to make it as any kind of writer. Or as an actor, we all thought.

"I mean no disrespect in saying that the Dean I knew was in no way impressive. He was an ordinary guy, showing no special promise scholastically, professionally, or socially. He was friendly in an aggressive way. He attained a modest popularity on campus because he worked for it. He knew everyone, and everyone knew Jim Dean, but perhaps that was not unusual at a junior college whose total enrollment was sixteen hundred. I knew everyone, too."

Not surprisingly, talk at the Schenk home turned to things sexual. "Jimmy said his main priority of the school term was to lose his virginity," says Swindell. If he was not being disingenuous, his declaration implied that his relationship with Bette McPherson had stopped short of penetration. Swindell reflects, "He openly wanted to lose his virginity, as opposed to getting laid. He wanted to know what it was all about."

A few months later, Dean was still pursuing the same goal. "Some of us planned a ski trip at Mount Waterman, which never materialized," Swindell relates. "One of our classmates had a place there; we would stay there and take girls. Jimmy was determined he was going to 'find his manhood' there. It was early 1950. I don't know why it fell through.

"Jim went after my friendship," Swindell continues. "He thought I was smart—and I was—in ways that he wanted to be. It's unlikely we would have had any close association at all, if not for his instigation. He must have sensed his deficiencies, because he latched onto people who possessed the traits he coveted—the Schenk brothers, Jim Wasson [later in *Macbeth* with him at UCLA]. There was also Dianne Hixon, a toothy, willowy blonde, taller than he, who was the homecoming queen. That's probably why he went after her, as a talisman of his upward mobility.

"Dick Schenk and I instituted rooters' buses to football games. Jimmy went with us to San Diego. We would sing 'Ninety-nine Bottles of Beer on the Wall,' that kind of song, and if it's true he couldn't carry a tune, that was the perfect situation for him to sing. And if there were ever a time when Jimmy was in his element, it was during the singing."

Dean had relatively little time to be a football fan because he was intent on making Santa Monica's basketball team. The school had won the conference championship the previous year, but the coach was now faced with the challenge of maintaining a formidable reputation with mostly new players. Practice sessions began in mid-October, and within three weeks fifty candidates had been winnowed down to fifteen. Dean was among them but would spend most of the season, which began December 2, on the bench. His best friend on the squad was Gordon Hein, a first-string forward.

"Dean was a third-stringer," remembers Hein. "His two goals at Santa Monica were to be a disc jockey and to drive in the Indy 500. I lined him up with a gal who would go with us to Dodgers games. Her father was a sportswriter, and she knew more about baseball than either of us.

"I also introduced him to Dianne Hixon, the homecoming queen. He told me he wanted to go out with her, I asked her if she wanted to, and she said it would be okay. Dianne used to walk around campus carrying a shoebox with a pet garter snake in it. She would take it out, curl it around her arm, and pet it. The homecoming queen contest was held at the high school. She stepped up on the pedestal and touched her elbows behind her back so her breasts would flex—and she had 'em. The audience ate it up, so she won.

"The college shared the cafeteria at the high school, and Dean and I ate there often. One day something happened that was right out of *Rebel Without a Cause*. Part of that movie was filmed at the same high school, of course, and the school seal imbedded in the sidewalk is really there. We walked on it and a couple of burly lettermen told us you weren't allowed to step on it."

Although SMCC's speech and theater program was small, it could boast the services of an extraordinary teacher, Mrs. Gene Owen, whose history of theater and beginning acting classes Dean had in fall semester. At the time, Owen said, Dean was ordinary-looking, not one to attract a second glance. Her earliest memories of him in her class were of a quiet, shy, small college boy who always wore glasses. The glasses were always masking a pair of eyes that Owen would not realize were "arresting" until she saw him on television two years later.

The Indiana freshman's speech, as she remembered, was even less auspicious. "His articulation was poor, he mashed his words, and he was somewhat difficult to understand," she said. "In class, someone pointed this out and blamed it on his Hoosier accent." But after class, Dean showed Owen his dental plate with the false front teeth attached, making her understand his difficulty in achieving the proper tongue positions for certain sounds.

To remedy these problems, Owen offered to work with Dean privately for the rest of the semester. "If anything would clear up fuzzy speech," she said, "it would be the demanding soliloquies of Shakespeare." When she suggested to Dean that they work on *Hamlet,* he enthusiastically agreed, wanting to delve right into the "O, what a rogue and peasant slave am I!" speech. But Owen wisely told him he would have to start from the play's beginning and work up to the renowned soliloquy.

"Early I found that Jimmy was not a very good reader, but if complicated parts of the play were explained to him, he would pursue the role of young Hamlet with intensity and originality," Owen said. When their second weekly session came around, he had memorized the opening speech. Owen cued him and then sat back in amazement at what she heard. "In only a dozen lines, he had established a deeply disturbed young Hamlet who touched my heart," she said. "I had seen the play with every great actor in both England and America in the role, and I had never heard those lines expressed quite so well." That night she told her husband she had finally found the right student to play Hamlet as the Prince of Denmark ought to be played.

"On we went through the play," she continued, "with Jimmy de-vouring every soliloquy, short and long, sharpening his articulation, and along the way developing and defining a vulnerable and troubled Ham-let that was artistry." Dean apparently relished this exercise; Dianne Hixon said he was often hunched over *Hamlet,* reading it aloud.

Dean appreciated Owen's friendship as well as the coaching. Sometimes he would wait for her in her office, sitting on the radiator until she returned from class, and they might talk for hours. However, his progress would for a time be apparent only to her. "He was not ac-cused of being talented," says Larry Swindell. "His professed ambition to be a stage and screen actor seemed unreasonable, especially in light of what most of us perceived as his physical shortcomings: short to begin with and thick eyeglasses. He was no Most Likely To Succeed candi-date. Among theater majors that designation belonged to his good friend Jim Wasson, who had movie star looks and was a much better actor.

"Robert Ringer, who later wrote *Looking Out for Number One,* was a young stand-up comic; he gave a program in the high school audi-torium. Jimmy introduced the program; in fact, he was warm-up man for Ringer. He was a rank amateur. He went over like the proverbial lead balloon. We didn't think he was much of a comic.

"In Gene Owen's class there were scenes from plays done, and stu-dents found out about them and would watch. I wandered into the class at Jimmy's invitation to see a scene from William Saroyan's *Hello Out There.* Jimmy played a man in jail; the scene was between him and a girl who took pity on him. He wasn't good."

Gordon Hein's memories of Dean's talents are more flattering. He relates, "Once Dean was in a skit about professional athletes being paid money under the table, a big topic in those days. He told me, 'I'm going to get the biggest laugh.' I asked him how. He got some Black Jack gum and used it to black out every other tooth. So, when he smiled in the skit and flashed his teeth, the audience howled. He knew what he had even then."

A chance encounter off campus highlighted what even then was Dean's gift of dramatic inventiveness. Charles Kersey, also an Indianan and Dean's same age, was studying at the Max Geller Theater Work-shop in Hollywood. One evening, Dean stopped by a friend's apartment and heard show music blaring from a record player inside. The friend was not in, but Kersey, the friend's roommate, let Dean in. Dean's mild curiosity about the music gave way to an even greater curiosity about two chairs facing each other about five feet apart in the living room. Kersey explained this was supposed to be a make-believe window.

"Our instructor wants us to make four entrances into this room in four situations." said Kersey. "Through this window, we're supposed to see someone we like, someone we don't like, an accident, and a sunset that a neighbor has just phoned about. The hard part is getting into the room. We just can't walk in, go to the window, and react. Watching the sunset is easiest, because of the neighbor's call. That gives a reason to go into the room."

Dean asked how Kersey intended to react to the sunset. "Well, I'll like it. I'll think it's pretty," he answered.

"Because your neighbor said it was?" Dean challenged.

"Not entirely. I like sunsets, too," said Kersey.

"Suppose," Dean suggested, "you were asleep at the time he called or busy doing something and couldn't be bothered?" Suddenly Kersey was impressed with Dean's imagination.

Dean also had an idea for the entrance involving a glimpse of a disliked person. "Go to an imaginary bookshelf, run your finger over the titles, and pick a book. Then squint as if you can't make out its title because the light's too dim. Go to the window for more light." Dean demonstrated the sequence as he went along. Pretending to hold a book at the imaginary window, he casually glanced as if at the outdoors. A dark look of hate spread across his face. "I was thinking of this guy I know at home," he explained.

Dean's friend arrived and the two had to leave for a movie. But as Dean left, he called out from the hall, "See you in the movies!" Kersey never got any major breaks as an actor, nor did he ever meet Dean again, but upon seeing *East of Eden* much later, he remembered those parting words.

At Christmastime, Dean sent earrings to Adeline Brookshire and a bracelet to Joyce Wigner back in Fairmount. To Bette McPherson, he sent a remembrance of a different nature: an empty beer bottle wrapped in a napkin on which he had written a few nostalgic and cryptic words about past shared beer-drinking sessions as well as wishes for a superb New Year.

A ten-day series of indoor camp meetings at Pasadena's Bresee Church of the Nazarene brought the peripatetic James DeWeerd to southern California in late January 1950. Dean dropped by to hear one of the minister's twice-daily sermons, and DeWeerd later cited his attendance as proof of a deeply religious nature that went unrecognized by the public.

The new semester began on February 1. From Gene Owen, Dean took voice and diction and radio workshop. Almost immediately he became one of the stars of the announcing crew at the college's radio station. His first assignment of note was to host a program entitled "Student Shares His Interest" on February 23.

Basketball season continued through March. Dean chalked up a grand total of four points: one basket in a February 17 match with Harbor Junior College after Santa Monica was so far ahead that victory was assured, and another in a March 3 game with San Diego. He may have played briefly in other games without showing up in the statistics.

During March, SMCC's newspaper, the *Corsair,* often mentioned Dean's name. It reported on March 1 that he would announce all Friday afternoon radio programs in the coming month. Following the school's annual variety show on March 9, the *Corsair* gossiped, there was a "terrific party" at a hangout called the Glen; among the couples in attendance were "Dean and Hixon." (Perhaps to Dean's dismay, the *Corsair* often noted Hixon's other dates—she was the homecoming queen, after all—with a UCLA man.) Finally, noting the prospects for track and field season, it listed Dean among five pole-vaulters "in good shape." That was his single notice as a vaulter; he apparently never placed in any meet.

In mid-March, the new members of the Opheleos were announced. Swindell explains, "Those of us who held over from fall semester—myself, the Schenk brothers, and others—were the ones who voted on who got in next time, and we got Jim in. The Opheleos supposedly were the outstanding twenty-one male students on campus, and for Jim 'outstanding' certainly implied something other than academic qualifications. He passed his courses, but it was a struggle."

One of Dean's private educational enterprises that year, entirely consistent with his publicly stated wish to lose his virginity, was to familiarize himself with the odysseys of memoirist Frank Harris. "I advised him who Frank Harris was—told him about *My Reminiscences As a Cowboy,*" says Larry Swindell, "and he began reading the autobiographical *My Life and Loves.* He then loaned his copy, with the bawdy passages underlined, out to several of his friends—Gordon Hein and Hans Holland, fellow basketball players, and some football players, too.

"Jimmy was just wild about Frank Harris's life. Largely because of basketball, he hated his own shortness and wished he were six-foot-two or -three. He would go on and on about how Frank Harris was five-foot-three and how women he had bedded would say, 'Oh, you big, strong man!' and said this was his ideal."

On the cultural side of Dean's life was the campus jazz club. "I initiated Jimmy into the lore of Dixieland jazz; 'trad' was what we called it as opposed to the then-current bebop craze," says Swindell. "Soon, he was more interested in trad than I was. With a few others we founded the SMCC jazz club in the spring of 1950. He and I made perhaps half a dozen trips to L.A. to listen to old jazz recordings at Ray Avery's Record Roundup on La Cienega Boulevard."

Although the Korean conflict had not yet started, there was a draft board office on the Santa Monica campus to enable convenient registration for men turning eighteen. "I knew of the draft office, but don't know under what auspices it operated," notes Swindell. "I went to it to apply for my student deferment. The Korean situation was about to erupt and it was a big, nagging worry. As I recall, there was no urgent sense of patriotism, nor was there any spirit of adventure, in contrast to the mood during World War II."

Whether Dean had any contact with this office is unknown; presumably his draft board in Indiana was keeping tabs on him. According to surviving Selective Service records, the portentous first step in the process of being drafted—the classification questionnaire—was mailed to him on April 7.

SMCC's annual May Day festivities came midway through the spring semester; by tradition the drama students presented a melodrama. In *She Was Only a Farmer's Daughter,* Dean played a proud, aristocratic father. Wrapping up the semester were the Opheleos' banquet, to which Dean came with Dianne Hixon; the annual spring sports banquet at the Elks Club; and final exams from June 5 through 14.

Dean is said to have spent the summer as an athletic instructor at a military academy in Glendora, which would have pleased his father—Gene Owen said Winton Dean expected his son to become a basketball coach. However, a three-week trip to Indiana with Winton and Ethel Dean interrupted the summer job. By this time, many of Dean's high school classmates had entered the military. One exception was Dean's good friend Rex Couch, one year his senior, who was studying premed at Indiana University in Bloomington. Dean and Couch drove down one day so Dean could visit Adeline Brookshire, who was working on her master's degree in speech and theater.

Dean told Brookshire he didn't feel his year at Santa Monica had been terribly useful in taking him where he wanted to go in acting. When he wondered aloud about coming to IU, Brookshire had a sudden idea. She took him to see Dr. Norvelle, chairman of the theater arts department. According to Brookshire, Norvelle said he would be delighted to welcome Dean to IU; that much of the interview Dean liked. But Norvelle stressed his belief that all theater arts majors should finish their degree and get a teaching certificate as a hedge against not succeeding as an actor. This was not what Dean wanted to hear, and his ambitions at IU never amounted to more than a whim.

Indiana University was not the only institution of higher learning Dean toured while on vacation. Within the previous year, James DeWeerd had been named president of Kletzing College, a Christian school in Oskaloosa, Iowa. Jennie Andrews Lee, a Kletzing professor, remembers DeWeerd's bringing Dean to see the Iowa campus.

Back from Indiana, Dean hung out with his Santa Monica buddies. "I was perhaps closest to Jim in the summer break between SMCC and UCLA," says Swindell. "When his car broke down and he couldn't immediately afford to have it repaired, he had to resort to double-dating with me in my car, twice. Dianne Hixon was his lady on both occasions. When we double-dated, I'd pick him up at school, a curious thing. It seemed he didn't want me to see where he lived."

Dean, Swindell, and Dick Schenk went to a three-lecture series held in Santa Monica High School's auditorium that summer, featuring anthropologist Margaret Mead, historian Will Durant, and author-folklorist Jesse Stuart. Durant's topic was "Is Progress Real?" Swindell said Dean was "powerfully impressed" by Will Durant's speech and "soon was often heard quoting Durant on the UCLA campus. Years later, when Jim was famous and we were entirely out of touch, I heard that he was still quoting Durant on the reality of progress."

The Santa Monica Theater Guild announced tryouts for another annual production of *The Romance of Scarlet Gulch,* but Dean felt he had had enough melodrama for a lifetime.

Exactly when Dean obtained his father's consent to transfer to UCLA is uncertain. He once mentioned the intended move to Gene Owen, and although she thought it would be a mistake, she kept her feelings to herself. Despite her instincts about Dean's talent, she felt that at that point in his life he would be overwhelmed by the bigger school's more rigorous academic standards. Even though Santa Monica lacked its own theater, she still felt Dean would be better served by its more intimate classroom settings and opportunities for individual help. She knew the cutthroat nature of UCLA's theater arts department, and Dean didn't seem secure enough to endure it. All of her premonitions would turn out to be right, but Dean had to find out for himself.

The Reluctant Bruin

"There are no stars at UCLA." If new students in the Theater Arts Department retained nothing else of Dr. Ralph Freud's[1] orientation lecture, that is the one idea he hoped would stick. "You're here to learn the craft of acting, set design, costumes, and lighting. You don't come here to be a star." The department's mission was to turn out professionals who understood all aspects of the theater.

James Dean, of course, was at UCLA precisely to become a star. For a brief time, he dabbled in the department's program, but his chronic inability to accept an environment of conformity doomed any possibility of his flourishing. As for academics, his status as a prelaw major was simply an accommodation of his father's revised wishes, an obstacle rather than an opportunity.

Enrolling at UCLA brought a change in logistics. Winton and Ethel Dean were now living in Reseda, several miles north of the university. Rather than stay with them and commute, Dean opted to seek housing on or near campus. When he registered, he specified his interest in joining a fraternity; based on personal information he provided—accomplished athlete, recipient of many high school awards—he was

---

1. Head of the Theater Division of the Theater Arts Department, his name was pronounced Frood.

steered toward Sigma Nu. His acceptance as a pledge entitled him to live in the fraternity house at 601 Gayley Avenue.

It was there that Dean first met a fellow pledge named James Bellah, a strapping, dark-haired youth who became a good friend. Bellah had just transferred from Johns Hopkins University in Baltimore. "We lived in the pledge dorm section of the house with bunks and lockers," Bellah remembers. "There were six to eight in a room. Dean was vacuuming the main room in the house when I saw him for the first time. He introduced himself. He grinned and was very warm."

Dean knew that his gifts in basketball and pole-vaulting were too minor for UCLA, so he took up other sports. Bellah introduced him to fencing, a pursuit he would embrace enthusiastically. "I had been a freshman fencer at Johns Hopkins, first saber," says Bellah. "I started at eight or nine years of age; my father had fenced. Dean wanted to learn it, so I started showing him some of the basics. He had an amazing athletic ability. The son of a bitch made a point on me the first time he held a foil in his hand! I was amazed."

The first letter Dean wrote to the Winslows from UCLA brimmed with enthusiasm for Greek life. He said it was too fabulous to describe verbally, so opted to send a picture instead. The letter was full of delight in fencing; Dean spoke of meeting Bellah and how he was picking up the fundamentals of fencing from this new friend. In fact, he added, both he and Bellah were on UCLA's fencing team.

Dean was inflating his claims to glory. According to Bellah, "UCLA had a fencing club, but not a fencing team. And Dean was not in the club. The only time I saw him fence was when I was showing him in an upstairs corridor of the house how to do it."

Dean also informed his aunt and uncle that he had learned to shoot a rifle, showing enough promise as a marksman to earn permission to use the rifle range at any time. Conceding that his newfound skills and fraternity life were taking their toll on his studies, he said he hoped to hold up. The letter was written just after the UCLA football team's October 18 victory, twenty-to-six, over Purdue, played on the Indiana campus. Dean tweaked his uncle about Purdue's loss and suggested that he visit California, where the Bruin team was robust and football taken seriously. He closed by saying his pledge brothers were complaining about his keeping his lamp on to write.

Larry Swindell, Dean's pal from Santa Monica City College, had also transferred to UCLA that fall. "Jim changed after he became a fraternity boy," says Swindell. "The change was that he became a jock, or, more accurately, a groupie at Kerckhoff Hall, the student union building, with the football players. In particular, he became a friend of Ernie Stockert, an end, and Dave Williams, a fullback." Both athletes were Sigma Nus. "Kerckhoff had a large veranda, and the football players had their turf," Swindell continues. "Jimmy was usually there with them. His wanting to climb became more obvious at UCLA, when it had already been obvious at Santa Monica!"

Another reason to hang out with the football jocks was that they had meal tickets. "The football players were highly privileged," recalls Charlotte Freedland, a theater arts student. "They had tutors. They ate in the Annex. And if you hung around with them, they took care of you—especially Ike Jones, a football player and motion picture major, handsome as Harry Belafonte. With him it was always, 'What do you need?' The meal tickets were issued to the athletes, but no one made an issue out of who ate."

On the romantic side of his life, Dean began dating Jeanetta Lewis, a young woman from Texas who was a Theta and involved in theater arts. He squired her to a Sigma Nu dance, where a photographer caught one of the broadest grins Dean ever managed.

Diverting as these activities were, his real purpose at UCLA was to act. Each semester, the Theater Arts Department presented four major productions. Louis Cutelli (later known as Lou Cutell) said general auditions began the first Monday of the semester and lasted the whole week. Applicants had to fill out a questionnaire and were then ushered in to read for all four directors. Callback sheets were posted each morning, and the directors debated the strengths, weaknesses, and ideal deployment of their talent pool until the following Monday, when final cast lists were posted. Among the selections for the fall semester of 1950 were *Macbeth,* to be directed by Walden Boyle, and *Papa Is All,* a comedy about an Amish family, to be directed by Edward Hearn.

"I was in an off-campus play and couldn't make general auditions," says Cutelli, who had recently transferred from Glendale College, "But I really wanted to be in *Macbeth,* so I asked Walden Boyle to give me a private audition. To my surprise, he agreed and told me to come read for him on Friday."

When Cutelli arrived, he found Edward Hearn sitting in with Boyle. "I read from *Macbeth* but didn't do very well," he says. "Then Hearn asked me to read from *Papa Is All.* I read it cold." Much later, Hearn told Cutelli that as of that Friday, James Dean was tentatively set to be cast as Jake, the male lead in *Papa Is All.* But Hearn was not completely satisfied with Dean and decided against him after observing Cutelli's reading. Cutelli was oblivious to Hearn's dilemma and left his audition feeling that he'd be lucky just to be a spear-carrier in *Macbeth.*

On Monday morning, anxious students crowded around the bulletin board. "I remember looking at the *Macbeth* list and being crestfallen because my name wasn't on it," Cutelli says. "But then I heard someone exclaim in disgust, 'Who the fuck is Louis Cutelli?' I had got the lead in *Papa Is All!*"

Dean, meanwhile, had been assigned to play Malcolm, elder son of King Duncan of Scotland, in *Macbeth.* Unaware that he had been passed over for a leading role, he glowed with happiness. Writing to the Winslows, he called his good fortune "the biggest thrill of my life." Three hundred and sixty-seven actors and actresses read and reread for the coveted roles, he said, and he had emerged among the chosen few. He called Malcolm a "wonderful lead" and a "huge part." "God! It's a dream, don't anyone wake me up," he exulted.

Malcolm is indeed a principal role, with many lengthy and demanding orations, including the play's final speech. Dean was too ignorant to be intimidated by its demands. Thanks to Gene Owen, who had coached him in *Hamlet,* he had some limited exposure to Shakespeare. But his only real experience in emoting the florid language of a bygone era was with Dickens's "A Madman's Manuscript" in high school.

Joel Climenhaga, who played Siward, general of the English forces, remembers, "*Macbeth* was produced under very strange circumstances. The scenery for Dunsinane castle was on the stage, while Birnam Wood was in the orchestra pit. I was supposed to lead the charge against Dunsinane, but I've always been extremely myopic and they didn't have glasses in twelfth-century England. I was afraid of falling on my face. So in rehearsals I suggested to Wally Boyle, 'I'm here to help

Malcolm; why don't you have him lead the charge?' Boyle thought that
was a great idea, so he told Jimmy to lead the charge.

"Jimmy took a big gulp and said, 'All right,' and then led the
charge. After rehearsal he came up to me and said, 'You're older than
me and less vain. That's why you wear glasses and most of the time I
don't. But I'm just as blind as you!' So it was a situation of the blind
leading the blind. Jimmy's horn-rimmed glasses were not a common
sight when he came to UCLA. He avoided wearing glasses in public at
all costs. In performance we sometimes stumbled on the eighth step or
so of the charge, and the audience would titter."

The curtain rose on *Macbeth* on Wednesday, November 29, 1950,
at eight P.M. (In all, there were four evening performances and a Thursday matinée.) The *Daily Bruin,* UCLA's student newspaper, favorably
reviewed the production but singled out only Macbeth, Lady Macbeth,
and the three witches for commendation. If Dean felt slighted at not
being mentioned, the *Bruin* made it up to him the following day, when,
as Malcolm, he was pictured on the front page in a scene with Macduff
and Banquo.

Specific reaction to Dean as Malcolm was uniformly bad, suggesting that his special affinity for Hamlet, sensed by Gene Owen back at
SMCC, did not carry over to Malcolm, or else that he was still too inex-
perienced to project that quality on stage. "He was overshadowed by
and in awe of Frank Wolff, who played Macbeth," explained student
Gail Kobe, "so he sort of stayed back."

Fellow students who saw the production were not impressed. John
Holden remembers thinking, "He just hasn't got it! He's never going to
be an actor." Larry Swindell grimaced, "Jim was terrible in *Macbeth*—
really terrible." Harve Bennett, the student reviewer of *Spotlight,* the
Theater Arts Department's newspaper, opined that Dean "failed to
show any growth, and would have made a hollow king." Bennett, later
cowriter and producer of many *Star Trek* movies, says Dean played Malcolm with an Indiana accent. "It was very wrong," he remembers. Reaction from actors in the production was even worse. Their objections are
pretty well summed up in Joel Climenhaga's comment that "stage acting was a cooperative art and Jimmy was not a cooperative actor."

But Dean seemed blissfully unaware of the complaints. To the
Winslows, he professed that he was now considered a competent actor

by his director, peers, and audiences. Even more delusional was his statement that the role had made him remarkably popular in a matter of weeks. If he could keep the momentum, he averred, he would surely make his mark in the theater world someday.

Many theater arts students from Dean's era have retained vivid impressions of him. To some, he was quite friendly; others were barely acknowledged. He complimented Rod Bladel, who played Macduff's son in *Macbeth,* on his articulation. "He said I was the only one in the cast he could hear without straining," says Bladel. "During *Macbeth* we would chat behind Royce Hall. He told me he wanted to do *Hamlet* someday.

"The only class we had together was anthropology, a huge lecture class. He tried to help me with the final during a cigarette break, but I flunked it anyway.

"He wasn't a hick or a hayseed. He seemed comfortable in urban surroundings. Nothing about him was compensative. Actually, he was a very ordinary kid, pleasant, friendly, down-to-earth—good-looking both with glasses and without. You know, we had no idea he had the talent that was later on display in *East of Eden.* We never dreamed that he would get all this mystique."

Lou Cutelli was already getting small parts in movies, for which Dean envied him. Says Cutelli, "Jimmy was always asking me, 'How did you do that?' Once he was sitting with me under a tree, and he kept saying, over and over, 'I gotta get myself an agent.' I thought that with the kind of looks he was blessed with, he ought to make it."

Encouraged by Cutelli's success, Dean enlisted Rod Bladel to help him prepare an audition for *I Want You,* an upcoming Sam Goldwyn picture starring Farley Granger. Dean wanted to use a scene from Sidney Kingsley's play *Detective Story* and asked Bladel to read the woman's lines. After Bladel critiqued Dean's interpretation, Dean began calling him "my old coach."

Morris Green, one of the construction crew on *Macbeth,* remembers Dean as very quiet, almost morose. "If you spoke to him," says Green, "all you would get out of him was a Gary Cooper–like 'yup' or 'nope.' But you had to notice him, because he intended for you to notice. You would notice him more than someone who was affable. And he always had *Daily Variety* or the *Hollywood Reporter* stuck in his back pocket. He was a poseur.

"He was always hanging around with Denis Sanders, a student filmmaker who would win an Oscar in 1954 for *A Time Out of War,* a two-reeler. Denis rode a Vespa [an Italian motor scooter] and Jimmy had a Vespa, too. You would always see them hanging around the shacks, a group of temporary World War II buildings. There was a parking lot over there. Denis Sanders had family money—it was a well-connected family. He was the only person I ever saw Dean with."

It is a rare student from that era who can remember Dean's spending time with or being close to anyone else in the department. "Jimmy was always distant," says Dick Altman. "It was common for a group of us to sit together on the lawn behind Royce Hall and eat lunch. Often you could look fifty feet away and see Jimmy alone under a tree. He never joined us."

Morris Green continues, "I felt that if you were someone important who could lead to Dean's future, he would go with you. If he could use you, he would. This was how I sized him up immediately. You just didn't exchange pleasantries or chat with him. As far as sexual orientation goes, I don't remember thinking of him as preferring either male or female. Simply put, his eye was on the target. He struck me as the kind who was killing time at UCLA until he connected."

Although Dean had done his gentlemanly duty on the dating front, some of his colleagues became aware that he occasionally hovered at the edges of the gay world. John Holden, a veteran attending UCLA on the GI Bill of Rights, said, "One night after a rehearsal or some late happening at school, Jimmy and I were walking to the parking lot. He sat in my car with me. I didn't know him well, but we were talking intimately. He wasn't attempting any seduction, but I could detect that he was seeking information about gay life in a very oblique way. 'Do you ever go to those bars?' he asked. I said I had been to some but was not amused and thereafter kept the conversation away from that subject."

Through Jeanetta Lewis, Dean had met two new friends during *Macbeth* rehearsals: Joanne Mock, who played Lady Macduff, and Bill Bast, her boyfriend. The four of them began double-dating and once, after a Friday rehearsal of *Macbeth,* decided on a whim to drive up the

Pacific coast to Santa Barbara for breakfast. "We used my father's car," remembers Mock, "and Bill forgot to put oil in it, so it broke down and we were stranded. Jimmy and I had to be back for our Saturday rehearsal, so Bill and Jeanetta stayed with the car and we hitchhiked. Jimmy made up stories to tell the people who gave us rides. He would say we were married and had been to see relatives in the country, or some such thing."

Not long after *Macbeth* ended, Dean got in and then out of a one-act play, *The Land of Heart's Desire,* by William Butler Yeats. "That semester," relates Joel Climenhaga, "Bill Bast and I both lived in the 'Kelton flophouse,' a rooming house for about twenty students at 555 Kelton. Bill had a part in *The Land of Heart's Desire,* and Ted Shank was the student director. However, we had a highly disciplined department, and if you missed a rehearsal, you were asked to leave the department.

"One Saturday night, Bill had had a late date with Joanne Mock. In fact, I was already up when he came in from it. He was still asleep at noon, and rehearsal for the one-act was to start at one. Somewhere between twelve-thirty and twelve-forty-five, Jimmy Dean came into the house, walked back into Bill's bedroom, and discovered Bill was still asleep. I was sitting in the kitchen, and Jimmy came in there and said, 'I thought Bill had a rehearsal this afternoon.' I told him that was correct. Then Jimmy mumbled hmmph and left."

At slightly past one, Dean walked into the rehearsal room. "As I recall," says Ted Shank, "Jimmy and Bill had both auditioned and I had cast Bill, not Jimmy. Then Bill started having problems getting to rehearsals. I discussed it with him and said, 'Let's just say if you're late again, we'll have to recast.' When Jimmy came in, he said, 'I heard if Bill was late again you were going to recast.' I said that was true, but he wasn't terribly late yet. Jimmy protested that he had just checked and found that Bill had slept through his alarm, so I told him the part was his."

Oddly, the *Spotlight* review of *The Land of Heart's Desire* doesn't list Dean (or Bast, for that matter) in the cast. "I believe what happened," says Climenhaga, "is that Jimmy couldn't get the Irish brogue necessary for the part, and Ted Shank was a perfectionist."

New Year's Eve was a perfect finale to what had been a good year for Dean. He joined others at a campus theater party hosted by Jim Wasson (Banquo in *Macbeth*). Larry Swindell was mildly surprised to see that Dean's date was Dianne Hixon, from SMCC. "Dianne hadn't transferred to UCLA with the rest of us," says Swindell. "I watched them kiss at the stroke of midnight. I hadn't known he was still in touch with her."

Sometime that winter, Dean's friend James Bellah did him an inadvertent but valuable favor. One of the few Sigma Nu pledges who was also interested in acting, Bellah had secured the services of an agent, Isabel Draesemer, through family connections. As Draesemer later explained, the problem with Bellah's getting into pictures was that he looked older, not younger, than he was. "I don't think I can do anything with you at this age," she told him, "but I'll try."

A potential break for Bellah came when Ken Dyson, casting director for Jerry Fairbanks Studios, called Draesemer about a Pepsi commercial. "He asked for kids who looked like they were sixteen through eighteen, but actually older," she said, "to avoid child labor–law problems. He said, 'They don't even have to be actors. I want to fill up the Griffith Park merry-go-round.'

"I realized this would be a good opportunity for a young actor to pick up a union card," Draesemer continued. "So I told Bellah, 'You're awfully tall for a teenager, but wear tight jeans and a floppy sweater and stay in the background, and maybe you'll get by.' I told him and others to bring their friends. All in all, I gathered up thirty-five kids.

"Ken Dyson invited me to come by for lunch at Griffith Park. So, rather than have thirty-five kids traipsing in my office to give me their dollar-and-a-half agent fee, I told them to bring it by while I was up there for lunch. Bellah gave me three dollars, and I told him it was only one-fifty—this sounds ridiculous in the current day and age—and he said, 'No, this is for Jimmy Dean.' And I asked who this was. Bellah said, 'They're doing a special shot of him and a girl getting the brass ring.' And I thought, 'Uh-oh! Of all these kids on that merry-go-round, they've picked this Dean kid for that shot. I'd better see about him.'"

According to Bellah, there was a second day of filming on the Pepsi commercial in a studio. "It involved a jitterbug and a piano," he says. "I was supposed to be the lead, but my dancing style is sedate. Dean was more wild. He got on stage and showed me how the dance should be done. So he got asked to do the second day of filming."

Isabel Draesemer remembers, "That night, Bellah phoned and he was all upset. He said, 'Do you know I had to drag Dean out of bed, and he was drunk'—Jimmy was drinking heavily at this time—'and he didn't care if he went or not. I told him, "You promised," and now they've called him back to work tomorrow in the studio for fifty-five dollars a day,' the union minimum wage then. 'He's going to work in the studio, and I'm not called back.'" Draesemer tried to be consoling, but hearing that Dean had now been singled out twice for close-ups activated her agent's instincts.

"I had him come in," she said. "He kind of draped himself into a couch; he would never sit. He just kind of flopped. I asked him if he wanted a career." Dean had already made it clear to colleagues that he fervently wished to be an actor, but he put on one of his acts for Draesemer. "Can I make a buck?" he replied casually.

Draesemer believed he could make a buck. "He had the advantage of looking younger, you see, and that is quite something." According to California's law, "under eighteen, you can only work four hours, and you have to have a social worker and a teacher. So I saw him as being able to play parts several years younger than he actually was.[2]

"It was a very strange time in Hollywood. You had to have a job to get your union card, but how can you get it if you can't get the job until you have it? Jimmy got his card through the Pepsi commercial. At that time, there was a fight between SAG [Screen Actors Guild] and AFTRA [American Federation of Television and Radio Actors). TV film had come in, and the problem was, which of the two unions should it come under? So, during this conflict, you could work under the Taft-Hartley Act for up to thirty days without belonging to any union. This is how Jimmy worked without having a card.

"As I saw it, Jimmy would need a studio contract with a rising salary over seven years—if he could last that long. Robert Taylor and Robert Stack rose to stardom under that system. He needed to make it by the time he was twenty-five. Otherwise, he'd be too baby-faced between then and forty to get much work.

---

2. Draesemer did not recruit Dean after watching him in *Macbeth,* as Bill Bast's biography claims; in fact, she did not attend *Macbeth.*

"I never had him sign a contract with me, though, because I didn't think he was that stable. I wasn't too sure of him. I didn't know.

"The photographer Wilson Millar, a friend of mine, agreed to do a full set of portraits of Jimmy for free. Wilson was a fairly famous man for his portraits of animals, which amused Jimmy. He also did all the stars appearing at the Griffith Park Greek Theater for many years. For women, he was fair, but his male studies were strong.

"I didn't want Jimmy to be a pretty boy. Actually, he wasn't. His profile was gorgeous, but in frontal view he was only nice-looking. His eyes were too close together, photographically, and being so nearsighted he was inclined to squint. In action, that was okay. But he missed being a romantic leading man or a strong 'heavy.' I classified him as a lead juvenile.

"Most often, an actor's eyes are the key feature on the screen, but Jimmy's prominent feature was his mouth. I thought he was a male Marilyn Monroe; all his romantic and sex appeal was the maneuvering and playing of that mouth.

"But anyway, I got him eight or nine jobs that year. These jobs were not big, but he would be in a scene. The major studios would look at rushes at night, and even if you were only in one scene, directors and producers would see you. Although actors griped about not getting anywhere, they were being seen this way."

Although Dean now had an agent, 1951 would not be so lucky for him. For starters, fraternity life turned sour on him. As revealed a decade later in *Delta,* Sigma Nu's quarterly magazine, there had been signs from Dean's first days as a pledge that he "was having difficulty adjusting to the give-and-take of chapter life. He remained aloof from chapter activities, preferring to stand on the fringe rather than get involved in the excitement of the period. He spent much of his time in his room, producing Salvador Dali–like sketches, such as a bloodshot eyeball suspended in midair and staring at a burned-over forest." (The eyeball motif, so prominent in the watercolors Dean painted during his brief suspension from Fairmount High, had carried over to his UCLA period.)

Manuel Gonzalez, chapter commander of Sigma Nu, said, "Whether or not these sketches are an insight into what was Jimmy's seemingly withdrawn nature, I cannot really say. However, I do believe they are indicative of the fact that he spent a great deal of his time in such individual endeavors rather than taking any part in any cohesive activities. Apparently, he was not comfortable in our group."

There are multiple versions of what Sigma Nu considered to be the last straw in the matter of James Dean, and all of them involve fists. One concerns housecleaning chores that pledges had to perform. Gonzalez, inspecting Dean's work, twice refused to approve it, prompting Dean to punch him in the nose. Another holds that Dean socked a different Sigma Nu member for impugning his masculinity because he was in theater arts. Richard Scott, a fellow pledge who lived with his parents and not at the house, says he heard the incident stemmed from a prank that the pledges had planned to play on the "actives" at dinnertime, which quickly degenerated into a food fight in which Dean slugged someone. Whatever the actual events, Sigma Nu asked Dean to give back his pledge pin early in the new year.

Richard Scott had liked Dean—they had double-dated—and so had the other pledges. On the night of initiation, Scott said, they banded together and told the actives they were going to walk out as a pledge class unless Dean was let back in. Somehow, pressure was brought to bear, and their rebellion folded after a couple of hours. But it was a kind gesture to Dean.

Summing up the pledge experience, James Bellah says, "I became an active member of Sigma Nu, but Dean didn't get in. It had to do with his personality. He was too eccentric. Mind you, I found him amusing. You never knew what he was going to do next. He was a born performer; he loved to take the stage. But Sigma Nu was establishment, and Dean was not establishment. He was just undesirable."[3]

Further disillusionment with UCLA came with Dean's failure to be cast in any of the spring semester's major productions. He wanted passionately to get the leading role of John, the witch boy, in *Dark of the Moon*, but Edward Hearn, its director, was the same one who had

---

3. Bellah doubts the story in Dalton's *The Mutant King* about Dean, as part of Sigma Nu initiation, being forced to lie spread-eagle on the bottom of a swimming pool while it was drained. For one thing, he said, Dean was booted out before the annual hell week, which in any case was not a brutal experience. Further, "there was no pool at the Sigma Nu house."

vetoed him for *Papa Is All.* The powers-that-be were not looking for Dean's special, camera-friendly quality, which had so captivated the Pepsi people. Dean pouted and withdrew from his friends, rather than take the loss in stride.[4]

He did land a good part in a one-act. "One of the student-written one-acts in the spring semester of 1951 was *The Axe of God* by Richard Eshleman, our superstar playwright on campus then," says Larry Swindell. "The 'axe' was Martin Luther. Jimmy was cast as a young monk. He went into rehearsal and thought *Axe of God* was a terrific play."

Richard Eshleman remembers, "Jimmy played a young monk who had come to the Wartburg seeking out Martin Luther in exile. He finds Luther in the company of [his future wife] Kathryn von Bora. Luther seems more concerned about his constipation than about God. Needless to say, the young monk is disillusioned and says he's going back to his order. Kathryn von Bora, played by Gail Kobe, tried to explain to him what Luther was all about. As playwright, I should have let the director and cast run with it, but the scenes between Jimmy and Gail were so exciting that I kept coming to rehearsals."

Kobe reports that Dean was always experimenting in rehearsals. "He was extraordinary," she said. "If you would go along with what he was doing, you could find wonderful things." Von Bora was pregnant with Martin Luther's child, which the monk finds so abhorrent that he insists she have an abortion. "His character had a point of view that was very strong, and so did mine," said Kobe. "So that made for a great conflict."

One night after rehearsal, Dean had an introspective conversation with Richard Eshleman. "He asked for a ride home, so I gave him a lift to Fraternity Row," Eshleman says. "But before he went in we sat in the car talking for a long time. He complained about fraternity life—said he'd been in a couple of fistfights there. He also told me how his father had urged him to major in prelaw. He was dissatisfied with everything and wanted to make some changes. He asked if I thought there was a

---

4. Charles Vorbach, the student who beat out Dean for the role, got an even worse review from Harve Bennett in *Spotlight* than Dean got for *Macbeth*. Vorbach, wrote Bennett, "basically wasn't right for the part," "never captured the animal strength of the 'Witch Boy,'" and "failed to delineate a specific brand of virility."

basis in his acting ability to justify changing his major from prelaw to theater arts. Based on what I'd seen in rehearsals, I said yes. But to change your major at UCLA, you had to drop out and then reenroll later. I urged him to do it."

The Axe of God was good experience, but it could not match the excitement of working professionally for the first time. "Not too long after the Pepsi commercial," said Isabel Draesemer, "Ken Dyson called me to say they were going to film an Easter show for the syndicated series *Father Peyton's TV Playhouse* at Jerry Fairbanks Studios, and they specifically wanted Jimmy to play John the Beloved." Dean was somewhat familiar with the dynamics of religious drama, having played a money changer driven by Christ from the temple in the Marion, Indiana, Easter pageant two years earlier. The show was called *Hill Number One,* a reference to Calvary, and John the Beloved had only a few lines but popped up in several scenes.

Billed by the *Hollywood Reporter* as "the most ambitious and imposing television film undertaking yet planned," *Hill Number One* had a cast of fifty, including some of Hollywood's prominent stars and character actors. Set to direct was Arthur Pierson, who, as a veteran of Cecil B. DeMille productions, was an obvious choice for a religious film.

Hill Number One was filmed during the last week of February. James Bellah, cast as a Roman soldier, says, "Dean was very sick with a bad case of the flu when he did the show. I gave him a ride to the studio in my Model A convertible, and it was cold. I literally forced him to work and probably damn near killed him in the process. At any rate, we both showed up for all calls. But because of his flu, his voice became quite hoarse. When the show was broadcast, a number of female members of the audience mistook this infirmity for sexiness."

Before the Easter show, Dean's exile from Sigma Nu had forced him to find other living arrangements. Characteristically, when faced with a crisis he was not too proud to ask for help. In this case, he turned to Bill Bast. Finding himself on a bus from Hollywood with Bast one evening, Dean plied his charm with considerable skill, flattering Bast with appeals to his intelligence and sophistication before suggesting that they go apartment hunting together the next day. After all, he cajoled, couldn't two people afford a place more easily than one?

The would-be roommates fell in love with a spacious three-room apartment decorated in Southwest style. Although it was more expensive than two students could afford, the decor and cheerfulness were too appealing to resist. The advance rent payment emptied both their wallets. A month later, just as it seemed that Dean would never come up with his share of the rent, his earnings from *Hill Number One* came through and saved the day.

By this time, Dean was cutting classes and driving his 1936 Chevy into Hollywood to look for parts or to hang out in Isabel Draesemer's office. Exhilarated by his Easter show, he understandably felt that Hollywood, not UCLA, was where his acting future lay. Then another auspicious opportunity arose. Bill Bast told him about an off-campus acting workshop to be led by actor James Whitmore.

The workshop owed its existence to graduate student John Holden, who had been close to Whitmore at the Yale University School of Drama. In the spring of 1950, UCLA had presented *He Who Gets Slapped,* in which Holden and Bast both played clowns. "Whitmore liked the way UCLA did its shows, so he came to see me in it," says Holden. "When Bast heard that Whitmore was coming, he begged me to introduce him. I asked Whitmore if he'd mind if a student joined us for a drink after the show. He okayed it, so Bast came with us—and ended up dominating the conversation."

The following spring, Whitmore called Holden and asked, "Are you coming to this class?" Holden said he didn't know what Whitmore was talking about. He was surprised that Bast had discussed the workshop with Whitmore without telling him. "Whitmore said he wanted me to come to the class because I was the only one he would know," says Holden. "So I went. It started out at the Brentwood Country Mart, but sometimes was held at other places, including my house in Santa Monica."

Whitmore said he agreed to lead the class "completely selfishly, to reaffirm things that I had learned in New York in the Actors Studio, and to see if they applied to young people and if they could be communicated to young people." Aside from acting exercises that heightened the use of the senses and imagination, Whitmore hoped to impress on the class the need to discover "what it is you essentially want as an artist." Thrilled with Whitmore's skill and knowledge, Dean quickly ingratiated himself with the veteran actor.

Back at UCLA, *The Axe of God* was set for March 21 but without James Dean. Richard Eshleman laments, "By urging him to drop out, I cooked my own goose, because he did drop out. As I recall, he gave us about a week's notice that he was leaving the play. Our stage manager had to take over his role." Larry Swindell, who was reviewing one-acts for the *Daily Bruin,* says he was completely surprised to discover the stage manager in Dean's role. With the exception of those who were involved in *Axe,* none of Dean's colleagues remembers his saying good-bye or even telling them he was leaving.

When reporters later asked why he had dropped out, Dean would offer a variety of rationales. "The school said I should leave," he told Mike Connolly, implying that academic standards were not met. To Howard Thompson of *The New York Times,* he said, "I busted a couple of guys in the nose and got myself kicked out. I wasn't happy in law, either." When Hedda Hopper interviewed him, he said, "I couldn't take the tea-sipping, moss-walled academicians, that academic bull." This last statement was probably closest to the truth.

During *Macbeth* rehearsals, Dean had a revealing conversation with Gail Kobe, who was working on costumes. "He came up to me while I was shredding plaid fabric to make fringe, and asked why I was doing it," she says. "I told him that I had to, since I was in costumes class that semester. I tried to explain that you were expected to learn all of the crafts that go into a theatrical production. He was unfazed. He said, 'I want to act. I don't want to do all that other stuff.' " By leaving UCLA, he proved that he meant what he said.

Heads or Tails?

Free at last of the constricting environment he found UCLA to be, Dean would soon learn that the real world had its own hurdles and sand traps. Despite his self-confidence and the best efforts of Isabel Draesemer, the early results of his pursuit of acting jobs would be negligible. Unemployment and its attendant agonies caused one of the most miserable periods of his life. The torment would drag on for months before an admiring benefactor, Rogers Brackett, gave him the breaks he needed to start building his career.

Dean and Draesemer harbored great hopes that *Hill Number One* would boost his profile and marketability. According to the *Hollywood Reporter,* every television station in the country aired it, reaching an estimated forty-two million viewers. Never again in his lifetime would Dean reach as large an audience. Moreover, the show's quality, for 1951, was considered impeccable. *The New York Times* praised the cast for "rendering one of the most nearly perfect performances ever seen" on the small screen. The *Hollywood Reporter* appreciated the "wealth of ability in the smaller roles."

The critics may not have taken note of Dean, but the grassroots reaction was favorable and enthusiastic. Dean told John Holden that he received a huge stack of fan mail. The loudest cheers came from Immaculate Heart High School near Griffith Park in Los Angeles, where a group of girls assigned to watch *Hill Number One* judged Dean to be a new heartthrob, tracked down Isabel Draesemer, and beseeched her to send her dreamy client to a party they wanted to give in his honor. He was pleased to oblige them.

Dean spent Easter Sunday with the Mock family, and they watched *Hill Number One* together. Joanne Mock had introduced him to her younger sister, Kay, whom he was dating. ("It was a thrill to be asked out by an older guy," says Kay Mock. "He was cute and nice but an odd duck—moody.") Elsewhere on Easter, Isabel Draesemer had asked casting agents to watch *Hill Number One*—many in the cast were her clients—then hosted an open house for both groups to mingle. But despite the legwork and hospitality, no one called to request Dean's services. "Jimmy was short and looked underage," Draesemer explains. "They were not interested in signing him for another Rock Hudson or Robert Taylor or glamour boy. At that time, for anything that was good, Jimmy was competing with stars who were in the age range for his kind of part, which made things quite hard. So he would have to break in through reputation."

Nonetheless, she gave Dean her best efforts. "He was presented to every talent department in town. There was no sense in his seeing producers and directors, since he didn't have any film credits. Sometimes I was there to present him to the talent departments, and sometimes appointments were made for him."

Without income, Dean could not cover his share of the utility bills, rent, or food. But though expenses were a constant irritant, what really irked him was the rejection implied in being an unemployed actor. He fell prey to the same ugly moods that had followed losing the part in *Dark of the Moon,* but now they were more frequent. Holing up in his room for hours at a time, he would sometimes grunt at Bill Bast's efforts to communicate or ignore him completely.

One of the few bright spots in this wasteland was James Whitmore's acting class. Margaret Ann Curran, who was UCLA's Lady Macbeth, recalls, "About eight of us met at Brentwood Country Mart for the Whitmore class. I don't remember any scenes being done. We did sensory exercises, one of which was to recall how many wires were strung into the building where we met, to get you to be aware of surroundings to draw on when you're acting. Jimmy and I became closer through the class. He certainly blossomed and flourished in it."

Joanne Mock attended one session of the Whitmore class where an improvisation was done. "Beforehand," she says, "Whitmore gave everyone a secret that they were supposed to keep. Then they all came together for what was supposed to be a club meeting, and I was the chairwoman. But I ruined it because I asked, 'How many of you are Communists?' and that turned out to be everyone's secret."

Whitmore believed that the "muscles of acting" are the imagination, the senses, and the emotions, and that they ought to be worked out regularly. Simple tasks were prescribed as exercises: "You peel an apple," explained Whitmore, "without the apple being there or without a knife in your hand—just using your imagination and your sensory equipment to make it be there. This is not usable on the stage, but it just heightens the organism you're using."

The class gave Dean an outlet for some of his pent-up energy. As for his miserably empty stomach, some kind soul would occasionally rescue him. Isabel Draesemer often invited him to dinner at her home. In May, Bill Bast's mother came from Milwaukee for a visit and took upon herself the mission of restocking the roommates' cupboards and cooking nightly dinners. But the most significant angel of mercy was seventeen-year-old Beverly Wills, daughter of comedienne Joan Davis.

Wills, who was an actress on CBS radio's *Junior Miss,* was introduced to Dean by Bast, who was dating her at the same time he was seeing Joanne Mock. One day at UCLA, Dean encountered Mock and invited her to coffee in Kerckhoff Hall. "While we were sitting there," Mock reports, "he told me Bill was two-timing me with Beverly. He was peering at me closely, as if he were most interested in seeing my reaction. I felt I was being observed. I went to the ladies' room and cried. It was the first time in my life I had been dumped! Jimmy and I were not close friends, so it was an odd thing for him to do."

Eventually, Wills began two-timing Bast with Dean. Even from their first encounter, a double date during which he scarcely spoke, Dean's moods were painfully evident to her. Her account of their few months of steady dating is so full of instances of his tormented, angry disposition and rude deportment that one wonders why she tolerated his company at all. Photos of Wills, however, reveal that the gift of beauty had passed her by. Actress Karen Sharpe, who was Wills's best friend at Hollywood Professional School, said, "Beverly always liked good-looking young men. I don't know if she and Jimmy were lovers, but I wouldn't be surprised. Beverly was very outgoing. She wasn't pretty by traditional Hollywood standards, but she had a strong, positive, and happy nature. That must have been attractive to sensitive and inhibited men. Fond as I was of her, I always wondered how she got all the good-looking guys."

Wills did witness a few instances when Dean's good qualities pierced the gloom. At a picnic, he amused her by climbing a tree and swinging from a high branch, pretending to be a monkey. When her senior prom at Hollywood Professional School rolled around, he seemed thrilled to wear a rented white tuxedo and escort her. So high were his spirits that when Joan Davis dropped by—she and Wills had prepared a mother-daughter skit as the prom's entertainment—he leaped up to help Davis off with her wrap. "Good heavens, I've never seen him like this before," whispered the surprised Davis.

But these happy moments were far outweighed by outbursts of anger or periods of listless silence. At Wills's home, Dean seldom acknowledged Joan Davis's presence. He would slump in her favorite chair and hang his foot over the side, making no movement for hours other than desultory stretches of the arm toward the fruit bowl until its contents were gone. Once Wills watched him blow up after spilling coffee on his only pair of slacks, angry that he couldn't afford a trip to the cleaners and fearing that the stain would give a poor impression at casting appointments.

Dean's festering disposition and failure to get jobs began feeding off each other in a vicious cycle, as Wills ruefully noted one day at a *Junior Miss* rehearsal. Dean sometimes tagged along to her early Saturday morning rehearsals. Hank Garson, the director, relates, "Once, before rehearsal, Beverly came up to me and said her friend would like to do something—did I have a part for him? I told her to send him to me. Dean came backstage; he looked like a young Frank Sinatra. I asked him to stand at the microphone and read some lines so I could check his voice. To my surprise, he said, 'Go fuck yourself! I don't do readings.' I just said, 'If you won't read for me, forget it.' "

Despite an April 1951 admonition from the *Hollywood Reporter* to the industry to "give these new young kids a break," casting people usually insisted on "name" actors. Those who would see Dean frequently rejected him on the basis of his looks. Some felt he was too short or not good-looking enough; others perceived him as more fragile and pretty than the "regular guy" they were seeking. "Usually, when the casting heads told him this, Jimmy would get so mad he'd insult the men right back!" said Wills. As Dean saw it, the issue was talent, but his confidence in himself was never contagious.

Dean exhibited a combination of naïveté and cocksureness in job interviews. Jonathan Gilmore, a friend in New York, wrote, "Jimmy would take off his glasses and squint miserably through most of the interviews, a kind of hazy nonfocus that had some agents saying the kid was on reefers." Rather than develop good interviewing skills, he simply became antagonistic toward those who did not adore him at first sight. Though he might fret over a coffee stain's weakening his chances in a casting office, he never grasped the importance of appearance and deportment.

Nor did he respect Hollywood protocol. "He even called the studios directly," said Art Marshall, a friend from UCLA. "Never got him much of anything—but the audacity!" Once when Isabel Draesemer arrived at Universal, she encountered him coming out of the casting chief's office. "Universal was one of my better studios; the previous week I'd negotiated several jobs there. Yet when I asked him why he was there, he answered, 'I don't think they know you too well.' When I went in the office, they said, 'Who *is* that kid?'"

"He was always working behind my back. But in Hollywood you couldn't just push for a part as in New York. You must be represented by your agent. Unless your agent can get you on an interview, with only two or three other contenders, that's it. You don't go barging in and say, 'Let me read.' You can't show your talents in Hollywood that way. Jimmy was too brash and insecure to be humble at the studios."

Shortly before another gathering of the Immaculate Heart fans, Dean was at Draesemer's home for dinner. "He was telling my mother about the girls as he watched her cooking," Draesemer recalled. "He said, 'I'm trying to think of as many dirty things as I can to shock them.' Now, who else does John the Beloved and then gets a fan club? He should've been thrilled! But he acts like this! Another time he was laughing about the decapitating of a square-dance caller in an auto accident."

In spite of Dean's shortcomings, Draesemer was fond of him. "When I knew him, he was generally very pleasant and likeable. His charisma made you reach out to help him," she said. "He laughed a great deal. I told him that I'd had a radio show during World War II called *Women's Journal,* and my radio name was Marie Dean. So he would be in a studio with me and say, 'Come on, Mom!' It felt kind of affectionate. Or maybe he was ribbing me for being older!"

Dean finally became desperate enough to take a nonacting job, so Bast, who was a CBS usher, persuaded his supervisor to hire him. While thus employed, Dean ushered his boyhood friend Bob Middleton into a few CBS shows. A seaman third class in the navy, Middleton was on an aircraft carrier dry-docked at Long Beach; he returned Dean's kindness by buying him cheap cigarettes at his ship's commissary. But the chance to show off for hometown folk did not improve Dean's humor, and he was as insolent to his CBS supervisors as if they were unyielding casting agents. He was fired after only one week. It began to look impossible for him to get any job.

Fear of being drafted for the Korean War may also have contributed to Dean's shorter and shorter fuse. After President Truman approved an increase in quotas in July 1950, draft boards across the country mobilized into a flurry of activity. Dean's board in Grant County, Indiana, had mailed him a classification questionnaire while he was still at SMCC. The few surviving documents in his Selective Service file show that he had a physical examination on April 28, 1951. But for reasons that he never disclosed publicly, he did not want to serve in the military. Part of his resistance may have stemmed from an intense desire to accomplish something before he died, a hope he once expressed to Wills during a mood of despair. Over the next few months he would wage an ultimately successful campaign to remain undrafted, protesting to his home board that he was both a conscientious objector and homosexual.

Bast, already worried about his roommate's mental health, said he grew even more anxious when Dean began taking all-night walks to the Venice Amusement Pier (now torn down), mingling until dawn with low forms of life on the prowl. Dean viewed walking as preferable to sleeping, since he had begun having nightmares about dying. "The nightmares," remembered Wills, "began to give him a certain phobia about death."

Just when it seemed that Dean had bottomed out emotionally, a few bits of luck started to come his way. Isabel Draesemer found a minor role for him on *Bigelow Theatre,* a television anthology series. Elsewhere, Ted Avery, a fellow usher he had befriended during his pathetic week at CBS, found him a job at Ted's Auto Park, adjacent to the studio.

The *Bigelow Theatre* job was in a filmed drama called "TKO"; Dean's part was too insignificant to be identified in reviews. The plot centered on a teenage boy (played by Martin Milner, later the star of *Route 66*) who becomes a boxer in hopes of winning money to help his father. Filming began on June 19 at Jerry Fairbanks Studios, then moved to Hollywood's American Legion Stadium for the fight sequence. Dean was paid forty-five dollars.[1]

The purely menial job at Ted's Auto Park, on the other hand, would facilitate a complete reversal of Dean's earlier misfortunes. Since April 1951, CBS had been airing a half-hour radio series on Saturday mornings called *Alias Jane Doe.* The director, Rogers Brackett, steered his car into the lot one morning while Dean was on duty.

Despite Dean's pronounced bitterness of the past few months, he remained fully capable of turning on the charm. The parking valet Rogers Brackett encountered was an animated, good-looking, seductive young actor, whose ambition was to play Hamlet. Brackett, too, was at his most charming. Dean left no account of his initial impressions of Brackett, but composer Alec Wilder described his own first encounter with Brackett years earlier in New York. "My first memory of Brackett is the sound of his loud, honest laughter in the Algonquin Hotel lobby," wrote Wilder. "I was instantly attracted by the genuine sound of his bellowing. He had grown up in Culver City, been an extra in many movies, knew half the Hollywood movie world and all the strange fringe

---

1. Dean may never have watched a broadcast of "TKO." It aired in Indiana on September 6, 1951, and his appearance was duly noted in the *Fairmount News.* But it seems not to have been shown in Los Angeles until late October, after Dean had left town.

people. . . . His cowboy walk was not an affectation, as he had spent most of his youth on horses—in fact, had been a polo player. He despised the cynicism of the advertising profession and the fact that he was giving his time and talent to a corrupt concept." This same combination of characteristics was what Dean saw.

Brackett resolved on the spot to audition Dean for *Alias Jane Doe.* Its story line was about a female reporter (Lurene Tuttle) who disguises herself to get stories, then publishes them under the signature of Jane Doe. Though Dean did get the job, surviving cast members cannot recall working with him. Madison Musser notes, "I was the love interest in the script opposite the marvelous Lurene Tuttle. I remember little about the show except what it did for me personally. It was, after all, a minor last gasp of a dying dramatic medium in this country."

But Lurene Tuttle, a prominent radio and television actress of the era, did remember Dean and was later named to the board of advisers of the James Dean Foundation. At a gathering of Dean's friends in New York in 1956, Tuttle met Adeline Brookshire, Dean's high school drama teacher. Tuttle told Brookshire that when Dean first worked in *Alias,* he would let each sheet of script flutter to the ground after it was read. The rest of the cast laughed at him for it, but it was what Brookshire had taught him to do.

Little is known about the way Brackett guided his radio actors.[2] However, a soprano whom Brackett directed in an Alec Wilder opera four years later recalls, "It was a riot! Rogers was great fun. He mostly just staged; he didn't get much into characterization. He was so funny that we mostly just laughed a lot."

John Michael Hayes, who wrote the scripts for *Alias Jane Doe,* says his records show that Dean worked in four episodes: July 28, August 11, and September 15 and 22. This helped to put Dean in the most stable financial condition he had enjoyed all year. His pay stub from the August 11 episode shows net wages of $56.99.

Even as Dean grew closer to Brackett, his living arrangement with Bill Bast was unraveling. Their frequent arguments over whose turn it

---

2. He was highly experienced in the medium, having directed *Vox Pop* and *We, the People* in the Forties.

was to borrow money to pay bills got to be too much for Bast. Earlier in the year, Dean had informed Joanne Mock that Bast was two-timing her with Beverly Wills; now it was Bast's turn to inform Jeanetta Lewis that Dean was two-timing *her* with Wills. Lewis reacted to the news with far more agitation than had Mock. A dreadful screaming and battering scene erupted when Lewis and Bast confronted Dean back at the apartment. When the smoke cleared, Lewis's mouth had been bloodied by Dean, Bast had packed and was chauffeured to a new apartment by Lewis, and Dean was left with sole responsibility for the apartment.

In August, Dean was hired for *Fixed Bayonets,* his first movie.[3] Isabel Draesemer says she got him this job, a walk-on role in a Korean War tale at 20th Century–Fox. His pay stub (net wages: $44.07) shows he worked on Saturday, August 11, so he must have reported to the studio after spending the morning working in *Alias Jane Doe.* His small bit as a sentry occurs almost at the end of the film. Helmeted, grimy-faced, and toting a rifle, he dashes in, crouches next to his commander, and pants, "I think I hear 'em comin'. . . . Could be the rear guard, huh?" His purpose is merely to herald the return of the remnants of the film's decimated platoon. The only comment in the reviews relevant to Dean was *Variety*'s crack about the failure of the soldiers' breath to steam in the supposedly freezing Korean mountains.

The trade press sarcastically called *Fixed Bayonets* "the most realistic war tale to date" because of nineteen separate injuries sustained by the cast. The first to fall was Bill Hickman (later one of the three men to accompany Dean on his fateful trip to Salinas, California, in 1955), who broke an ankle when he fell down a movie mountainside. Other casualties included a bayoneted foot, a hand burned in a shell explosion, a fractured elbow, and a wrenched leg.

While on the set, Dean befriended Tony Kent, a young man in the cast. Through Kent, Dean would meet Jack Larson, the original Jimmy Olsen on TV's *The Adventures of Superman,* that same summer. "At the time of *Fixed Bayonets,* James Dean was nice-looking, lively, and agreeable," Larson remembers. "Tony Kent was charming and Jimmy seemed so, too."

---

3. In preproduction and early filming, the movie was called *Old Soldiers Never Die.*

Though Kent had billing in the movie and Dean did not, three years later Kent would still be floundering while Dean was wrapping up his first major motion picture. In August 1951, however, they were living the same struggle for recognition and survival. There is no clearer picture of it than in Kent's 1954 letter to columnist Sidney Skolsky (in response to a column on discouragement in the acting profession).

"I studied, breathed, thought, and dreamed and worked for acting," Kent wrote. Walking into an agent's office one day, Kent was signed and immediately put to work in a picture, *The Two-Dollar Bettor,* in which he had one line. Then came *Fixed Bayonets,* which Kent was sure would be his break. "From the makeup man to Richard Basehart, the star, I was told, 'This is it,' " he recalled.

But after *Fixed Bayonets,* Kent's career stalled; he had no film work and drove a truck in Hollywood. After several months, he decided to try his luck in New York, but had to work as an elevator operator, book salesman, and typist. Finally, he found work in summer stock, where a noted actress told him to keep the faith and something would surely come through for him. He returned to New York fortified by good work and good reviews, but soon became downhearted again. Some television work came his way, but then that dried up, too. "Thanks again for that column," Kent concluded, "because it's tough trying to make it."

Dean's work in *Fixed Bayonets* is an unsung but major irony. At precisely the time the movie was filmed, he was fighting to avoid the hazardous action in Korea that he was portraying on screen. According to the late Robert Custer, former Indiana state director of Selective Service and a lifelong resident of Marion (Dean's county seat), Dean asked for a deferment based on his claim to be a conscientious objector. (Such a claim, if based on Dean's Quaker religion, could be legitimate.) This was attested by a letter from a California minister.

Custer also said Dean wrote a letter claiming he was homosexual (presumably in hopes of being deferred). Custer learned of this through Nelle Hines, clerk of the local draft board in 1951, who discussed it with Custer even though he was not a member of the board.[4] He added that

---

4. Nelle Hines devoted much of her long life to the Selective Service System. She was Indiana state field coordinator during World War II, checking on all local boards to

the board rejected both the conscientious objector and homosexual claims, so Dean appealed their ruling to a national board. The case would not be resolved until the fall.

Interspersed between struggles with the draft board and Dean's various new jobs were weekends spent with Brackett. Sometimes, after wrapping up *Alias Jane Doe,* they would head for Tijuana and the bull-fights.[5] "No doubt two things attracted Jimmy to bullfighting," director Nicholas Ray would later observe. "There was the ritual, the matador's inescapable endurance test, the challenge of proving himself; and there was its physical grace." Thanks to James DeWeerd, who back in Fairmount had shown him home movies of bullfights in Mexico, Dean was already familiar with the sport. Now, bolstered by what he saw in Tijuana, he rapidly became hooked.

Sunday afternoons sometimes found Brackett and Dean at the Malibu cottage of Miles White, a leading Broadway costume designer. "As I remember, 'Hamlet' came every Sunday with Rogers," said White. "I was in L.A. that summer to design costumes for both the L.A. Civic Opera and Barnum & Bailey. I was living at 18674 West Topanga Beach Road. Rogers and Ralph Allen, my assistant, and I would be going on with our repartee, and Hamlet would just have a beer in the corner; he wouldn't say anything. He used to irritate Ralph, who couldn't understand why he wouldn't join us."

---

ensure they operated efficiently, and in the Vietnam years was local Selective Service director. During the period of James Dean's application for deferment, she was often quoted in the Marion newspaper on matters of military induction.

Decades later, Adeline Brookshire asked Hines in a grocery store what the real story behind Dean and the draft was. Hines said Dean had written the local board a letter saying, "You don't want me in your man's army." In 1987, Brookshire telephoned Hines to confirm this; but Hines, who was then nearly ninety, hung up. Whether she was the source who in the early Fifties leaked the contents of Dean's letter—which circulated rapidly throughout Fairmount—cannot be determined. But she did pass the story to Robert Custer.

Brookshire had known of the rumors all along. Five days after Dean's death, she had a long talk with Burl Ives, who had been in *East of Eden* with Dean. Ives asked her if Dean had homosexual tendencies. Brookshire wrote to her mother about the Ives incident and reminded her of the earlier draft board rumors.

5. There were regular advertisements of bullfights in the trade papers; to attend was *au courant* in Hollywood.

As the summer wore on, Dean came to realize that, left to his own devices, he faced discouragement and failure; when he joined forces with wealthy or well-connected admirers, breaking into acting was much likelier to happen. Within the latter course of action lay two options. On the one hand, Beverly Wills and he had talked about getting married and moving to New York, where Dean hoped to act on the stage, living off money Wills had saved from her radio work. On the other hand, Rogers Brackett had invited him to share his quarters in the elegant Sunset Plaza Apartments.

Isabel Draesemer remembers Dean approaching her with a "heads or tails?" situation: "What can I do to further my career: marry Beverly Wills or move in with Rogers Brackett?" "I'd say nuts to both," Draesemer replied. "Do what you want." As she saw it, "It was just a matter of what he could leech onto." Beverly Wills may or may not have been serious about marrying Dean, but Brackett was evidently the more persuasive, because Dean moved into the Sunset Plaza and gave it as his address to 20th Century–Fox.

Brackett and Dean would read La Mure's *Moulin Rouge* together or, more in Dean's native vein, the works of the Hoosier poet James Whitcomb Riley. Brackett's most far-reaching contribution to Dean's literary refinement was introducing him to Antoine de Saint-Exupéry's *The Little Prince*. Dean's love for the book became legendary, and he insisted that all his close friends familiarize themselves with its message: "What is essential is invisible to the eye." Brackett had learned of *The Little Prince* through Madison Musser. "Several times," said Musser, "I read it aloud for friends, and one time Rogers was in the group. He was reduced to tears by the beauty of the book and wanted to secure the recording rights for me to do it as a reading. Upon inquiry he found that, as I recall, Hedy Lamarr, of all people, owned the rights, so that was that."

Once, Dean took Brackett to Reseda to meet his taciturn father and stepmother, an experience Brackett found bizarre. Brackett reciprocated, bringing Dean home to his mother in Culver City. "Rogers and Tess [his mother] were very close and adored each other," said Madison Musser. "Like Rogers, Tess was in constant movement." When Brackett and Dean went out, they sometimes enjoyed the bluesy performances of Stella Brooks, a renowned saloon singer of the era. Once, between sets, Dean asked Brooks what her extraction was, and she sarcastically retorted, "Do you want to know if I'm a Jew?" Dean, she later recalled, gulped and said yes. "I'm a Jew," she confirmed.

After Dean's death, Brackett shared memories of him with a friend, Martin Russ, in the course of a drunken monologue in New York's Blue Ribbon restaurant. "Rogers talked about how charming Jimmy was," said Russ, "and told me that once after they had eaten chicken for dinner, Jimmy made a remarkable mobile out of the bones. Another time, after Rogers had had a minor car accident, Jimmy put a Band-Aid on the fender. Rogers was not only touched by these gestures but associated them with Jimmy's remarkable aptitude for stage business.

"During the course of our conversation, Rogers took a photo out of his wallet to show me. It was Jimmy, sitting naked in a tree. No, the genitals were not showing. It was clearly Jimmy. Rogers cried when he showed it to me."[6]

Madison Musser remembers, "Everyone thought it was a joke where Rogers and Jimmy were concerned, Rogers taking this social naïf under his wing and teaching him which fork to use. I had letters from people in California saying in essence, 'Rogers has this kid in tow, Hamlet, that he's trying to be Svengali to.' But Rogers loved to form people."

The change in Dean's status was apparent to Isabel Draesemer the next time she took him to lunch. "He got all upset because they didn't have Roquefort dressing," she recalled. "I asked him, 'Why are you upset at that, when last week you'd have been glad just to have a sandwich?' He said, 'I've been getting around, and I have some new clothes.' "

---

6. Russ said he had heard about the infamous but blurry and unverifiable photo allegedly showing Dean with an erection in a tree, subsequently published in Paul Alexander's *Boulevard of Broken Dreams,* but the snapshot in Brackett's wallet was not it.

"The kid in Paul Alexander's book in the tree isn't Jimmy—isn't even close," says Jonathan Gilmore.

The rumors of nude photos of Dean in a tree are nonetheless true, according to *Theatre World*'s John Willis, who says he has seen them. They were taken, he says, by Earle Forbes, staff photographer to Daniel Blum, Willis's predecessor as *Theatre World* editor. Willis says both Blum and Forbes kept sets of the photos of Dean and many other young men.

Beverly Wills had moved to her father's place in posh Paradise Cove, out past Malibu, for the summer, a change Dean initially found diverting. His old nemesis from Sigma Nu, Manuel Gonzalez, happened to live in Paradise Cove, too. "I did have occasion to see Jimmy several times after he left the chapter, when he visited friends who were neighbors of mine in Malibu Beach," said Gonzalez. "On each of these occasions he seemed quite friendly and appeared to be far happier outside of the fraternity than I am sure he would have been within."

Early in August, Wills was back in Bel Air to preside at her eighteenth birthday party, hosted by her mother. Dean was one of her guests, and they enjoyed each other's company. But Wills's move to Paradise Cove eventually came to emphasize the immense chasm in class between her and Dean. Expenses, for one thing, were a problem. "Why can't you meet me in Hollywood?" he complained. "It's such a long drive, I'm always running out of gas."

"I felt at home at the beach," Wills rationalized. "I was with a lot of happy kids whom I'd grown up with every summer, and we were having lots of fun. Somehow, in this happy-go-lucky atmosphere, surrounded by boys and girls who didn't seem to have a care in the world, Jimmy stuck out like a sore thumb. When Jimmy came by, they looked at him as if he didn't belong. He was very sensitive, and it hurt him very much to be looked down on."

The last straw came at a dance one night. Despite Dean's exuberant sense of rhythm and movement, he was unfamiliar with the dances being done. One of the local boys cut in on Dean as he tried to dance with Wills, and Dean snapped. "He grabbed the fellow by the collar and threatened to blacken both his eyes," recalled a mortified Wills. Flustered and angry, she ran out of the dance down to the beach. Dean followed, and they had a final argument. He had surely hidden the nature of his relationship with Brackett from her, so the breakup would alleviate the awkwardness. Yet he genuinely missed Wills and the good times they had, according to Karen Sharpe.

"Jimmy was very brokenhearted and shocked that they had broken up," Sharpe says. Dean had become friendly with Sharpe while he went with Wills, and now turned to her for moral support. "He spent a lot of time with me after the breakup," she says. "I was his consoler. He usually arrived at our apartment in the afternoon. My mother would invite him to stay for dinner. He would always accept each invitation. She was the perfect mother—accepting, never judgmental—which he liked.

"Jimmy was fun and witty and bright. There was a quality of madness in him, in a funny way. We used to go into department stores or into a Laundromat in Westwood and improvise that we were married. We would talk with the owner or the customer about the little things young marrieds talk about. It was a test of our talent. Often we would go down to the courtyard at my apartment, and Jimmy would pretend to be a matador. I had to be the bull and he would call out, *'Toro, toro!'* He would pretend to pass a cape in the matador fashion, then laugh with glee. It made him happy but bored the hell out of me!"

Sharpe knew nothing about Dean's private life. "I never pried," she said. "I never knew where he lived; he always came to my apartment. I never saw him with anybody. He was never one to discuss his goals in the normal way; he seemed quite secretive about his plans. Without warning, he would disappear for weeks at a time. But he knew I was there if he needed me. We were never lovers, just friends. There were never any strings attached; he could come by when he wanted. He felt comfortable that way."

Brackett kept up his efforts in opening doors for Dean. He sent him to the home of Leonard Spiegelgass, a screenwriter at MGM. Spiegelgass was known as an aggressive homosexual, said Miles White, "very forward on the attack," not at all good-looking, and quick to take umbrage. Dean flicked cigarette ashes on the rug and otherwise behaved "like an animal." Spiegelgass told him to get out of his house.

The last episode of *Alias Jane Doe* aired on September 22, 1951, and Brackett was asked by his company to produce a children's television program, *Meadow Gold Ranch,* in Chicago. With the trade papers full of references to radio's slow death—"Radio is tightening its belt for the most critical year of its starry career," noted the *Hollywood Reporter*—Brackett saw this not only as a necessary move but as a stepping-stone to working in New York City. The one hitch in this plan was what to do with his young friend. But it turned out that Dean was willing to move with him.

Whether Dean ever considered staying in Chicago with Brackett is unknown, but moving to New York had been on his mind for some time. Certainly Draesemer, James Whitmore, and many others had told him it was the best way to gain acting experience. Margaret Ann Curran remembers discussing it with him over coffee at Tip's in Westwood Village. "He was asking my opinion about whether he should go," she recalls. "He really hadn't been very good at Shakespeare, and I didn't think he had that much talent. But he wanted so very much to be an actor; I can't tell you how strongly. So I encouraged him to go, because I knew how much he wanted this and would never be happy unless he did it."

As fate would have it, just as Dean was weighing the pros and cons of uprooting himself, jobs started coming his way. He landed a part in his second movie, this time at Paramount in a Dean Martin–Jerry Lewis comedy, *At Sea with the Navy*, later renamed *Sailor Beware*. He played one of two managers of an amateur navy boxer who had drawn Jerry Lewis as an opponent. As Dean massages his fighter in the locker room, they overhear Lewis spouting off tough, exaggerated boxer lingo in hopes of gaining a psychological edge. Lewis's gambit works; Dean exclaims, "That guy's a professional!" Unfortunately for Lewis, Dean and his trio conspire to bring the amateur's older, professional brother to the fight to make it an even match.

The job involved three days of work, the first two in the actual fight scene, where Dean is glimpsed climbing in and out of the ring through the ropes, throwing a towel over his shoulder, and at the end, helping his KO'd fighter out of the ring after Lewis has accidentally but not surprisingly won. The locker-room sequence was filmed on the third day.

Sailor Beware was a small personal milestone of sorts for Dean: for the first time, his name appeared in the *Hollywood Reporter,* under "Castings." It may also have been the occasion for Dean's acquaintance with a man who would later be very important in his career, Dick Clayton.[7] Although Clayton is now a top Hollywood agent, he was then a

---

7. Although Clayton insists he met Dean on the set of *Sailor Beware,* the filming logs show that he worked one day only, September 6, 1951, while Dean didn't start work until September 29.

minor actor who had one day's work in *Sailor Beware* as a yeoman.

Clayton recalls, "I had decided by then that I didn't have the talent to be an actor. I told Jimmy I was going to try to become an agent and asked him what he was going to do. He said he was planning to move to New York. I told him to be sure and look up Jane Broder and Jane Deacy, because they were good agents. He eventually went with Jane Deacy, of course. Maybe he never got to the other Jane."

As soon as Dean finished his work at Paramount, he took his 1936 Chevy in for a transmission job so it could be sold. He was wrapping up his affairs as quickly as possible, but two important matters remained before he could leave: a job in a third movie and a second armed forces physical examination, both scheduled for October 9.

Each of Dean's early movies was renamed after filming began; the third, at Universal-International, started out as *Oh Money, Money,* but in the end was called *Has Anybody Seen My Gal?*. Its stars were Charles Coburn, Rock Hudson, and Piper Laurie. Dean and Rod Bladel, his UCLA friend and fellow Draesemer client, were hired for the same short scene.[8]

Coburn's character was a wealthy man who takes a job as a soda jerk to hide his privileged status. Dean and Bladel played brash college students. As Coburn slides an ice-cream soda down the counter to Tony (Bladel), who quips, "Got it, Gramps," the camera follows the soda and pans onto Dean, who is leaning insouciantly against the counter. He demands a chocolate malt made to exhaustive specifications: "heavy on the choc, plenty of milk, four spoons of malt, two scoops of vanilla ice cream, one mixed with the rest, and"—as he jauntily plops a fedora on his head—"one floating." In a nice comeback, Coburn asks him to come back later for a fitting.

Bladel recalls, "Isabel Draesemer had shown our pictures at the casting office. One afternoon I came home and there was a message to report to Universal the next day, where an assistant director approved Jimmy and me. But he didn't hire us on the spot. Other kids were called as well. Then I got another phone message saying I had been cast as

---

8. Bladel acted under the name of Rod Barkley.

Tony. We were each paid fifty-five dollars. It wasn't an early-morning call, and we didn't have to wait long to be filmed. They were very well organized.

"We were being photographed for wardrobe tests when Piper Laurie came by and complimented us on our costumes. It struck me as a nice way for a star to treat a couple of bit players. We had a talk with Charles Coburn while we were waiting to do the scene. Jimmy asked, 'How long have you been in the business?' Coburn answered, 'You mean the theater?' " Coburn, who was considered the best poker player in the Motion Picture Alliance, talked with the young men about gambling and said he thought the California law prohibiting gambling in one's own home was abominable.

"Jimmy had to do his part more than once," Bladel continued. "He got very little direction from Douglas Sirk. Sirk just told him to 'act superior and offhand.'

"After it was over, Jimmy drove me back to campus where I was rehearsing *Candida*. He came into rehearsal for a few minutes to say hello to his old friends." Bladel and the others had no idea, nor did Dean inform them, that he would be leaving California in a matter of hours.

Before Dean's afternoon call at Universal, he had an appointment for his second armed forces physical examination, a rare step in an induction system where a single examination usually sufficed. His records give no explanation for it and say only that the end result was rejection. The basis for the rejection is lost to history. However, Brackett later disclosed that he had paid for Dean to have a series of psychiatric visits through which he would be certified as homosexual. Perhaps the October 9 appointment was merely a formality to deliver the psychiatrist's certification to a military physician. The purpose of such a psychiatric finding, to bolster Dean's original claim of homosexuality, would be useful only if the Grant County draft board had disallowed the claim because they didn't believe it.

Two years later, Dean would discuss the draft with his friend Jonathan Gilmore in New York. "One night in a cafeteria on Broadway," Gilmore reports, "Jimmy said one could get out of being drafted by claiming to have bisexual tendencies—which included having homosexual tendencies, of course, but one was afraid of being branded queer. He pointed out that the Selective Service was not dumb and would see you were trying to hide the real facts from them. 'It's like saying you've just got a little bit of leprosy,' he said." Dean told Gilmore he hadn't been drafted yet because he was below I-A due to poor eyesight but above IV-F because he wasn't blind.

Dean may have left Hollywood the very next day, since by October 15 he was in Fairmount, Indiana, and had already been in Chicago. Karen Sharpe said he had come to dinner at her apartment the night before he left. He had been telling her for some time that he was thinking of going. "I've figured out how to do it," he said, "and when I come back I'll be a star." He did not say how he was getting to New York or that he would stop in Chicago and Indiana. Whether he and Brackett went to Chicago together or whether Brackett went ahead is uncertain, although Brackett's friends believe they went together. Beverly Wills said Dean called after their breakup and told her "a friend" was giving him a free ride to New York.

After taking a room for himself and Dean at the Ambassador East, Chicago's most expensive hotel, Brackett immediately went to work on *Meadow Gold Ranch*. His company also assigned him to WMAQ, an AM radio station, as a commercial supervisor—not directing, but making sure commercials went smoothly.

Dean left Chicago almost immediately to pay a surprise visit to Fairmount. Three days before his arrival, Fairmount High School's newspaper, unaware he was coming, ran a short article on him based on a not-so-recent letter to his family. First, it reported Dean was spending "most of his time making pictures for the Bigelow Theater," mistaking the anthology series for a film studio. "Although he performs in a considerable number of these movies," it noted, "they are cut so much before they are released that Jim doesn't always know whether his part will appear in the final film. His most recent production is *Fixed Bayonet* [sic].

"Archery and golf are two sports he has become proficient in. A recent trip to Mexico made a bull fighting enthusiast out of him, so much so, that he intends to become a matador. Besides all these activities Jim finds time to appear in an occasional television show. Living only twenty miles from his father's home, he frequently visits there. His last trip to Fairmount was about one year ago."

As soon as he set foot in the town, Dean reverted to the wholesome, "no different than any other" Hoosier lad that Fairmount believed him to be. Except for his increased knowledge of acting, the street smarts he had acquired in the past two years were suppressed and not displayed. Although his draft classification would not be official until November 14, rumors of his telling the draft board he was homosexual may already have surfaced. He may have believed that such information was confidential and would not go beyond the draft board. If, on the other hand, he knew about the rumors, it was courageous of him to come.

He looked up Adeline Brookshire and asked presumptuously if she could arrange for him to present a convocation to the student body, a scheme she went along with. While Brookshire was busy assuring a skeptical principal that Dean would not ask to do it if he weren't capable of pulling it off, Dean hurried back to the Winslow farm to grab his matador cape. That the principal allowed the convocation shows that Fairmount was somewhat awestruck at the major strides in acting they assumed Dean had made. He was granted fifty minutes but took ninety.

Dean harangued the student body as he walked up and down the center aisle of the auditorium, recounting his adventures in the Pepsi commercial, at UCLA, and in Hollywood; and plugging the fine arts. At one point he fixed his stare on Brookshire and rhetorically demanded, "Why didn't you teach us Shakespeare?" Although she remained silent, she wondered why the Shakespeare he was taught didn't seem to have registered.

After the extended monologue came a bullfighting demonstration, which no student ever forgot, especially the young women. They remember that Dean was dressed in a cream-colored jacket and slacks, white shirt with red stripes (open almost to the waist), and a gold chain around his neck. A senior boy was pressed into service as the bull and ran time after time across the stage carrying a long stick, serving as horns. Dean whirled his cape and delighted the students with his grace.

A few basketball players remember Dean's joining them during a practice session, then dramatically crawling to the showers from the gymnasium pretending to be an old man and terribly out of shape.

Almost as much a part of Fairmount lore as the bullfight convocation was Dean's directing a rehearsal of the junior play, *Men Are Like Streetcars,* at Brookshire's request. He viewed the task as a crusade to bring James Whitmore–level acting techniques to a group of shy, small-town high school students. Before the rehearsal began, said Bill Payne, "We were all in the drama classroom, and he was asking each of us what our character's background was. When he got to me, I said, 'I don't know,' and he didn't like that, so he moved right on to the next person."

Dean seemed especially concerned with entrances. Lola Small, the female lead, had to come on stage and pick up a hammer, a maneuver that Dean made her repeat several times. Valarie Pace, who played a maid, could not say a line at her entrance to Dean's satisfaction. He took her into another room but instead of trying to coach her said, "Now we'll give everybody something to talk about!"

Jill Corn's character had to be spanked, but when the spanker did not meet Dean's expectations, Dean threw Corn across his lap to demonstrate the correct way to paddle her. In the process, Corn's cheekbone caught the corner of the chair Dean was in, and her eyes watered. Dean was apologetic when he saw this. Just before midnight, Brookshire's husband came into the auditorium and complained that irate parents were calling him demanding to know why their offspring were not at home. "Mrs. Brookshire never kept us past ten o'clock," said Corn. "And here it was midnight, and we hadn't even got through the first act. Jimmy gave me a ride home, though."

At the conclusion of Dean's rather busy week, the *Fairmount News* reported, "James Dean and Rev. James DeWeerd left Saturday morning [October 20] for Chicago where they will transact business for a few days. Mr. Dean had spent five days with Fairmount relatives." The presence of James DeWeerd in Chicago created certain logistical problems for Dean. Whether Dean told DeWeerd about Brackett (or Brackett about DeWeerd), whether he introduced them to each other, and whether he failed to notify Brackett that he was back cannot be answered. Although Dean could have enjoyed the luxury of the Ambassador East at Brackett's expense, he chose to stay with DeWeerd in more modest lodgings while they were transacting business. Without specifying the sleeping arrangements in Chicago, DeWeerd told a reporter that Dean took one look at a rickety four-poster bed and cracked, "Once you taught me to pray. Now let's pray this thing doesn't fall on me."

Eventually, Dean did return to Brackett. But he was exceedingly restless and Brackett thought it best to send him on to New York. Brackett called his friends Alec Wilder, who lived at the Algonquin Hotel, and Madison Musser, the actor who had worked in *Alias Jane Doe,* asking them to show Dean the ropes when he arrived. Then he bought Dean a ticket on the Twentieth Century Limited and sent him on his way.

Dean's experience in California throughout 1951 offers intriguing insights. He saved trivial pay stubs and minor financial records; he wanted to document his activities. Yet he exerted tight control over information concerning his private life, as with his letter quoted in Fairmount High's newspaper. He had accurately reported his interest in archery and golf without mentioning Beverly Wills, who had been his partner in those sports, and his enthusiasm for bullfighting without mentioning Rogers Brackett.

Had Dean remained in Hollywood, he would not have lacked for work. "The day he left," Isabel Draesemer said, "Fairbanks Studio called again to ask for him in the next big religious show, once again as John the Beloved. I called four hotels in Chicago trying to find him."[9] But, without his impending New York apprenticeship, Dean might not have found a suitable context for his naturalistic, nontraditional acting gifts, even though hints of them could already be glimpsed in his movie bits. New York had called, and Dean was ripe for what it had to give.

---

9. Jerry Fairbanks Studios was loyal to its players. Ruth Hussey, for example, who played Mary in *Hill Number One,* had already played the same character in an earlier Christmas broadcast.

Manhattan 101

The mutual courtship of James Dean and Manhattan was inevitable. "Jimmy was an individualist, an original, and anyone who came in contact with him felt it," his friend Christine White observed. That individuality would not fully flourish until he was swathed in the absolute freedom that only New York could bestow. In those post–World War II years, seminal forces in many artistic disciplines—painting, ballet, jazz—were concentrated in New York, and its artists felt they were getting the same nourishment that Paris had given earlier generations. As essayist E. B. White noted, the ability to create is contingent on the absence of distractions, and Manhattan's vastness affords a splendid isolation.

In 1949, the Denver Zephyr had carried Dean to the National Forensic League competition, an event that took him far afield from his limited Indiana experience. Now, two years later, the Twentieth Century Limited transported him to a rendezvous with destiny in New York, for here he would complete his transformation to his fullest self. He was in some ways, to be sure, a congenital country boy, but he had been born to come and go as he pleased, to sleep when and where he wanted with no regard for what the neighbor or aunt or minister might think.

Dean was carrying a list of Rogers Brackett's referrals; on it was the name of Brackett's best friend, composer Alec Wilder, who lived at the renowned Algonquin Hotel on West Forty-fourth Street. Dean devised—or perhaps Brackett put him up to it—a novel way of presenting himself to Wilder. In a play on the Antoine de St. Exupéry book he had come to love, Dean telephoned Wilder as soon as he arrived and cooed, "Hello, Mr. Wilder, this is the Little Prince."

"The fact that Dean was the center of Rogers's life was all Alec needed to be extremely generous and helpful," explained Wilder's close friend and collaborator James Maher. When Dean called, Wilder told him to come right over to the Algonquin dining room. "He ate a large and expensive breakfast and then started to fabricate his own sources," recalled Wilder. "It was kind of amusing. Immediately started to tell me—I don't remember what it was—some nutty story about a fire in Chicago."

After breakfast, Wilder helped Dean rent a room at the more modest Iroquois Hotel just a few steps to the east. But Dean would spend most of his time at the Algonquin. Maher relates, "Alec performed a great service to Dean by bringing him into his personal world, which meant introducing him to the gang at the Algonquin— bellmen, deskmen, concierge, waiters. It was an enormous piece of luck for a young guy coming to New York, not knowing anything or anyone.

"The bellmen knew Alec was looking after Dean, and would sit and talk with him on the bench opposite the desk. They were a nice group of friends to have—truly family to Alec—so it was more than just providing shelter. Dean, a stranger, walked into a nest, thanks to Rogers and Alec."

Brackett, too, had done Dean a great service by sending him to Wilder. A perennial recipient of encomiums and tributes, Wilder was praised posthumously by *The New Yorker*'s Whitney Balliett. Taking issue with jazz pianist Marian McPartland's assertion that Wilder's "greatest" and "most lasting" gift was his music, Balliett wrote, "I'm not sure that Wilder's greatest gift wasn't his complex, brilliant, echoing self. Look at the hole he's left." Wilder shared this remarkable self with Dean freely. Playwright Arnold Sundgaard says Wilder's nurturing of Dean was "only one of many mentor-avuncular relationships that he had with similarly gifted young men over the years. They saw in Alec some kind of older statesman–father to whom they could turn for encouragement and advice, and Alec was never at a loss to offer both."

Wilder found Dean engaging. "He was short, physically strong, weak-eyed to the extent that he needed glasses, cheerful, uninformed, a prankster, and most certainly not a reader," Wilder wrote two decades later. "He came from a poor farming family, had no money, but was possessed by the desire to act. He behaved in a very masculine manner, but was homosexual. Until [*See the Jaguar*], he was a pleasant companion, a cheerful, noisy kid."

Although Dean left the Iroquois and moved to the YMCA on West Sixty-third Street to save money, he continued to hang out at the Algonquin. Sometimes he would sit in the lobby with Wilder, amusing him with imitations of persons they both knew. "He was hanging around, doing nothing, sitting on the bellboys' bench at the Algonquin most of the time," wrote Wilder. "Somewhere along the way, he bought himself a recorder. I used to write little tunes for him, and he called me and tried to play them back over the phone."

During those early, loosely structured days, Dean collected an unusual assortment of friends. One was Richard Gearin, a native of Massachusetts.[1] "I was just back from Korea when Jimmy came to New York," Gearin said. "I had a part-time job with Greyhound Bus. Jimmy would come into the terminal on Fiftieth Street carrying stacks of books—Hemingway and others."

"He lived with me, off and on for a year, whenever the YMCA didn't have rooms on a given night. My apartment was at One hundred-and-tenth and Amsterdam. I had other roommates there, too. The building was torn down later."

Jerry's Bar at Fifty-third Street and Sixth Avenue was one of Dean's earliest New York watering holes. "Jerry Lucci took me and

---

1. In the mid-Eighties, Gearin presented himself at the Winslow farm in Fairmount and was virtually adopted by Marcus, Jr., and Mary Lou Winslow until his death in September 1987. He always talked as if he had known Dean well, and many fans accepted his story. "I destroyed my letters from Jimmy years ago," Gearin said; "I don't want no publicity. Jane Deacy [Dean's agent] and I have lots of unpublished photos. Jane told me not to share them with the public. She said, 'They already have enough.' Jimmy had mailed them to me."

Jimmy under his wing," said Gearin. "He fed us for no charge when we needed it. He would tell us to get spaghetti out of the fridge and not worry about it. Jimmy was a good cook, though; Jerry taught him to make spaghetti."

Dean once said he was too intimidated during his first weeks in New York to do much beyond watching movies, a fact that Richard Gearin corroborated. "Do you know what Jimmy's favorite film was?" he asked. "It was *A Place in the Sun*. He took me to it and we watched it continuously from eight A.M. to two A.M." One movie Dean would not have missed was the first film he ever worked in, *Fixed Bayonets*. Its "gala public premiere" was on November 20 at the Rivoli Theater, Broadway and Forty-ninth Street. His second film, *Sailor Beware,* opened in New York at the Mayfair Theater, two blocks away, on January 31, 1952.

Within his first few weeks in Manhattan, Dean wrote an upbeat letter on YMCA stationery to James DeWeerd. He said the city's possibilities were already revealing themselves to him in strange and fascinating ways. His favorite pastime was ice-skating at Rockefeller Center. Unplanned expenses such as new glasses and a new coat were eating away faster than he had hoped at the money DeWeerd and others had loaned. But signs on the career horizon encouraged him: his appointment calendar was brimming and two agents were already giving him close scrutiny. Although he felt he had to keep running to get his foot in the door, he expressed relief to be young enough to endure the fatigue.

There was a down side to Dean's New York life as well, readily apparent to Louis Fontana, who cut hair in the Iroquois's barbershop. "Jimmy and actor Paul Burke lived on the same floor," Fontana relates, "and Burke sent him down to me when he needed a haircut for an appointment. He had no money but paid me later. He was depressed and didn't talk much. He used to sit on the steps of the barbershop, mad that he couldn't pay rent or buy food. He had no work that winter and was often broke, and the hotel wanted to throw him out. I told the management, 'Don't evict him, he's a good actor and a good kid. He'll pay later.' And he did, too. He would tip me."

When Beverly Wills accompanied her renowned mother, Joan Davis, to New York that winter, she contacted Dean at the YMCA. A familiar face from Hollywood was a welcome sight to him, but his demeanor was a shock to her. He was wearing the same jacket and slacks that he always wore in Hollywood, and his initial air of bravado quickly deflated when he confessed that he had yet to find acting jobs. "He was depressed, and he was hungry, too," she later wrote. "I insisted that I buy us both a spaghetti dinner, and he took me up on it. I think it was the first square meal he had had since he left Hollywood." He told her that if he couldn't find work, he would go to Mexico and become a bullfighter.

Once Dean overcame his fear of the city and began pounding the pavement, he got some long-armed help from Rogers Brackett in Chicago. Brackett telephoned Madison Musser to ask him to give Dean a hand. "When I met Jimmy," said Musser, "I knew I had seen him in Hollywood and might have been introduced to him in the CBS radio building, where I was on the ushering staff. Someone had told me that he parked cars next door. I'd done very well in TV in New York and could make introductions for him, which I did. I made a point of introducing him to everybody, and everybody I introduced him to gave him a job. The only one I remember now is Marion Dougherty, who was casting for Kraft.

"He seemed to be interested in my approving what he did. He wanted my critique but wouldn't accept it. Once he was doing a reading and asked me to see it. All the actors in it were asked to wear dark clothes—suits, dark dresses. But Jimmy turned up in a transparent fishnet shirt and the tightest bloody jeans you ever saw. He had a wonderful body, but I was incensed! I told him afterwards, 'I thought you were rotten! But I might have felt differently if you hadn't dressed so obviously!' He was totally selfish and undisciplined as an actor."

Another important contact was James Sheldon, an aspiring young director. "I was supervising commercials at Young & Rubicam but wanted to get into freelance directing," says Sheldon. "This was either late in '51 or early in '52. Jimmy showed up at the office and I had him read. You give somebody a scene and tell them to 'look it over, take your time. When you're ready let me know.' Some can be great actors but terrible readers. When Jimmy read, I sensed the intelligence; he was terrific."

Through Sheldon, Dean bagged what may have been his first television job in New York, *Mama*. Sheldon sent him to assistant producer Doris Quinlan to read for the part of Nels, the son, when its then-current occupant, Dick Van Patten, was about to be drafted. "Jimmy reminded me of Brando," explains Sheldon, "and Brando had originated the role of Nels when *I Remember Mama* was on Broadway. And I had worked with Dick Van Patten, too. So I sent Jimmy over to the *Mama* people and they liked him. I wanted to direct that show, so I wasn't about to do him that kind of favor if I didn't think he was any good."

Rosemary Rice, who played the teenage daughter Katrin, said Dean first appeared as an extra and then briefly played Nels. "He wasn't good," said Rice. "Dick Van Patten was somewhat crazy and played it with a wild sense of humor. Jimmy on the other hand was very serious. He absolutely wasn't right for the part. Although I liked him, he was a very dark person and made me nervous."

According to Dick Van Patten, Dean, Paul Newman, and Jack Lemmon all played friends of Nels on *Mama*. "Jimmy Dean was supposed to replace me," Van Patten recalls, "but I wasn't drafted, so I reclaimed the part. He was very disappointed. But he and I were friends. See, I was also on Broadway at the same time, and he thought that was wonderful. He became my flunkie. After the show, I'd take him along to actors' poker games in the Forrest Hotel on Forty-ninth Street. I'd send him out for cigarettes or Coca-Cola. We'd sometimes play until four A.M. He didn't ever play; he'd just sit there and watch.

"Sometimes he'd meet me at the stage door of the Alvin Theater after my show, and we'd go out for coffee. He loved to talk about acting. He told me that he thought real acting technique was *not* to know the lines too well, 'So it looks like you're searching for the words,' he'd say."

A squib in the *Marion* [Indiana] *Leader-Tribune* of Saturday, January 19, 1952, said, "Friends of Jim Dean, Fairmount High School graduate in 1949, will have a chance to see him on TV today in a play scheduled to begin at three P.M." This happened to be the first showing of *Mama* in Indiana. (In New York it aired on Friday evenings.) The episode and part that Dean played cannot be identified.

On January 27, Dean had a small part on the *CBS Television Workshop*. This experimental Sunday anthology series revived for television the prestigious radio show *Columbia Workshop* (the program on which Orson Welles had produced his famous Martian broadcast). The producer, Norris Houghton, described Dean's episode as a "semidocumentary on jungle warfare based on war correspondent John Hersey's account of his first action on Guadalcanal, *Into the Valley*. Dean played one of the dogfaces." The role was reminiscent of his bit in *Fixed Bayonets*.

James Sheldon's benevolence to Dean continued. He recalled, "We had a very platonic, friendly relationship. But being older than he and being a little more connected, I think he leaned on me. I remember enjoying being with him, but also feeling that he was taking more than he was giving, I suppose. I was helpful to him, always trying to do something for him. He would borrow a few bucks. He was a very attractive and sexy and lovable fellow and had a wonderful helplessness about him, subconsciously turning it on when he needed to.

"I remember one day walking up the street, stopping at the Y, and seeing his room—the only time I'd ever been in a room at the YMCA, and they were such small cubicles. But he never lived with me.[2] We were friends, but I was married, and the first five years of my marriage I was a very good husband."

One day while making the rounds, Dean met a young woman who invited him to a meal at the Rehearsal Club, the residence for single female performing artists at 47 West Fifty-third Street. Thereafter Dean loitered frequently in its lobby, where male visitors were permitted to stay until midnight curfew. "The women I knew there regarded Dean as a lovable child," said James Bellah, Dean's friend from Sigma Nu, who came to New York the year after Dean did. "They'd feed him—half a sandwich from one, a Coke from another."

One rainy afternoon, Dean was sitting in the lobby, imploring various women to loan him an umbrella, but having no luck. A young dancer, Elizabeth Sheridan (known in those days as Dizzy), felt sorry for him and loaned hers to him. He struck her as pathetic and insignificant, and she was not at all impressed with him. But after the umbrella incident, they kept encountering each other. One evening he asked to tag along to a club in Harlem where she and her two male dance

---

2. David Dalton's biography, *The Mutant King,* misidentified Sheldon as the man with whom Dean lived in a loft in the West Twenties; it was actually Rogers Brackett. Sheldon lived on Gramercy Park South with his wife all through Dean's New York years.

partners had a performance. "Jimmy was smitten from the first time he saw me dance," Sheridan remembers.

After the show in Harlem, the small group went for drinks at Jerry's Bar, which was only half a block from the Rehearsal Club. Sheridan ordered Champale, a brand of beer, but the waiter mistakenly brought a bottle of champagne. Dean did a double take because champagne was far beyond the range of his pauper's budget. "He didn't have a cent, and he was borrowing from everyone in town," Sheridan says. But rather than inform the waiter of the mistake, Dean improvised, grandiosely boasting of his ability to afford the champagne. Sheridan was amused and began to have feelings for him.

Back at Jerry's a few nights later, Sheridan and Dean were chatting with another couple in an adjoining booth. Suddenly it dawned on Sheridan that "his ideas and my ideas sort of jelled." Dean drew pictures on a napkin, as was his wont in restaurants, and Sheridan found herself appreciating his artistic gifts. Jerry's became a charmed place for them. They met there a third time on Dean's twenty-first birthday, and he told her it was the best birthday he had had in a long time.

After that, they saw a lot of each other. "It was a desperate kind of feeling he had toward seeing and talking to me any time that he had a spare moment," observed Sheridan, "almost like he didn't have anybody else, either. He just sort of hung on, and I guess I must have been particularly lonely at the time, too."

As Dean was growing closer to Sheridan, who was two years older than he, television jobs began falling into his lap. On February 20, he was in "Sleeping Dogs," an episode of *The Web* on CBS, with Anne Jackson and E. G. Marshall. One of the forces behind Dean's successful audition was Eleanor Kilgallen, a casting agent at MCA. Kilgallen says she met him when Maynard Morris, a "legendary" MCA agent in the legitimate [stage] department, brought him into a meeting one day in hopes of signing him with their agency. "We would have these periodic caucuses so we'd be 'up to date in Kansas City' on these new kids," she explains. "The legit department would bring them in to introduce them to us in TV, the 'illegitimate' department." Kilgallen and several other agents attended. "Morris had seen Jimmy in a theatrical reading of some sort. He had no agent then.

"Jimmy was very intense. He looked at the woodwork and stared, but he had an attention-getting quality. And it so happened that Franklin Heller over at CBS had a script with a part for an eccentric." Kilgallen called Heller to warn him that she was sending over a boy who, although strange, was perfect for the vagrant part in "Sleeping Dogs."

Kilgallen's warning was an understatement; Heller thought Dean was rude, badly dressed, and something of a mess, and he wanted no part in hiring such an inauspicious newcomer. But Kilgallen put her foot down. "Frank," she scolded, "I'll never recommend a good person to you again if you don't take this boy, because he's going to be a big star!"

Anne Jackson confirms that Heller's reservations were not far-fetched. Dean was "a pain in the neck," she says, because "he took up unnecessary time with the director. Generally, actors knew when they took a role in a TV melodrama that they had a job to do and you had to be a team player. With eight or nine actors there was so little time for each one."

Management of James Dean in those early days was done by Archer King of the Shurr Agency. "Jimmy had come into the office to see someone who had already left," recalls King, "and he was just standing there, so I helped him. During *The Web* rehearsals, someone called to say Franklin Heller was upset that Jimmy wouldn't get to his marks for the cameras. Cursing, I went down to CBS. Jimmy said, 'I'm trying to get my character.' I told him that what concerned me was that this was his first job [with me], and I didn't know how he'd survive. 'You've got to work,' I said. 'You need the money!' "

Dean played a boy trying to solve his brother's murder; Jackson's character, who is eventually shown to be mad, admits that she killed the brother after he came on to her. Despite the trouble Dean caused, Jackson found him likable. "I got to admire him when he wasn't competing—I'd never seen such an appetite for being another Brando. Still, he could be disarming and sweet," she recalls.

Lela Swift, the director, says she had faith that Dean could do the part even through the rocky rehearsals. "He was very dependent on me," she says. She remembers that he went to extreme lengths to get the feel of his part. "You fake actions in rehearsals," she says, "but Jimmy let himself be hit in the face. He was lying on the floor bleeding. He didn't get up or verbalize any pain."

In Chicago, Rogers Brackett was paying close attention. "I remember," says Brackett's friend Jim Harelson, "joining Rog to watch one of Jimmy's shows, something directed by Lela Swift. It wasn't a big part, but noteworthy. When it was over, Rog called him to critique his performance. He was very much interested in Jimmy's career; he thought he was going to be a hell of an actor."

When *The Web* aired, Dean was so good, Archer King says, that *Martin Kane, Private Eye* on NBC called the next morning wanting to hire him. Unfortunately, Dean caused the same problems as on *The Web,* and this time the producers were not as tolerant; he was fired. "I was furious with them," says King. "I tried to explain how good he would be. They had to pay him anyway, because he was union." King felt sorry for Dean and let him stay in his apartment. "He used to baby-sit for us," the agent adds.

Dean needed the sense of validation he got from his friends' critiques. At his insistence, Sheridan would sit in on his television rehearsals and performances, marginal as they might be in those early New York days, and gave him her notes when they were over. "He seemed so insecure in his acting," she wrote. "Yet he must have thought he was good because he had no doubts about getting to the top." It was clear to Sheridan that Dean had supreme confidence in his future as an actor. "He never for one instant thought that he really couldn't make it. He always knew that he would one day be a star, and there was no question in his mind about it at all."

Two weeks later, Dean played a hotel bellhop in "Ten Thousand Horses Singing," a *Studio One* episode. He was on screen for no more than forty seconds, during which he spoke one word, "yes," proffered a nice profile during a slow elevator ride, and grimaced when the star, John Forsythe, was punched out by an irate hotel guest.

After another two-week interval, Dean had his best television part of the entire year in *Lux Video Theatre's* "The Foggy, Foggy Dew." He was in all but one of the scenes in the half-hour program and had almost as many lines as James Barton, the featured star. The story was based on the English folk song of the same title, which is sung by a man whose son's eyes constantly remind him of his dead wife. Dean played Kyle McCallum, a nineteen-year-old boy who unwittingly encounters his biological father while on a hunting trip. This man is an odd-looking, guitar-toting drifter who two decades earlier was working incommunicado on a steamship in the Orient when his wife died in childbirth; his name is also Kyle. Young McCallum has no idea that he isn't his parents' natural offspring, but the drifter almost instantly recognizes him as his progeny.

The man visits the McCallums, an influential and well-to-do couple, wanting to reveal his identity to young Kyle. Since they never told the boy he was adopted, they beg the drifter not to upset the status quo. When the boy arrives home, the evident affection between him and his parents persuades the drifter to leave without spilling the beans—but not before a lusty rendition of the last chorus of "The Foggy, Foggy Dew" with its lyrics about the fair young maid and the son's eyes. It was one of the few times Dean would play a happy, well-adjusted person. Kyle Senior was played by James Barton, who was then on Broadway in the Lerner and Loewe musical *Paint Your Wagon;* the McCallums were portrayed by Muriel Kirkland and Richard Bishop.

Muriel Kirkland recalled that Dean rebuffed James Barton when the veteran actor tried to help him with his part. "Mr. Barton was a most generous person and had always helped others and especially the newer people," said Kirkland. "Dean's attitude was peculiar. He seemed nervous and his acting was highly strung, much more so than what his part called for."

Of the five shows Dean worked in through March 1952, all were on CBS, which meant he put in many hours of rehearsal at Grand Central Station.[3] "When Grand Central was built," explained Franklin Heller, "they thought they could persuade the stock exchange to move uptown, so they had two enormous areas intended as trading floors built on the third floor, directly over the south waiting room area. Of course, the stock exchange never came, so CBS eventually rented the space for very little."

Dizzy Sheridan went faithfully with Dean to rehearsals whenever possible, and they reached the point where they were seeing each other every night. A couple of times, she says, she and her friends successfully

---

3. He would have had one NBC appearance to his credit as well had he not been fired from *Martin Kane, Private Eye.*

conspired to sneak him upstairs to her room at the Rehearsal Club. Finally they decided it made sense to live together, so they took a tiny room at the Hargrave Hotel (still standing, though in a newer incarnation, at 112 West Seventy-second Street).

Now a successful television actress *(Seinfeld, Alf)* in Hollywood, Sheridan reminisced about her time with Dean one afternoon in a Ventura Boulevard bistro. "Everyone left us alone during that time," she said. "We were two people against the world. We both felt pretty separated from life. That's why we were so good together. We had our own way of talking. Later in *Rebel Without a Cause,* he said things that were lifted right from the way we would talk. One of them was drawing out the word 'sure'—su—u—u—re—which he spoke in the empty swimming pool scene."

There was tenderness and desperation between them, and there were also old-married-couple habits that crept into their routine. Dean would send clothes to the cleaners and forget about them, so Sheridan would bail them out. "I used to wash his underwear in the sink," she said. "He bought me *The Little Prince* and would read a chapter at a time to me; then he would ask me to tell him what he had just read. He was taking classes in mime and would come back to the room and act out Pierrot and Pierrette. Even then he would talk about the actor in him turning into a director.

"I've had letters from crazy people about him. One was from a gay man who asked, 'How dare you claim Jimmy? He's ours!' As to the question of whether he was gay, I really don't know. But I can tell you that we very much enjoyed each other when we were together. It was very intense and very heated."

Once when Dean was out shopping for groceries, he impulsively telephoned Sheridan because, he told her, he was suddenly consumed with the thought of getting married: "We must get married before we get caught up in all this." She had no idea what came over him between leaving the Hargrave and arriving at the store, but she remembered his being inexplicably afraid that night. Asked why she didn't take him up on his marriage proposal, she gave no specific answer.

Sometimes when they had all they could take of New York, they would visit Sheridan's mother in Westchester County. "We would borrow her Plymouth," she says, "and drive to a bird sanctuary I knew. Near its lake there was a house that no one knew about. Or we went to a hotel on Long Island Sound in Larchmont—which was very romantic. You could hear the water." Oddly, Dean told Sheridan he didn't want to drive and always asked her to do it.

"Jimmy was very sweet to the elderly and the needy. I remember Moondog [the blind street musician, famous for his horned Viking helmet and triangular drums, with whom Dean often talked]. And it was a very strange thing about his mother. He was so sensitive about that. Over and over, as we would lie in the dark, we would talk about the things closest to us, and his mother came up all the time."

Their relationship weathered quarrels over the lack of money. Sheridan had a job retouching photos, and Dean's work was sporadic at best; after "The Foggy, Foggy Dew," his funds were scarce or nonexistent. When Sheridan announced that she had quit because her job was keeping her from pursuing dancing, Dean became so angry that he walked out.

Knowing that Dean was in financial straits, Franklin Heller, the producer who hired him for *The Web,* had helped him get a job as a stunt tester on *Beat the Clock,* a game show in which contestants from the audience had to perform stunts successfully within a sixty-second time limit. The stunts were devised by CBS staff writers Frank Wayne and Bob Howard.

The stunts were first tested in their garages in New Jersey and brought into New York for a second round of tests in the cellar of the CBS studio. Finally, the stunts were rehearsed in the studio three times for the benefit of the cameramen and technicians. "We used professional actors to substitute for contestants," continued Heller, "trying to react as if we'd just brought them up from the audience to be on the show. We paid five dollars an hour.

"Dean was very poor, had no money at all, so we had him on. But we had to fire him after a short time, because he could do anything—he was the best-coordinated human being I ever knew! There was no trick or stunt that he couldn't accomplish with the greatest of ease; we had balancing stunts and all that jazz—nothing he couldn't do. He had absolute unerring control over his body."

Frank Wayne echoed Heller's memories of Dean's poverty. A sponsor made tapioca pudding and supplied *Beat the Clock* with copious quantities of it for the live commercials. Once Dean asked Wayne if he could keep the tapioca if they were going to throw it out. When Dean explained he had not eaten for two days, Wayne gave him the tapioca and took him to dinner as well.

A *Beat the Clock* connection was responsible for Dean's meeting Martin Landau, who became his good friend. Dean and another stunt tester, Tommy Tompkins, and Landau were all being put through their paces at a CBS open casting session one morning at the Mansfield Theater. Tompkins pointed Dean out to Landau: "That's James Dean, who was on *The Web* not long ago. He was great!"

Afterward, Tompkins introduced the two aspiring actors, and they walked along together. "Our stroll came to an abrupt halt in front of a building under construction," recalled Landau. "Jimmy just had to watch the work, with keen attention to every detail. We were there for twenty minutes." Landau would come to realize that such curiosity was typical of Dean. Later, over coffee, they discovered that they were both gifted at drawing and sketching.

The two friends began spending considerable time together, sitting in Central Park discussing Marlon Brando and Montgomery Clift, listening to classical music, or riding in tandem on Dean's motorcycle. "I don't like bikes, and I don't like motorcycles," Landau commented, "but I'd ride with Jimmy." Once while riding behind Dean, Landau said, he was carrying a stack of his books and Dean's record albums and had to hold onto the collar of Dean's coat with his teeth.

Meanwhile, with only a few dollars now and then from *Beat the Clock,* Dean and Dizzy Sheridan were so broke that all they could afford to eat was Shredded Wheat. Sometimes to make the situation less desperate, Sheridan added a macabre humor to their plight by lighting candles while they ate. Finally they had no choice but to leave the Hargrave Hotel and find separate quarters.

Dean moved in with Rogers Brackett, who had recently arrived from Chicago and taken a flat on the top floor of 132 West Twenty-third Street. Lyricist Marshall Barer visited them a few times while Dean lived there. "Jimmy had his own special kind of wit," said Barer.

"There was a toy animal stuck to the ceiling of the apartment. I asked, 'How did that get up there?' Without missing a beat, Jimmy said, 'Suction shoes.' " Another time, Dean was on the phone with Mary Chase, author of *Harvey,* trying to get an audition for her newest play, *Bernardine.* When he hung up, he said, "I think she's going to change the name of the play from *Bernardine* to *Jimmydine.*"

Sheridan found a room on Eighth Avenue that was so small it could barely contain a bed; the door could not be opened all the way because the bed blocked it. Although Dean was living with Brackett, he spent a few nights there with her. Not surprisingly, Brackett and Sheridan became rivals.

Sheridan's memories of Brackett are at best remote. "I met him more than once, I think," she said. "He was tall, thin, dark wavy hair, horn-rimmed glasses. Jimmy had run away from him in Chicago. He was an evil man and wanted to control Jimmy. Jimmy wanted me to stand up to him. I only remember sitting in their apartment and being very much aware that this man resented me and my position in Jimmy's life. When I left, just outside in the hallway, Jimmy hugged me because he was thrilled at what I'd done. But I don't remember what I said."

Brackett's interest in Dean had very likely turned possessive, but Dean's coming to New York with a ticket purchased by Brackett was hardly running away from him. Sheridan may be the only person on earth to have considered Brackett evil. Those who knew him say variously that he was "unforgettable," "unique," "compassionate," "the most companionable and enjoyable of men," and possessed of a "tenderness that was fairly rare."

Whatever the case may have been, Brackett's interest in Dean's well-being never wavered. He saw to it that Dean was hired as a crew member on *Hallmark Hall of Fame.* Actor John Kerr was doing a bit on the *Hallmark* just then and remembers, "The final credit at the end was a shot of producer Albert McCleery's signature on a card. Jimmy's job was to underline the signature with a piece of chalk. I remember McCleery saying to Jimmy, 'Shoot the cuff,' meaning get the cuff of your shirtsleeve in the shot." But even with that little chore, says James Maher, "Dean made trouble for Rogers in the agency by breaking the chalk or some such shenanigan. Instead of protecting Rogers, he contributed to Rogers's business problems by being a pain in the ass."[4]

Hallmark Hall of Fame was hosted by Winston Churchill's daughter Sarah, who had once been in Brackett's summer stock company in Marblehead, Massachusetts. "She showed up at the Algonquin at various times, usually quite high," recalls Arnold Sundgaard, "but Rogers was a staunch supporter of hers. He had a key to her Central Park South apartment." Churchill held postbroadcast soirées at her place every Sunday, which Dean and Brackett enjoyed attending.

When Brackett had to go to Europe on business, he asked his friends Jan and Ahmet Ertegun if Dean could stay with them during his absence. "Jimmy lived with us for about a week, in the East Seventies between Lexington and Third. I don't think he was working then, but my ex-wife, Jan, listened to him read lines and coached him," recalled Ahmet Ertegun, now cochairman of the Atlantic Recording Corporation. "Jan was a stage designer. Rogers was one of her best friends, and we were like family to him.

"Jimmy was interested in exotic things—bullfights and sports cars. We played matador with the cape and horns, taking turns being the matador and the bull. We talked a lot about cars, how one double-clutched and things like that. I took him for a spin in my Jaguar and even let him drive it. I taught him how to shift down.

"We became pals in the few days he was with us. He liked me because I was somebody who had lived half of my life in Europe. He wanted to know about Europe, where Hemingway ate in Madrid and Paris, how tables are set. He was a young man with a tremendous amount of curiosity and an obvious innate flair for things that were elegant."

Sometime during Dean's first months in the city, he also stayed with other friends of Brackett, writer David Swift and his wife, actress Maggie McNamara, who first met Dean when he was at Brackett's hotel in Chicago. "We always had a lot of starving actors over to our apartment on East Sixty-first Street," recalls Swift, "and also at our

---

4. Right after Dean's death, the *Chicago Sun-Times* noted that he had been scheduled to return to *Hallmark Hall of Fame* in November 1955 to make "The Corn Is Green" after having worked as a backstage assistant on the same show.

place on Fire Island. When we gave parties, Jimmy would be sitting in a corner, unhappy about being so poor in New York. We took lots of stereoscopic pictures of him brooding, but none of those pictures survives.

"We introduced him to actress Norma Crane and they hit it off. [Crane's mother died when she was an infant, and she was raised by relatives, which qualified her as a Dean soulmate.] He lived at her apartment for a while. Norma's boyfriend at the time was actor Gene Lyons, and although Gene had his own place, he was practically living with Norma. Even though Jimmy's sexuality wasn't a threat, Gene wasn't too pleased with that arrangement."

Dean continued hanging out with James Sheldon, an association which led to his introduction to his future agent, Jane Deacy. "When I first met Jane," said Sheldon, "I was not married. She was a switchboard operator at the Shurr Agency. I wanted tickets for a show that Shurr handled, and the agent said there were none left. 'But,' I was told, 'our switchboard operator's husband doesn't like the theater and she has tickets; why not go with her?' So Jane Deacy was a 'blind date.' We got along very well. . . ."

By the time Dean came to him, Sheldon had already known Deacy for a few years. "Jimmy had become a responsibility, and I had a wife, and a social life, and a career," Sheldon continued. "He started to be a pest—in a nice way—and I didn't have much time for him. I sent him to Doris Quinlan on *Mama,* Bob Stevens on *Suspense,* and to other people. But I realized he needed someone to take care of him, and thought Jane Deacy would be good for him. He needed someone to talk to, and she would be good, instead of him talking to me. It wasn't that I was annoyed by him; we were always friendly. It was just a matter of who could help him more.

"Jane was then a very warm lady, tall, attractive, a little overweight, who came from Ohio, and had a son. She had ambitions to do more and had a very good eye for talent. Her early clients were mostly musical; she had a very good ear for singers and dancers. Much later she would handle only George C. Scott. She was a good negotiator—fearless. She had a very winning way with her people and defended them. She always was a very stubborn woman. She also was very foresighted in realizing that TV was about to break forth, and encouraged her clients to do things on TV.

"As a woman, she was very motherly with all her clients. Gentle, sweet, unlike many agent people who are real hard dealers, even some of the ladies. Jane was always very soft and nice. When Jimmy died she was really, genuinely destroyed. It was a close friendship. Not just the success of him, but he was like her baby.

"She used to keep a picture of him on her desk with a new flower every day. One day, George C. Scott said, 'Look, I'm leaving you unless . . .' and Jimmy's picture was put away. Then eventually George became so successful that for years she has only handled him. Jane gets very close to her clients. When someone says they don't like something, she gets upset. That's a good agent's job, and there aren't that many left."

Since Deacy has never wavered in her refusal to talk about Dean to writers, it is impossible to fix the dates of her first meeting with him and signing him as a client, although an educated guess would be May 1952. As such, she had no role in Dean's early television jobs, which he got principally through Sheldon and Brackett. When they met, she was still with the Shurr Agency; she became a solo agent in August 1952.

Whether Dean was surprised at the next development in his life is uncertain. Bill Bast relocated to New York to look for a job, arriving on a muggy morning in May. He phoned Dean and then found his way to the Brackett-Dean residence on West Twenty-third Street, only to discover that his old friend had fallen back into a heavy sleep.

Later that day, Dizzy Sheridan made them both laugh when she innocently suggested that they find a place together. (Dean apparently had told her very little if anything about Bast.) But they quickly realized that they had forgotten and forgiven the ugly confrontation at the Santa Monica apartment the previous summer. So they rented a room at the Iroquois Hotel. Dean relished the élan of playing Bast's guide to Manhattan after living there only seven months himself.

April had been a dry spell for Dean in acting jobs, but in May things began to look up. On May 11, he had a part in a one-hour radio drama about Abraham Lincoln, "Prologue to Glory," on *Theater Guild on the Air*. John Lund and Wanda Hendrix were the stars; Dean played Denny, a young friend of the future president.

Lincoln was a popular subject that month. Many programs about his life were broadcast, which had the effect of confusing later scholars as to which ones Dean was actually in. On May 26, he was back on tele-

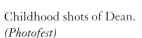

Childhood shots of Dean.
(Photofest)

Dean's mentor Alec Wilder *(left)* and patron Rogers Brackett confer during the dress rehearsal of a Wilder opera Brackett was staging in May 1955, a few months after Dean stopped associating with them. *(Fran Miller)*

An early publicity still of Dean by photographer Wilson Millar, 1951. *(Photofest)*

Dean's close friend Christine White, from the 1952 movie, *Man Crazy,* made soon after she met him. *(Photofest)*

Michel (Louis Jourdan) tells Bachir (James Dean) that he eats disgustingly in *The Immoralist,* 1954. *(Photofest)*

Constance Ford, Roy Fant, Arthur Kennedy, and Dean on a mountain top in *See the Jaguar*. *(Photofest)*

Dean *(right)*, in *See the Jaguar,* tries to stay one step ahead of a pursuing mob with the help of Ford, Kennedy, and Fant. *(Photo by Fred Fehl. Courtesy of the Billy Rose Theater Collection, New York Public Library for the Performing Arts)*

In the final, climactic scene of *See the Jaguar,* Kennedy helps Dean escape from the jaguar cage as Ford looks on. *(Photo by Fred Fehl. Courtesy of the Billy Rose Theater Collection, New York Public Library for the Performing Arts)*

Dean *(front)* visits Marlon Brando (in sunglasses) on the set of *Desirée*, 1954. *(Archive Photos)*

Dean escorts Pier Angeli to a celebrity showing of *Gone With the Wind,* August 10, 1954. *(Photofest)*

Publicity still of Dean and co-star Julie Harris in *East of Eden*. *(Photofest)*

Aron (Richard Davalos) menacingly eyes Cal (Dean) as his girl, Abra (Harris), gets too close. The sheriff (Burl Ives) observes. *(Photofest)*

East of Eden publicity still of Dean. *(Photofest)*

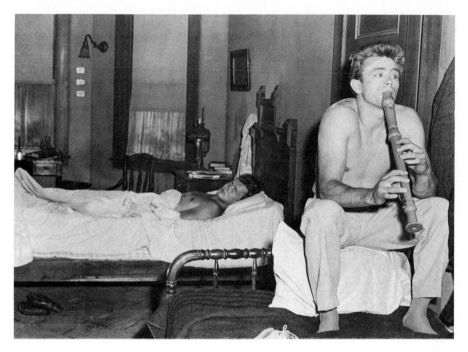

Davalos watches Dean playing his recorder in a scene that was cut from *East of Eden*. *(Photofest)*

Brothel keeper Kate (Jo Van Fleet) warily converses with Cal (Dean), her long-lost son, in *East of Eden*. *(Photofest)*

Dean's passion for bongo drums was almost as strong as his love of fast cars. *(Photofest)*

Actress Terry Moore, in "a wool job with a neckline so high she could chin herself on it," is escorted by a bored Dean to the September 22, 1954, Hollywood premiere of *Sabrina. (Archive Photos/Albin)*

Publicity still of Dean from "The Unlighted Road," *Schlitz Playhouse of Stars,* which was filmed in January 1955. *(Photofest)*

vision in *Studio One*'s "Abraham Lincoln," with Robert Pastene in the title role. Dean gave an excellent performance as a Union soldier about to be shot for falling asleep on guard duty. Lincoln, who is visiting General Grant, asks to speak to the soldier. When Dean is brought in, he hardly dares look at the president, stealing only an occasional furtive glance. (This kind of reaction is what Dean did best.) In questioning him, Lincoln learns he is from Vermont. "We have a place, a big farm up there," Dean stammers. Lincoln wants to know what the soldier means by "we." After much hesitation, Dean mutters, "My mother, sir."

This maternal information touches Lincoln, and as he contemplates what to do, Dean weeps. His sobs were authentic and he may actually have thought about his own mother during the scene. Finally Lincoln writes an order discharging him and sends him back to his regiment. Dean grins widely as he hurries away.

After little more than half a year in New York, despite a lot of hunger and discouragement, Dean had a lot to show for his time in the city.[5] Through Rogers Brackett, he had met and become friends with some of the most distinguished names in New York—Wilder, Ertegun, and Churchill. As distasteful as he found the business of hustling acting jobs to be, he had many good credits to carry in his actor's portfolio, especially "The Foggy, Foggy Dew." Sheridan said he had affixed a sarcastic label, "Matters of Great Consequence," to the portfolio.

Two related events illustrated just how much of a New Yorker Dean had become. During May, the city was swarming with graduating high school seniors on class trips, including Fairmount High's Class of '52. On the evening of May 18, some of them, including Dean's old friend Larry Lee Smith, met with him; they thought of him as a sophisticate, and he was not one to disappoint them.

Another opportunity to be the man about town had come one week earlier. Jane Addams Reed, who had grown up just down the road from him in Fairmount, was chaperoning another school's trip to New York. The only person in the city she knew was Dean. She tried

---

5. Before dropping his anchor at the Iroquois with Bill Bast in May, Dean had had almost too many residences to count: the Sixty-third Street YMCA; the apartments of Ertegun, Swift, Crane, King, Gearin, and Brackett; the hotel room with Sheridan; and a previous short stint at the Iroquois.

phoning him all day, not finding him in until she was about to climb in bed.

"In New York, it's just time to live," Dean informed her with the savoir faire of a native. He convinced her to get dressed and go out on the town with him. When he first met her in her hotel lobby, she sensed he was posing. "Wonderful to see you, dear," he gushed. "Would you like to go for a drink?" Reed demurred, owing to her chaperone status. Then he grinned broadly, as he might have in Fairmount, and told her he couldn't afford to drink but was merely behaving as New York social customs prescribed. They went to a restaurant for sodas and talked until two A.M.

At the restaurant, Dean's countenance turned grave. Reed noticed that his coat was shabby and his hair was long. He chain-smoked and fidgeted during their entire visit. He told her he was subsisting on milk shakes because solid food was too expensive. (Better that she believe he was starving than know about the living arrangement with Brackett.) What stuck in her mind was his intense explanation of his philosophy of acting.

"I can't do something just because somebody tells me to do it," he said. "If I get a part as an old man, I watch an old man, listen to him, and then I mock him until I feel like an old man, too. If I get a part, even if it's washing dishes, I'll go home and get a dishpan and wash and wash until my hands peel and I know exactly how it feels to wash dishes. That's the way I have to act. That's the only way I can act." (That would explain his eagerness to be hit in the face in *The Web*.)

He was rapidly mastering the ways of the city. "New York is vital; above all, fertile," he would later say. "I fit to cadence and pace better here [than in Hollywood] as far as living goes."

The Unbearable
Lightness of Acting

Dean learned about the Actors Studio, the temple of the naturalistic Stanislavsky "method" of acting, from James Whitmore, and held the dream of being admitted even before he moved to New York. When he worked with Anne Jackson in *The Web,* he was terribly impressed with her Studio membership and peppered her with questions about how to get in. To be helpful, she encouraged Lee Strasberg, the Studio's revered artistic director, to watch Dean's performance when the show aired.

Despite his enthusiasm for becoming a member, the last auditions of the season were fast approaching and he had not chosen a scene or a partner; possibly he intended to wait another year to audition. But the right conditions dropped into his lap, and he had the clarity of vision to recognize and seize the opportunity. It came about when he went to the Shurr Agency early in April 1952 in hopes of becoming Jane Deacy's client.

Wearing a black suit, black tie, and white shirt (a clear sign that he wanted to make a favorable impression), Dean stepped into the reception area. Beyond it was an anteroom with a secretary's desk. A young woman in a red jumper and matching velvet hat sat at the desk typing, deep in concentration, but she was not the secretary. Dean wandered in and peered over her shoulder. "I can't believe—was he raised in a barn?" the woman asked herself in annoyance. Heaping on the irritation, Dean asked, "What are you doing?" "Typing!" retorted Christine White huffily.

White, who had been in New York for seven months, had already appeared in several television shows and one Broadway play, *The Long Watch,* which had just closed after only twelve performances. Thrown back on her own resources, she was writing an original scene that had grown out of a "weird early morning compulsion." She was a Jane Deacy client and had permission to use the typewriter while the secretary was at lunch.

The young man hovering over her, White thought, could not be an actor; he looked like a delivery boy. "He doesn't have any right to be back here in the office," she thought; "he should wait out there with the rest of the cattle." Dean "threw himself back against a file cabinet and draped his arms around it." Then he asked, "Are you an actress?"

At the end of her rope, White answered, "I don't know whether I am. *They* will have to answer that. But right now I'm trying to write a play."

"Oh! You're trying to write a play," Dean repeated. White thought, "I'm going to smack him in a minute." "Yes," she seethed. Dean wouldn't quit. He asked, "What about?"

"I can't believe the chutzpah here," White remembers thinking. "So he came over, and that's when he started to read it. I figured he wouldn't understand it if he read it, so I let him look." Dean kept looking until finally White complained, "You're breaking my concentration, and you really have to move because this machine is not mine." Finally, he went out quietly.

"I finished as best I could, and it was a good ten to fifteen minutes," White continues. "I packed up and went across the outer office and through the outer door, and then I stopped, and I don't know why. But I saw him out of the corner of my eye, sitting in the corner, and that's when I said to myself, 'You were rude to that boy.' It was such a big stop. I don't know what made me do it. It was a very abrupt stop, and I reopened the door and went back again, and I apologized to him. 'I'm sorry. I know I was abrupt with you. I was short of time. Are you waiting for an interview?' He said, 'Yes, but I've waited long enough. Can we go have some coffee?' I didn't expect that. I said, 'Okay, well, if you want to.' We went to the Blue Ribbon on West Forty-fourth."

White learned that Dean was unemployed and trying to make up his mind whether to be an actor or a bullfighter. Unable to get comfortable in the booth, he kept shifting around. He spoke of his wish to audition for the Actors Studio, and White said she, too, hoped to get in, using a scene from Ibsen's *The Master Builder*. Dean did not tell her of his living arrangements with Dizzy Sheridan. White didn't know where he lived when they met; trying to remember decades later, she says, "He may have been sleeping in Central Park."

Dean was "absolutely hep" on reading the scene that White had just finished typing, and he asked her to read some of the lines with him. It was set on a beach at Cape Hatteras, North Carolina, in the path of an approaching hurricane. The young woman, Clayton, has run away from home and been picked up in a bar by Sam, an "intellectual beachcomber." Its theme was alienation from society and family.

"When you write something," White recalls, "you're not impressed; you always think you'd better redo it." So she was surprised at Dean's enthusiasm for the scene. He was taken by its outdoor setting and the iconoclasm of the male character. But White objected. "This guy is considerably older than you," she said, "and he sort of takes her under his wing because he's been around, rejecting the world." But this only whetted Dean's interest even more.

After two hours White had to leave, so Dean walked her to the bus stop. "You didn't give me your phone number," he said to her. "AT 9-0049," she intoned, and he stood there repeating it to himself. Although she had found the afternoon interesting—Dean had struck her as someone who, like herself, was "ready to hear the call" of naturalistic acting as espoused by the Actors Studio—she had no idea it would turn into anything beyond a one-shot encounter. She later reflected, "Everybody's from somewhere out of New York, and I knew he was reaching out for some place to confide, to share."

The next morning, White's roommates had all gone to work, but "I was an actress, so I could sleep in." She was still in bed when the phone rang. "This is Jim Dean," said the voice at the other end. White wasn't sure who it was. "The scene," the caller persisted. "You know, yesterday. I called the Studio and fixed everything. We can audition together, and you can do it under the Ds [for Dean] with me." (The auditions were scheduled by the alphabetical order of the candidates' surnames.) All of this hit White like a ton of bricks. She didn't have the same sense of urgency. "He was in such a hurry. It really put a great big lump of fear in me. I thought, 'I'm not ready yet, I've got time here!' " She still felt he was wrong for Sam, who was supposed to be much older than Clayton; Dean, in contrast, was five years younger than White. She also resented his wanting her to assist him by using her own scene.

Dean clarified his intentions. Although Studio auditions were supposed to involve two people (monologues were discouraged), generally only one of the two was auditioning. Dean wanted White to do a joint audition. Showing the same chutzpah as in Hollywood, where he had called movie studios directly, he had already phoned Lee Strasberg at the Studio to get his scheme approved. He reminded White that she could get in under the Ds this way, instead of waiting for the Ws. "He was selling me my own play," she continues, "saying things like, 'There's so much you can play on a beach!' "

From the other end of the phone Dean announced, "I know this scene calls for beer, so I'll go buy some, and then I'll be there." White was astounded and began to protest. "What, you mean you have an appointment today?" he asked. Having exhausted all of her excuses, she had to admit that she did not.

"And then he was at the door almost right away!" White figured Dean must have called from around the corner (she was living at 51 East Ninety-first Street). "He had a bag with two apples and two cans of beer. That's all I think he had any money to buy. That was it. He couldn't get over the apartment. He said, 'God, what a great apartment you've got. This is fantastic!' I replied, 'Yeah, three other girls live here, too.'

"So we went upstairs and there's no room to sit in my bedroom. There's the bed, the bookcases, night table, phone, one small chair right next to the bookcase as you come in. So we went out on the roof, and he exclaimed, 'This is perfect! We'll rehearse here.' So we brought some pillows out, and then we attacked the scene. He told me to spread my coat as if it were a blanket on the beach: 'You're running away, so you wouldn't be carrying a blanket.' I used the same coat at the audition.

"We would put the pages down and put books on top of them so the wind wouldn't blow them away. While we were learning it, we'd have to lean over to get the lines. The scene was all down on the floor most of the time anyway, because we were supposed to be on a beach. So, we could easily see the script. That's how we really learned it. He would be lying back, and forget, and say, 'Oh, God!'—and he'd pick it up, and read it, and say, 'Oh, I know what it is.' We would block it that way and of course change it a lot every time we did it.

"We decided to keep the scene stylized, because we were down on the blanket most of the time. 'My God,' we'd say, 'how do they move with their lines? Who can we tell they're lying down on the blanket all the time?' So we had to ballet the thing, which he's very good at, choreographing the scene, sitting up, getting back down—arm movement. We thought, 'We're going to stay on this quilt, like you do on the beach, and choreograph it without getting on our legs until the end of the scene. Then we're gonna let them have it!'

"At the end, when he invites me into his shack, he had a grand Shakespearean gesture when he reached out to me, saying, 'Come . . .' At first he was reluctant to do that, but eventually he said, 'I can do this. . . . I feel comfortable with it.' "

Both Dean's and White's roommates were pressed into service as audiences. Bill Bast oversaw a rehearsal and gave them his criticism. "We did the scene in their room at the Iroquois, and there was no room!" White recalls. "We always asked people what they thought. I don't know if it made any difference, but we would ask."

Once after coming inside White's apartment after a heavy rain, they rehearsed the scene for her roommates and Barbara Dalton, a friend from the next block. Dean had taken off his soaked shirt and trousers and hung them up to dry; he went through his paces wearing a raincoat over his underwear. Another time, White asked Dean if they could do the scene for a man she had dated, but he refused. "He would do the scene for women but not male rivals," she says.

They even ran the scene for Jane Deacy in her office. "We were both nobodies," emphasizes White. "Jimmy was not her client then; it was the first time she ever saw him perform. She was just as interested in what I was doing as in what he was doing. We sat on the floor in her office, leaning against the wall, playing in imaginary sand, and—I'll never forget—Jimmy let out a stream of cusswords. I don't know if it was because the phone rang, but I said, 'God, Jimmy, don't do that, please!' I looked at Jane, and there was a big frown on her face. I don't know what she thought.

"The cry of the day was cusswords. The greater you could cuss—I mean, even girls—like sailors! I can't believe the language we used in those days. When I first got to New York, I didn't, but when you got into the nest of upcoming actors and in the main gang, which we were, it was rough, it was tough, it was street talk. He would get mad, and say, 'Oh, fuck that!' I got used to it after a while, but I wasn't used to it in Jane's office."

White says she introduced Dean to Deacy. Informed that James Sheldon claims credit for sending Dean to Deacy, White replied, "The day I met Jimmy in the secretary's office—why was he there? Sheldon must have sent him. But he didn't get to see Jane that day."

Since Deacy has never given interviews, the exact details of how she took Dean on as a client are unknown. However, the way White became Deacy's client was quite informal. Arriving in New York late in the summer of 1951, White's first act was to buy a red hat at Saks. Then, wearing the hat and her favorite red jumper, she met a friend from summer stock for dinner in Greenwich Village. The friend had asked Deacy to meet them. When Deacy saw White, she exclaimed, "What an incredible profile! Come to my office Monday morning and wear that outfit!" From then on, White wore the hat and jumper whenever she wanted to make an impression. She had been wearing them, of course, when she met Dean.

Out of the blue one day, Dean told White he wanted her to meet Louie Fabrikant, proprietor of a Manhattan jewelry store. White was not particularly interested but went along. Dean presented her to Fabrikant, who said, "She's a lovely young lady. You can bring her to dinner tonight."

"See?" Dean teased. He hadn't told White anything about the dinner scheme. Dazed, White asked, "What are you having?" "Anything you want," replied Fabrikant. What Dean had up his sleeve soon became clear. "Now," he said to Fabrikant, "what we can do for you is, we will do our scene." Suddenly, he threw out his first line. "You want to do it *here?*" asked White. "Of course we want to do it here," Dean insisted, "and then we'll do it again tonight."

"So we started the scene," said White, "and of course, customers were there, the phones are ringing, and we got not even halfway through it. Fabrikant was listening, but he kind of went back into a corner because I think he was embarrassed. He finally said, 'By the way, if you'd like to have an audience, you can ask some more people to come to dinner.' Jimmy said, 'That's a great idea.'

"We wondered, should you dress for the part or dress for dinner? In the end, Jimmy wore black and white: a black raincoat that was too big in the shoulders, baggy black pants, a white shirt, no tie. Everything he wore that night was borrowed. I was in my usual uniform, red jumper and peasant blouse and loafers. Jimmy said, 'We can't be late,' and of course, we were hungry."

Fabrikant greeted the thespians in a suit and tie. "He was altruistic," says White. "He was just interested in us; we couldn't give him anything." After a sumptuous dinner prepared by his cook, he said, "I thought you were going to do something." Dean replied, "I've asked a couple of people to come for dessert," a plot twist that did not sit well with White at all.

"Sure enough," she continues, "four girls came to the apartment. I don't know where he found them; some of them didn't seem to know his name. I thought, 'He's directed this whole scenario!' " After Dean and White had retreated to a bedroom to prepare for the scene, she protested, "What are you doing with these girls in here? I am not in the mood for this!" Dean tried to persuade her that the girls were just part of the audience and this would be good rehearsal time for them.

"Then," relates White, "the girls began to wander into the bedroom! They didn't want to sit out there and talk with Fabrikant; they wanted to talk to Jimmy. I said, 'I just don't think we should be doing this. Let's not bother with it right now.' I was put out because he hadn't brought me in on his plans; he was doing the big creative number here, and there were other girls around. Maybe if one other girl had come, I'd do it, but with four I didn't know what to do. If he brings one, then you're in direct opposition with her; but if he brings four, that's not the same thing. I didn't know if he wanted an entourage or an audience or what, but we did not do the scene, because Jimmy's partner—me—was not going to do it. I was miffed, and that was it.

"Fabrikant did not want me to go at all. He said, 'Why can't you stay here and talk to me?' I thanked him for his generosity, but I was not in the mood to handle the situation. When I left, if Jimmy's eyes ever widened, they widened then. I don't know if I did that just to get a rise out of him, but he was stuck with his plan, and I left him with it. If you have a partner in a scene and a dinner partner and date, you're going to bring her in on what you're doing.

"So, he never did anything like that again. He never again failed to consult me about what he was going to do. He would call the shots quite frequently—'Now we're going to do this, now that'—but then he would say, 'Okay?' as a means of consulting me. With Fabrikant, Jimmy was really, with his enthusiasm, trying to make a hit for a meal and trying to find security within a normal kind of home. But it was a night that did not materialize in terms of progress on the scene."

May 4, 1952, was White's twenty-sixth birthday. Dean gave her a series of drawings, one for each month of the year, that he had done. "There were twelve cards with different pictures, beautifully done," White elaborates. "Some had buildings or something graphic for what he wanted to say. For my month, May, he drew a cute little blond girl who was trying to draw *me* as a child. So it was very childlike." Each drawing was accompanied by a short poem. "It was something like, 'Happy Birthday, Christine, you're a pal.' That's not it exactly; I'm paraphrasing. Each picture was as different and diverse as he was able to be.

"There was one drawing of his mother, maybe for the month she died. I only remember the drawing vaguely: sort of a profile with wavy hair; abstract. The verse was, 'My mother died when I was wee; Maybe that is why I'm me.' It was as if a little kid had written it.

"That was his present, to draw something for me, because he knew I would appreciate it. I loved the way he drew, and I had told him I did. He was good at it; I wasn't just telling him that. Later, when we were both living at the Iroquois, his desk was always full of rulers and pens and paper whenever I'd stop in. He was always automatically doing things with his hands.

"He handed the drawings to me in an envelope. I looked at them rather quickly. And I didn't take it too significantly, except that he didn't have money to buy a present. I put them inside a book which I could reach from my bed. When I changed apartments, they were left behind. I tried to locate them later when people were hounding me for them. I looked up the owner in Cape Cod, who said, 'Oh, I don't have that apartment anymore.' "

As the day of the Studio audition drew nearer, Dean and White realized they had to clock the scene. Neither of them had a watch, so once while they were rehearsing behind the Metropolitan Museum of Art, Dean asked a stranger to time it for them. The result was fourteen minutes, and the Studio had a five-minute limit. They made cuts, but when they couldn't shorten it to less than eight minutes, they decided to take their chances with the buzzer.

The road leading to Actors Studio membership was more often than not long and winding. "The auditions were not advertised or announced. Preliminaries were held monthly between October and April," explains longtime member Salem Ludwig. "Approximately sixteen hundred auditioners were heard through the season. Then, there was one final yearly audition for the approximately thirty to fifty applicants who had passed the preliminaries. Of these, usually between eight and fifteen were accepted as members. In Dean's year [1952], the finals would have been in late May."

White, the exclusive source on the Studio audition in all Dean biographies, insists that despite the usual requirements of preliminary and final tryouts, she and Dean auditioned only once. "It could be," says Salem Ludwig, "that since they were seen by [Elia] Kazan and [Cheryl] Crawford and Strasberg [the Studio's ruling triumvirate] instead of a preliminary jury, there was no need for them to do it again." Somehow, Strasberg had been persuaded to let them audition with the semifinalists.

Actress June Havoc, it is said, vomited just before her Studio audition; Al Pacino was terrified before his. A very young Paul Newman agonized over not feeling up to the Method. So it is no surprise that when the moment of truth came, Dean suffered his worst known instance of stage fright. Arthur Storch, one of the finalists that day (who was admitted), remembers seeing him curled up on top of a radiator, sleeping. White chatted with some friends, only to turn around and discover Dean "mesmerized" on the radiator, staring into space. "I can't do it," he choked. "I'm not ready yet." White suggested that they drink the beer they planned to use in the scene to calm down. But when their names were called, Dean refused to do the scene with empty beer cans, so he ran out to buy more. They had to be rescheduled after the other candidates, but the physical exertion of running finally soothed Dean's anxiety.

"When we did the scene," says White, "we'd already gone over the time limit and hadn't been buzzed. Jimmy had his hands in the air, and it wasn't clear we were through. So he said, 'That's it!' meaning, 'It's over.' " Kazan and Strasberg both praised their work and asked who wrote the scene. "I did," said White, running back on stage. Now she and Dean would have to await the results. The panel's decision would be delayed by Kazan's trip to Europe to scout locations for his next film *(Man on a Tightrope)*.

Over the course of Dean's rehearsals with White, she says, he "became adhesive." Dizzy Sheridan remembers, "Once late at night when I was alone in bed in the hotel, Jimmy called to say he was working late on his scene with Christine and would have to stay overnight at her apartment. He kept asking, 'Is that okay?' and then he said 'I love you' just before hanging up." Dean took pains not to have any overlapping between these women. White says they all met by chance on the street once, with Dean cheerfully finessing introductions ("This is the one I've told you about"). Sheridan soon left to do summer stock in Ocean City, New Jersey, freeing up more of Dean's time for White. Then, Sheridan returned to New York just as White was leaving for three months in Hollywood. So Dean was spared much of whatever rivalry might have developed if the two women had been in New York at the same time.

White's early memories of Dean parallel Sheridan's. "He talked a lot about not having money," she relates. "It was very painful—'Lend me twenty dollars or I'll starve.' " In what had become a rite of passage for all Dean friends, White was expected to learn and love *The Little Prince*. "Oh my God," she tells her interviewer, "you just brought that back to me now. He gave me a copy and autographed it. What have I done with it? Yes, he loved that book. And we never really had time to read very much of it, just an excerpt here and there, or, 'Get this!' That would be it; he'd go off into something else. The things he read were sort of a personification of himself."

About this time Walter Winchell wrote that White was dating actor Tom Tryon and eloping to Connecticut; Dean spotted it and called her. "I see you're going out with Tyrone Power," he joked. It was his play on the name Tryon. White retorted, "He's as handsome as Tyrone Power." Then Dean said, "I thought you said the press isn't interested in what you're doing, but they *are.*"

"Jimmy wanted togetherness," White asserts. "It was always, 'Can I go, too?' We—in fact, everyone—went to each other's TV rehearsals. Assistant directors were told whom to let in. Whoever had the appointment, we would go with the other person, wait for them, joke around. If they didn't get it, we'd laugh. We didn't care, because we were not going to get down. Nobody was going to reject us. If we got rejected, we'd say, 'Tough luck, you missed it!' It was their fault; it was never ours. 'Blind as a bat!' Jimmy would say, 'Damn guy can't even see!' So we were always there. Always the actor's courage has to stay much higher than the average person."

While awaiting word from the Actors Studio, Dean worked in an episode of the *Hallmark Hall of Fame* called "The Forgotten Children." He played Bradford, a young Georgian aristocrat, one of his few non–juvenile delinquent roles. The program was a vehicle for Cloris Leachman, who played one of America's foremost educators, Martha Berry, as a young woman.

"The Forgotten Children" begins in 1887 at the Berry family's annual barbeque. Questioned about her future plans, Martha says she might found her own school. After all, she says, she is an emancipated woman. Here Dean gets a brief but nice close-up, showing his wavy, slicked-back hair as he quips, "The only emancipated woman I ever knew lived on a side street in Memphis." Some of the young ladies are aghast at such an improper remark.

Unbeknownst to the revelers, an illiterate hill country girl hides in the bushes watching the festivities. Dean spies the girl and seizes her, with a warning not to "bring your trash around here, you little dervish." His part in the plot is at an end, but the experience leads Martha to establish a school for the uneducated, "forgotten children" of the Georgia hill country.

Though the Bradford role is brief, Dean manages to establish a well-delineated character. Tics and gestures that would later brand him as an Actors Studio member are very much in evidence. Slouching on porch steps next to Martha in the party scene, he is unable to keep his fingers off his face, variously scratching his head, eyes, and nose. If he's not doing that, he's letting his hand droop.

"The Forgotten Children" was Dean's last known television job in 1952, but sometime that year he appeared in an unidentified episode of *Suspense*. (He listed it among his television credits in his first *Playbill* biography later that year.) The director was Robert Stevens. In a 1959 article about the capacity of television directors to recognize talent in the rough, Stevens commented, "Dean seemed to me to be very ambitious and intense, but he didn't strike me as being a very good actor. That just proves how wrong I was." His perfectly discreet statement glossed over a connection that transcended business.

According to John Peyser, another director for CBS, Stevens "was a very unstable homosexual and CBS never knew when he would blow his cork, and I would be there to take over. He sometimes disappeared, and I went on with *Suspense*." But producer Franklin Heller elaborates, "Stevens was exceptionally talented at a time when the production capacities were rudimentary, and imagination and talent made a big difference. That is why he was tolerated by the management."

In 1987, Stevens met James Sheldon on the street. Sheldon, who had sent Dean to Stevens so long ago, recalls, "Bob invited me to lunch, and out of the clear blue, he said, 'I want to thank you for sending Jimmy Dean to me.' He told me they had been involved sexually."

In the Seventies, Stevens, by then quite prominent in the industry, had forbidden the use of his name when speaking about Dean to biographer Jonathan Gilmore. "The way he worked," said Stevens, who appeared in the Gilmore biography as Ben Sherman, "was that all the personal feelings he had in himself would just come up through the parts he was playing—it was like a massive psychological ejaculation. Made me think of what I'd read about the way Soutine painted: the individual tearing himself apart—a kind of volcano of emotions—but restrained, too, and fitting right into whatever he was doing."

Dean's *Suspense* episode could have been any of three in the first half of 1952 to feature William Redfield. In a *New York* magazine interview, Redfield said he and Dean had worked together and that Dean played a punk gunman. Redfield described an incident similar to Lela Swift's story about Dean's masochistic rehearsal for *The Web*. "Eventually in the show I had to hit him. Well, I had done a little boxing at the YMCA. So we staged the fight, and we got to the run-through. And I threw this so-called knockout punch at him, and of course I missed him by about *this* much. And he stopped the run-through and he said, 'Billy, hit me.' And I said, 'No. I don't want to hit you. I'll hurt you.' And he said, 'But we gotta see blood or there's no scene.' I said, 'We're not supposed to put each other's eyes out.' And Jimmy says, 'No. *Hit* me. Or at least promise me when we get on the air you'll hit me.'

"Well, I did. I hit him. And he did bleed. It was a hell of a shot and he hit the ground, banged into the bar. Doesn't seem like much now because we've had so much violence since, but it was unusual then. So later on I went in to see him. He had a swollen jaw. I said, 'Jesus, you asked me.' But he said, 'Oh, it was *good. Good.* That was really good.' "

In the first week of July, some of the happiest news a young actor could receive reached Dean and White: both received postcards welcoming them as new members of the Actors Studio. Legend has it that Al Pacino had to audition three times, Dustin Hoffman at least seven times, and Geraldine Page nine times before getting in. Although these failures were blamed on poor-quality scenes, few members got in on their first try, making Dean's and White's achievement all the more remarkable.

White treated the good news with great casualness in a short note to her parents, dated July 7, giving it less wordage than a request that they send her bathing suit. For Dean, the triumph was tempered by the menace of poverty. Reduced to asking for money from the Winslows, he explained that he anticipated a scarcity of television jobs during the summer months and was having to forfeit dancing and fencing lessons. He said he felt terribly guilty always to need something whenever he wrote, but the present situation seemed desperate. The Winslows replied within a few days, sending more than the ten dollars he had asked for.

Some of Dean's friends from UCLA found their way to New York that summer. His former pledge brother James Bellah came in hopes of finding acting jobs. "I sought Dean out as a career contact," Bellah explains. "He was living at the Iroquois with Bill Bast and embarrassed me when I came to his room because he opened the door dressed in jeans, but no shirt, and embraced me.

"He took me to the Rehearsal Club, and I met Dizzy Sheridan there. He fixed me up with another girl there who later became my ex-wife. Another time I went to the Shurr office to respond to some casting calls, and Dean was there. He said, 'I've been a professional house guest on Fire Island.' " Bellah returned to California at summer's end, not having found any jobs beyond a cigarette commercial.

John Holden remembers him at a party in honor of three UCLA women who were on their way back to California from Europe. "Because of his good looks," Holden says, "people were titillated." Margaret Ann Curran spent a couple of weeks in New York at the end of a stint in summer stock. "There was a reunion for UCLA people, and Jimmy was there, wearing jeans," she recalls. "He was very much a loner. He was on the outskirts, sitting in a window seat, just staring out the window. But I really liked him because he was a very sensitive person.

"He pulled me aside and asked me how long I'd be in New York. 'I'd like to have you meet some people here who might be of help,' he said. I thanked him profusely, but, I thought, who in God's name could he possibly know? He kept looking over his shoulder as if someone might eavesdrop. He said, 'I really mean it,' but he was very into himself and wasn't specific. He didn't mention the Actors Studio.

"I had a few more days in New York but never followed up with him on this. So I got back to California and was later surprised to read in *Variety* that he was in *See the Jaguar*. Ever since that experience, I've never told anyone who wanted to take risks to be an actor not to try it, because Jimmy defied everyone who said he couldn't do it."

Marion Rothman, an alumna of the Whitmore class, was surprised to encounter Dean on a New York street with his bullfighter's cape; he gave her a "self-dramatizing" greeting. The most amazing incident, however, comes from Joanne Mock, who was working as a program assistant at ABC. "I was up in the sponsor's booth for a show," she reports, "and Tallulah Bankhead was in it. Jimmy was there and came running up to her, jumped, and she caught him. His arms and legs were wrapped around her. But I was too shy to go down and say hello."[1]

---

1. How Dean met Tallulah Bankhead is unknown. There is no record of their working together in television. Bankhead's only appearance on ABC during Dean's career was on January 5, 1954, in the title role in *Hedda Gabler* on *U.S. Steel Hour*.

In July, Dizzy Sheridan had a break from summer stock and visited the city. Coincidentally, *Has Anybody Seen My Gal?*, the third movie Dean worked in, had just opened at the Mayfair Theater, so he, Bast, and Sheridan went to see it. When his brief soda fountain scene came along, all three friends stood up and cheered. Sheridan, who found Dean depressed, talked him into going back to Ocean City with her, but the anticipated psychological benefit did not materialize; he seemed unhappy and in a hurry to get back to New York.

Later in the summer a meeting was called for newly accepted Studio members. Christine White reports, "Jimmy wasn't there; I think he was away. Kazan came over to me to talk. I was so scared I wanted to jump out the window, or wished I'd had roller skates on." Kazan has been quoted in recent years as saying he never saw Dean at the Studio, an assertion White disputes. "Kazan said, 'I really liked your scene, and I thought the guy was great. Where is he?' So it isn't true that Kazan never saw Jimmy at the Studio."

The Actors Studio, said member Geraldine Page, was a "high-powered postgraduate course" for actors. The sessions were held every Tuesday and Friday at eleven in the morning. Lee Strasberg, the artistic director, would enter the room and announce the scene about to be performed and the actors in it. At the scene's conclusion, Strasberg always began by asking the performers to explain what they were trying to accomplish.

Strasberg's objective was "to explore the vast array of what you can do," said Geraldine Page, "what all actors can do if they know how to do it—so that they are forced to examine what they just repeat because it was good once—imitate themselves. He continually makes you work back to some initial source."

Ironically, to act at the *Actors* Studio was taboo; members were continually exhorted to *be* or to *do the work*. The worst thing one could be told, they recall, was "You're not doing the work" or "You are acting, not being." Strasberg explained, "I stress the difference between the actor who thinks acting is an imitation of life, and the actor who feels acting is living." This was achieved by careful contemplation of what had gone on in the character's life before coming onstage. Members were expected to convey a sense of being in a place rather than on a stage. Not to do so invoked Strasberg's caustic rebuke.

In such an atmosphere did James Dean begin to imagine the work he would do as one of the fold.[2] He developed his first idea for a scene with television actress Grace Raynor, who was not a member. It involved looking at a map to choose a destination in Europe.

"It was only an incomplete, one-page draft, much of it in Jimmy's handwriting," says Christine White. "Then Grace Raynor gave it up, and I started working with him on it. In this scene, we were newlyweds. It was a comedy. He wanted to go to Spain and the bullfights. At one point, he used the map as a *muleta*. I wanted Switzerland and mountains.

"Jimmy was standing up most of the time, and I was sitting at a table," she continues. "He might say, 'If we do this, down here, then we can easily make Paris!' Since we had to have movement in the scene, I might get up from my chair and say, 'You can't do that; it takes five days!' The scene was very funny; it was a domestic thing and we thought it was as cute as could be.

"The inspiration for it was, we loved globes and maps. Jimmy had a medium-sized globe in his room. We would often play a game where one would point to a spot on the globe and the other would have to guess which country by asking questions. We learned the globe that way. Also, Jimmy had bullfight-itis.

"The only thing is, the Actors Studio never did comedy, as far as I could tell. They were never into laughs; it was always yo-heave-ho Volga boatmen, always very discordant and down and depressed. The more depressed you could be, the better for your art. We did the scene as a 'preliminary,' where nine or ten others would 'sit in the weeds'—in other words, they were there but they weren't there—to see if it could be performed in class. Their verdict was that it wasn't ready.

"Jimmy had a fit, but he managed to control himself until afterwards. He had two objections to the preliminary jury. He said, 'They didn't turn on the goddam lights! How can you do a comedy in the

---

2. When Dean and White auditioned in May 1952, the Actors Studio was still in the CBS Radio Playhouse at 1697 Broadway (at Fifty-third Street), but by September 1952 it had moved to the top floor of the ANTA Theater on West Fifty-second Street. By the time of the Dennis Stock photos of Dean visiting the Studio early in 1955, it was meeting at the Malin Studios, 1545 Broadway (at Forty-sixth Street), Room 610.

dark?' Then he said, 'It's the material. It's not *zaftig* [juicy] enough.' Yet that's why so many didn't get into the Studio; their scenes were too frivolous. Jimmy loved comedy. I frequently saw him laugh so hard that he shook."

One of the earliest benefits of membership for Dean was meeting Frank Corsaro, a young director of great talent. Corsaro was moderating a session when Dean, seated on the far side of the room, stood up and with a grandiose gesture pointed directly at him. "Afterwards," he recalls, "Jimmy explained that meant he wanted to meet me." By bringing Corsaro, now the Studio's artistic director, into his orbit, Dean was simply continuing his practice of collecting friends whose knowledge and sophistication were useful to him. "Corsaro," notes Christine White, "is an intellect and extremely excellent wit, and you could be in his company for hours and never stop laughing." Bill Bast wrote that Dean came to consider the director his most intellectually stimulating friend, learning from him a great deal about modern writers and composers.

Since Dean's entrance into the Studio coincided with the zenith of his passion for bullfighting, he settled upon a dramatization of Barnaby Conrad's *Matador* for his maiden scene. "His matador scene was non-verbal," White explains. "He kept his back to the audience because he assumed the matador's posture so beautifully. He did exercises matadors use to warm up—that he had taught to me—and *muleta* passes with his cape.

"I saw the scene done for Strasberg, but then I had to run off to CBS and couldn't stay for the critique. I heard through the grapevine that it didn't go too well. He waited about two weeks to tell me about it; he wanted some space between the critique and when he told me. Strasberg had really lit into him."

According to member David Garfield, Strasberg's critique of Dean was "long and penetrating." Dean "listened impassively, but the color drained from his face. When Strasberg had concluded his remarks, the young actor slung his matador's cape over his shoulder and silently walked out of the room." Dean was so unnerved by this experience that he almost never worked at the Studio again. Frank Corsaro later wrote, "In all the years at the Studio, Dean performed once or twice for the aggregate and retired thereafter in abject terror of the

Studio's sophisticated and high-standard judgments. He would never submit to Lee's supremacy as a guide."

Arnold Shulman, a playwright member of the Studio who would later write one of Dean's television scripts *(I'm a Fool),* says that he—like all members interviewed for this book—cannot remember Dean doing any scenes at the Studio. "He was just sullen, and who wants to be around a sullen person?" Shulman asked. "I wouldn't have bet a quarter on his future."

Years after Dean's time at the Studio, Lee Strasberg remembered almost nothing of his work. He told David Garfield, "It was my feeling that Jimmy didn't go far enough. It seemed to me, as with many other people, that he was not using enough of himself. . . . My impression is that while the work continued, it did not make any progress that I remember or was aware of."

When Dean died, a Studio member in Hollywood called Strasberg with the sad news. "It somehow was what I expected," Strasberg revealed a year later. "I didn't cry. I just said, 'I knew it. I knew it.'" When a reporter solicited Strasberg's comments on Dean's death, he said, "His behavior and personality seemed to be part of a pattern which inevitably had to lead to something destructive. I always had a strange feeling there was in Jimmy a sort of doomed quality."

Did the Actors Studio have an impact on Dean's acting? His colleagues and friends almost uniformly fail to list it as an influence, with some even disavowing its significance in his eventual career. Director Vivian Matalon, who acted with him in *The Immoralist,* asserts, "I think the Studio has little right to claim him. He seemed tremendously influenced by Brando and Clift—sort of the offspring of them. I thought he had a very poetic quality and was tremendously talented."

Most sources agree that Dean's best work came under rarefied, idealized conditions, not under a barrage of criticism such as Strasberg's. In *The Immoralist,* he would flourish under the empathetic supervision of Herman Shumlin and the friendship of Geraldine Page, as he would in *East of Eden* under Kazan and with the selfless Julie Harris at his side. Not so in *Giant* under George Stevens and especially not in *The Immoralist* after Daniel Mann had taken over as director. In *Rebel Without a Cause,* Nicholas Ray understood that "for a successful collaboration, Dean needed a special kind of climate. He needed reassurance, tolerance, understanding."

Dean considered whatever he may have learned about the Method to be secondary. "The most important thing I learned studying in New York," he told Hollywood columnist Erskine Johnson, "was how an actor takes care of himself; how to protect himself from Hollywood, from the stage, and from television. There are tricks to every trade, and there are tricks actors can use to overcome bad scripts, bad stories, and bad direction."

At the time Johnson printed these remarks, Dean had just finished working in *Rebel Without a Cause*. Johnson asked if he had needed to deploy his bag of tricks. "Not yet," Dean replied, "but I've got 'em, just in case."

Pleasing the Skipper

See the Jaguar, which closed after five performances, is remembered today only as the vehicle for James Dean's Broadway debut. Fans hold that no one but Dean could credibly have played Wally Wilkins, the excruciatingly naive, weak-minded mountain boy, an opinion reinforced by one critic's comment that Dean gave "an extraordinary performance in an impossible role." Thus, it is easy to forget that the ill-fated play was far more important to Dean than he was to it. He was not the first choice for the part and was cast only at the last moment, long after more urgent questions of backing and leading roles were settled. Wally Wilkins was a well-written but secondary part and could have been played by any number of actors.

Bolstering the mythology, Hollywood later propagated an account of Dean's getting a part in *See the Jaguar* through sheer ingenuity and cunning: fast-talking his way onto a yacht as a deckhand, though secretly he knew nothing about sailing, betting on the likelihood that the skipper, who had clout on Broadway, would favor him and arrange an audition for him. Although the yacht trip did occur, the actual circumstances were quite different from Hollywood's version.

As with most of his other breaks in the previous year, Dean's association with *See the Jaguar* began with Rogers Brackett. Undaunted by Dean's decreasing interest in him, Brackett was still the best asset and most ardent backer Dean had going for himself. Sensing yet another opportunity to advance Dean's career, Brackett took him as his guest to the Stony Point (Rockland County, New York) estate of his friends Lemuel and Shirley Ayers. Although Dean's initial encounter with them was nothing more than a pleasant outing in the country, it would culminate in his Broadway debut.

Lemuel Ayers had distinguished himself as scenic designer in the original production of *Oklahoma!* Later, itching to try the theater's financial side, he branched into production (as coproducer) with *Kiss Me Kate* and *Out of This World.* Ayers took over the option on playwright N. Richard Nash's *See the Jaguar* in April 1952 with the intention of coproducing and designing it that fall.

These credits were even more impressive in view of Ayers's youth; he was only thirty-seven. "He was a famous man with good taste," remarks James Sheldon, "and very contemporary at that time, having pulled away from the standard people like Robert Edmond Jones, Jo Mielziner, and those great scenic designers. Lem brought a little more color and and a little more fun to the things he did."

The Ayerses' Stony Point salon was a remarkable slice of posh, postwar New York theater world life, sustained by Shirley Ayers's family money and a yen for having guests. ("Lord, they could spend money," observed her sister. "I never knew two people who could spend like them.") The likes of John and Elaine Steinbeck, Mitch and Fran Miller, Mel Ferrer, and producers Arnold Saint-Subber and Martin Manulis were among their frequent guests. Dean, freshly admitted to the Actors Studio, was not without credentials in this august assemblage.

Martin Russ, a Marine who, on weekend leave, frequently went along with Alec Wilder to the Ayerses' place, says, "I remember thinking, 'If I ever get rich, this is how I'd like to live.' Everything—the silverware, the pillows on the couch—was perfect. I was totally dazzled by their place." The beautiful 1849 mansard house (which the Ayerses rented) was situated on eleven sloping acres too heavily wooded to permit a view of the Hudson about a mile to the east.

The Ayerses' daughter, Sarah, remembers her childhood home as "a very rarefied adults' arena. There were always lots of luminaries from the theater and the artistic world around the house. My older brother, Jonathan, and I were allowed to mingle with the grown-ups on weekend holidays as long as we showed interest. Everyone stayed up, drinking and smoking like crazy, then gathered the next morning at the breakfast table in bathrobes, picking up where they had left off. They all drank like fish. My brother and I used to talk at length about who was more blotto than whom. There were regulars of whom we would say, 'They're on their sixth drink; they'll be stumbling soon.' "

Talk of *See the Jaguar* pervaded these heady weekend gatherings. Michael Gordon had been signed as director and Arthur Kennedy was leading man, but the other roles were up for grabs. It soon became clear to Dean that finding favor with Lemuel Ayers could open up an auspicious career opportunity. He began a campaign to make himself irresistible to each member of the Ayers family. Marshall Barer, a frequent guest, says, "Jimmy was courting the Ayerses. He was smart enough to know you didn't act like Brando around them. He was suddenly a different person, offering a chair to Shirley, being obsequious."

Sarah Ayers, who was seven when Dean frequented her parents' place, says, "Jimmy had a remarkable ability to create magic. My brother and I were madly in love with him. I had an unbridled expectation of him; couldn't wait to see him. He and Rogers used to arrive burning rubber. He drove very recklessly. Once they hit a deer. The car was totaled."

Martin Russ, also a great pal to the Ayers children, says he never crossed paths with Dean at Stony Point or anywhere else, "but it was just as well; I would have been jealous of the way he charmed the kids." The children loved to watch Dean climb a tree and act like a monkey, the same tactic with which he had delighted Beverly Wills the year before.

Composer David Diamond knew Lemuel and Shirley Ayers well. "Lem was a very obvious homosexual," he recalls. "People were surprised that he had married. Shirley, with her deep, masculine voice, may have had just enough masculine strength for him.

"He was extremely uptight about it. When I would go up and give him a big hug, he would say, 'I wish you wouldn't do that in front of the children.' I would say, 'Lem, relax!' I would have three drinks and then play up to him in front of Shirley—oh, *especially* when she was there!" The dynamics of the marriage were such that Shirley Ayers and Alec

Wilder carried on an open affair in those days, of which Lemuel Ayers was fully aware.

Lemuel Ayers was no more able to resist Dean's charm than Alec Wilder, Rogers Brackett, or anyone else upon whom its seductive intensity was focused. The consequence, however, was not the part in *See the Jaguar* that Dean coveted but an invitation to share a maritime adventure. The Ayerses, as befitted persons of their privileged station, were fond of chartering a yacht every August and organizing an entourage of friends to accompany them. As the day of departure drew nearer, they found themselves needing an extra crewman, and their new young friend James Dean seemed the perfect candidate.

The yacht trip, which lasted about ten days and went from the Hudson River to Martha's Vineyard and back, has always been shrouded in mystery. What little is known about it comes from Alec Wilder, who said the sea was so rough in the first couple of days that he and others disembarked at New London, Connecticut. The yacht was called the *Typhoon,* but the other guests cannot be identified. Back in New York, Dean spoke enthusiastically of the fundamentals of yachts and sailing to his friends but would say nothing of the trip's events until three months later. He had had a good time but was scarcely less uncertain about getting into *See the Jaguar* than before.

Rogers Brackett later claimed to have put a bug in Ayers's ear about casting Dean even before the cruise, but Ayers demurred on the grounds of Dean's lack of experience. But Brackett, who was not on the yacht trip, also claimed Ayers's opinion of Dean warmed up enough over the course of the cruise for him to agree to let Dean read for a part at an unspecified future date.

Brackett refused to give up. Soon after the trip, Ayers began putting on readings of *See the Jaguar* for potential backers, at which actor James O'Rear was engaged to read the Wally Wilkins part. "The first reading was held at Shirley Ayers's aunt's Fifth Avenue apartment in a beautiful living room," recalls O'Rear, "with the furniture pushed back and folding chairs set in rows like a small theater. Sitting down in front was a man I had met at Lemuel Ayers's place named Rogers Brackett. Seated next to him was a young man whom I didn't know. At the next reading Rogers Brackett was there again with this young man next to him. And then again at the reading after that. They got to be a gag! The last reading was at the Warwick Hotel, because the audience had grown. Brackett and the young man, who was James Dean, were there. I was mildly curious as to why, because the readings were really for potential backers."

O'Rear says Boris Karloff had attended one backers' reading and afterward raved to friends about how outstanding O'Rear had been in the Wally Wilkins role. "But I was then in my late thirties," O'Rear notes, "and the part was a teenage boy. I could have done it on radio, but not on the stage. The part was very well written, and I think anyone who played it would have had more or less a success with it." Wally Wilkins was a seventeen-year-old boy kept locked in an icehouse by his mother to protect him from the brutality of the world. Set free at her death, Wally sees his crude community for the first time and is obligingly illiterate and helpless. Fed berry pie by a kind man offstage, his face is affectingly slathered in the dark, gooey fruit when he reappears. He has never seen or comprehended paper money before and wads it up in little balls and tosses it in a river.

As September wore on, the only thing Dean heard from Ayers's office was a deafening silence. The production was being held up by a lack of money. The *New York Herald-Tribune* took note of the dilemma on September 27: "Lemuel Ayers doesn't seem to be worried about being able to raise the rest of the money for *See the Jaguar*. Mr. Ayers has gone ahead with out-of-town bookings [in Hartford and Boston]." As Dean's adviser throughout the process, Brackett realized that patience was the best course of action.

With nothing to do but wait, Dean tried to settle back into the rhythms of ordinary existence. His return from yachting coincided with Dizzy Sheridan's return from summer stock. "For some strange reason or other I was on a bus one night," she related. "I didn't know when Jimmy was due back in the city, and the bus was just passing Jerry's, the place around the corner from the Rehearsal Club where we first went for drinks. All of a sudden I saw Jimmy walking down the street going towards Jerry's. I leaped off the bus and I saw him turn into this bar, and I went in after him. When I got there he was in a telephone booth trying to locate me, and I rapped on the door of the telephone booth, and I had never seen him more shocked. We had a great big mad love scene right in the middle of the floor."

A common and urgent need for housing would bring Sheridan and Dean together as roommates once again. Bast and Dean had quit the Iroquois and were rooming with a friend from UCLA in her West Forty-sixth Street sublet. But they had to leave when the lessees returned from Europe and exercised their preemptive rights. They joined forces with Sheridan and moved uptown to 13 West Eighty-ninth Street, an apartment they would come to associate with hunger, bare mattresses, and Dean's bullfighting practice, in which he was always the matador and they had to be the bull. "We used to spend a lot of time in Central Park, and we used the cape that he dragged around with him," said Sheridan. "I was a dancer and I liked to dance in the middle of the street. So we would always wait until the street cleaners would come and it was six o'clock in the morning, and we were always dancing."

What little money each of the roommates earned went toward paying rent; the pantry was almost always bare and they always felt hungry. Relief came in a letter to Dean from his dental technician father, offering to supply him with a new dental plate if they could meet within a few days in Fairmount. Since there had been no word on *See the Jaguar* and no television work, Dean saw no reason not to go—not even lack of money for transportation. Dangling the prospects of his aunt's home-cooked meals in front of Sheridan and Bast, he persuaded them to hitchhike to Indiana with him.

Early in the morning of October 9, the three friends rode a bus to the New Jersey side of the Lincoln Tunnel and put their thumbs up. By nightfall they had reached the end of the Pennsylvania Turnpike, but Ohio still lay between them and Fairmount, Indiana, and all they had eaten was ice cream. Luck was with them as they were spotted by the driver of a Nash Rambler who introduced himself as Clyde McCullough, catcher for the Pittsburgh Pirates. He was a National League all-star and was driving all night in order to make Dubuque, Iowa, the next evening for the first game in a barnstorming tour.[1] McCullough was the

---

1. Not Des Moines, as Bast's biography reported.

soul of kindness, buying them dinner and offering them encouragement (which they accepted) and cash (which they declined) before dropping them off at dawn at a point where Marcus Winslow could retrieve them.

The next few days were a revelation to Sheridan. "It was the freshest air the three of us had smelled in a long time," she rhapsodized. "I wish everyone could have been with us in Indiana to see the way Jimmy treated the animals, even the dirt around the farm. The love he had for nature showed me how completely simple he was." They were up early each morning, horseback riding, target shooting, watching Dean perform stunts on his old motorcycle—and eating, eating, eating. Winton Dean kept his commitment to meet his son there. "He gave Jimmy two new front teeth," Sheridan laughed.

Dean visited Fairmount High School, where Adeline Brookshire, in what was becoming an annual event, again turned junior class play rehearsals over to him. Repair work on the auditorium that fall had forced the juniors into the gymnasium, where they would have to perform their play, *Meet Corliss Archer,* as theater-in-the-round, without any painted sets. Cast members thought Dean was hard on them, but they admired what they perceived as his sophistication. The *Marion Leader-Tribune* would note, "James Dean, New York City, a former Fairmount drama class student, who has starred in television shows and has held parts in film productions, was in Fairmount last week, conferring with Mrs. Brookshire and her students. He was accompanied to Fairmount by William Bast and Elizabeth Sheridan."

As if to wake the interlopers up to reality, someone—most likely Brackett—telephoned to summon Dean back to New York to read for *See the Jaguar.* He asked his friends to join him in a short visit to his mother's grave in Marion before they were dropped off along the highway, forced once again to depend on their thumbs. The glad tidings from New York were not enough to assuage the gloom of leaving the farm. "We were very, very depressed, especially going into New York through the tunnel, because we didn't want to get back into the city," Sheridan said.

Legend has it that Dean got the part after besting scores of other actors who auditioned. In reality, he was not the first choice for the role; he got it only after another actor, Wright King, had turned it down.

King had appeared in both the stage and movie versions of *A Streetcar Named Desire*. "I was ten years older than Dean was," King explains, "but I was playing a lot of young guys. He and I were up for a lot of the same things. We knew each other from making the rounds. At the time I was pretty hot. I'd done *The Bird Cage* with Arthur Laurents and was doing a lot of TV and was up for another play.

"My agent sent me to read," King continues. "I don't remember whom I read for, but it was a backers reading. I had never met Ayers before. Michael Gordon gave me some direction between the first and second acts. Afterwards, he said it looked good for me. So I waited and waited and waited to hear, and I kind of put other things off because *Jaguar* appealed to me. I made an attempt to get in touch with Ayers's office, but they forgot about me. I assumed someone else had the role. Finally I gave up hope and took a job in television production.

"Then Ayers's office called, leaving a message with my wife that they wanted me to play Wally. I told my wife I was going to ignore it, but they called again and again. She told them I wasn't interested. Finally, to give my wife some peace, I called Lem Ayers. He said, 'Wright, we want you badly for this. We just got mixed up around here. Tell your new job that you'll come back; all we need is for you to open in New York.' But I said no. Actually, I gave Ayers a lecture. I told him that I hoped he could learn from such a mistake."

Without Wright King, there ensued a bit of a scramble for an actor to play Wally Wilkins. Dane Knell, a cast member, asserts, "Wally was one of the most difficult roles to cast. Every agent in town was trying to cast it. I was sent to read for Wally by Alan Brock, a friend's agent. 'You're not quite right physically for the part,' they said, 'but why don't you understudy Jeejee?' That part was intended for an older actor, but eventually they put me in it. I was also understudy for Wally." Jeejee was the show's comic relief, a stooge who seems borderline retarded.

"We were casting," remembers playwright Nash, "and couldn't find the right person. I thought Wright King was too tall and looked too old. One afternoon, Michael Gordon, Selma [Tamber, Ayers's assistant], and Lem went to lunch while I stayed behind in the office working. A young man came in, looking disheveled—torn clothes—and with a swagger. He said he had come to read Wally. It was Jimmy Dean. I asked him, 'How did you get the script?' He said, 'I won't tell you.' We talked about the play, and he spoke intelligently about it. He seemed to understand it."

The others soon returned from lunch. Nash's description of Ayers's attitude toward Dean is perplexing, but not necessarily inconsistent with other accounts. "Lem wanted him out of the office almost immediately," Nash says. "Lem was a very fastidious man and Jimmy Dean was not. Michael was neutral about him. Finally everyone agreed that Jimmy would read. He did read—miserably. He mumbled, skipped speeches. It was awful.

"Jimmy was crestfallen. He knew he'd done badly. I followed him out because in type I thought he would be perfect. The others were glad to see him go! I asked him what had gone wrong. He said, 'I couldn't see!' He showed me his glasses, and one of the lenses was cracked. So I gave him ten dollars and told him to get them fixed and come back and try again. That was the first moment I saw him smile.

"I told the others about this. Lem was adamantly against Jimmy, saying he didn't know anything, didn't have any stage experience. Michael was very neutral and only reluctantly said, 'We'll have him back.' The director has final say."

Persistent, gentle persuasion from Dean's advocates may have softened Ayers. Alec Wilder wrote, "Between Brackett and myself, we persuaded Lem to let Jimmy read for a very difficult role. I gather that Jimmy read so well he was instantly hired." Shirley Ayers may also have been influential; she later told Wilder how pleased she was that Dean got the part.

According to Nash, when Dean came back "he was brilliant. Again I followed him out of the office and noticed that he hadn't fixed his glasses. Instead he had bought a knife that dangled on the end of a long chain. I asked him how he could have done so well if he still couldn't see. He said, 'I memorized the part!'

"Selma asked him who his agent was. He said, 'I don't have one.' She said, 'I want to deal with an agent' and recommended Peter Witt, who had done a lot of the casting for me in another show. I did know who Jane Deacy was, but didn't know she was Jimmy's agent."

For Dean to say he had no agent seems, to put it mildly, surprising. Although Jane Deacy was his agent, it seemed she was the only one in town *not* to claim some credit for getting him into *Jaguar.* Peter Witt, in the documentary film *James Dean: The First American Teenager,* said he told Dean about a job in *Jaguar* that might be right for him—entitling Witt to collect the customary five percent agent fee. "But he was so poor," said Witt, "that I was embarrassed to charge him $3.75 commission on an Equity minimum of seventy-five dollars a week. I needed it, but I just didn't have the heart."

Alan Brock, the agent who sent Dane Knell to audition, later wrote in *Classic Film Collector* that Dean's name had been suggested to him as a possibility for Wally. Brock had never heard of Dean, so he invited him to his office. "During the questions and answers, I was aware of a quiet insolence directed at me," he said. "I also saw that Dean was giving me the 'X-ray stare' to the point of exaggeration."

No sooner had Brock begun speaking specifically about the Wally part than Dean leaped up and announced that he had already been sent for by another agent. "Before I could comment on his odd behavior," said Brock, "Dean's attitude swiftly shot from rudeness to outright hostility." Dean had kept the appointment only to exploit an opportunity to vent his accumulated resentment at all casting agents, feeling they had ignored or rejected him.

"How come all you agents never pay us any attention until someone else gives us a tumble?" Dean shouted. "We bust our backs making the rounds, going from office to office every day, trying to see you guys, and not a chance. We've got feelings, too! Then, when we get our own break—bam! You all jump on the bandwagon. All of a sudden, we're popular." Brock tried to explain the exigencies of his profession, but it was no use.

See the Jaguar was set in the "backwash of civilization," where gas station owners attract customers with signs to "See the Fox"—or ferret or other trapped animals—while tanking up. Dean's character, the feebleminded Wally, served as the pawn between the evil mob—led by a ruthless hillbilly racketeer (Cameron Prud'homme) who owns the town's gas station and general store—and a small band of good guys, consisting of an idealistic schoolteacher (Arthur Kennedy), his intemperate tattoo artist "Gramfa" (Roy Fant), and pregnant girlfriend (Constance Ford), who also happens to be the villain's daughter.

The mob spends half a day in hot but fruitless pursuit of Wally until the hero, in a moment of weakness, leads them to him in exchange for the villain's daughter's hand in marriage. Enraged that Wally threw away his mother's money that they were after, they lock him in a cage that had been intended for an elusive jaguar. The play ends as the hero is shot to death for setting Wally free.

Rehearsals began on Monday, October 20, 1952, and Dean showed his elation by being the first to arrive. The next day's *New York Herald-Tribune* mentioned that Dean had been cast, possibly the first time his name appeared in a New York paper.[2] By now, Ayers had canceled the out-of-town tryout in Boston; city officials had warned that, although they considered the play inoffensive, some of the lines violated the laws against indecent speech. (They had not heeded Walter Winchell, who wrote in his column that *Jaguar* would "win every theatrical prize of the season.") Playwright Nash refused to permit any alterations in the script, so Boston was out. *Jaguar* would now try out in Philadelphia.

Dean was thrilled to have his own dressing room, the first trappings of having hit the big time; he plastered its walls with bullfighting posters. He was also thrilled to have a mentor in Arthur Kennedy. "He took Jimmy under his wing," said Dane Knell, "and advised him on such things as investing money wisely." But opinions on whether Kennedy's influence was for the best were mixed. "He seemed completely different," said Dizzy Sheridan, "once he got involved with Arthur Kennedy." Dean would come home from rehearsals and still be under Kennedy's spell, acting "big, blustery, drinks and is loud—which Jimmy wasn't," complained Sheridan. "Well, that wasn't so good." Much later, Wilder would lament, "I watched the leading man brainwash Jimmy into believing that no one in any production was of any consequence but the actor. And," he added, "I've always believed that this attitude accounted to a great extent for Jimmy's shocking behavior when he hit the big time in Hollywood."

But Wilder was still fond of Dean at that time and kept his reservations to himself. Wilder was very much a part of *See the Jaguar,* in-

---

2. In Hollywood, shooting on Warner Brothers' *Trouble Along the Way,* which some filmographies mistakenly list among Dean's credits, began at the same time as *See the Jaguar* rehearsals. Dean was not in Hollywood during the filming.

vesting nine hundred dollars in it and composing its incidental music at Ayers's behest. Paltry funding made hiring an orchestra out of the question, so Wilder wrote a score for *a cappella* chorus, which was tape-recorded by sixteen singers conducted by Mitch Miller.[3] One critic would call it "trembly Eliza-crossing-the-ice music, added to keep up the excitement during set changes," but director Gordon felt it was so well written that "sometimes the play seemed to underscore the music rather than the other way around."

In the final act, while caged and half delirious, Dean had to reprise a simple lullaby, "Green Briar, Blue Fire," sung by his demented mother in the first act. Bast and Sheridan shouldered the burden of helping him learn it at home, a formidable challenge given Dean's ineptitude at carrying a tune. "He could sing in more different keys during the course of one song than anybody I've ever heard," remarked his friend Kent Williams. Though the process was "ear-wrenching," wrote Bast, Dean finally mastered the six-line tune.

One cast member who came to know Dean well was Phillip Pine, who played Hilltop, a vulgar hunter who lusts after Constance Ford's character. "Jimmy was a mixture of naïveté and driving ambition, but the ambition was instinctual, not thought out," remembers Pine. "He was completely taken with his own momentary need. Everything was judged by 'What do I feel *now*?' He represented something in the theater that made me unhappy: he was undisciplined. But I never met anybody who was more appealing to the maternal sense in all women."

Rapport invariably grew between members of the cast. "We'd be walking down a side street, or even Broadway," says Pine, "and Jimmy would whip off his jacket and do olés at passing cabs. Kennedy egged him on in this." This was typical, according to Arthur Batanides, who played one of the villain's rustic minions: "Jimmy loved to create a situation with a disturbance."

There were three weeks of rehearsals before the first out-of-town tryouts in Hartford, Connecticut. With one week to go, Dwight Eisen-

---

3. During a musicians' strike a decade earlier, Wilder wrote "vocal orchestra" arrangements for Frank Sinatra's first Columbia recording sessions, so his work for *See the Jaguar* was well within his métier.

hower defeated Adlai Stevenson in the presidential election. In August, Dorothy Kilgallen had reported, "Practically all the Broadway shows scheduled for fall will hold off opening until the elections are over. The producers feel Ike, Adlai, and the general interest in politics are just too much competition." Certainly the *Jaguar* schedule reflected this.

Dean had turned twenty-one the previous February, and this would be his only chance to vote in a presidential election. "Many of us voted," says Pine. "I did, my wife did, Arthur Kennedy, Connie Ford, Lem Ayers—and all for Stevenson. But I doubt if Jimmy voted. We all talked about the election a lot, but any mention of it turned Jimmy off completely."

The cast left New York on November 11 to prepare for three evening performances and one matinee at Hartford's New Parsons Theater. "There was a party before we left New York," notes Pine, "then opening parties in Hartford, Philadelphia, and New York—not to mention some closing parties. We had more parties than performances!" Dane Knell remembers long three-way conversations on the train with Dean and the avuncular Wilder. Knell was Dean's roommate on tour, while Pine and Dean were assigned to the same dressing room.

"In Hartford," says Batanides, "Arthur Kennedy, Jimmy, and I had gone out drinking one night. Those two got quite drunk, and as we walked back to the hotel, they were knocking over garbage cans and making a scene—loudly enough to make the cops come. I talked to the cops and smoothed things over. Kennedy went back to the hotel, but Jimmy and I went on to a Greek restaurant.

"At the Greek place, I got to wondering how Jimmy got the part. For one thing, during rehearsals, I couldn't figure out why he wasn't fired. He was a pain in the ass. Most of the time you couldn't even hear him say his lines. For another thing, I'd heard that others were up for the part. So I asked him.

"He was still pretty drunk. He told me that he'd gone on this yacht trip with Lem Ayers and that they'd dressed him up like the god Neptune and put him up on a throne, which is what they generally do on ships as they cross the equator. Jimmy was giggling and rolling his eyes as he told me about it. I gathered that there had been a thing between him and Ayers. They hadn't gone out there to fish!"

Dean himself believed there was a connection between the yacht trip and his casting, because he later told the Warner Brothers publicity department about it when they were compiling his studio biography. Warner Brothers in turn bowdlerized it, to wit: "Dean hired out as a hand on a yacht whose skipper was connected with show business. The skipper got him an audition for *See the Jaguar*." In this form, the tale was parroted ad nauseam by reporters and fan magazine hacks.

There was a perception in the New York theater community, despite Ayers's negative attitude toward Dean that Nash saw, that Dean got the part because of events on the yacht trip. Both Pine and Knell heard rumors about it. "My God," said Pine, "it was all over town: 'Where did this boy come from? Why, Lem Ayers's boat.' "

The late media expert Robert Wayne Tysl stumbled across an anonymous source on the Ayers connection—although he treated it cryptically—when he was collecting information for his 1965 dissertation on the James Dean image. "The curling toes of the habitually shoeless farm boy," wrote Tysl, referring to a cast portrait of Dean as Wally Wilkins, "demonstrate part of the bucolic charm Dean *must have used* on Lemuel Ayers. . . . [later] the *sponsorship of Ayers* and Dean's good reviews kept him working in television."

Elsewhere in the dissertation Tysl took Hollywood reporter Joe Hyams to task for "pussy-footing and hewing to the established Hollywood line, rather than revealing, or at least seeking, the truth" in Hyams's profile on Dean in the September 1956 issue of *Redbook*. "As an instance, this is the Hyams version of how Dean was able to get his first Broadway role: 'He got [it] himself by talking himself into a crewman's job on a yacht. One night he told the skipper that he really wanted to be an actor. The skipper had a friend . . .' "

Tysl clearly had sensitive information on the Dean-Ayers connection. "Certain aspects of Dean's personal life prompted those who did know him to disclaim knowledge," he wrote. "The inside story of how one becomes a star . . . is not always a particularly wholesome story. It is, in fact, unprintable."

The inevitable stress of fine-tuning the play for its expected run on Broadway caused the early rapport to fray. Margaret Barker, cast as the crazy mother, said Dean had the dressing room next to hers and was practicing his recorder. "I like quiet and concentration before a play starts, and so I admonished Jimmy—perhaps a bit too harshly—

requesting that he shut up for the rest of our sakes."

Once when director Michael Gordon was belaboring a point with Dean about interpretation, Dean stopped the rehearsal. "Why is it," he asked, "Phil can do what he wants, and you always question what I'm doing?" "It was petulant," said Pine, "like sibling rivalry. He wanted you to think he was not being given the same consideration as his peers."

Broadway legend holds that Dean pulled a knife on someone in Hartford. According to Nash, it was Gordon. "During a rehearsal or maybe a scenery setup, Jimmy stood on the apron of the stage and flashed a knife at Michael and said, 'You come up here, you son of a bitch, and you'll get this!' I'm not sure what provoked it, but I was there, and those were his exact words. I hadn't been paying attention, but I did see that incident. A stagehand broke it up. Jimmy got on well with the stagehands but not with Michael, who was a formalist and believed in doing the professional thing. There was never any artistic quarrel between them; Jimmy just didn't go by the rules. He would come late to rehearsal, or he would pretend to forget the lines. But Michael wouldn't have fired him; you can't fire someone that good."

Opening night in Hartford had its share of glitches. Due to problems backstage, the curtain rose nearly a half hour late. Then, at the end of Act Two, where Gramfa is clubbed to death and Wally is captured, Dean threw in some unexpected business. It was crucial for Pine to drag Wally offstage as the lights came up on a dying Gramfa. But in this performance, Dean surprised Pine by struggling with him, even though he had previously been submissive. "Did I miss a rehearsal?" Pine wondered to himself. With no time for argument, Pine stomped on Dean's foot. Offstage, an aggravated Dean protested, "I was only doing what my character would have done." "Well," Pine countered, "that's what *my* character would have done in response."

The reviews the next day were favorable to the ensemble but not to the play. They complained that the ideas Nash intended to convey were hopelessly obscure, to the point of "keeping the audience coughing and rattling its program." One critic felt Nash showed considerable promise as a dramatist but inevitably lost his audience when his splendidly earthy characters broke character to spout philosophical cant.

This first engagement of *Jaguar* was reviewed by both local papers and *Variety*. All three singled out Dean for praise, with the *Hartford Courant* being most enthusiastic. "Give a special accolade to James Dean in a tender, touching role as a simpleton," it said. "He plays the part beautifully." To the *Hartford Times* he was "exquisite," and to *Variety* "good."

From Hartford, the troupe traveled directly to Philadelphia, where they opened on November 18 for two weeks at the Forrest Theater. Gordon, Nash, and Ayers realized that, despite the positive reception in Hartford, the show needed work if it was to pass muster in New York. "There were furious rewrites in Philadelphia," Pine says, "but Nash seemed to get more and more confused about what he'd written. To tell the truth, it was an opera!"

The Philadelphia papers appreciated the play and the players. "Lemuel Ayers has been enormously successful in selecting the right cast for playwright Nash's unique approach," the *Inquirer* asserted. It said Dean made "an impressive stage debut." The *Bulletin* questioned why the play would have appealed to Kennedy but called it "taut and well-constructed." It commended Dean's "good character portrait."

The late hours after each night's final curtain were the only time the cast had to blow off steam. "In Philadelphia, Jimmy went out with girls from another show who were staying in our same hotel," said Knell. "But if he overnighted with any of them, it wasn't in our room."

Playwright Tennessee Williams was a good friend of Lemuel Ayers and came to Philadelphia to see the show. One evening he joined some of the cast for drinks at the Variety Club. "Jimmy thought Tennessee had the hots for him," Pine remembers.

Living in the same Philadelphia hotel for two weeks forced the ensemble to interact in a way that would not have happened in New York, where each had his own place. "Once," says Pine, "Jimmy, Kennedy, and I were having beer and sandwiches in Kennedy's hotel room, and Jimmy asked me, 'Wanna wrestle?' I replied, 'Not particularly.' Finally he said, 'Ah, come on!' and Kennedy, who was a bit of a troublemaker, said, 'Why not?' So, being in a hotel room, I didn't want to hurt him or get hurt. I think he thought that by physical contact with me, it would enhance his character. A real bizarre thing! Childish . . . idiotic!"

Phillip and Madelyn Pine threw a party for their daughter Macyle's ninth birthday in Philadelphia, and Dean delighted her as he had dazzled Sarah Ayers. "Jimmy connected to Macyle immediately," says Pine. "He danced and carried on. It was the only time I ever saw him go out to another person." Dane Knell was also struck at Dean's winning ways with Macyle and other cast members' children. "He wasn't condescending to them," says Knell.

Jaguar closed in Philadelphia only four days before the Broadway opening, at the Cort Theater, the following Wednesday, December 3; a special Tuesday night preview was given for American National Theater Academy (ANTA) members. "Kennedy was not a stupid man," observes Pine. "He—and we—knew it was not going to run. He fell apart in New York. The play was wrong! A kid in a cage—you're defying human credibility. For it to work, you'd have to have music or poetry coming out of it."

Back in New York, thanks to the suggestion of George Ross, press agent for *Jaguar,* Dean appeared on a Sunday evening radio show hosted by Jack Shafer. A book about the Aztecs that Dean had carried to the interview caught Shafer's attention. Dean admitted to a fascination with the Aztecs' fatalism. He said he agreed with their philosophy of getting the most out of life while life was good. As Shafer later told it, Dean said he wanted to live as he sensed the Aztecs had, as intensely as possible, feeling his experiences right down to their roots. Dean came across as friendly and serious-minded; it was good publicity for him, but whatever was said about *Jaguar* was not significant enough to impress itself on Shafer's memory.

In his *Playbill* biography, Dean was silent about the Aztecs but candidly confessed that his "great passion," besides acting, was bullfighting, "which he says he just lives for." He duly noted his state high school dramatics championship but, gambling that the handful of persons who knew better would never see the *Playbill,* ratcheted up his showing in the Longmont, Colorado, nationals from sixth to first place. Six television shows, three movies, and membership in the Actors Studio were his acting credentials. Neither UCLA nor SMCC was mentioned.

Opening night was a parade of disasters. Gordon said, "I vividly remember badly botched scene shifts in Act Two that caused catastrophic delays between the scenes." The tape-playing equipment malfunctioned, depriving those scene changes of their effective musical interludes. And a stagehand failed to provide a gunshot at the moment when Wally shoots a jaguar offstage.

"I was standing next to the prop man backstage," reports Arthur Batanides, "and was surprised when I noticed he hadn't reached for the gun. It was an important cue, because those on stage were supposed to react to it. Arthur Kennedy didn't wait for it; he grabbed Jimmy and dragged him on stage. His back was to the prop man, and he was going forward with the scene, when suddenly the gun went off. Kennedy turned around and gave a cold stare to the prop man. He could have the most deadly stare in the world. It was a total look of hate. He wanted to kill him."[4]

While Dean and Pine recuperated in their dressing room after the unlucky performance, a young actress named Constance Lena Hoffman barged in to congratulate them. "She was gushing about how great we had been," recalls Pine, "calling both Jimmy and me by name, which was the strangest thing, because I'd never seen her before. I assumed she was Jimmy's date, and Jimmy assumed she was a friend of mine. She kept talking, wouldn't leave, and managed to hang on Jimmy and come into Sardi's as if she were with him."

At Sardi's, Phillip and Madelyn Pine and Arthur and Midge Batanides had taken their seats at the main table for the opening night gala. "Elaine Perry, who was the money in the show and was footing the bill for the party, had been held up," says Pine. "But her date was Bob Patton, an actor who was younger than she, and he was there with us. Jimmy brought the Hoffman girl over and pawned her off on us, and she sat next to Bob Patton in what was supposed to be Elaine's seat." What ensued was worthy of Noel Coward. "Elaine showed up," Pine continues, "and got mad because she saw this girl and thought Patton was two-timing her. On top of that, Midge Batanides thought the stray

4. In the version of *See the Jaguar* published in *Theatre Arts* magazine, Kennedy is onstage when the gunshot occurs. But as noted, there were constant rewrites. The *Theatre Arts* version includes one character, Orie, who had been written out of the play by opening night. Kennedy could have been offstage in whatever version was used that night.

was a secret love of Art's, and *she* got mad. Everybody was fighting. It was one of the damnedest scenarios I've ever witnessed."[5]

Dean's official date for the party was Dizzy Sheridan, but there was little joy in the occasion for her. With hindsight, she traces the disintegration of their relationship to Dean's "getting swept up in the theater." An early sign of it was Dean's annoying her with his assimilation of Arthur Kennedy's less attractive characteristics. Then, after a few weeks of separation while Dean was on the road, he called to say he was back, and they went out for a drink. Something seemed to be bothering him. "The way he talked," Sheridan said, "it was so hard, and his gestures and everything were hard and sort of an I-don't-give-a-damn kind of thing. He wasn't warm at all the way he used to be."

Then came opening night and Sardi's. "The whole experience was very uncomfortable for me," she remembers. "I was wearing a cloth coat, while all the other women wore fur." As she sat watching Dean circulate among the other tables, deluged with enthusiastic congratulations, she knew the private world they had shared was melting away for him.

Sheridan and Dean left the party together, walking east on Forty-fourth Street to the Royalton Hotel, where Dean was staying as a reward to himself for his Broadway debut. "We went up to his room," Sheridan recounts, "but the management called him up and made me come down, because they knew we weren't married. Jimmy came down with me and put me in a cab." Although the awkwardness of the moment was superimposed on them by external forces, the experience was metaphorical for Sheridan. "I had a horrible, sinking feeling just then. As it turned out, that really was the end of the relationship. His knock came earlier in life than mine, and he was clearly moving on in his career before I was in mine."

The following morning, playwright Arnold Sundgaard called on Alec Wilder at the Algonquin and found Dean there. It was the first time he ever met the young actor. "I had not seen the morning papers,"

---

5. Four months later, Constance Lena Hoffman wed bachelor Broadway actor Sam Levene, the original Nathan Detroit in *Guys and Dolls,* who was twenty-five years her senior.

Sundgaard says, "but apparently the notices for *See the Jaguar* were not good. Whatever it was, Jimmy seemed distraught, not only for the future of the play but for himself. But there was something more than that, some kind of conflict with the director or other members of the cast, that was troubling him as well. I can no longer recall the exact details except his trying to pound the bed and pace the confines of that tiny room.

"What is revealing, however, is that the morning after his New York debut it was Alec to whom Jimmy turned for consolation, understanding, and advice. He did not turn to Rogers Brackett, who had been his sponsor, nor to the Ayerses, his patrons. I think it was Alec for whom he had the greatest respect. It was a role Alec enjoyed and had played with many others before Jimmy."

Indeed, the morning papers carried dismal news for Ayers, Nash, and their company. Without exception, the New York journals took an ultimately dim view of the play, calling it everything but a success: "pretentious," "bewildering," "wildly ineffectual," and "a disappointingly contrived evening." Even the *Hollywood Reporter* carried a bad notice that morning: "Nash stubbed his typewriter badly on this one," it groused. The play "is moody and muddled, weighted down with dramatic symbolism that never seemed to pay off."

The weeklies weighed in soon after with equally desolate pronouncements. A "hollow triumph, the good try that misses," sniffed *Newsweek*. *The New Yorker* labeled it "one of the season's major catastrophes" because the script "came dangerously close to sounding like nonsense." *Cue* condemned Ayers "for bringing the piece to town in the first place."

The ensemble of *See the Jaguar,* on the other hand, was uniformly praised. If any of them came across as unconvincing, it was blamed on the playwright. Kennedy earned accolades for his "honest and exciting theatrical images." Pine displayed "individuality" as a stereotypical mountain bully. Dean impressed the majority of the critics; the consensus was that he achieved "the feat of making the childish young fugitive believable and unembarrassing," according to Richard Watts of the *New York Post*.

Friends of Dean who came to the show ranged from Bill Bast to John Holden (from UCLA) to Ahmet and Jan Ertegun. James Sheldon went on opening night specifically to see Dean. "His performance was just fabulous," Sheldon remembers. "He was a weird little boy, an animal mountain boy. He was electrifying." Terese Hayden, who would be instrumental in casting *The Immoralist,* saw Dean in *Jaguar* and thought he was "fantastic."

Christine White returned from Hollywood, where she had worked in two films, just in time to catch the closing performance. "Jimmy got me my ticket," White says, "and it was confusing to me. I couldn't understand basically what the play was all about, and I couldn't stand him being in the cage! I thought, 'He's such a free individual, and he has such great rhythm, and here he can't use his legs. He's really being squashed; this is ridiculous!' I went backstage after the performance, and we went out."

The only negative comment from the inside crowd was voiced by seven-year-old Sarah Ayers, who was "very disappointed that there wasn't a real jaguar in it."

Composer David Diamond, who had never seen Dean before, was sufficiently impressed to make perhaps the earliest written comparison of Dean to Marlon Brando. In his diary, Diamond wrote, "Alec [Wilder] phoned to say there was a preview of *Jaguar* and that 'this wonderful boy you'll love' is to be seen to be believed. I found the play a mess, but like Marlon in *Truckline Café,* Jimmy was *it.* This tiny boy who looks thirteen has a lot of Marlon's mannerisms but a wholly different sensibility."

Dane Knell later reflected, "I knew he wasn't just another actor. It wasn't because of Method acting that he was special; it was just that with him, it was more real than with other actors. What he did really worked. It was the same way I later felt about Dustin Hoffman. You knew immediately they were going to go far."

Alan Brock, the agent whom Dean had told off, attended a performance to watch Dane Knell. Afterward, Brock encountered Dean in a backstage hallway. "Hiyah, Brock! What do you think of me now?" Dean railed. "Don't tell me, I know. All you guys are saying the same thing: Dean's a great actor. Nuts to you all!"

Now it was Brock's turn to have his say. "What's all the shouting for, Jimmy?" he protested. "Sure, you gave a fine performance, and you've finally made the grade. But don't forget there are many actors on

Broadway right now who could have been just as good, and don't forget it's the best part in the show. Every actor believes he is the best if only given a chance. But can they all have the genius they so firmly believe they have? What do you expect of an agent?"

Brock started to walk away, when Dean stepped in front of him and surprised him with a smile. "Okay, Brock, don't get sore, maybe I'm wrong. This is all new to me. I don't know your side. Maybe you're not such a bad guy." Brock could only conclude that Dean was difficult to figure out.

"A couple of years later," says James O'Rear, who read the Wally Wilkins part at several backers' auditions, "I was passing through Cromwell's at Rockefeller Center and felt a tap on my shoulder. I turned around and it was James Dean. I knew who he was by that time because he was becoming famous. He smiled and said, 'I saw you read the part I played in *See the Jaguar* and I want to thank you, because I thought you were great. I tried to do everything you did in the part.' It was the only time we ever spoke."

To apprehend the remarkable progress Dean had made, one had only to compare his highly praised role in *See the Jaguar* with his substandard rendition in *Macbeth* at UCLA exactly two years earlier, both of which ran for half a week. In *Macbeth,* Dean got bad reviews in a good show, and most of his peers felt certain that the only result of his pursuit of acting would be heartbreak. In *See the Jaguar,* he got good reviews in a bad show and immediately became a much more marketable actor. By following his instincts and opting for on-the-job training in New York, rather than toughing it out in an academic environment, Dean had taken the path that was right for him.

Lonely Shepherd
of the Iroquois

When Dean went out of town for the tryouts of *See the Jaguar,* he bade a permanent farewell to the communal life as it had been lived in the West Eighty-ninth Street apartment. He stayed briefly at the Royalton Hotel when he returned, but it was too expensive to make a habit, so he decided to drop anchor at the old reliable Iroquois Hotel across Forty-fourth Street. For the remainder of his short life he would choose to live alone, except for spells when he was either broke or relocating.

The Iroquois would be Dean's headquarters until the end of spring. Here he would have a unique opportunity to deepen his standing friendships with Christine White and Bill Bast and to be nurtured by a new friend, the composer David Diamond. Yet the hotel also represented a starkly solitary period of his life. Each of these friends was struck by his diffusion of an overwhelming loneliness.

Christine White was just back in New York after being in Hollywood for twelve weeks, going to auditions and making two pictures. She had given up her place on East Ninety-first Street before leaving and was set to take over a friend's sublet upon her return. But the friend's trip to Europe was postponed, so White was in the lurch and needed lodging in a hurry. When she called Dean at the Iroquois and mentioned the situation, he immediately insisted, "I can get you in here!"

"So it was a fast thing," says White, "and the room was furnished.

I never had any furniture in New York. I just went there with suitcases and mementos, and I moved in right below him one floor. What a bleak place! Jimmy was always trying to fix up his room. He'd pound on the floor with his boot. That meant come up, because I've fixed one of my walls! And there would be matador shots around and he had bull horns. He had no fridge, so he kept his milk and beer out on the fire escape. It was in the dead of winter. I remember he had crackers on the desk. There were two plants I had brought him. He would bathe the leaves in milk. His room was never a mess at that time.

"Often we would talk until three or four in the morning, settling the world's problems. One of these sessions was out on the fire escape; it was one of our deepest exchanges. Jimmy wore a windbreaker and I wore lots of layers. It actually wasn't too cold when we were out there. We were smoking cigarettes, drinking beer, and dropping the bottles to watch and hear them break. We even wrote part of a western film script out there—westerns were in at that time. I later developed it and gave it to Dick Clayton, my West Coast agent. I don't know what happened to it.

"We had many exchanges about God and what Jimmy's theological viewpoint was at that time. We discussed it very often and deeply. Jimmy was no Puritan; to him Jesus was a champion. 'Any guy who would do all that has got guts and balls,' he said. '*That's* what I like. All that theological, ideological ritual crap is nothing but boring.'

"I know that his roots were grass roots in an underprivileged way; that's what he said. He was used to lack, to going without; he had no regard for wardrobe, clothes, or anything. He was completely involved in 'What you think or what you feel is more important than the shirt you're wearing.'

"Jimmy's mother's death did not preoccupy him heavily, because you do forget those things, but at the same time . . . he had a leak in his heart, is the best way to describe it. It would be for anybody, to lose a parent. He couldn't figure it out. His fretting and annoying others came because he could not get a grip on that. A mother's influence would have rounded him out a bit more, because his father was basically not too encouraging. I think he felt a lot of lack there. I think he felt his father could have made a move, and had wishful thinking in that area. There was a lot of profanity involved in reactions to his father. The

Actors Studio indulged the most horrifying language you can imagine, so we were all beginning to pick it up. This helped Jimmy to put a cover over whatever he felt about the absence of his father's approval. You can be cocky and talk like that and throw it off.

"He didn't really go on a lot; didn't really have patter at his command. If he were excited, the rhythm of his speech might be up and up. But if you were alone with him, as I was so much, he would completely relax and open up, and all the nuances would come out. But basically, he was not your big talker. He didn't pull out a lot of bio, 'I did this; I did that.' He was not a party bore that brought out all these different aspects of himself. He would just as soon skip it.

"He was not known as a great intellect, but when he opened up, I thought Jimmy was borderline brilliant, absolutely brilliant. I would think that for his education, which hadn't gone on too far, his eagerness to learn—his personal studies of Shakespeare, Lorca, sculpting, this and that—his desire to grow was way above average. He was on a big musician kick and learned to play his recorder. He gave me the music from *Romeo and Juliet* as a present."

White kept a low profile during the two months or so she was at the Iroquois Hotel. Dean told her, "People think you're still on the Coast." She retorted that she had planned it that way. "I had sequestered myself for two reasons," she explains. "First, being squeamish about that movie I made. I was embarrassed by the title, *Man Crazy!* I joked that I would go away on an ocean liner when it was released. Second, I had auditioned for *My Three Angels* on Broadway but was sexually harassed by Jose Ferrer, the director. That really devastated me. I never told Jimmy about it, even though I generally told him everything."

On the nature of her relationship with Dean, White was evasive. Asked how she managed to refrain from falling in love with him, she says, "That's an interesting question because I asked myself that. But there were a lot of guys around, always people to date, to go out with, that you would meet. When Jimmy came along, we sort of paired off, but we were always with other people as well. But I think we were so in love with what was going to happen to our careers more than anything.

"But there were many times when Jimmy would make a pass, but it was very . . . he knew me pretty well. It was a look, or we would hold hands in a movie, or it would be walking down the street, or he would make a sudden move. Yes, he would. Then if I would laugh or something like that . . . or sometimes we would stand in the street and hug each other. It wasn't that there was any reason not to fall in love. But it would be—what I really think about it was—we were planting a foundation.

"He said he was a virgin, once removed. We used to kick that thing around. We used to say it all the time; I told him that, too. And so he said, 'That's okay.' We would spend the night together. But everything was fun and just like 'getting to know you.' It was like building a relationship, a very solid relationship, on trust, on fun, on friendship, and companionship. In the back of our minds, it would be like, 'If there is going to be somebody, it's probably going to be you'—something like that. The serious nature of it was on a layer that we really didn't act on. But it was pretty deep. The respect for one another was very deep. I think that's what we had. I think he needed that.

"Virgin once-removed means one time you did. And then you didn't. Either you fell and you didn't want to fall anymore, or the conscience was at you and you felt guilty. It came from me; he said, 'Oh, yeah, me too!'

"As I said, it did become romantic at times. But as you can tell by the kaleidoscope of his career, he's there—and then over there; he's with so-and-so—and then with so-and-so. Then he's in the Village riding his motorcycle. Then he's in Indiana. Then he's in *The Immoralist,* and he's busy! Multiply it with what I'm doing at the same time. I did show after show. I was working much more than he was. That didn't bother him, because girls were much easier to cast than guys.

"The reason why we were not intensely close-knit together at that time is that we thought we had forever—didn't think it was going to end. And all we could do was grow bigger and better. That was the underlying attitude. And always the paramount thing was, if you don't take any risks, you're not going to do anything. So we were never afraid of a challenge."

Through White, Dean had vicarious entrée to two important personalities. At that time, Marlon Brando lived on West Fifty-seventh Street across from Carnegie Hall. Whenever Dean and White passed the building, Dean would muse, "I wonder if the General is in tonight."

Eventually White was invited to a party for theater people; advance intelligence had it that Brando would be there. "By prearrangement," she says, "Jimmy called me at the party, hoping I could arrange to have him come up. I just couldn't invite him. The dynamics were such that I could have brought up a girl—but a fellow, no. When I got back to the Iroquois, he made me recite what Marlon had done in minute detail. He went at it like a director: 'Wait a minute, back up. Say that again! Okay, let's take it from the top again.' "

While making *Man Crazy!* in Hollywood, White had been at a party at Judy Garland's home, seated on the floor with many others, listening to Garland sing. "I met Sammy Davis, Jr., for the first time there; he offered me his seat on the floor. He was Mr. Wonderful even before the play! I said, 'You really are a gentleman.' He had a tremendously ingratiating personality. Jimmy was intrigued. He said, 'Why didn't you call me? I would've talked to him!' " Dean, of course, would meet and become friends with Davis in Hollywood.

White left the Iroquois Hotel in February, moving to the East Eighty-second Street sublet vacated belatedly by her friend. Summing up the time she spent as Dean's downstairs neighbor, she said, poignantly, "He was so lonely. He didn't know how much. Of course, he refused to admit it. Maybe this quality made girls want to mother him. He was an impulsive, immediate creature who thought nothing of crying."

Dizzy Sheridan's one brief experience with Dean at the Iroquois Hotel was anything but positive. As far as she was concerned, he had simply "disappeared" after their fiasco on the opening night of *See the Jaguar*. "It took me about two months to find him," she reported. "I found out he moved back into the Iroquois, so I called him one night and went over to see him. He seemed in an even worse condition than the night when he'd been so hard and bitter about New York business right after out-of-town tryouts."

Dean inexplicably seemed unwilling to open up to Sheridan. She had felt, when they first met, that he was afraid and hung onto her. But once he began to make a name for himself, it was she who became afraid. "Then I started to hang onto him," she said, "and he didn't seem to want the responsibility of having anybody hang onto him, because he was going up too fast. That was just extra weight."

No sooner had White left the Iroquois than Bill Bast, "out of necessity," came back to it. This time he and Dean would keep separate quarters, though on the same floor and directly across the hotel's small courtyard from each other. Bast said they would often signal to one another through their windows. But when Dean's shade was drawn, Bast knew it was his Do Not Disturb sign to the world.

Bast resided there until he left New York in the late spring to take a job in Hollywood. On the plane to California, thoughts of Dean's isolated nature swirled in his head, and, as with White, images of Dean and his recorder remained vivid. Bast had often seen Dean at night sitting by the window in his room, practicing tunes that Alec Wilder had written for him. Dean reminded Bast of a lonely shepherd.

But Dean was the muse of not one but two composers on West Forty-fourth Street as he doggedly expanded his musical prowess. The second was David Diamond, who was biding his time while waiting to return to Florence, where he had lately been a Fulbright scholar. He had taken Room 73 at the Iroquois; Room 74 was Dean's.

Diamond's diary of February 22, 1953, notes, "Alec [Wilder] introduces me to a charming young actor (I think he said he was studying at the Actors Studio, with Kazan). Very handsome, short, muscular. Has a provocative way of looking at you, then suddenly smiling. Said he loved my *Romeo and Juliet* music and *Rounds;* that he played the recorder. Works on TV. Now what is his name? Can't remember. Only his eyes (without his eyeglasses he seems near- or far-sighted)."

The nameless youth with the great smile was unmasked on February 27. "The young actor Alec introduced me to (of all things!) has the room next to mine. Asked him in as we left the elevator. His name is James Dean. I can't be certain . . . he seems more lonely than anything else; or perhaps it's as Alec says, 'He thinks you're famous.' He hopes to 'get a break' in the theater. I think Irene [Lee, assistant to producer Hal Wallis] should see him. I give him a letter to her. I'd stake a million on him. Only Marlon made me feel this way."

Serendipity had given Dean an immediate and devoted friend. He and Diamond went with Wilder to a film starring Buster Keaton and Charlie Chaplin, *Limelight,* the following evening; Diamond noted that Dean was "in tears" during one of Keaton's scenes. The following week, Diamond, who still teaches at the Juilliard School of Music, took Dean on a tour of the school and lent Dean his copy of Dashiell Hammett's *Red Harvest,* which "fried him." On March 7, Diamond wrote, "Jimmy is serious about me writing something on the recorder for him. There's a wonderful way he has of looking down at his feet, then up into my eyes, and then after a second of non-expressiveness, a glowing smile bursts forth. One wants to hug him."

Oddly, Diamond has no recollection of Bill Bast, and Bast seems not to have known of Diamond. It is hard to imagine how, given their respective importance as Dean's friends and proximity to him on the same floor in the same hotel, this could be so. It may have simply been another instance of Dean's painstaking compartmentalization of his friends.

Nearly four decades after their introduction at the Iroquois Hotel, Diamond spoke of Dean's modest quarters there and how their friendship developed. "Jimmy's room had a white, enameled bed, on which he was always stretched out playing his recorder, and a badly beat-up chair. He was not one for sitting; he was always on that damn white bed, leaning his head against the slats. I'd say, 'Jimmy, use a pillow!'

"Though not to the extent as with him and Alec, it was a father-son relationship with Jimmy and me. I think the reasons he liked me were that I was known—my music was being played by the Philharmonic—I was older [Diamond was then thirty-seven], and I never made a pass at him. He really wasn't my type. One thing about me, even from the time I was small, was that when I would find beauty in a person, I would look at them in a certain way—worshipful. Warmth was what I got back from Jimmy. But there was nothing taunting in his reaction to my warmth. He called me Sneakers because I could run so fast. He couldn't believe it. When I couldn't get a cab, I'd run after it!

"The night porter at the Iroquois was a large, heavy black man called Chuckie. He adored Jimmy and vice versa. Jimmy loved pastrami sandwiches. Once I said, 'I feel like having a pastrami sandwich,' and Jimmy exclaimed, 'Oh, yeah!' These are the kinds of things I remember about him. He was a simple, mixed-up, but not complex youth. Hollywood ruined him, and mythology has defaced him completely.

"I would buy him Chapsticks, because his lower lip would crack—a shame, because that was the most beautiful part of him. The camera captured his mouth, his whole aura, beautifully. This wouldn't have come through on the stage. What the movies don't preserve is his short stature or his well-developed pectorals and thighs. He also had a crazy look without his glasses, which is not preserved."

One day Dean, Diamond, and Wilder were lounging around in Dean's room. "Jimmy was wearing crazy boxer shorts and looked ridiculous," Diamond recalls. They were discussing the journalist and former member of Congress Clare Boothe Luce, who had just been named ambassador to Italy. "She has a cold face and colder eyes," Dean observed.

Diamond was a fortunate resource for Dean's natural curiosity about music, just as Leonard Rosenman and Walter Gieseking would later be. "Jimmy had a record player and would play the balcony scene of my *Romeo and Juliet* over and over, and say, 'Here's where Romeo is on the balcony!' I'd say, 'Jimmy, I don't want to hear it anymore. I wrote it!' Once he insisted on knowing how a three-staves Bach organ piece could be orchestrated. I brought a twenty-four-line orchestra score sheet to show him how it was done. His face was like a child.

"Jimmy cherished the recording I gave him of Sinatra conducting Alec's pieces. I had an old set of Alec's harpsichord and wind octets, an album of small-size seventy-eights, which Jimmy jiggled around to in sort of hillbilly dance steps. He also liked to play a record of Marian Anderson doing four Brahms songs and the Stokowski arrangement of Bach's *Come Sweet Death.*"

Live concerts were also part of Diamond's informal program of educating Dean. On March 29, he took him to a Leonard Bernstein concert at Town Hall featuring four compositions specially commissioned by the Koussevitzky Music Foundation. Afterward they had a long conversation in the Algonquin lobby with playwright Edward Albee and his companion Bill Flanagan, who was studying composition with Diamond.

Diamond echoes White and Bast in his impressions of Dean's isolation. "I felt such an agony in the boy," he emphasizes. "It was something very clear to me, always very clear to me. He was the loneliest person I ever knew. Sometimes he would cry." Despite his affection for Dean, Diamond was wary of entanglement with so emotionally needy a person. One morning at the corner of Forty-fourth Street and Sixth Avenue, Dean unsuccessfully entreated Diamond to have coffee with him at an Automat. "Where are you always going?" Dean asked. "But I'm always on my way somewhere," confided Diamond in his diary. "I didn't want to be any more involved with him."

When Dean asked Diamond why Wilder didn't take him around the way Diamond did, he replied, "Because you're too short!" (Wilder was six-feet-three.) Wilder once gossiped to Diamond, "Jimmy's a little bit jealous about your fondness for Martin Russ." While Diamond and Russ were friendly, there was never any sexual relationship between them since Russ was not, and is not, homosexual. "When I asked Jimmy about this," Diamond avers, "he answered, 'Oh, well, you know, uh . . .' And I gave him a big hug. He blushed. I was so touched. This was in the small lobby of the Iroquois. Another time when I hugged Jimmy, he rested his head on my shoulder. It was because he played one of my pieces so beautifully on his recorder."

Shortly before Diamond returned to Italy, Dean's unstated feelings for him apparently bubbled up in a troubling way. "J. calls this afternoon," Diamond's diary reads. "He knows I'm his friend, isn't that enough?" Diamond later explained, "If people became problematic, I'd only use their initial in the diary. Jimmy was jealous because I had Ciro, a lover in Italy."

Nonetheless, Diamond said he never saw Dean act out any homosexual feelings, despite ample opportunity to do so. "Once he asked me to massage his neck. He got in the tub," Diamond recalls. "He was always complaining about his neck, was always twisting it around. So often, there in his room, he'd be nude in the tub, or on the bed, and even if there's nothing there between two people, sooner or later, if he were gay, he would have asked or intimated that he wanted to be satisfied. But he never asked me, say, to use the soap to lather him up down there. Oh, he may have been semierect some of the time, but nothing ever happened. Alec would ask. The implication was, 'I knew I could trust him with you.' Once, when I was massaging his neck, he asked, 'Are there any blackheads on my back?' There weren't. I would massage his shoulders, sometimes to the rhythm of Tchaikovsky's Sixth.

"He was a very blond, fair person. He didn't seem to have any beard. I guess he must have always shaved close. The hair on his legs was a blond down. He had three or four hairs on his chest. His pubic hair was blond.

"Jimmy exuded such a sensuality, an aura. It was lush, a kind of purity. There was no badness in him. He even smelled good, even when perspiring."

Dean frequently joined Diamond, Wilder, Rogers Brackett, and several of their friends in drinking sessions at the Blue Bar in the Algonquin. In a sense, these gatherings carried on the hotel's renowned heritage of sidesplitting repartee established by the wits of the Round Table in the Twenties. Wilder wrote, "Rogers and I met in the claustrophobic Blue Bar and have laughed ourselves into exhaustion ever since." Arnold Sundgaard remembers, "Puns were Alec's specialty, and Rogers was his equal. Rogers made bull's-eye observations that took me days to comprehend. I'm sure it took Jimmy just as long to know what was going on as I did. I can see Alec now, slapping his thigh in uproarious laughter."

"Rogers's style," observes Brackett's friend James Maher, "was to speak from Olympus but at the same time to allow his listeners the special cachet of being fellow insiders. Even if you weren't privy to whatever world he was dissecting, Rogers let you feel that you were—a gracious little piece of trickery. His punch lines were delivered with a very sober, altar boy–like expression, his head canted slightly, reverentially, his eyebrows raised. The only problem with his manner was that he was always on. You could almost sense him waiting for his cue, for the appropriate instant to deliver a perfectly distilled—and perfectly rehearsed—*mot.*"

Not surprisingly, the homosexual members of this circle took a special interest in Dean. According to Madison Musser, they called him the Marshmallow Brando. Diamond says, "Marshall Barer had a crush on Jimmy. Bradley Saunders, a tall, aristocratic air force pilot, was crazy about Jimmy; he said he liked them young. George, the legendary bartender, always scolded me if I put my arm around a man; Alec would sometimes egg me to do it to rile George. Mr. Martin, the hotel's manager, was flauntingly gay—and crazy about Jimmy—so I don't know why George was so uptight."

Only rarely would Dean catch the spirit of these "drinking-near-hysterical punning series," as Diamond calls them. "Jimmy loved it when Alec would imitate actress Julie Haydon, wife of the critic George Jean Nathan. With Alec being so tall, mustache and all—to see him act so coy, and to put his hands in the praying attitude at the side of his face like Haydon—it's the only time I ever saw Jimmy in hysterics."

Once in a great while, the talk would be dark and somber. "There were times," says Diamond, "when it was only the three of us at the bar, and Alec would be quite drunk and tell grim tales about his father's treatment of his mother. On Jimmy's face I could see torture. He was going through inner hell listening to Alec."

More often, the sessions tried Dean's patience. "Jimmy always had a Coke or soda; he didn't drink with us," says Diamond. By this time, it seemed, what had once been a source of enlightenment and engagement to Dean—Brackett's clowning and wit—were now annoying him. "I saw something was about to break between Rogers and Jimmy," remembers Diamond. "At the Blue Bar they barely spoke to one another, and Rogers rarely came to the Iroquois.

"Jimmy couldn't abide effeminacy, nor could he abide what he called 'hot-shit talk.' He would either walk away or else mutter, 'Aw, nuts!' his eyes always looking down just before he took off. Though homosexual myself, I am always slightly uncomfortable with the effeminate or 'flying' grotesques. After a while, Jimmy would give me the wink, and we'd go to the China Bowl down the street. He would ask me how I could stand that group. I only went there for Alec. Sometimes even Alec would get fed up with the camping of the guys in our crowd and repair to the Red Lobster on Forty-fifth Street."

Marshall Barer recalls, "Once when I arrived at the Algonquin in a cab, Jimmy rushed over. He had a beautiful girl with him, an up-and-coming actress, and said, 'You can settle the argument: Which one of us is more beautiful?' " Barer says he called the contest a draw.

It was during this time that Dean sent a postcard to the Winslows that typically gave no clue as to the worldly and frequently sophisticated people and events he was coming to know so well. He berated city dwellers and proclaimed everlasting fidelity to his origins as a country boy, adding that he had been ice-skating a lot. A reminder of his upcoming mid-April appearances in *Danger* and *Treasury Men in Action* was given. He closed with an urgent demand that his cousin Marcus, Jr., send more artwork for his walls at the Iroquois Hotel.

"Vaguely I remember some puerile drawings, crayons, on his walls," Diamond says, "but I thought they were Jimmy's! Ice-skating, yes—and how! He was off to Rockefeller Center often. I can still picture the skates in a duffel bag."

Meanwhile, the social life that Dean knew through Diamond continued right up until Diamond sailed for Italy on May 1. There was dinner at designer Paul Morrison's apartment (Diamond's diary: "Jimmy liked him a lot"), an evening of jazz at Eddie Condon's, and drinks at the Russian Tea Room. The day before Diamond departed, he presented Dean with another composition for the recorder. In his diary, he wrote, "Jimmy seemed touched and clutched my hand, kept pressing it over and over again as he thanked me."

By the late spring of 1953, Dean was working too infrequently to afford even the Iroquois, so he spent the summer living in apartments of friends and strangers. But he retained a fondness for the Iroquois, as shown in his admonition to correspondents to write to him in care of "the old hotel" because he continued to stop by regularly.

Barbara, Betsy, and Bates

Fortified with favorable reviews from *See the Jaguar,* Dean was soon working in television again. Nineteen fifty-three would be his banner year for television work, with appearances on sixteen programs.

He would still know lean times, because these jobs were his only known source of income and there were occasionally long stretches between them. But the small screen laid the foundation for his movie career, both as an apprenticeship through which his unmistakable mannerisms, movements, and attitudes evolved, and as an introduction to Hollywood talent scouts. His screen test for *Oklahoma!* came about because director Fred Zinnemann's assistant had "spotted him in a TV show" and was "very impressed." George Stevens, his future director in *Giant,* would recall that "long before the movies or anyone else in Hollywood had heard of Dean, I saw him in a half-hour television play. It was the first time that I ever watched anxiously for the credits so I could find out who this brilliant, sensitive young actor was. His was an extraordinary talent."

Throughout 1953 Dean would have three principal residences: the Iroquois Hotel until June; Jonathan Bates's apartment during the summer; and beginning in the fall, 19 West Sixty-eighth Street, eventually the most famous of his domiciles. The year also brought a changing of the guard among his friends. Rogers Brackett faded from preeminence—Madison Musser remembers Dean's frequent bad-mouthing of Brackett by this time—and Dizzy Sheridan moved to St. Thomas to pursue dancing. Only Christine White and Martin Landau carried over from 1952. Newer friends came up through the ranks: Frank Corsaro, Eartha Kitt, Jonathan Gilmore, Claire Heller, Betsy Palmer, Arlene Sachs, and especially Barbara Glenn, with whom Dean had one of his most exceptional relationships.

According to Glenn, she and Dean met in Cromwell's coffee shop on the day *See the Jaguar* opened. Sitting with Rusty Slocum and other friends, she spotted a "magnificently gorgeous" but "withdrawn" Dean in a corner by himself and asked Slocum to invite him to their table. He seemed uptight and insecure, and his attempts at conversation were pathetic, yet Glenn found Dean attractive and fascinating. She also sensed in him an overwhelming aura of self-destructiveness. The combination of good looks and danger was irresistible to her. "He related to me differently than anyone I'd ever met," she says.

The next time they met, Dean gave her a short story by Truman Capote and then called her to hear her reaction to it. Conversation drifted from Capote and the theater into Dean's confidences about his mother; Glenn said he went so far as to tell her she reminded him of Mildred. Although she hated his motorcycle, she would occasionally ride around New York with him, hanging on for dear life. She could see he was a highly vulnerable person, wary of letting anyone get close and terrified of rejection, and she felt she was "walking on eggshells" with him in those first few weeks.

Eventually Dean realized Glenn was a kindred spirit and began to confide everything to her. She soon learned that if he were upset about anything, she could count on a phone call in the middle of the night. They maintained a mostly private relationship. "I was very much apart from the rest of his life," she said. "The group we were part of was very small. We didn't go out and meet people." His letters to her over the next two years compose the single best resource on James Dean as he really was.

The flip side of this trusting relationship was extreme volatility. Glenn says they could not be together for any length of time without a fight erupting, and when Dean was angry, he withdrew and refused to communicate, rather than shout and carry on, which only multiplied her aggravation. Somehow, the combination of tenderness and combustibility would sustain them for over two years.

Dizzy Sheridan would see Dean one more time before her move to St. Thomas. She had become the proud owner of a Great Dane and invited Dean to come to Central Park to meet her pet. "We must have spent a good hour there," she recalled, "just running with the dog and throwing things for him, and having him run and bring it back to us." As a closure to their intense and recently painful partnership, the visit was somewhat healing.

Interwoven with the drama of Dean's personal friendships were his televised dramas. His first two jobs in 1953 echoed his rustic Wally Wilkins role in *See the Jaguar*.[1] On the *Kate Smith Hour* of January 15, he was an angel in hillbilly garb in a short skit, "The Hound of Heaven." An Appalachian man, Hyder (John Carradine), and his dog, Rip, wait at the gates of what they assume is heaven. The gatekeeper (Edgar Stehli) welcomes Hyder but bars Rip. Hyder goes nowhere without Rip and won't enter. Dean as a winged messenger appears, calling for Hyder. When Hyder says he can't go through the gateway because to exist without Rip would be hell, the angel tells him it *is* hell in there. The gatekeeper was trying to trick Hyder and knew Rip would smell the brimstone and warn him. The angel has the last word, observing that a man will walk into hell with both eyes open, but even the devil can't fool a dog.

Two weeks later Dean played Randy Meeker, teenage son of a mountain moonshiner, in "The Case of the Watchful Dog," an episode of *Treasury Men in Action*. To convince his father, Clay, that he is mature enough to join the moonshine syndicate, Randy borrows a hot rod to deliver two hundred gallons of bootleg liquor to a "floating depot." Treasury agents pursue him, but their car is no match for the hot rod and he escapes. But his admiration of his father turns to contempt when Clay shoots the family dog, whose barking compromises their hideout. Randy angrily dares Clay to shoot him, too, but agents burst in just at that moment. Completely disillusioned with Clay, Randy reveals the floating depot's location to the agents.

---

1. Robert Tysl alleged in his dissertation on the Dean image that "the sponsorship of Lemuel Ayers" was responsible for Dean's post-*Jaguar* work in television.

When he wasn't working in television, Dean was spending much of his time with Frank Corsaro, who was becoming increasingly influential in his life. "He liked me because I was Italian, very smart, and a good director," Corsaro recounts. "I found his sensibilities heightened, but his knowledge limited. We used to read poems and stories. One afternoon we spent reading *The Little Prince* and had a strong emotional reaction to it. He was in tears. I was in tears.

"He had ways of arousing the protective sense, and then the Pandora's box would open. He didn't believe he could sustain friendships; they all had to be tested. I constantly tried to get him to go to a therapist, so he could improve his interpersonal relationships. He was beginning to isolate himself from people. He was in desperate need of help yet distrustful of almost everyone who could help him."

Eartha Kitt's remarkable friendship with Dean began when the two of them met in the Syvila Forte dance studio; later he would take dance classes with her at the Katherine Dunham studio. Kitt had grown up even further removed from anything resembling an intact home than Dean; thus both had worldviews that were shaped by what they missed. They developed what Kitt said was an unusually clairvoyant, trusting, spiritual relationship. On top of that, she claimed to have tutored him in her brand of stage presence. They would often roam New York together in silence, she said, but each knew what the other was thinking. Kitt was one of the most frequent recipients of Dean's infamous middle-of-the-night telephone calls, and she indulged him in the habit.

Dean marked his twenty-second birthday by playing Robert Ford in "The Killing of Jesse James," an episode on *You Are There,* a new television program featuring historical events as if reported live. John Kerr had the Jesse James role. "Most of the show dealt with what was going on politically, leading up to the shooting," Kerr explains, "so neither Jimmy nor I was on until the last four or five minutes. I came on after being out on a horse—stopped at a well for a drink, then went inside a saloon. I stood on a chair to straighten a picture, and Jimmy shot me in the back. He had a line that shooting Jesse James would make him famous and he would collect the reward. It was only a small part, but it didn't take a lot of brains to realize he was talented. I thought he was first-rate and would be a wonderful actor."

Vivian Matalon, a young English actor who watched the show, had been one of many to read for the Wally Wilkins role in *See the Jaguar.* "I felt better about losing the *Jaguar* part when I saw Jimmy in 'Jesse James,'" Matalon says, "because it was no disgrace to lose it to someone that good."

One of Dean's surviving pay stubs is from the *Hallmark Hall of Fame* and dated March 8, 1953. Yet he was not in that day's episode, "Horace Mann's Miracle." The probable explanation is that he was fired before the show aired; the student who takes up a collection to help Horace Mann keep a college solvent was ultimately played by John Kerr. Although much ado has been made about how similar Paul Newman's career was to Dean's during these years, Kerr's career actually paralleled Dean's more closely. Both were up for the same roles in *Bernardine, East of Eden,* and *Cobweb;* both were on Broadway in early 1954 in plays with homosexual themes; and immediately after Dean's death Kerr took the part Dean had been slated for in "The Corn Is Green" on the *Hallmark Hall of Fame.*

The following month, Dean had back-to-back television jobs. On April 14, he appeared for the first of what would be four times in the popular CBS crime series, *Danger.* Two days later he returned to *Treasury Men in Action.*

The *Danger* episode, "No Room," featured Dean as a safecracker whose brother talks him out of participating in a burglary. Back in Indiana, the *Fairmount News* proudly announced the appearance and regretted not reporting more. "Jimmy," it added, "has appeared in a number of programs not being shown in the central Indiana area." The Hill twins remember announcements over Fairmount High's public-address system whenever a Dean television appearance was imminent.

"The Case of the Sawed-Off Shotgun" on *T-Men* was notable because Dean worked with the gifted Ben Gazzara. Though both played teenagers, with hindsight it is amusing to contemplate Gazzara's playing a wholesome boy who tries to persuade Dean's small-town tough-kid character, Arbie Ferris, to attend Boys Club meetings. Arbie refuses, preferring to work on his scrapbook of clippings about his favorite criminals.

Hearing that Blackie, a renowned bootlegger, has just landed in town, Arbie schemes to meet and impress him. To his consternation,

Blackie (played by Joseph Downing, a veteran B movie gangster) tells him to beat it, so he steals Blackie's sawed-off shotgun and plans a gas station robbery to earn his respect. But he bungles the robbery and flees, leaving the shotgun at the crime scene. An annoyed Blackie tracks him down, beats him up, and is about to abduct him forcibly when federal agents save the day. Arbie gets off with probation under the custody of Gazzara's model citizen father.

Christine White was working even more frequently in television than Dean, but they still found time to keep in touch. She was now living in what she called her "crazy Germantown apartment," a fifth-floor walk-up at 533 East Eighty-second Street. Dean always wore motorcycle boots when he visited, and usually tried to persuade her to ride with him. He would cajole, "I'm a great driver!" to which she would reply, "I believe you are." But she feared he would drive recklessly and would say no thanks. Instead, she and Dean would take walks along the East River, only a block from her apartment. Dean would ask, "Are the tugboats out tonight?" which was White's cue to impersonate a tugboat horn.

It was not Dean's style to discuss his friends or arrange for them to meet each other. White said he never mentioned Eartha Kitt or Barbara Glenn to her; "Was she on the coast?" White asked about Glenn years later. "He never spoke about any other girl to me except Dizzy [and, later, Pier Angeli]. He was smart; if he were with another girl, he wouldn't do that. He was very closemouthed, and that's nothing because we all had loads of dates and loads of options. So nobody was being pinned like you were on campus. It was a very open season." However, when White heard that Beverly Wills had written a fan magazine article entitled, "I Almost Married Jimmy Dean," she exclaimed, "Well, I never even said that, but I would be more a candidate than anybody!"

In May 1953, Dean met Jonathan Gilmore, a handsome eighteen-year-old actor, at breakfast in a drugstore. Their eventual sexual involvement (which fell short of consummation, amounting only to a few feints) has come to overshadow other aspects of the friendship almost completely. "We were sporadic friends," Gilmore recollects, "jumpy and spotty, but we'd connect like electric wires and it made sparks. It had to do with his being perverse about things and drawn, as if by a magnet, to what struck him as perverse. He saw me as a kind of teenage

Rimbaud who didn't like anybody, and he liked that. I'd been told that I was misanthropic and that it was a bad situation to have negative thoughts, but Jimmy liked these. He always joked and laughed about the things he'd say that were derogatory about people, and he'd encourage me to say bad things about people, especially to their face.

"It was like two bad boys, though neither of us was bad in the delinquent or criminal sense, and I encouraged whatever craziness he'd think up. The physical side or attempts at it were extensions of the intensity of this relationship. It was kind of an affair between bad-boy spirits."

Dean discovered right away that Gilmore shared his enthusiasm for bullfighting and motorcycles. They also liked to drink and discuss acting and colorful personalities they admired, such as John Hodiak, Tallulah Bankhead, Edith Piaf, Jean Cocteau, and Jean-Louis Barrault. "I'd met Piaf at the Chateau Marmont in L.A. in '52, and Jimmy was most excited to talk about her," Gilmore relates. "I played her records for him. With Bankhead, Jimmy said she was a 'superb prima donna bitch.' He was fascinated with her mouth; he said it was a kind of living thing with a mind of its own, apart from the personality, and that it gave him a hard-on, and he wanted to stick his dick in her mouth."

Gilmore may be Dean's only close friend not to be subjected to the legendary fanaticism for *The Little Prince*. However, Dean did confide his most personal feelings about his mother and father to his younger friend. "He would talk to me about his mother when he was drunk, how they related, and how he lacked a 'line' to her, such as he said was still possible for me to sustain with my mother, who was alive," explains Gilmore.

Spring commencement exercises were at hand, and for the second year in a row, Dean met Fairmount High seniors who had come to New York on their class trip. He visited with them at the Paramount Hotel, then went to an Automat with two or three who had been his neighbors in Fairmount.

Perhaps the contact with hometown folks prompted Dean to type a letter to James DeWeerd on May 20. Addressing DeWeerd as King of the Wood, he mentioned his recent Broadway debut with its critical accolades and stated his pride at supporting himself through acting. The irony, he said, was that despite his success with varied roles, he had no idea who or what his true self was.

Some measure of what Dean had absorbed from intellectual friends can be seen in the letter's pretentiousness. Latin phrases infested its four paragraphs, not to mention his current favorite terms, "harpies" and "metaphysical whoo-haas" (he also used them to inscribe a gift to Bill Bast around the same time).

On May 1, 1953, Dean had a small part in *Tales of Tomorrow,* one of only two times he worked for ABC in New York. The plot centered on a dangerous new chemical formula that produced evil and even suicidal tendencies in anyone unlucky enough to ingest it. Playing Ralph, a lab assistant to Rod Steiger's eccentric scientist, Dean had only one scene in "The Evil Within," but it was probably the only role in which he actually saw what he was doing: he wore his glasses, since they enhanced the part.

"The Evil Within" would be Dean's last job for two-and-a-half months. Without income he could no longer cover his rent at the Iroquois, so Frank Corsaro came to his rescue. "Jimmy never did stay at my apartment," said Corsaro, "but I arranged for him to stay with Jonathan Bates, who I knew through the Actors Studio. Bates was Irish, a cherubic-looking guy, and trying to write for the theater."

Bates was a twenty-eight-year-old purser for TWA and usually worked the trans-Atlantic routes. He had dogs and was glad to have Dean living there to take care of them during his frequent absences. Christine White remembers that Dean appreciated the rent-free arrangement but was not pleased about the dogs. One rainy Sunday afternoon he called her to ask for a twenty-dollar loan: "Float me, Baby. I'm flat." White says, "So I met him across from Rockefeller Plaza. He told me, 'I'm going nuts. I've got these dogs to walk!' He liked the dogs, but they weren't his and they were cutting in on his time. Once he couldn't sleep because of them, so he spent the night on my couch. He wore my apricot pajamas. That's all I had that wasn't a nightgown."

Madison Musser visited Dean at Bates's apartment: "It was above the Brown Derby [40 West Fifty-second Street], a cabaret whose [electric sign] flashed on and off. He wanted me to hear him play the recorder."

While between jobs, Dean acted in at least three stage ventures, for little or no pay. At the Actors Studio, Calder Willingham's *End As a Man,* a play about sadism in a southern military academy, was in workshop. Reports that Dean played the cadet Starkson are erroneous, says Willingham. "He was only a 'walk-on' or actually a 'sit-on,' as an amanuensis at the inquiry by the general into the goings-on of Jocko [Ben Gazzara] and the others. Jimmy sat there at a table in a cadet uniform and pretended to take down the proceedings in shorthand. He had no lines, no action, nothing. That was his 'part': pretending to scribble in a notepad."

End As a Man rehearsals were held from ten P.M. to two A.M. to accommodate the daytime jobs of cast members. The director, Jack Garfein, remembers Dean playing duets of baroque music on his recorder with another actor, William Smithers, during breaks. The play was done for Studio members only on May 10, then for potential backers on May 17 and June 11, in the Studio's spartan quarters on the top floor of the ANTA Theater, a forum without even a curtain or a real stage.

Willingham gave a post-workshop party at his Twenty-eighth Street apartment, an event notable for Dean's uncharacteristic public gregariousness. "Although Jimmy had had no real part at all in the play," the playwright remembers, "he totally dominated the party, with jokes, narratives, speculations, mad comments, mimickings, dances, leaps, gurgles, slobberings, fartings, goosings of girls, collapses, sudden dramatic recoveries from apparent death, and all kinds of other attention-getting ploys and stratagems. To do that to a room full of actors of some considerable talent—Gazzara, Tony Franciosa, Pat Hingle, Bill Smithers, Albert Salmi, Mark Richman and others—is no mean feat. As I observed his incredible nonstop performance, the thought came to me, 'This boy is going to be a star!' "

End As a Man found its angel in Claire Heller, a twenty-three-year-old actress and daughter of a wealthy San Francisco investment banker. Over the summer, as Heller prepared the show for its September opening off-Broadway—and while Barbara Glenn was away in stock—she and Dean became friendly. Willingham remembers their leaving his party together.

Actress Carroll Baker said she often saw Dean and Heller at

soirees convened for classical music appreciation. Baker's autobiography describes Dean's sitting in a corner without speaking, sometimes beating bongo drums along with the music. "His girlfriend, Claire, told me that he loved attention from girls, even though he went to extremes not to be noticed," she reported. "Their relationshp was most unusual because while they spent hours and even days and nights together at her apartment [45 Tudor City Place], they were never seen socially. He confided in Claire, and she was careful not to betray his trust, so I couldn't get her to tell me why they never went out together. His attitude toward her was somewhat cavalier and at times almost rude. Claire, on the other hand, was refined and gentle and understanding. More than anyone else, she understood the troubled rebel in him."

Barbara Glenn spent the summer at the Cragsmoor Playhouse in the Catskills. The tension of a pending separation usually provoked an argument between her and Dean, and this particular instance was a classic. Glenn's friends decided to give her a bon voyage party at Dean's (Bates's) apartment, an idea that triggered an unusually foul mood in him. "The night of the party he just got nastier and nastier and surlier and surlier," she said. Although he was ignoring her, she said good-bye to him and walked two blocks to Jerry's Bar, where she sat crying in a booth with a friend. Not surprisingly, Dean appeared. "He didn't have much to say," said Glenn, "but he held my hand and we sat there. Then we spent the night together and that was it."

One of Dean's letters to Glenn that summer, written in a six-thirty A.M. mental haze, rhapsodized the madcap ambience and cacophony of his block, which besides the Brown Derby could also boast the raucous dance hall Leon & Eddie's, the Famous Door, Jimmy Ryan's, the 21 Club, and several restaurants.[2] He also referred cryptically to the contents of a drawer in the desk he was sitting at, saying it contained photographs and drawings that were "imaginative" and "not so subtle." The artwork in question apparently belonged to Jonathan Bates, as Dean claimed simply to have stumbled upon it.

---

2. This happened to be the block known in the jazz world simply as "The Street." By 1952, much of its glory had faded, and *Variety* called it "that moldering midway of strip and clip joints."

An experience related by David Swift clarifies Dean's meaning. "Once Jimmy invited us to hear him play his expensive recorder. We had all been out to dinner; Norma Crane was with us, too. Maggie and I had picked up the tab for dinner and drinks; and Jimmy, who had drunk a lot, was in a good mood, feeling expansive. It was the first time I heard him talk about his homosexuality. He pulled out some bad drawings of sailors seducing a man, holding a man down, and so forth. I was pretty shocked."

In mid-June, Dean had a small part in *The Scarecrow,* one of four plays in a landmark repertory series at the Theater de Lys. Much of the action concerns a magic mirror that reflected the true nature of a man's soul. A lady blacksmith (Patricia Neal) schemes with the devil (Eli Wallach) to torment a judge who jilted her. They create a man out of a scarecrow (Douglas Watson), who falls in love with the judge's niece (Anne Jackson). At the end, the scarecrow sees himself in the mirror and knows that all men are scarecrows, to whom love alone gives a soul.

Directed by Frank Corsaro, *The Scarecrow* was put together and rehearsed in only one week. Dean had a brief and unbilled role as the scarecrow's mirror image. "At first, I felt he was not old enough, not experienced enough," says Corsaro. "But then I started thinking, maybe he could. After all, there were a lot of Studio people in it. He helped out in a sense, reflecting the inner aspects of man."

Terese Hayden, the producer, remembers, "Jimmy was beautiful as Doug's mirror image. Such physical grace! To me, his walk-on part made a difference. There was something distinguished about what he did. He caught the flavor of that potential passion, that Doug Watson did not, in whatever he did in that mirror."

Despite his minuscule role, Dean made important and even crucial connections during the short run of *The Scarecrow.* Hayden; David J. Stewart, who acted in another play in the series; and Vivian Matalon, a production assistant; would all come together with Dean later that year in *The Immoralist.* Stewart, in fact, would be responsible for getting Dean cast in it.

However, good training and connections could not fill an empty stomach. At the end of the play's weeklong run, Dean wrote Barbara Glenn, lamenting the dearth of television work, thanking her for sending him a check, and apologizing for the inconvenience it caused her.

He also alluded to doing a reading with New Dramatists, the playwrights' workshop. This was Jonathan Bates's play *The Fell Swoop,* which was read on June 23 at the Palm Gardens (the New Dramatists' usual venue) on West Fifty-second Street. Jonathan Gilmore remembers that Dean also did a workshop reading that same summer of a play based on Kafka's *Metamorphosis.*

The Scarecrow was slated to resume for two weeks in early July, and Corsaro had told Dean he would replace Watson as the scarecrow. But Watson stayed with the show, and Dean decided not to continue on as the mirror image. Corsaro also envisioned directing August Strindberg's *Ghost Sonata* at the Actors Studio later in the summer. "Jimmy would have been perfect for Arkenholz [the student with second sight]," he said. "But we didn't do it. Then I had an argument with Jimmy about Bates's apartment, and so we didn't see each other for awhile."

Jonathan Gilmore says Dean was "very stingy and tight about money. Once we were in an army- and navy-surplus store on Forty-second Street, and he bought a pair of army fatigue pants with pockets on the side lower legs, no back pockets, like Brando wore in *The Men.* Jimmy moaned and groaned and dickered around to squeeze the price down from the marked-down sale price. He always made sure someone else was going to pay for the coffee or whatever. And usually someone always did, so he got to expect it."

Although Gilmore and Dean confided in each other a great deal, Gilmore kept silent about his discussions with playwright John Van Druten about a possible part in a new play. "I knew that if I told Jimmy," relates Gilmore, "he'd make inroads to Van Druten and go to bed with him in order to get the part, and I was up for it without yet having had to go to bed with Van Druten and was hoping to keep it that way."

Employment finally materialized in mid-July when Dean bagged a juvenile delinquent role in a new NBC series, *Campbell Soundstage.* Joe Adams (Dean), just out of jail, sincerely wants to go straight, but two obstacles stand between him and that goal. First, he wants to be seen carrying what he thinks is a badge of respectability: a briefcase. (The catch is, he must pull off one final robbery to afford one.) Second, the ringleader of Joe's petty crime syndicate expects him to come back to work and is prepared to use violence to enforce his wishes.

Joe tries to rob Noli (Susan Douglas), a pretty ballet student, but he's a soft touch and melts before her pleas for mercy. She gets him interested in the Bible, he wins the money for his briefcase in a pool game, and all looks well until Joe's old boss leans on him to help with an imminent heist. Joe warns that an anonymous girlfriend will give the boss's identity to the police if Joe is killed; it is a bluff, but the boss falls for it. Joe and Noli reunite and celebrate their future by quoting Holy Writ. (Dean reads the Bible here with far more alacrity than he later would in *East of Eden,* where his irreverence provokes a paternal rebuke.)

Donald Medford, who directed Dean, remembers his being "absolutely brilliant" in an early rehearsal. "So I sent the rest of the cast home," Medford says, "and kept him behind. I told him, 'I want you to think of what stimulated that performance.' This was how we worked together. For him, every moment in a show was a first. He didn't retain anything from one rehearsal to the next. I tried to improve his retention."

For the first time, Dean was mentioned by name in a television review; unfortunately, it was one of his few purely negative notices. *Variety* said the script of "Something for an Empty Briefcase" was "out of the Dead End Kids school of literature," and called the casting of Dean "confusing" because his interpretation did not evoke a habitual petty gang member. "His mugging and repetitive hand gesturing were on the ludicrous side, if their intent was to show the sensitivity and groping of the suddenly awakened thief," sighed the reviewer, whose opinion of Dean differed drastically from Medford's. Still, Dean had reached a watershed of sorts: his roles were now big enough to ensure that his subsequent career would be well-documented.

Soon after "Briefcase," Dean took his first vacation of the year: another yacht trip with Lemuel and Shirley Ayers. He wrote to Glenn that he'd had his "annual" yacht racing thrill but, rather than identify his hosts, dubbed them the "New York Yacht Club." He claimed that the entire party had to lash themselves to the helm during a severe storm and that he got seasick.

In his next job, "Sentence of Death" *(Studio One Summer Theater),* he worked with a pretty young Indiana native, Betsy Palmer. "I had just come back from summer stock and was saying hello to people at CBS," said Palmer. "I didn't have any jobs lined up. Somebody asked, 'What are you doing?' They told me to hurry downstairs and read for *Studio One,* because someone had just dropped out of the lead. I got the part."

The part was Ellen, a mink-wrapped dilettante who saunters whimsically into a mom-and-pop drugstore and orders a turkey sandwich just in time to witness a man shoot and kill the proprietor. At a police lineup, the hysterical widow and two other witnesses identify Joe Palica (Dean) as the killer. Ellen tells the police that she is skeptical, but eventually Palica is tried, convicted, and sentenced to the electric chair. Then one evening Ellen recognizes the real killer in a bar; he turns out to be the widow's boyfriend and Palica is saved.

In a scene on death row, an officer offers Palica a cigarette, which he refuses. The line, "I never did pick up the habit," carries great irony coming from chain-smoking Dean. Martin Landau reports that Dean wanted to vomit on camera in this scene. Both that idea and the alternative of dry retching were vetoed by the producers. "I never did figure out if he was putting them on or not," said Landau.

Wendy Sanford, a member of the CBS production staff who worked with Dean on *Studio One,* had a simple explanation for Dean's look of great concentration and emotion: "he was nearsighted." She also had "the weirdest feeling something was going to happen to him" because "he was driven."

One week later, Palmer and Dean were teamed again in one of his best-known performances, "Death Is My Neighbor," a *Danger* episode. The eminent Walter Hampden was cast as Clemens, an elderly building superintendent. Dean played JB, an itinerant boy who cleans apartments in exchange for permission to sleep next to the furnace. Palmer's role was Netta, a photographer's model who rents a room in the building and decorates it with samples of her work. From this, JB surmises that Netta is loose, and plots to rape and murder her and then frame Clemens. But the police intervene and thwart JB's aims.

John Peyser, the show's director, says Dean's friend Eleanor Kilgallen recommended him for the part. "Though his publicity had made him out to be incorrigible, I had yet to meet an actor I couldn't handle, so we decided to take him on," remembers Peyser. "He turned out to be no tougher than, say, Rod Steiger.

"On the first day of rehearsal, up in the halls above Grand Central

Station, Walter Hampden arrived before any of the other members of the cast. He asked me to rehearse the company very hard, as he knew that age had crept up on him and made retention of lines and action quite difficult. When Dean arrived, I took him aside and told him the problem and asked him to help out.

"We started the first reading and Jimmy was, to say the least, discourteous. In fact, he was downright rude, mumbling his lines, not coming in on cue, and doing everything possible to be difficult. We finally reached an emotional scene between Jimmy and Mr. Hampden. They read through it, and when they had finished I asked them to read it again, this time letting me see some of the passion in the scene. When it came to Mr. Hampden's big speech, he really turned it on. His voice broke, tears came to his eyes and coursed down his cheeks. When he came to the end, he turned to me and calmly asked me if that was what I wanted. I said, 'Lovely reading.' Jimmy's eyes were wide open, his mouth agape.

"From that moment on, Mr. Hampden could not open a door, get a chair, need a pencil, but that Jimmy was right at his side. When Mr. Hampden wanted to go over a scene, there was Jimmy, ready to do his every bidding.

"The show went very well. We televised it live in a CBS Theater on Third Avenue around Seventy-eighth Street. When the performance was over, Mr. Hampden invited Betsy and Jimmy to share a bird and a bottle with him at the Friars' Club. Jimmy had come to work in a pair of jeans and a T-shirt. He was living at that time in a cold-water flat several blocks away. Somehow he left the theater, got to his digs, and was back in Mr. Hampden's dressing room, wearing a suit, shirt, tie, and shined shoes, before the old actor had finished changing back into mufti."

The *Variety* review couldn't say enough good about Dean; it's as if it were compensating for the earlier negative comments on "Briefcase." Dean, it proclaimed, outshined two "top stars," Hampden and Sir Cedric Hardwicke (who had appeared in the show right before *Danger*). His performance was called "magnetic" and deemed responsible for enlivening the show. "He's got quite a future ahead of him," the review concluded.

The immediate upshot was that Dean could now afford an apartment, so he settled on a tiny fourth-floor walk-up on West Sixty-eighth Street. He had already left Bates's apartment and had been imposing on various friends. "Jimmy knew an artist named Donato Manfredi," recalls Gilmore, "a painter and photographer who lived at Thirty-third and Third Avenue. The three of us drank beer at the San Remo. Don took artistic nude photographs of me, and he said he took some of Jimmy in '52, but I never saw them."

Betsy Palmer says, "I gave Jimmy blankets, pillows, and sheets for his first apartment on Sixty-eighth Street. I was living on about West Sixty-sixth, but I never got to see his place. I never met any of his friends." Palmer said Jane Deacy kept him on a strict allowance. "We didn't have the money to hang out at Sardi's. We mainly stayed at my place. I would cook dinner. Maybe we would get a cheap ticket to see a play. We shared record albums. He gave me Albert Roussel's *The Spider's Feast,* a ballet-pantomine.

"Both being from Indiana drew us together. We were good friends, and actually—briefly—lovers. Friendship was more important than the sexual part. Nurturing was really the thing about our relationship. He was a lost lamb. I never felt he would live to be old. Something hovered around and shrouded him, an air of 'I've got to get this done quick.' He was a skyrocket, a comet."

Dean followed up his memorable *Danger* performance with a role in NBC's *The Big Story,* a weekly dramatization of crimes solved by reporters. His episode was set in Joplin, Missouri, where the *Globe and News*'s Rex Newman had helped authorities uncover a trail of robbery and murder by a trio of teenagers. There was a large cast, including John Kerr. "Jimmy and I played brothers," says Kerr. "One was sent to prison—that was me—and he was plotting to break me out."

From this point until he began rehearsals for his second Broadway play, *The Immoralist,* Dean's television roles would be distinguished and lucrative. On October 4, he appeared in William Inge's one-act television play, "Glory in Flower" (*Omnibus,* CBS). Jessica Tandy and Hume Cronyn were the stars; Dean played Bronco Evans, a volatile teenager who jitterbugs with other kids at a small-town bar with a jukebox. He insists on partnering Tandy in some "atomic age" gyrations, only to send her sprawling on the dance floor. Later, when he mouths off at the bartender (played by Cronyn), who has reprimanded him for underage drinking and smoking marijuana, he lands on the floor himself when a self-righteous bully knocks him down.

Ten days later Dean played Jim, a student at the center of a college cheating scandal, in "Keep Our Honor Bright" (*Kraft Television Theater*, NBC). Forced to recount how he obtained an advance copy of an exam, Dean cowers before the honor committee in a tortured, invertebrate slouch. The committee dangles the possibility of a lighter penalty in exchange for his naming the students with whom he shared the bootleg exam.

Dean is effective in a scene where, after a suicide attempt, Jim is visited in the hospital by Sally (Joan Potter), another cheater whose name he revealed. When she enters his room, he keeps his head turned, out of shame. She draws him out by placing a toy spider on his chest and making it jump with an air pump. He giggles with the same childlike delight he would later show with a toy monkey in *Rebel Without a Cause*. But he sobs over the irony in being most ashamed of his one act, naming names, for which the committee lauded him.

Actor Bradford Dillman made his television debut in "Keep Our Honor Bright." At that time, he says, he saw Dean two or three times a week in various casting offices (and they had been in *The Scarecrow* together). "We competed for the role of the Sensitive Young Man, a role Dean won more often than not. Yet, for all our encounters and conversations, I can't say I knew him at all. Our personalities were dissimilar.

"Jimmy was not at all gregarious or forthcoming. You could never describe him as friendly, nor indeed as particularly likable. His offstage persona was very much what survives on the screen. He did have an impish sense of humor and enjoyed shocking people. I recall a party where he sat alone on a couch, sulking that others seemed to be having such a good time. Eventually he intruded himself in a circle and fired off some irrelevant, scatological observations, delighted that it dispersed ladies to the far corner of the room.

"Even then I was tremendously impressed by, and envious of, his singular talent. And he had his priorities in order. My one vivid memory of Jimmy is a late afternoon at that actors' oasis, the coffee shop [Cromwell's] of the RCA Building, where hopefuls mingled, unwound, and shared casting rumors. I slumped onto a stool next to him and, unsolicited, launched into a bitter recitation of my rejections of the day.

Abruptly he turned on me. 'Who asked you?' 'What?' I said with surprise. 'I said, who asked you?' he repeated. 'You think I give a shit you want to be an actor? You think that guy over there, or that woman in the booth, cares about you being an actor? Oh, maybe your mother does, I don't know, but get this straight: Absolutely nobody in the world gives a flying fuck. You want to be an actor? Fine. But never, ever bitch about it.' Advice I've heeded to this day."

Dillman is not the only person to remember Dean, *Kraft Television Theater,* and Cromwell's. Patty Magda, a teenage girl from the Bronx, had noticed and appreciated Dean on television and, with a group of like-minded friends, began following his career. Whenever her group learned he would be appearing on *Kraft,* she said, they would head for NBC a few hours before air time. They knew they could find Dean in Cromwell's and were bold enough to strike up a conversation with him. Carried away with teenage rapture, the girls bestowed every superlative they could think of on him. Magda's fondest memory is of Dean's treating her to a sundae at Cromwell's on her fourteenth birthday. She cajoled the waitress into giving her the check after he left. Magda would later become president of a New York area Dean fan club.

An even more interesting reaction to Dean on *Kraft* came from a student at Manhattan's High School of Performing Arts, Arlene Sachs. She was so captivated that she mustered her courage and phoned him, using the proverbial line, "You don't know me, but . . ." They arranged to meet at the Museum of Modern Art.

Sachs, who was then seventeen, told Dean biographer Joe Hyams that Dean became her first lover. Their relationship was conducted principally at night, and consisted of walks in Central Park, sessions of listening to classical music, reading literature and poetry out loud, or, when being together wasn't possible, talking on the phone until six A.M. Sachs said she soon came to realize that Dean was involved with men as well as with other women and would never be exclusively hers.

Two days after his impersonation of a college cheater, Dean returned to the *Campbell Soundstage* in "Life Sentence," the story of Jean (Georgann Johnson), an unfaithful wife who lives near a prison. He played Hank Bradon, a convict who works in the prison garden and often detects Jean staring provocatively at him from her porch. One day he slips away to confront her, inviting her to go away with him after his imminent release. Dean's portrayal of an emotionally unsound thug who fantasizes about what Jean looks like in a bathing suit is excellent.

Jean's husband infuriates her when he admits he moved them to the prison town not because of a promotion but to keep her away from other men. She shoots and kills him, then concocts an alibi which the police believe—temporarily. Bradon, newly released, returns and urges her to run off with him, but the police arrive to arrest her and tell Bradon to get out of town.

Before *The Immoralist* interrupted his newly dynamic television career, Dean brought off three challenging roles within twelve days in November. The first, *Kraft Television Theater*'s "A Long Time Till Dawn," was also his first leading role. He played, yet again, an ex-convict, Joe Harris, who embodied many contradictions: both a poet and a gangster, smart but having the logic of a child. Freshly out of jail in New York and furious to discover his wife missing, he kills an elderly neighbor who advised the wife to leave him.

As the police close in on him, Harris snaps and reverts to childhood. It was one of Dean's most challenging tasks in television, and he never became entirely comfortable with it. There were seven grueling days of rehearsal and Dick Dunlap, the director, despaired of getting through to him. Then Dunlap happened to introduce Dean to his father, an Iowa farmer visiting New York, and the two avidly discussed the care and feeding of hogs. Once Dean realized he and Dunlap were both farm boys, he became fully compliant.

Dean's difficulty with the role was evident thirty-five years later, when a clip of the performance was featured in *Hello Actors Studio,* a documentary about Method acting. To a *New York Times* reviewer, Dean's "jittery performance" demonstrated "how annoying the mannerisms of the Method can be."

Both the second and third movements in Dean's November sonata were directed by his friend and promoter James Sheldon. "The Bells of Cockaigne" (*Armstrong Circle Theatre,* NBC) presented Dean as Joey Frazier, an underpaid stevedore with the financial burden of an asthmatic son's medications. Gene Lockhart portrayed an old Irish janitor who dreams of winning the lottery and returning to his native land. On payday, as the janitor discovers he has the winning serial number on his dollar bill, Frazier gambles with his fellow workers and loses all his wages. The saintly janitor gives Frazier the winning bill, forfeiting his pilgrimage but saving the day for Frazier's ailing son.

Lockhart, who had already worked with Dean in *Hill Number One,* was not nearly so charitable off-camera. James Sheldon remembers, "Lockhart was very professional and a very nice man. He complained to me about Jimmy, who was late for dress rehearsal and holding everyone up. I said, 'I'll handle it. Don't worry.' I found Jimmy downstairs in the drugstore drinking coffee. He was unaware of the trouble. It wasn't malicious; he was so wrapped up in himself that he wasn't thinking of other people. Without mentioning Lockhart specifically, I said to him, 'People are getting to dislike you. You're late, and you know how much it costs to wait with the orchestra. You're being hostile.'

"Completely oblivious, Jimmy retorted, 'Gene Lockhart loves working with me!' He was very apologetic about his tardiness but was in another world; he didn't realize the time. I don't remember the excuse he had, but he had certainly changed from the earlier days."

Dean played the first half of "Cockaigne" shirtless, and his torso appeared more taut and defined than in *Rebel Without a Cause* a year-and-a-half later. John Kerr recalls Dean's comment that NBC made actors look "longer and skinnier" while CBS made them look "shorter and squarer." "Whenever he was on NBC," said Kerr, "his family would invariably express concern that he wasn't eating enough."

"Harvest," a Thanksgiving special, was Dean's single appearance on NBC's *Robert Montgomery Presents.* For director Sheldon, it was a personal turning point, "my first important dramatic show. I remember asking for Jimmy and discussing it with Jane [Deacy]. Except for the star parts in those days, the director cast the show, within the confines of money. Frances Head, an English casting agent, would do the bargaining and try to get them for less. I just said, 'This is who I want.' The producer would take charge, but Mr. Montgomery didn't have much to do with it; he was a figurehead, except he might come to a run-through. I also got Reba Tassell on the show; she made me a belt because she was so pleased to be on. She worked with Jimmy very well; they had love scenes.

"Jimmy was introspective and into his little thing, although 'star' isn't the right word. He had his own world, and he didn't connect with other people. But on 'Harvest,' everybody liked him. I would've heard to the contrary."

Dean's character was Paul Zelenka, the youngest son of a farm couple (Dorothy Gish and Ed Begley); he loves Arlene (Tassell), the daughter of well-heeled city parents. Paul courts Arlene at her parents' country place but ultimately loses out to a more sophisticated fellow. His dejection impels him to join the navy, but in a happy ending, he is granted leave to join his family on Thanksgiving.

Donald Medford said the secret to working with Dean was discipline. "After he made *East of Eden,* I ran into him in New York," relates Medford. "We had coffee together. He told me that Elia Kazan and I were the only two directors who gave him a sense of what he was doing and a sense of craft.

"He was not difficult to work with, but he could be frustrating. I would just stage him and let him go. Most live shows had three cameras; however, I always had a fourth camera on Jimmy and followed him wherever he went. It was worth it."

From Bachir to Cal

The June 8, 1953, issue of *Show Business* predicted that producer Billy Rose would have a tough task getting just the right actors for *The Immoralist,* a stage adaptation of André Gide's 1902 novel of a young French couple honeymooning in Algeria and trying to come to grips with the husband's homosexuality. Acknowledging that the husband role would be "delicate," the piece also said, "Finding the three African boys who are very handsome, slightly effeminate but very athletic will not be easy."

Both the director, Herman Shumlin, and the female lead, Geraldine Page, were set months in advance of rehearsals. "It's an actress's dream," Page exclaimed of her role as Marcelline. "I get drunk, go mad, and die!"[1] Unfortunately, there was no such enthusiasm among the early choices for the male lead; Marlon Brando, Montgomery Clift, Richard Burton, and Tyrone Power all declined. Not until mid-October did Shumlin, Rose, and playwrights Ruth and Augustus Goetz approve Louis Jourdan for the role, and by then the production had been pushed back two months.

The "three African boys" were actually Arabs, two shepherds,

---

1. An early draft of the script may have had Marcelline dying in the end, but in the published version of *The Immoralist* she lives on.

Moktir and Dolit, and the servant, Bachir, later described as a "color-fully insinuating scapegrace" and "completely corrupt he-slut with a hundred itchibay [polite critics in those days couldn't say "bitchy"] tricks." When the *Show Business* item appeared, James Dean was rehearsing with the *Scarecrow* company and surviving on money borrowed from friends. Although the connections he made in *The Scarecrow* led to his important role as Bachir, it would not happen until November.

The labor involved in presenting *The Scarecrow* and the other three plays in the Theater de Lys series had exhausted producer Terese Hayden, so she went to work for Herman Shumlin as an aide-de-camp. "Shumlin was out of touch with the new currents in New York theater," Hayden explains. "He knew that I had created the *Players Guide* and that I had been with the Actors Studio since its inception, so I was in a position to know the best young talent in town. On this matter, he trusted me almost one hundred percent."

For the part of Moktir, the philosopher-shepherd who interprets the homosexual life to Michel, the husband, Hayden recruited David J. Stewart, a Theater de Lys series alumnus. Stewart was a decorated World War II paratrooper and "a very savvy theater man," according to Hayden. Knowing that the role of Bachir was still unfilled, Stewart suggested James Dean.

"I knew who Jimmy was from *The Scarecrow*, and I had seen him in *See the Jaguar* and at the Actors Studio," Hayden continues. "I said uh-uh to David because I felt Jimmy, though tremendously talented, was a tricky and tough little cookie. But David convinced me not to be put off by Jimmy's behavior and encouraged me to fight to get him in the show."

Hayden summoned Dean to read for the director. "So, Jimmy comes up to Shumlin's office looking like a junior Marlon," she recalls, "and Shumlin tells me, 'Get him out of here!' Shumlin was genteel, and he was put off by Jimmy's slovenly mode of dress. But I told him, 'That's the boy, believe me.' David had reassured me that Jimmy could handle the part, and then I passed the same reassurance on to Shumlin."

The director's own casting methods were unusual. Phillip Pine, who eventually replaced Dean as Bachir, recalls how he missed out on being in the original cast. "I went in to see Shumlin and was prepared to read for Bachir and Moktir. Shumlin just stared at me interminably—it was a matter of five minutes! Finally, he said, 'No, too old for Bachir, too young for Moktir.' He'd been waiting for vibes!"

Dean still had to read for the Goetzes, and he asked Studio member Arthur Storch to help him prepare. "He was nervous about it," recalls Storch. "We went to Central Park, sat at the edge of the Pond, and I read lines with him for a couple of hours." The advance preparation paid off: Ruth Goetz said Dean was "perfectly seductive" when he read, which is precisely what they wanted.

Once Dean had the part sewn up (and once he was finished with his work on *Robert Montgomery Presents*), he set out on his motorcycle (a Royal Enfield) for Indiana, arriving in Fairmount just in time for Thanksgiving. The prospective journey of several hundred miles through snow, ice, and freezing temperatures alarmed Barbara Glenn, and she had pleaded with him not to do it. But he would not be deterred.

While on the farm he studied T. E. Lawrence's *Seven Pillars of Wisdom,* which he believed would give him an insight into Muslim culture. He also drove into Marion to see radio announcer and sportscaster Bill Fowler, whom he had known from his days on the high school basketball team. Ushered into Fowler's office, Dean slouched down in his chair and giggled. He announced his upcoming part in *The Immoralist* and asked, "Do you want to interview me?" Years later Fowler recalled making several ten-minute tapes of their conversations. "I sure wish I knew what happened to those tapes," Fowler laments.

Dean's return trip distressed his Aunt Ortense Winslow, who insisted that he wear a ski mask and heavy gloves. Near Harrisburg, Pennsylvania, a fuel bearing gave out on his motorcycle, fulfilling his loved ones' worst expectations and stranding him for four days. Initially it was simply a matter of waiting while a new fuel bearing was on order, but the repair shop happened also to be an Indian motorcycle franchise. When he spotted a maroon Indian 500 with gold stripes in the showroom, its allure exceeded his resistance, and he negotiated a trade-in of the disabled motorcycle. He had to stay in a boardinghouse while waiting for the Royal Enfield's papers to be sent from Fairmount and for Jane Deacy to send the money from New York. An employee at the repair shop remembers that Dean used two payroll checks from *Kraft*

Television Theater and *Robert Montgomery Presents.*

In New York, Dean found his composer friend David Diamond back from Italy for a few weeks. "There was a bar called Tony's where Alec Wilder and I would gather, often with Jimmy, just before *The Immoralist,*" Diamond relates. "I had known André Gide—my *Psalm for Orchestra* is dedicated to him—and Jimmy was anxious to know all about him. Jimmy was reading a copy of another Gide novel, *The Counterfeiters,* and I brought him my copy of the French to show him how much finer it was than the English translation."

"Jimmy did say that playing Bachir was a tough assignment," Diamond continues. "He said he would not ape David Stewart's voice in the show; that two hissing Arab ephebes were one sound track too many." Although Stewart's close friends say he did not lisp, Diamond says Dean privately mimicked him as if he did. (As with his mocking of James DeWeerd, Dean was not above making fun of benefactors behind their backs. It was a prime example of the perverseness Jonathan Gilmore described.)

"I remember telling Jimmy to go easy on darkening the skin, that there were lighter-skinned Arabs," says Diamond, "and to be seductively enticing without resorting to Western homosexual affectations. And he said, 'I can do it all with my eyes,' to which I retorted, 'But don't roll them'—upon which he slid from his chair and onto the floor giggling like a little kid. He was like a beautiful child, and I remember as I looked down at him from behind the chair, his lips looked even more sensual and tempting upside down than in normal glance. He was a very beautiful young man."

Dean's understudy would be Bill Gunn, a young black actor who was also cast as a nonspeaking Arab boy. Just after getting the part, Gunn was in Cromwell's and spotted Dean, whom he recognized from television. He introduced himself and said, "I'm your understudy!" Dean immediately asked what, if anything, he knew about Arabs. They spent the evening listening to Arab music and drinking wine in Dean's apartment.

When Dean asked Martin Landau for advice on how to sound Arab, Landau made the misguided suggestion that he hang out at a rug store. Dean did just that, talking to everyone entering and leaving. He discerned an accent, practiced it, and passed it on to Gunn. But Shumlin told them it sounded Spanish, so they worked on perfecting a rhythm of speech rather than an accent.

The script called for Bachir to perform a dance with scissors to prey upon Michel's weakening resistance to male flesh. Bill Gunn claimed that he was assigned, based on previous dancing experience, to work with Dean on coming up with the movements. David Diamond recalls, "Once Jimmy and I were in a cafeteria, when suddenly he got up—we were at a table and all to ourselves—and started doing dance movements as Bachir. It was spontaneous. He pinned his gunnysack [the burnoose, or hooded Arab cloak, that he would wear in the play] around his neck and began doing motions with his fingers, like Gide's young Arab friend Athman. Athman and other Arab boys would do those motions to entice the westerners to follow them into the whore districts."

The dance that Dean came up with left quite an impression on one critic, who wrote the following season, "I have not seen such interesting sexual gyrations since James Dean, the Arab boy in *The Immoralist,* attempted to work his wiles on Louis Jourdan." But the ensuing years have eroded the memories of those who saw Dean play Bachir, and no one can say what made the dance so striking. But when Phillip Pine replaced Dean in the role, he was advised by director Daniel Mann "to give the impression in the dance that you're gradually sitting on Michel's cock." There was no physical contact, but whatever he did seemed effective, said Pine—who is heterosexual—because often "there would be a man waiting for me with flowers at the stage door afterwards!"

Rehearsals began on December 18 at the Ziegfeld Theater. Although Hayden had put up a small Christmas tree backstage, there was little to be joyful about, because the cast, playwrights, and producer were all having difficulty adjusting to Herman Shumlin. Vivian Matalon, cast as Dolit, says Shumlin made him feel like a whipping boy. "He would summon me by beckoning with his finger—he never called me by my first name. In fact, he insisted that I be listed in the program as V. Matalon instead of Vivian. He said he didn't want people pointing a finger and saying, 'It's *that* kind of play, and it's got *that* kind of an actor in it!' I was in torture every day, always thinking, 'What's he going to do to me next?' David Stewart and I were very close friends, yet I was so humiliated during those early rehearsals that I barely spoke to David."

Neither did Dean and Shumlin get along in the beginning. "In those days," Hayden explains, "Actors Equity had the five-day clause, under which you could fire an actor within five days of the first rehearsal and not have to pay them anything. Shumlin wanted to fire Jimmy under the clause, and Lucia Victor, the stage manager, supported him.

"Finally I took Shumlin aside and said, 'Do me a favor. Say to Jimmy, "Do what you want to in today's rehearsal," and then don't say a bloody thing!' And then Jimmy did the most exquisite rehearsal! Very seldom do you have an actor who is an organic being, but Jimmy was. Shumlin fell in love with Jimmy when he saw how stunning Jimmy was. He was simply enraptured by the talent and the gift of the boy. He not only didn't fire Jimmy, he adored him, and Jimmy responded with affection and respect. Once you caught Jimmy's attention and let him see that what he was doing was appreciated, he was malleable."

Now that Dean had made an ally of Shumlin, he would walk up to him, rest his hands and head on Shumlin's shoulder, and agonize until the proper motivation for a particular line gelled in his mind. Vivian Matalon reports, "Shumlin would say, 'That boy was wonderful!' Clearly, that was what Jimmy most wanted. He was a seducer par excellence. The way he dealt with people was on a seductive level. Male, female, child, or animal, it made no difference. It showed in the way he spoke to people, giving his apparent undivided attention when listening to them."

On December 31, Adeline Brookshire, who was in the city for a speech teachers' convention, came as Dean's guest to watch a rehearsal. He brought her into the Ziegfeld via the stage door and introduced her to Shumlin. The director noticed a cigarette butt on the floor of the stage and picked it up. "How was this young man when you taught him?" Shumlin asked. "Did he throw cigarette butts around?"

In the afternoon, Ruth Goetz approached Brookshire to ask what kind of student Dean had been. Goetz told Brookshire she thought Dean had "the soul of an artist." In the first days of rehearsals, Goetz said, "I thought he was the most undisciplined boy I had ever seen. He seemed to be absolutely uncontrolled. But as I watched him develop in his role, I realized that this young man is one of the most disciplined actors I have ever seen."

Ruth and Augustus Goetz were increasingly disillusioned with Herman Shumlin. They had written the play specifically to bring the subject of homosexuality into the open (although the word was never in the script) and to show compassion for homosexuals who had married and then reaped the whirlwind. "We were confused and disoriented by Herman's attempts to bowdlerize the play and negate the drive of the novel," said Ruth Goetz. "He decided to sentimentalize Marcelline's situation so that Michel seemed the villain. He insisted audiences couldn't relate to a homosexual husband. We concluded that Herman couldn't."

Out-of-town tryouts were set for Philadelphia's Forrest Theater. On January 3, 1954, a large ad in the *Philadelphia Inquirer* featured a lengthy message from producer Billy Rose about the glory of the play and production: "As for the director—and I write this after watching a run-through—if I had my choice of anyone in the whole fool world for this particular play, I'd still pick Herman Shumlin." Rarely in theatrical history has there been a case of more unfortunate timing. On the very day the embarrassing ad appeared, Rose fired Shumlin. The Goetzes had summoned Rose to a rehearsal to observe what they felt was the disintegration of their play, and he agreed with them.

Among those who did not agree with the decision to fire Shumlin were Terese Hayden and James Dean. "When Billy Rose gathered everyone to announce that Shumlin was fired," says Vivian Matalon, "Terry hit him with her baseball cap and said, 'I'm sorry Mr. Rose, but I think you're a son of a bitch.' She resigned on the spot." Hayden later called the incident "an act of passion." She also said Dean thought Shumlin's firing was "a crock."

With the cast set to leave for Philadelphia in less than a week, a new director had to be found at once. A month earlier, Daniel Mann, a veteran stage and screen director, had wrapped up the movie *About Mrs. Leslie* in Hollywood and then headed for Manhattan for what he thought would be a one-month vacation. Instead, Billy Rose persuaded him to take over *The Immoralist*. While this may have been good for the show—the Goetzes never complained about Mann—it was a tragic move for Dean because it triggered the psychological nadir of his career.

After Shumlin's nurturing, Dean felt he got not a whit of understanding from Mann. He also blamed Mann, rightfully or not, for a gradual diminution in the importance of his role.[2]

While Shumlin had no connection to the Actors Studio, Mann, ironically, had taught there in its early days and ought not to have been fazed by qualities Dean shared with other Method actors. However, Mann once had a major argument with Lee Strasberg, whom he called the Jewish pope. He said Strasberg's school was peopled by actors who could peel an imaginary orange and feel the juice running out but couldn't walk up to another actor and say hello. Whatever their source, the problems between Mann and Dean were "personal rather than professional, and obvious and public," as one cast member told Robert Tysl.

Opinions on Mann's talents were mixed. Phillip Pine thought Mann was "totally dedicated to acting." Mann's wife, Sheri, says, "Danny loved actors. He knew how to open up a creative space in their head." On the other hand, actor Jack Larson remembers Mann as distant. "Mann had convinced me to accept my part in *About Mrs. Leslie* by saying, 'Trust me,'" Larson says. "But then I had a serious mental block about the part, and he never helped me." Dean's problems with Mann may have been similar to Larson's, though far more severe.

The enmity, unfortunately, was mutual, and it developed quickly. When Phillip Pine and his wife and daughter traveled to Philadelphia to see the show, Mann asked to see him afterward. Mann complained to Pine that Dean was "like a fox fucking a football—he's all around it but can't get in." Mann was disturbed that Dean never did a scene the same way twice. Geraldine Page, Mann felt, was the same way, "but you can rely on her."

Mann offered Pine the role of Bachir on the spot. To accept, he would need a release from his job as male lead in a soap opera, which he could not get. His daughter Macyle had not forgotten being charmed by Dean during the Philadelphia run of *See the Jaguar,* and when her father told her Mann wanted him to take the part, she protested, "You can't do that! It's Jimmy's part!"

---

2. Daniel Mann had been Lemuel Ayers's first choice to direct *See the Jaguar.* Fortunately for Dean, Mann was not available for that job.

Another problem was Dean's distaste for Louis Jourdan, whom he considered wooden. Jourdan was not completely comfortable with English and had to translate the lines into French to learn them emotionally, a burden Dean may not have appreciated. According to Sheri Mann, during a rehearsal in Philadelphia, Dean brought a scene with Jourdan to a halt by taking some imaginary object out of his pocket, licking it, and holding it up to the light. "Danny said, 'You can't do this. We're in a play!' He jumped across the footlights and chased Jimmy out of the theater and down Walnut Street, yelling, 'You son of a bitch! If I catch you I'm gonna kill you!'"

Years later, Mann said, "You know, he was a very sick young man. He was outlandish and sadistic. You're talking to a man who painfully suffered the impact of this type of behavior."

Dean's loss of confidence and interest in *The Immoralist* was immediate once Mann took over. Feeling a keen lack of moral support in Philadelphia, he wrote to Barbara Glenn, begging her to come visit him. He complained that rehearsals were confusing and that he had no sense of how the play would be received. "Looks like a piece of shit to me," he groused. "Hate this fucking brown makeup."

Valiant attempts were made to Arabize Dean, with varying results. "Getting the right makeup job was a cinch," said Bill Gunn. "Keeping his hair black was another story. He tried the do-it-yourself tints and rinses, but they wouldn't take. Finally he had it done by an expert beautician, and arrived at the theater a bona fide brunet—with an itchy scalp." So Dean washed his hair to relieve the itching, and "within two minutes he was a blond again," Gunn continued. "Fortunately the shoeshine boy near the theater was well-supplied with black polish that night."

"He was supposed to be an Arab boy," recalled Geraldine Page, "and he looked less like an Arab boy than anybody you could imagine, with that face and blond hair. But the way he behaved gave such an image—it had nothing to do with the way he looked on the surface."

The public's response in Philadelphia was gratifying. On opening night there was a record-setting blizzard, but by and large it didn't keep ticket buyers away. A review the following morning said Dean was "colorful as a thieving, blackmailing Arab boy." Later that day, Dean quoted that same phrase in a letter to Glenn—but, says Glenn, he was not pleased; the review only reinforced his enmity toward the show. He told her he had approached his role as a tragedian but was disgusted to have been turned into the comic relief. Never before, he grumbled, had he worked with such a boring show and cast. Once again he pleaded with her to come down on the train, even guaranteeing to pay her way.

The second week was sold out. The Goetzes listened carefully to the audience's reactions and struggled to improve the play accordingly. Geraldine Page remembered "thirty-two different third acts in thirty-two consecutive days" and credited Dean with helping her cope with the changes in her character. "I'd show him the new rewrites," Page said, "and he would come up with some idea that would be so intriguing to my imagination that I couldn't wait to get on the stage and try it.

"For instance, they decided to change the scene when we come in from the desert. It's about how hot and dusty it's been. And he was walking around thinking about it and saying, 'Now, what do you do when you're hot? Try to get cool! You take a cool cloth and put it here on the insides of your wrists, the insides of your elbows, and you put it behind your neck.' Well, with that little bit of business to incorporate into it, the whole scene took on a kind of shape, and then all the dramatic values and all the content, the words, gathered around this simple little thing."

Page and Dean had never met until rehearsals began, but they became "good friends right away." She, Dean, and Matalon often ate together in Philadelphia and she called them "the three musketeers." What struck her about Dean was his "tremendous intensity and curiosity about people—always fascinated by everything around him. Most people would be frightened by this kind of intensity. He made people look at themselves and not like what they saw. Unless you kind of welcomed that look at yourself, because it gave you a chance to reassess yourself, Jimmy was a very uncomfortable person to be around."

Dean's UCLA friend Rod Bladel attended *The Immoralist* in Philadelphia and went backstage to see him. Dean brimmed with sarcasm about the play and Daniel Mann. "Jimmy called Mann an anal-ist," reports Bladel. "He described some of the mental images that Mann wanted the cast to use—dried vomit was one of them. They were revolting! He said to me, 'You could play this part.'" Bladel, a very small man, thought that was preposterous. "Doesn't Bachir say, 'I am strong'?" he reminded Dean. "All that means," Dean deadpanned, "is 'I can fuck.' " He autographed some paper money that was used as a prop and gave it to Bladel. The inscription read, "To Rod, with best wishes for the future—your future—James Dean (a bunch of shit)."

Back in New York, the cast and playwrights had a week of rehearsals to work out the kinks. However, the Goetzes and Billy Rose remained unsatisfied with the play, and Rose finally took a desperate step: He kept the February 1 opening night but called every major newspaper in town and persuaded them not to review the play until February 8.

"In the week between Philadelphia and New York," remembers Vivian Matalon, "Jimmy did the most audacious thing. Danny Mann was giving us notes after a rehearsal, and Billy Rose was meandering up and down the aisles. Rose was muttering, 'I'd give this show away for a nickel, but no one would take it.' At the same time, Jimmy was being impertinent to Mann. Rose noticed it and said, 'Okay, Dean, you behave! This is Rose speaking!' and Jimmy cupped his hand to his ear and retorted, 'What was that name again?' "

Ortense and Marcus Winslow came from Indiana to attend the February 8 opening at the Royale Theater. Dean had introduced them to Barbara Glenn during their previous visit to New York, and they passed a note back to her asking, "Aren't you the young lady we met?" During a "stormy" run-through of the show just before the opening, Ortense Winslow had shyly approached Ruth Goetz and asked if "it had all been worth it." Winslow confided her anxiety about her nephew's living on the edges of poverty and hunger and his refusal to work at a regular job, and wanted Goetz's reassurance that he had enough talent to justify all the hard times. Despite Goetz's private reservations about Dean as a person—his "dreadful manners" and "absolute inability to get along with human beings"—she told his aunt that he was an exceptional and brilliant actor.

At the curtain call on opening night, Bill Gunn said, "each member of the cast had to come forward, bow, and step back into line. When it came Jimmy's turn, instead of bowing he picked up his burnoose, spread it out until his knees were showing, and delicately curtsied. The audience went wild. So did Mr. Rose, but our producer's mood was of a different nature, to say the least." Mann also hated Dean's curtsy, saying, "He would taunt me with it!"

Reacting to Dean's performance, James Sheldon says, "The dirty, evil, seductive part he had down pat; *that* he knew how to do. But I never really believed him as an Arab boy. I just felt that physically he was too Indiana to convince me. But it worked." Edna Ferber, author of *Giant,* agreed, saying she thought he was "miscast." Christine White, at Dean's suggestion, failed to attend. "He told me about his fights with Danny Mann, and you've never heard anyone so mad in your life. He was poised to kill; 'sadistic' and 'son of a bitch' were some of his kinder terms. He said, 'Don't bother to come,' so I didn't."

The opening night party at Sardi's, which coincided with Dean's twenty-third birthday, was as dreadful an experience for Barbara Glenn as it had been for Dizzy Sheridan with *See the Jaguar.* Dean tried to enter the restaurant dressed in ragged dungarees and T-shirt but was naturally refused. While he went home to change into a suit, a process he disliked thoroughly, Glenn found herself trapped in a "nightmare" situation. "It was like a bad Hollywood novel, everybody gossiping and bitching" at her table. Dean returned sartorially upgraded but temperamentally degenerated; he seethed and would not talk to anyone, including Glenn. She suggested that they go have a drink on their own since he clearly wasn't enjoying the party, but he insisted on staying. Finally, Glenn told Dean she could endure no more. He left with her, but a match had been set to a highly flammable situation and they had a violent argument; it would be a while before they spoke again.

On or about opening night, Dean tendered his two weeks' notice, simply bailing out at the earliest opportunity permitted under Equity rules. The mythology behind his quitting, however, has consistently held that by so doing he got even with or had the last laugh on the powers-that-be. That is far-fetched, says Barbara Glenn. "There had been problems between them and Jimmy ever since Philadelphia," she emphasizes, "and while it's true he wanted out, they very much wanted him out, too. His notice would have been no surprise to them."

All of Dean's reviews were good, but perhaps the most complimentary came from Wolcott Gibbs of *The New Yorker,* who felt that only Dean's and Jourdan's performances were memorable, with Dean playing "the amoral Arab—corrupt in every sense of the word—to villainous effect." At the end of the season he won a Daniel Blum *Theatre World* award as one of the twelve "most promising newcomers" on Broadway. He would not be able to attend the awards ceremony in late May because of his commitments in Hollywood.

Dean's remaining two weeks in *The Immoralist* were even more interesting off stage than on; in fact, they were a personal renaissance. While temporarily on the outs with Glenn, he turned to Arlene Sachs for company. Sachs had a knack for making introductions between complementary persons; her newest inspiration was to bring Dean to the studio-apartment of Roy Schatt, an accomplished photographer of theater personalities. Schatt had never heard of Dean and remembers that he appeared disheveled and utterly undistinguished as he mumbled his trademark inaudible response to Schatt's greeting. Sachs described Dean's work in *The Immoralist* and his "magnificent" dance with scissors. Suddenly Dean sprang to his feet and did his dance, amazing Schatt with his radiance. Schatt was one of the rare persons Dean decided at first blush that he liked, no doubt due to Schatt's obvious prominence and nonthreatening countenance. By the end of the visit, Dean had recruited him as his photographer and photography instructor.

Another milestone was appearing in a reading of Ezra Pound's new translation of Sophocles' *Women of Trachis,* which inaugurated a series of Sunday night dramatic readings at the New School for Social Research in Greenwich Village. The Sunday schedule allowed Broadway actors to participate on their day off. Roy Schatt photographed Dean and other cast members (Eli Wallach, Anne Jackson, and Adelaide Klein, who was also in *The Immoralist* as a servant) at a rehearsal, and the single performance was given on Valentine's Day. The *Brooklyn Daily Eagle* said Dean (as the son of Herakles and Daianeira) "lent good support."

Perhaps Dean's biggest fringe benefit for being in *Women of Trachis* was meeting twenty-nine-year-old composer Leonard Rosenman. Howard Sackler, director of the New School series, had asked Rosenman if he'd be interested in composing incidental music, and the answer was affirmative. "It was my first experience in scoring any kind of drama," Rosenman remembers. "After the performance of *Women of Trachis,* there was a cast party, and my first wife [Adele] and I played piano duets. Jimmy was quite impressed at this. Sackler introduced us. Later when I asked Sackler about Jimmy, he replied, 'Tough kid. Sleeps on nails.'

"Soon afterwards, Jimmy showed up at my apartment door in the middle of the night, dressed in black leather, to ask me to teach him piano. I said I would and eventually gave him six or seven lessons. But he was lazy and never practiced. He couldn't understand why he couldn't play a Beethoven sonata without first practicing scale and finger exercises.

"I became his role model. If he saw me carrying a book, then he'd start carrying it. In fact, they were my books! Kierkegaard and other philosophers—I don't think he ever read them.

"Adele and I were separated at the time, and I was living on and off with her. I needed a place to keep my things. So Jimmy let me use his place on West Sixty-eighth Street. I don't think he and I ever stayed there at the same time. In the famous photos of that apartment, those paintings on the walls are mine!"

Important as the Sophocles play and introductions to Schatt and Rosenman were, they paled in comparison to Dean's meeting with Elia Kazan to be considered for the part of Cal Trask, a boy who schemes desperately to win his father's love, in *East of Eden,* a new Warner Brothers motion picture Kazan was to direct.

The genesis of Dean's movie career began with Paul Osborn, a good friend of Ruth and Augustus Goetz, who helped convince Billy Rose to produce *The Immoralist.* Osborn also happened to be adapting John Steinbeck's novel, *East of Eden,* for the screen. He alerted Kazan, who was just beginning the casting process, that he "ought to see" Dean in the play. Kazan knew who Dean was but had never seen him do anything at the Actors Studio except hunch over in his chair and pretend to be Brando. He took Osborn's advice and saw the play but found Dean's performance inconclusive, so he summoned him to his office.[3]

Warner Brothers' records indicate that Dean must have swept

---

3. Ruth Goetz later expressed anger at Kazan for "stealing" Dean away from their show, but Dean had no solid offer from Kazan until March 1, long after he had turned in his two weeks' notice.

Kazan off his feet. On February 2, Kazan had lunched with John Kerr, star of *Tea and Sympathy,* hoping to persuade him to play Cal; then cabled Jack Warner that he believed Kerr to be the star of the future and, though Kerr had commitments through June, worth waiting for. Only three days later, however, Kazan could hardly contain his enthusiasm as he wired Warner that he'd found a wonderful new actor (Dean) who could work right away, making it unnecessary to wait until June. He said he would have Dean and Patricia Smith, a promising Broadway actress, screen-tested on February 16.

Kazan recounted that initial meeting with Dean in a 1976 interview with *American Film.* "He did a thing that always attracts me: He wasn't polite to me. He made me feel he wasn't straining to butter me up, that he had a real sense of himself. He said, 'I'll take you for a ride on my motorbike.' It was very hard for him to talk, and riding me on the back of his motorbike, which I did like a damn fool around the streets of New York, was his way of communicating with me. He had his own way, and I thought he was perfect for the part. I thought he was an extreme grotesque of a boy, a twisted boy. As I got to know his father, as I got to know about his family, I learned that he had been, in fact, twisted by the denial of love."

Elsewhere, Kazan revealed what he typically sought while casting. "If they've got something," he reflected, "the shine and shiver of life, you could call it, a certain wildness, a genuineness—I grab them. That's precious. That's gold to me. I've always been crazy for life. As a young kid I wanted to live as much of it as possible, and now I want to show it—the smell of it, the sound of it, the leap of it."

Another factor in his ardor for Dean was the physical grace that Terese Hayden had noted in *The Scarecrow.* Larry Swindell says, "Kazan told me he was first attracted by Dean's wonderful use of a very athletic body and that body-acting is a natural faculty that can't be taught." Isabel Draesemer, Dean's first agent, had noticed the same thing: "To me," she says, "his sex appeal lay in his mouth and below—the use of his body."

Before his screen test, Dean approached Eli Wallach during a *Women of Trachis* rehearsal and confided his nervousness about the test. "Jimmy was a young innocent and rather timid about it," Wallach recalled. "He said to me, 'Kazan asked me to do a screen test. I don't know what to do.' " Wallach says he urged Dean to go ahead with the test.

Actually, Dean was no stranger to screen tests. The previous year he had met with director Fred Zinnemann at the Hotel Pierre to discuss the musical role of Curly in the film version of *Oklahoma!* Arriving forty-five minutes late, disheveled, and in cowboy garb, he explained to Zinnemann that hotel management had taken one look at him and thrown him out. Finally he had sneaked onto a service elevator. "Dean made a sensational test with Rod Steiger in the 'Poor Jud Is Dead' number," wrote Zinnemann. "His singing voice may not have been equal to the task, but that test was a classic. I wish I knew if it still lies hidden somewhere in some attic or garage, or whether it has been destroyed."

Dean had also tested for the Warner Brothers picture *Battle Cry* just after returning from his icy journey to Indiana. Warners executive William Orr, who had come to New York on a talent search, met with Dean and initially had a difficult time persuading him to test. Once he finally agreed, he was paired with a fledgling actress called Ruda Michelle, *née* Ruda Podemski.

"Jimmy and I met for the first time when Warners introduced us for the screen test," Podemski remembers. "We were poor and would go to Cromwell's with our sandwiches in a bag and just order coffee. Or we'd meet in the Village. It seemed we were always having coffee together. He immediately started calling me 'My Podemski,' which became my nickname.

"I went up to his apartment to rehearse for the test, and he was standing there with his face and body covered by a bullfighter's cape. I said, 'What is this, Halloween? I know who you are!' He told me, 'We're good together, we don't need to rehearse.' Instead, he put on a record of *Carmina Burana* and said, 'Just sit close to me.' We listened to the music and that was our rehearsal! Neither of us got into *Battle Cry,* but they told us, 'We think you're the best we've seen in New York.' "

Besides the test with Podemski, Dean also tested with Walter Matthau for a different part. Orr's report noted that Dean's physical appearance was not what they were looking for, although he was clearly more talented than the other candidates and reminiscent of Marlon Brando.

Kazan was informed about Dean's *Battle Cry* test and requested that it be airmailed to New York so he could evaluate it. Then on February 16, he oversaw Dean in new tests for *East of Eden,* pairing him with Patricia Smith, Joanne Woodward, and Paul Newman. One week later, Kazan wired Jack Warner that he was certain Dean was the right choice for Cal. Then he got cold feet and informed Warner that he needed more time to think and would make a final decision on March 1.

The Cal role was clearly the most important to Kazan; later he said he had a strong and personal identification with Cal. When his self-imposed deadline arrived, he wired Warner that Dean was his choice. With that decision made, Kazan felt comfortable enough to go on a month-long vacation in the Bahamas and leave other casting decisions until April. On March 5, Warners' New York office wired the main office in Hollywood with an order to draw up a nine-picture contract between the studio and Dean. His salary for *East of Eden* would be ten thousand dollars, increasing with every picture until it reached forty thousand on the ninth film. No more than two pictures were to be made per year without Dean's consent. Dean would be free to work on Broadway after the third picture; television and radio guest appearances were also permitted.

As soon as the part was his, he called Christine White and ordered her to "come over right away." White says they sat on the stairs outside his apartment while he gave a blow-by-blow account of how it happened. "We were laughing and falling down the stairs about going Hollywood—women in high heels and leopard-skin shorts," she recalls. "After he'd spent years trying to get real, he asked, 'Now that I've got all this depth, why am I going out there?' I told him, 'Pour it in the part, and put blinders on!' Later, when we were walking along the street, he told me Julie Harris was doing it with him. But he'd wanted me to do it."

Although Harris was a favorite actress of Kazan's, she was not initially considered for Abra, the female lead, because she was on Broadway in the title role of Jean Anouilh's play *Mademoiselle Colombe.* But her show closed after only a short run, and she was suddenly available. To reassure Jack Warner of the soundness of casting Dean and Harris in the leads, Kazan sent them to the Fourteenth Street studio of *Life* photographer Gjon Mili to make yet another screen test, in color but without sound.

Except for an insignificant encounter at a party, Dean and Harris had never met before the Mili test. Dean, inspired by the carnival scene in the *Eden* script, brought along some balloons, blew them up, and then popped one during the test with a burning cigarette; Harris squealed and jumped. For the camera's benefit they also did a slow and romantic embrace and kiss. "When I met him I adored him," Harris later said.

The eventual winner of the role of Aron, Cal's twin brother, was Richard Davalos, an usher at a movie theater. Vivian Matalon remembers being in Dean's apartment while Davalos was there. "Davalos was being tested for *East of Eden* at the time," notes Matalon, "and both of them kept up this 'Hey man, Yeah man' talk as if each were trying to out-macho the other."

The two months between Dean's quitting *The Immoralist* and going to Hollywood was pretty much his to use as he wished, and he took full advantage of it. He sat in on a few sessions at the Actors Studio and was entranced by a touring company of Kabuki dancers who gave a special performance there at Lee Strasberg's request. Henceforth Dean would rave animatedly about the art of the Kabuki theater to friends. Whether or not he ever did any further work at the Studio, however, is uncertain. The report most likely to be genuine is that he assisted actor Joseph Anthony in a scene from Chekhov's *The Seagull*.[4]

Dean relished the company of Leonard Rosenman and Roy Schatt, hanging out with and acquiring artistic knowledge from both men, the principal difference being that Rosenman would ride behind Dean on his Indian 500 and Schatt would not. Dean brought Kazan to one of Rosenman's concerts and introduced them, which led to Kazan's hiring Rosenman to write the *East of Eden* score.

Roy Schatt was charismatic and magnetic, says actor Bob Heller, "a little pedantic, maybe, but a great father figure." Once Schatt and Dean met before dawn to wander in search of photographic subjects in the earliest morning light; they waited at the Plaza Hotel's fountain as the sun rose. During a separate expedition they encountered some police and hoodlums brawling near Washington Square. They moved in

---

4. Arthur Storch, who was in the Studio's production of Edna St. Vincent Millay's one-act *Aria da Capo,* says that contrary to various reports, Dean was not in it.

closely with their cameras and snapped away, only to discover that Dean's lens cap had not been removed and Schatt's camera had no film in it, sending them into fits of hysterical laughter. They enjoyed gathering on the roof of the Museum of Modern Art with friends—Heller, Bill Gunn, Martin Landau—to smoke and talk endlessly of acting and art.

Schatt found Dean "intellectually curious," with a "screwball" sense of humor and a "flair for daredevilry." As a student, however, his attention span was short, and he became exceedingly bored with developing negatives or any process in which patience mattered a great deal. Eventually, Dean became reckless with the friendship of this benevolent man and accused Schatt of cashing in on his celebrity. The friendship ended when Dean talked Schatt into photographing him for *Life* magazine and then betrayed him with another photographer. "Nobody was ever a close friend to him," Schatt would ultimately conclude. "He only used people to learn things he wanted to know."

On March 16, columnist Dorothy Kilgallen reported, oddly, "Clifton Webb is playing star-builder. His protégé is James Dean, who just snagged one of the leading roles in John Steinbeck's *East of Eden.* Young Dean might be described roughly as in the Marlon Brando style—dungarees and T-shirt more often than the blue serge suit."

Although Kilgallen and Webb were friends, her source for this tidbit is lost to history. Clifton Webb and Dean were both native Indianans but appeared to have little else in common. Actor William Redfield told *New York* magazine that "the rumors were rife that [Dean] was Clifton Webb's protégé." To be sure, Redfield once lived directly across Fifty-second Street from Dean but was candid enough to say he had only rumors, not facts. Webb's only known assist to Dean came several months after the Kilgallen item appeared, when he persuaded Hedda Hopper that she had made a mistake in boycotting an *East of Eden* preview.

Although Dean had left *The Immoralist,* he still kept an eye on it. His UCLA friend John Holden attended in hopes of seeing Dean in it, but "unfortunately he had left the cast. But before the play I saw him come in with a redheaded woman on his arm. I decided not to talk to him because he had seemed so off-the-wall whenever I had bumped into him in New York, and I assumed his play credits would have further inflated his ego. But at intermission I felt a tap on my shoulder and I turned around, and it was Jimmy, with the redhead. He was very friendly and asked what I was doing there. I told him it was too bad I wasn't seeing him in the role, and he said, 'But this is a lousy play.' He was in a good mood that night."

The Immoralist had kept Dean out of television for a few months, and when he did return, it was in an episode of *Danger*. To his credit, his impending Hollywood career caused no slump in the quality of his work in "The Little Woman," which aired on March 30. He played a counterfeiter on the lam who befriends and hides out with an impoverished little girl (Lydia Reed) who lives in a playhouse in a slum alley.

Director Andrew McCullough was working with Dean for the second time. Although author Joe Scully had written the part specifically with Dean in mind, McCullough informed Dean right up front that he wanted no nonsense from him, especially because Reed was only eight. Dean was able to be generous and cooperative; his gift for interacting with children was fully evident.

Just before leaving for Hollywood, Dean encountered his old friend Madison Musser in a Sixth Avenue bar. "Jimmy was at the end of the bar, and there were lots of actors standing at it," says Musser. "He yelled, 'Hello, Madison! I just wanted you to know I've signed a contract with Elia Kazan!' By this time I was not too happy with Jimmy because of his callous behavior towards Rogers Brackett. I yelled back, 'Well, I think it's time you got out of town.' There was a look of fury on his face, and when he left, he passed by me, deliberately saying nothing."

Kazan had initially expected that Dean would go to Hollywood while he was in the Bahamas, but Dean's commitment to *Danger* kept him in New York. So Kazan and his discovery flew together to the film capital on April 8. The director was amazed and amused to discover that Dean owned no luggage and had his few belongings tied up with brown paper and string. Dean told him it was his first flight.

After they arrived, reported Kazan, "We were heading toward the studio when Jimmy said, 'Can we stop here a minute? My father lives in there.' We stopped and he went in and got his father. Out came a man who was as tense as Jimmy was, and they hardly could look at each other. It was the goddamnedest affirmation of a hunch that I had ever seen. They could hardly talk; they mumbled at each other. I don't know what the hell Jimmy stopped to see him for, because in a few minutes he said, 'Let's go.' "

Every Eden Has Its Eve

The Hollywood that Dean confronted was as superficial as he and Christine White had imagined. That very week, columnist Sidney Skolsky wrote, "It's the younger players, the dating set, and the special group eager for publicity, who frequent the restaurants, nightclubs, and every party. This crowd believes they must be seen, and realize that items in the columns and photos in the fan magazines are important and necessary to their careers. Almost at every party and nightclub opening, you can find Terry Moore, Zsa Zsa Gabor, Jane Powell, Rita Moreno, Jeff Chandler, Tab Hunter."

Dean wanted no part of the Hollywood social scene, fearing he would be respected less for his work than for being a nice guy. Director Nicholas Ray later explained, "Everything Jimmy did suggested he had no intention of belonging to the place. He shied away from social convention, from manners, because they suggested disguise. He wanted his self to be naked."

He would be managed by his old friend Dick Clayton, by then an agent with Famous Artists. "When *East of Eden* was being cast," explains Clayton, "Jane Deacy told me Kazan was looking at Jimmy, so I called Kazan and put in a good word. Then when Jimmy was set to come out here, he told Jane, 'I want to be with Dick.' "

Beverly Linet, a fan magazine writer and close friend of Clayton, recalls, "The night Jimmy Dean arrived, Dick and I went to a press screening of *Indiscretions of an American Wife*. Afterwards, we had to go home to wait for Jimmy to call. I was annoyed, as I wanted to go out for ice cream." It was only the first of many annoyances Dean would inflict on Hollywood.

Kazan wanted Dean to look like a handsome, corn-fed farm boy in *East of Eden* and ordered him to get a tan. According to Bill Bast, Dean appeared at his door early one morning to announce that they were going to the desert to comply with Kazan's mandate. Bast was evidently willing and able to drop all his writing projects to accompany Dean; he suggested they go to Borrego Springs, forty miles beyond Palm Springs in the California desert. Bast's 1956 biography says they were away for a week but is silent on how the restless Dean spent his time.

On their return, Dean and Bast met with Clayton at Famous Artists. As a conscientious agent, Clayton was the soul of helpfulness and within the next month would arrange for Dean to buy a car (a sleek, red 1953 MG), rent an apartment across from Warner Brothers, and meet starlets to date.

One of those starlets was Terry Moore, another Clayton client, who had been in Kazan's *Man on a Tightrope*. Stopping by Clayton's office one afternoon, Moore said she discovered a boy sleeping on the window seat. "I walked over and ever so lightly tickled his nose with the Venetian blind cord," she wrote. "The next thing I knew, I had been tackled and was rolling over and over on the floor with this exuberant youth." It was Dean, of course, and he said Kazan had talked about her.

Dean assured Moore that even if his name meant nothing to her, it would when *East of Eden* hit the movie screens. So disarming was his unorthodox appearance and behavior that Moore invited him to her parents' home for dinner that evening. "My father," she chuckled, "never recovered from the shock of watching Jimmy unzip his pants and let out a belch after dinner."

Moore said Dean was soon following her everywhere. She was booked for a summer engagement in Las Vegas and maintained a grueling daily rehearsal schedule. Dean would accompany her to Goldwyn Studios, where she was put through her paces. Already familiar with ballet stretches and barre work from his dance classes with Eartha Kitt, he practiced right along with her.

Moore was an outwardly devout Mormon whose Scripture toting

and abstinence from tobacco and alcohol were well-known in Hollywood. While the thought of James Dean sitting still through Mormon Sunday school may seem incongruous, Moore claims he attended with her, wearing his scarred motorcycle boots and a dark blue suit. Dean considered Moore a bimbo and claimed to Barbara Glenn that he said so to her face. But that didn't keep him from feeling she had something to offer him.

Dean looked up Gene Owen, his former dramatic arts teacher at Santa Monica City College. Not sure she would remember him, Dean told her his name. Owen replied that not only did she remember him; she had seen him on television and written him a fan letter that he apparently never received. Dean became a frequent visitor to Owen's home. Once he took her and her ten-year-old daughter for a spin in his MG. They never forgot his demonstrating the car's ability to turn "square corners." "The quiet streets of the Pacific Palisades," Owen said, "have never heard such squealing of tires. My daughter was completely charmed by him. He was so sweet to her."

On May 4, Julie Harris arrived in Hollywood and was ensconced in an apartment near Warner Brothers. Dean appeared at her door that night and insisted that she come for a ride in the MG. "I would have preferred to unpack," Harris said, "but I didn't want to put him off. So I rode with him into the Hollywood Hills at a terrific rate of speed. I was holding onto the sides of the car and thinking I would die before the picture even started. But I knew enough not to say I was frightened or ask him to go slower, as that would have made him go faster. So I just kept saying, 'This is great!' When we got back I think he had decided that he couldn't scare me."

Harris was a close friend of writer Christopher Isherwood and his companion, artist Don Bachardy, who lived in Santa Monica. "Julie told us that her leading man was new but would turn out to be a great star," says Bachardy. At the end of her first week, Harris hosted a gathering at her apartment for friends and *Eden* personnel. "Jimmy was a very shy, brusque, tousled-looking guy, just sitting on a couch," Bachardy continues. "We didn't get it through our heads that this was her costar. Later we asked her which of the guests had been the leading man. When she said it was the boy on the couch, we were shocked. But she protested, 'Oh, no—he's going to be a great star!' Not long after that, we went with Julie, Jimmy, and Richard Davalos to a screening of *On the Water-front.*"

Between arriving in Hollywood and starting work on *Eden,* Dean wrote five letters to Barbara Glenn, replete with desperate declarations of misery. He detested smoggy Los Angeles and yearned to finish the picture and get back to New York. In particular, he agonized over his persistent and deliberate antagonism to just about everyone, wondering why he treated people that way. Kazan, Tennessee Williams, and even Julie Harris were objects of his scorn. He realized this was not good. Preliminary work at Warner Brothers, wardrobe and makeup tests, re-pelled him. His only salvation was the new diversions he could buy with his suddenly full wallet: his MG, a motorcycle, and a palomino he called Cisco.

Just as he had done while in Philadelphia with *The Immoralist,* he tried to coax Glenn into visiting him. He especially lamented being away from Leonard Rosenman, who he said was his only friend and the only one who understood him, and eagerly awaited the composer's ar-rival to begin scoring the movie.

In a drugstore near Warners, Dean bumped into Karen Sharpe, his confidante from the days of his romance with Beverly Wills. Sharpe's star had also risen since they last saw each other; she was work-ing in *The High and the Mighty* at Warners. Her mother and her Hun-garian agent were with her in the drugstore. "My agent was uneasy with my talking to someone in a leather jacket and jeans," she said. But she told the agent to go have coffee with her mother so she and Dean could talk.

Dean told Sharpe he would love to get together, but the *East of Eden* company was about to go on location in Mendocino. "Then he said the most interesting thing," Sharpe remembers. "He told me, 'If anyone comes in here, you'll see me change. Just play along with me.' And someone did come in that he knew. He did act strangely—brooding, in-coherent, and staring into his coffee, not looking up. Later I came to un-derstand that his notorious 'strangeness' was just an act. But he played that part so long, maybe he became the act." Terry Moore had the same opinion. "I believed his mannerisms were premeditated," she wrote. "I think his behavior was an act." Moore felt it had to do with his wanting to get to the top.

The *East of Eden* company left on a chartered plane to Mendocino, which in the film was supposed to be Monterey, on May 26. Leonard Rosenman had flown in from New York only that morning, taken a cab to Warner Brothers, and arrived just in time for the chartered flight.

After five days of filming in Mendocino, mainly of Cal (Dean) stalking his brothel-keeping mother, Kate (Jo Van Fleet), the company traveled south to Salinas for seven days of exterior shots. The first of those days was devoted to the scene of Cal in the bean field. Kazan had contracted with a local farmer to have the bean plants three inches high in the first week of June. "That scene where Cal's watching the beans grow," said Julie Harris, "lying in the furrow and peering at them, was all Jimmy's inspiration."

The company was bused back to Hollywood on June 11 and began two months of filming at the studio the next day. Among the first scenes done there was Cal's being made to read Bible verses by his self-righteous and arid father, Adam, as punishment for willful property damage. Cal infuriates his father by reading the verse numbers in addition to the text.

Kazan initially hoped to get Jimmy Stewart, Gary Cooper, or even Spencer Tracy for Adam, but in the end was delighted to have Raymond Massey because of the antagonism that grew between him and Dean. In fact, Kazan claims to have made the mutual distaste explicit to both actors so it would spill over into the film.[1] In shooting Massey's close-up during the Bible-reading scene, Kazan secretly assigned Dean to insert obscenities into the verses to provoke Massey into an on-camera rage.

The scenes in Kate's bordello were done in the last week of June, allowing Jo Van Fleet and Lois Smith, who played a barmaid, to finish and return to New York. Smith got her part after first auditioning for Abra (Julie Harris's role). The barmaid role had been coveted in turn by Dean's UCLA friend Gail Kobe, who after testing unsuccessfully for it was invited by Kazan to be a student in a crowd scene instead. "I was

---

1. Raymond Massey's autobiography professes no ill will toward Dean, only consternation at the bizarre and time-consuming preparations he underwent before going into his scenes.

somewhat humiliated after not getting the part," Kobe remembers. "But Jimmy was absolutely wonderful to me.

"One Sunday while *East of Eden* was filming, I was driving through Burbank with my mother and aunt from Michigan to show them Warner Brothers. At a stoplight, Jimmy pulled up to us on his motorcycle and yelled, 'Hey, what are you doing? Let's have coffee.' So we went somewhere near the studio, and he charmed both of these older women. During a moment when they stepped away, he encouraged me with my acting. 'Hang in there, it'll be fine, you'll make it,' he said."

Upon Dean's return from Salinas, a momentous letter from Barbara Glenn awaited him. She informed him that she had met a man who wanted to marry her. "Basically, what I said in the letter," recalls Glenn, "was, 'I think I want something else.' There was an agony in [our relationship] that I wanted to overcome, and for the first time I was able to verbalize that I didn't really want what I had with Jimmy. I was able to say, 'I'm not here anymore.' "

Dean answered right away. He felt immensely pleased that she had written with such integrity and said he wanted her to be loved and to have all her dreams fulfilled. He knew he couldn't marry her—he believed he would prove to be a completely inadequate mate—but confessed that it was still very hard to release her.

Elsewhere on the Warners lot that June was an actress in need of consolation herself. Pier Angeli, on loan from M-G-M for *The Silver Chalice,* had broken off her engagement to actor Kirk Douglas the previous New Year's Eve, but in the spring, reporters noted that they were dating again. "She says that she and Kirk were never in love, just good friends," explained a close friend. "But he was the first man of any consequence in her life. When Kirk ran off to Vegas and married, Pier was a little taken aback."

Angeli's romantic pride sustained another blow at singer Eddie Fisher's June 17 Cocoanut Grove opening, where both she and Debbie Reynolds sat at ringside tables. "Eddie had invited Pier to be his date also," recalled Reynolds. "He just hadn't met me when he asked her. And there sat Pier thinking she was with Eddie Fisher, too. Until Eddie came down to my table and the photographers descended on us. When Pier realized what he had done, she left."

Doubly devastated, Angeli decided that when the going gets

tough, the tough go shopping. "We hear one day on the *Silver Chalice* set that there is this kid on the Kazan picture," she said. "They say he is very good. I say to myself, 'Anna, maybe you better look.' So I look." Angeli (*née* Anna Maria Pierangeli) chose to stroll over to the *Eden* set only days after Barbara Glenn's letter had taken its emotional toll on Dean. He was a virtual sitting duck for Angeli's enchanting aura.

Hollywood commentators felt Dean bore a certain resemblance to Kirk Douglas; one would soon write that his physical similarity to Angeli's former fiancé was the "inside reason why his romance with Pier created such a stir." Angeli may have been struck the same way. "I was amazed," she admitted. "I have never seen a young actor like Jimmy. I have great respect for his talent. We are introduced. Soon he is visiting my set. I am visiting his set."

The affair flared like brushfire. June 14 was Angeli's first day on the *Chalice* set; she met Dean sometime that week. That Saturday was her twenty-second birthday, and already he was sufficiently mashed on her to give her a matching gold bracelet and necklace. On Sunday she was helping him scrub down his palomino, and before anyone knew it they were spending every spare moment together. When Dean had a break from filming, he would hop in his MG and zoom over to the *Chalice* set to see Angeli; on her breaks, she drove her baby blue Cadillac to wherever he was. She showed him all her new *Chalice* costumes. A publicist on the *Chalice* set once watched Dean roar down one cross street to her dressing room, barely missing her because she had just driven down another street to his set.

Being attracted to Dean, who at twenty-three was only a year older than she, was a new sensation for Angeli. "I have never been interested in a boy so young," she marveled. "I have always liked older men. They are interesting. They can talk of something besides baseball and jitterbug dancing. But Jimmy is different. He loves music. He loves it from the heart the way I do." Besides her considerable external charms, Angeli had the secret ingredient that so often attracted Dean, the void of losing a parent at a young age. "Pier talked about her dead father all the time," recalled Kirk Douglas.

Dean, on his part, felt Angeli was genuine and poised. "Everything about Pier is beautiful," he said, "especially her soul. She doesn't have to be all gussied up. She doesn't have to do or say anything. She's just wonderful as she is. She has a rare insight into life."

One Sunday afternoon Dean and Angeli called on Gene Owen. "This was the first time Jimmy had brought a young lady to our home," said Owen. "She was exquisite in a white blouse and pale blue slacks. She had grace and Old World charm. My husband and I were planning a European trip the following summer, and Miss Angeli told us of her life in Italy, suggested the places we should visit, and told us how much we would enjoy Rome and Florence. Jimmy spoke of travel, too, and was quite elated that Miss Angeli had been able to teach him a few Italian phrases, which he repeated with a fine accent." If Dean's bringing Angeli to meet the Owens reflected a subconscious desire to create a familial atmosphere, it is revealing that he didn't take her instead to meet his father and stepmother.

The press was barred from the *Eden* set, but the Warners publicity machine saw to it that Dean-Angeli rumors leaked out. Its news releases depicted the two of them running up more mileage between their sets than on the highways, or spending their Sundays horseback riding together in Griffith Park. Hollywood gossips were only too happy to take up the chase. In late June, columnist Sidney Skolsky advised, "James Dean has the lead in *East of Eden,* and you'll be hearing of him." Teasingly, he added, "Pier Angeli has discovered him already." A week passed and Skolsky smelled a real story. "The *East of Eden* set," he carped, "is closed to every visitor except Pier Angeli. She's James Dean's Eve, regardless of denials."

Sadly for all involved, the scourge of denial quickly infested the relationship. Just after Skolsky unmasked Angeli as Dean's Eve, columnist Louella Parsons whispered, "Hollywood is talking about . . . the confusion and difference of opinion between Pier Angeli and Warners studio workers over whether she and James Dean are romancing. The studio workers saying she's constantly on his set, and Pier insisting that she has never dated the stage actor." A subsequent Parsons column exposed the reason for the denials. "Pier Angeli's watchful Italian mama, who thoroughly disapproved of Pier's romance with Kirk Douglas, now thoroughly disapproves of her romance with James Dean," it said. "This is the main reason Pier's been denying to columnists that she's seeing Dean at Warner Brothers almost every day—which she is."

The denials began even before Dean and Enrica Pierangeli met face to face. Angeli sensed, after her experience with Kirk Douglas, that her mother would develop an almost maniacal antagonism toward Dean, and she turned out to be right. Although Dean's first offense was nothing worse than tardiness, it nonetheless evoked a strong maternal reprisal: "Reason James Dean's dates with Pier Angeli are now limited to daytime," announced *Daily Variety,* was that "her mama got mad when he brought her home after curfew." After a second encounter that was even less to her liking, Signora Pierangeli's disapproval escalated swiftly. "Jimmy told me," recalls columnist Kendis Rochlen of the *Los Angeles Mirror-News,* a close friend, "that on the set one day, Mama Pierangeli found Jimmy visiting in Pier's dressing room. Mama had a friend with her, an Italian count who wanted to watch Pier work, and she was scandalized to find them in there unchaperoned. Jimmy said they had not been in the sack, but still Mama started screaming and ranting in 'that goddam Italian.' "

Kazan grew concerned after Dean started showing up in the mornings looking exhausted and then not performing well, and he assumed that Angeli was the reason. "I was anxious that he was going to do something terrible," said Kazan. "I didn't think he would complete the picture. So I moved him into a dressing room at the studio, and I moved in next door." In such close proximity, Kazan could tell when Angeli was inside with Dean. But the groans and gasps emanating from the Dean dressing room were not the most frequent sounds to breach the thin walls. Kazan said it was more common to hear him and Angeli arguing. With the considerable tension between Dean's and her mother's clashing demands on Angeli, Kazan's observation is not surprising.

But there were nonsexual conflicts as well. Julie Harris remembers, "Once Pier had asked some friends to have lunch in the commissary, and I guess she'd said to Jimmy, would he come to lunch? And he came without a shirt, dirty from the set, in his old dungarees. Pier was a beautifully perfect little creature, always in an ensemble, always completely perfect—bag, shoes, everything, and just a little hat or bandanna. She burst into tears when he appeared at lunch this way, and so they weren't talking for a time."

As troubles mounted, there was an air of inevitability to the next blow to fall. "One day, Mama found Pier's diaphragm," relates Kendis

Rochlen. "She confronted Pier with it, and Pier started talking back to her. Mama was fit to be tied. She stormed into Jack Warner's office and flung the diaphragm on his desk. 'You've got this punk kid,' she bellowed, 'and my daughter's going to be a big star. I don't want him to see my daughter ever again!'

"I never knew Jimmy to be so mad. Over the phone I could hear him pounding the wall with his fist. He sputtered, 'I'm not allowed to see Pier again. I was summoned to Warner's office. The big mogul said, "I want you to stop fuckin' that broad, or you'll be off the picture." ' Jimmy was offended that Warner called Pier a broad. He snarled, 'The old lady wouldn't let me marry her if I were the goddam pope!'

"Pier told me that her mother called Anna Maria Alberghetti's father [another pushy and protective Italian stage parent] for advice on how to deal with her Jimmy Dean crisis. He told her, 'You do what we do in the old country: lock them up. You do whatever it takes to keep non-Catholics away from our beautiful women.' From that point on, Pier was virtually under house arrest."

For the sake of *East of Eden*, Kazan was happy at this turn of events—he said Dean's gloomy solitude suited his purposes—but he was the only one. Dean's disquietude was painfully obvious from the way he glumly spent his free time. "All he had was his camera," said Kazan. "He used to stand in front of the mirror in his room and take roll after roll of close-up photographs of his face, with only the slightest variation of expression."

The drama in Dean's personal life paralleled the romantic conflicts in *East of Eden*. In July there were three weeks of night filming on such scenes as the carnival, where Cal and Abra finally act out their attraction even though she is his brother's girlfriend. The forbidden kiss occurs as they are suspended in midair in a Ferris wheel seat. Kazan had the set cleared to put Julie Harris at ease for the scene, and one publicist's news release claimed that folksinger Burl Ives, who was playing a sheriff in the picture, played his guitar and sang to put Harris and Dean in a romantic mood.

One night during carnival sequences, Marlon Brando came on the set at Kazan's invitation. Press accounts of the visitation said Brando hoped to pick up some pointers on directing from Kazan, but Kazan later claimed he invited Brando specifically to watch the effect of the great actor's presence on Dean. It may have been their first introduction. Kazan said Brando was gracious to Dean, who "was so adoring he was miserable." The next day Dean returned the compliment by visiting Brando's set at Twentieth Century–Fox *(Désirée)*.

Another guest on the set at this time was Dick Clayton's friend Beverly Linet, who was seeing Dean for the first time. "When I saw Jimmy, he was leaning with his head against a sort of picket fence, trying to concentrate," Linet relates. "I said to Dick, 'Let's go over.' But Dick said, 'No, he's deep in preparation.' I had never seen 'preparing' before in my life. Jimmy was like that for fifteen minutes. Then out came Julie Harris, and the cameras rolled. Jimmy and Julie walked down a street together, and then Jimmy asked, 'Are you going to the carnival tonight?' and Julie replied, 'Yes, I'm going.' Then someone yelled, 'Cut! Print!' That was the extent of it. I would be generous in saying it lasted thirty seconds. I knew about Method acting, but did he need to go through all that? Dick took me over for a brief introduction, and that was it."

Dean would finally get the girl in the picture, and for a time it looked as if the same luck might apply in real life. Though he was in official exile from Pier Angeli's life, his remarkable resourcefulness was equal to the task of circumventing Signora Pierangeli's edict, and he enlisted the help of experts. Kendis Rochlen says, "Jimmy consulted with me about how he and Pier could get around Mama. He obliquely asked if they could use my place to rendezvous. I said, 'I can't do that.' But I became their go-between. I had Jimmy's phone number, which no one had, not even [Warners publicity man] Ted Ashton. I had Pier's phone number. I even had a code name. Pier would give me the appropriate phone number when she was with the girls. Jimmy, in turn, would give me the number where he could be reached. So, he and Pier were still seeing each other, but I would write in my column that other girls were dating him."

Signora Pierangeli had their home phone number changed as an additional means of keeping Dean at bay. Ever the deferential agent, Dick Clayton obtained the new phone number through his own connections and then took it to Warners, where he stood talking with some executives. "Along came Jimmy," he said, "and he hopped right over, and I slipped him a piece of paper and said, 'Here's the number you want.'

So he screamed and howled and grabbed me and gave me a kiss on the mouth, and he was just like a kid. It was like giving him a great prize."

East of Eden filming concluded on August 9. Dean was called back to the studio for postrecording on August 10 and 18, but other than those tasks nothing stood between him and the escape to New York that he had so eagerly craved in his letters to Barbara Glenn. Mike Connolly of the *Hollywood Reporter* sized up the situation: "James Dean is hanging around, even though *East of Eden* is finished. Pier Angeli . . ." By this time, a few Hollywood scribes were reporting that Signora Pierangeli's wrath had inexplicably dissipated. Erskine Johnson claimed she "stopped ruffling her maternal feathers" after experiencing Dean's charm firsthand. "A couple of Sunday night suppers on the family patio turned the trick," Johnson quipped. Louella Parsons wrote, "Pier Angeli and James Dean continue to see each other. Obviously Pier's mother no longer objects." The most obvious sign of the rapprochement was their very public date to an August 10 celebrity screening of *Gone With the Wind,* captured in their radiant formal attire by a bevy of photographers.

Finally Dean flew back to New York for a television commitment ("Run Like a Thief" on *Philco TV Playhouse*). "I drove him to the plane," said Angeli, "and he was on the same flight with Debbie Reynolds.[2] I introduced him to her so they'd each have someone to talk to during the trip. But when Jimmy called me after he arrived, he said that Debbie was sick most of the flight, and anyway, he was sleepy."

Dean and Reynolds were on a red-eye flight from Los Angeles that touched down at Idlewild (now Kennedy) Airport early on August 27. Reynolds, accompanied by her mother, was on a whirlwind trip to New York to see her beau, Eddie Fisher, before going into rehearsals for M-G-M's *Hit the Deck.* She had suppressed her malaise by the time the plane landed, because she presented a radiant picture for a gaggle of reporters waiting to watch her reunion with Fisher, a diversion that allowed Dean to slip away from the airport unmolested.

Roy Schatt noticed that he was unusually subdued and preoc-

---

2. Reynolds and Dean had already met at Beverly Wills's birthday party in August 1951.

cupied, and that Pier's name kept coming up in his conversation. Finally, Dean asked if he could go in Schatt's darkroom to call Angeli in Hollywood. Through the door Schatt heard Dean's voice "starting to rattle like a machine gun." Suddenly, Dean opened the door and asked Schatt to come in the darkroom and talk to Angeli. "He was blushing," Schatt recalled. "His eyes seemed larger and sadder than they'd ever been and just about to spill over." When Schatt took the receiver, Angeli asked him to tell Dean not to get so excited. Schatt had never before seen any indications of Dean's emotional self.

Before flying to New York, Dean had confided to Rochlen his unease over being away from Angeli. "He was worried," notes Rochlen, "and said to me, 'They're getting to her. I'm gonna lose her. Keep in touch.' He gave me his phone number in New York before he left. One morning at two A.M. [Pacific time] he called me to talk about Pier. 'I'm so sad,' he mourned. He said he was gazing at the stars as he talked." Besides Rochlen, Dean had also been pouring out his Angeli woes to Barbara Glenn by telephone throughout the summer.

His insecurity was not unwarranted. Two nights after he left, Angeli attended what was billed as the Hollywood party of the year, hosted by Sonja Henie. Reporters noticed that Angeli's affections were the coveted prize of the evening. "Pier, stag, fought off sundry wolves throughout the entire enchanted evening," wrote one. Columnist Sheilah Graham took her aside for a lecture. "See here, Private Angeli," Graham scolded, "this sort of solo nonsense has got to stop. Why didn't you bring a guy?" "Because there was no guy to bring," Angeli replied. Neither she nor any reporter acted as if she were not single and available.

She and Dean had made plans to reunite at Lake Arrowhead upon his return from New York. Her twin sister, Marisa Pavan, and other friends gathered there with them. The weekend may have reminded Dean of the times he and Bette McPherson spent at Arrowhead with the Armstrongs five years earlier. But it was not the salvation of the relationship that he and Angeli counted on. Within days, she was spotted with new suitors. She even turned down a date with Marlon Brando, not in deference to Dean, but to watch a movie at home with Allan Grant, a *Life* photographer. Sheilah Graham babbled that Angeli had resumed dating Jacques Sernas, the blond French actor. Sidney Skolsky did a double take when he spied her at an *Ice Follies* opening on the arm of Donald O'Connor. ("Now, how did *they* get together?" he mused.) Angeli's appearance with O'Connor, who was only two months divorced, quickly became the Romance of the Week. "Donald O'Connor was very quiet and very solemn and very attentive in the darkest corner of the Captain's Table with Pier Angeli," gossiped Mike Connolly. By September 25, Hedda Hopper was gushing, "I've rarely seen a cuter couple than Pier Angeli and Donald O'Connor."

In the wake of his progressive estrangement from Angeli, Dean went on a rare public date—escorting Terry Moore, who was the Hollywood press's reigning piñata, to the September 22 premiere of *Sabrina*. A premiere was precisely the kind of Hollywood event Dean despised, and the buxom Moore was bound to attract the kind of attention he loathed. Photographers were waiting as their limousine disgorged them in front of the Paramount Theater. Moore's wardrobe that evening, "a wool job with a neckline so high she could have chinned herself on it" as one newsman jested, seemed painted on. "Terry Moore had the screen's latest hot bet, James Dean, in tow," said Sidney Skolsky. "Terry was herself and Dean didn't get to say a word over the mike. He just stood there without saying a single word." Other journalists accused Moore of stealing Dean away from Angeli.

Moore refuted all such allegations. "I knew Jimmy before Pier knew him," she said. "I only went out with him because Dick Clayton pleaded with me. Dick said Jimmy didn't have a date and it was important for him to be seen." As for hogging the microphone, Moore said, "They called me up to the mike. They ignored Jimmy. I said, 'Don't you want to talk to James Dean? He's going to be an important star. He's just finished *East of Eden.*' I was helping Jimmy. He's a boy who doesn't have very much to say. That night at the mike he couldn't say a word. I tried to save the day by talking for him."

Having seen Dean with Moore, Kendis Rochlen telephoned Angeli, who "insisted there wasn't any tiff. 'I was too tired to go to the premiere,' she explained. 'They're always such big productions, and I'd rather go see the picture a few days later and eat my popcorn and relax. I've just been terribly busy with dancing lessons and costume fittings for my *Green Mansions* [her next scheduled film] tests.' "

While Dean adjusted to Angeli's diminishing presence in his life, he kept busy shooting extra *East of Eden* scenes. Kazan was now telling colleagues that the movie would be a good one. He thought that Dean, in spite of his inexperience, had instinctively played most of his scenes right. What pleased Kazan the most was the movie's originality: he said Dean had portrayed a kind of hero never before seen by moviegoers.

There was a last effort at a Dean-Angeli reconciliation. On the day of Dean's fiasco with Terry Moore, *Daily Variety* casually mentioned that Angeli had asked him to escort her to the September 29 world premiere of *A Star Is Born*. But only two days later, it announced that Dean and Angeli had "phffft," offering no further details.

They did go to *A Star Is Born,* where it was clear to veteran Hollywood watchers that the romance was over. But neither Dean nor the press foresaw the events of the following weekend, when Angeli and popular singer Vic Damone decided to ride into the sunset together. Angeli went to M-G-M on Friday, October 1, to test (unsuccessfully) for *Green Mansions.* After her test, she dropped in on the set of *Hit the Deck* to see Debbie Reynolds and other friends. Just as her fateful visit to the *Eden* set had had immediate romantic consequences, her spontaneous appearance on the *Hit the Deck* set would now yield similar results. When she arrived, Vic Damone was being filmed singing an Italian ballad. Noticing her, Damone asked her to stay on the set until all his takes had been shot. Then he invited her to the Retake Room, a bar and grill across the street from M-G-M, for Cokes. He plied the jukebox with coins, and Cokes gave way to champagne. Then came the coup de grâce, "September Song."

"Nobody ever dances at the Retake Room, but we did for about an hour," Angeli recounted. "Everybody was staring at us. Then I got this funny feeling in the pit of my stomach and knew it was the real thing at last. So when he said, 'Why don't we get married?' I replied, 'Why *don't* we?' " To make sure that Damone was serious and not simply giddy with champagne, Angeli met him on the golf course the following morning to reaffirm his proposal. That night, Damone asked Signora Pierangeli for her daughter's hand.

Damone had told reporters he was itching to wed—"I've had enough of living alone; besides, it'd be nice to have somebody to sing to"—but his dating pattern during 1954 gave no clue that he would impulsively settle on Angeli as his intended. He had squired a long list of starlets, actresses, and other notables throughout the year, including

Anna Maria Alberghetti (who was his date at the Eddie Fisher opening that had been so embarrassing for Angeli), Mona Freeman, Maureen O'Hara, Judy Spreckels, Sheela Fenton, Nancy Sinatra, Pat Crowley, and even Marisa Pavan, Angeli's twin. In July he was serious with Joan Tyler, but at the end of that month, according to *Daily Variety,* he and actress Patricia Hardy flew to New York to announce their engagement to his parents. Then, less than a week before Damone proposed to Angeli, Sidney Skolsky wrote, "Damone, who admits he and Joan Tyler are romantic, have kissed and made up. They didn't see each other for about a month." Damone's surprise betrothal to Angeli would have dumbfounded anyone trying to make sense of his recent love life.

But he and she had a history, about which Dean knew nothing. When Angeli was in Munich in 1952 to make *The Devil Makes Three,* Damone, who was stationed there with the army, phoned and asked her to make a special appearance on a variety show he was helping to put on for the soldiers. He called her onto the stage, cuddled her in his arms, and sang "September Song" to her, the ballad he would later exploit so strategically in the Retake Room. For the next two months, they dated, chaperoned by her mother, and on the eve of her return to America, Damone proposed marriage. Signora, however, had not approved, and they had no intervening dates before the Retake Room. "But we saw a great deal of each other, even if we didn't date," Angeli explained. "We saw each other every day at the studio, and we had long talks. Both of us had an electric sensation whenever we met. And he spent a lot of time at our house when he was dating my sister. We danced and talked and had a lot of fun."

Despite the startling developments of the previous twenty-four hours, Angeli kept a date with Dean that Saturday evening. "She broke the news to me the night before she announced her engagement," Dean would soon tell Kendis Rochlen, "but she wouldn't tell me who the guy was. I was floored when I learned it was Vic Damone. I figure that when I went back to New York after finishing *East of Eden* her family and friends got her ear and changed her mind about me. I won't try to pretend I'm not sorry—Pier's still okay with me. Oh well, maybe she likes his singing. I hope they'll be happy."

In print, Rochlen made Dean sound magnanimous in defeat. Her account of what he really said, off the record, paints a less gracious picture: "I don't give a shit. But I know how we can cure her of Damone. We lock her in a five-by-five room plastered with pictures of him *before* his nose job." (Now it was he, instead of Angeli's mother, who wanted to lock her up.) Dean vented the same feelings over dinner with Christine White when he was back in New York in early November to work in a *Danger* episode. "He called Damone a jerk, among other four-letter words," recalls White. "He couldn't believe that out of all the competition, Damone was the one to beat him out."

The wedding was set for November 24, the day before Thanksgiving, at Saint Timothy's Catholic Church in Westwood. Invitations were a hot ticket; many Hollywood insiders were miffed at not receiving one. Rochlen, who did have an invitation, chose not to go. "However," she says, "I knew Jimmy would be there. He told me his plans. He said, 'I'll give Mama a present. I'll be in my black leather jacket'—she hated it—'on my motorcycle, and I'll gun the shit out of that thing!' " Various scribes reported that Dean had indeed been across the street; some mentioned the motorcycle.

"I hate to sound cynical," Sheilah Graham wrote, "but a group was taking bets on which marriage of the engaged Hollywood couples would last the longest. Pier Angeli and Vic Damone received the best odds." In spite of Graham's hopeful prediction, the marriage got off to a rocky start. Reports of marital discord during their Las Vegas honeymoon circulated almost from the day the new couple arrived. "Pier Angeli and Vic Damone had their first spat. It was over his gambling," wrote Mike Connolly. Twelve days later came more blissful news: "Check with the Vic Damones," wrote Skolsky in one of his *Memos to Myself*. "The talk is that they returned from their honeymoon very happy because they expect a baby."

The baby, a boy named Perry, arrived on August 22, 1955, about ten-and-a-half months after his parents became engaged. (Rumors of James Dean's paternity are titillating but groundless.) But despite the child, the marriage was not a happy one; Angeli divorced Damone in 1962. Her second marriage, to Italian bandleader Armando Travajoli, was no more successful.

If Angeli really loved Dean, why didn't she marry him? Why was she willing to plunge into a bad marriage at the drop of a hat? If not for the maternal obstacle, would Dean really have married her? Both principals are long dead and cannot speak for themselves, but the facts of the relationship permit reasonable conclusions.

Clearly, Dean and Angeli were strongly attracted to each other during a time of emotional rebound for both. Her mother was a bête noire to him for the first several weeks they were dating, but somehow she eased up in her opposition, and they dated openly again. Dean accused Signora Pierangeli of working behind the scenes to get rid of him, but she could not have prevented an elopement. The causes of their dissolution—there was no formal breakup—were inherent in them and not due to any outside enemy.

First of all, the relationship was never exclusive. Although Dean had celebrated Angeli's birthday by giving her expensive gifts, she spent part of the same birthday with Eddie Fisher, even giving him a gift for the occasion. She continued seeing Fisher during the rest of June while Debbie Reynolds was out of town, all the while spending lots of time with Dean on the Warners lot.

Dean maintained outside interests, too. On August 4, *Daily Variety* reported, "Pier Angeli found out James Dean was dating an extra—and on her picture, yet, *Silver Chalice.* She's miffed." Even though Dean was officially banned from her life at that time, Angeli had expected him to be true. So she started seeing other men in August. The August 23 *Hollywood Reporter* tattled that she had gone to Ciro's with Mack Gray, calling them the "oddest twosome" there.

There were aspects of each of their characters that would have severely impaired the viability of a marriage. Kirk Douglas wrote that during his engagement to Angeli, he met her at a hotel in Venice; all over the mirror in her room were pictures of Douglas from a movie they made together. Years later, Marisa Pavan told Douglas that until fifteen minutes before he arrived at the hotel, Angeli's mirror had been plastered with pictures of a young Italian boy. Douglas also revealed that in the spring of 1954, just before his new fiancée arrived in southern California, Angeli rang his doorbell one night at eleven P.M. "Pier, who could never go anywhere without her mother's permission, had driven up to my house all by herself. She wanted to see me. The game she was playing was clear to me. I said no, it was too late, we could talk some other time. She was devastated. She couldn't accept the fact that it was over . . . That was part of her sickness. I closed the door on Pier."

Dean apparently had a vile habit that could doom any marriage. Leonard Rosenman said that when Dean imbibed, he tended to be a mean drunk and "had a reputation for beating up his girlfriends." According to Rosenman, Dean physically abused Angeli "once too often."

There is no evidence that Dean ever formally proposed to Angeli. He made a telling statement to Kendis Rochlen when she asked him if he and Angeli would get engaged. "We've got to grow up a little first," he answered. "Anyway, I'm too neurotic. Right now I couldn't take care of Pier the way she should be taken care of." He had earlier told Rochlen, "I ain't never getting married."

Although Angeli loved her mother, she was rapidly finding her ironhanded rule more and more intolerable. Until the summer of 1954 she wasn't even allowed to have her own checkbook. She began to talk back to Mama, which she had never done before. During the days of Dean's exile, the *Hollywood Reporter* carried a revealing item: "Understand Pier Angeli's threatening Mama she'll leave. But Mama still has the contracts." With her mother indisputably holding the upper hand, Angeli's only way out was marriage. Vic Damone was Catholic, of Italian heritage, and well-off, and so he became her ticket to freedom.

Once Dean had dated Angeli, his taste in women tilted decidedly toward the exotic and foreign: Dana Wynter, Lili Kardell, and Ursula Andress were yet to come. Andress, in fact, may have had the last word on Angeli. Shortly after Dean died, she told a reporter, "Jimmy explained to me what happened with Pier. He said her family objected to him, and all the time they would have to sneak around to see each other. He found out it was more a joke with her, exciting because nobody was to know."

Meet the Press

Dean had achieved moderate public visibility before returning to California. Some of his television roles had earned favorable reviews in *Variety,* and both Broadway appearances were praised by the critics. But this was news, not publicity; there were neither photos (at least not of Dean) nor promotional ballyhoo. His career in New York was devoid of the trappings of star-building machinery—fan magazine articles, studio press agents, press books, and world premieres. His closest brush with that way of life had been winning a *Theatre World* award but work on *East of Eden* had kept him away from the presentation.

He was completely unprepared to assume his ceremonial duties at Warner Brothers. Though he wanted to be an actor and even a star, he believed he could ignore the commercial concerns inherent in becoming studio property. Thus, his reactions to being marketed as a commodity were often hostile. He wanted the rights but not the responsibilities of stardom.

But once he signed on the dotted line, Warner Brothers owned him, and they had other plans for him. So did the Hollywood press, whose bread and butter depended wholly upon the manufacture of prose irresistible to avid followers of stars' lives. Hollywood was then embroiled in its well-known struggle to remain profitable in the face of competition from television, and as film scholar John Francis Kreidl points out, to lure Dean away from television and into the movies was as much a Hollywood survival strategy as the invention of CinemaScope. In addition, Marlon Brando, Hollywood's reigning rebel, was growing too old to retain that title. "The replacement chosen was James Dean," wrote media expert Robert Tysl, adding that the campaign to invest Dean with Brando's old image was "obvious and undeniable."

For his first several months in Hollywood, Dean enjoyed a period of grace during which he was shielded from press importunity, thanks to Kazan's gag order on the *East of Eden* set. "Kazan put out orders that no one was to talk to Jimmy," explains Kendis Rochlen. "He knew Jimmy didn't know the rules and wasn't equipped to handle the imbeciles who covered the studios."

By no means, however, did the press embargo exempt Dean from star-building responsibility. As a Warner Brothers contractor, he was obligated to submit to the publicity department's machinations. The first order of business was to prepare an official studio biography. Although Dean cooperated, his attitude toward the finished product was later revealed by Hedda Hopper. While she was interviewing him, "he fished his official studio biography out of his pocket, glanced at it, rolled his eyes up toward heaven, and threw it away."

The other step in this process was the assignment of a press agent, Ted Ashton, to the *East of Eden* company. Ashton's duty was to collect newsworthy incidents and anecdotes from Dean (and all other actors in the company) and then pass them on to the Hollywood press. Hedda Hopper, Louella Parsons, Harrison Carroll, and other scribes may not have been allowed to ferret out news on the *Eden* set, but Ashton was expected to shovel it to them prolifically.

Being in exile did not keep the press from detecting that something intriguing was afoot, especially Kendis Rochlen, a young columnist being groomed by the *Mirror-News* as a new Hedda/Louella for evening newspaper readers. Her husband, a functionary in the Warners publicity department, came home with the news that "there was a kid who walks into a scene and is magic. . . . You haven't seen anything like it since Brando. . . . He's shy and won't talk to anyone."

"So I said to myself, 'I want to talk to this kid!'" Rochlen remembers. "I knew how to pretend to be a secretary. I called the *Eden* set and found Jimmy in the Green Room.[1] I may even have said I was Dick Clayton's secretary. I used to say anything!

"Jimmy came to the phone. I introduced myself. His first words to me were, 'Go fuck yourself!' I hooted! He said, 'I've never heard of you before.' So I said, 'I've never heard of you! Listen, I've met people more interesting than you. And I've worked the police beat and there's not a four-, six-, or eight-letter word you can say that will shock or frighten me!'

"He was so astounded that now he laughed! I suggested, 'Why don't we knock off this talk and get to know each other? I write my column to please only myself. I want to talk to you about making the movie.' He said, 'Okay, fine. I'll give you my number.' We agreed to meet.

"I think he called a day or two later. He'd picked up the *Mirror-News* and read my column. I asked him how he liked Warners. I told him it was a better lot than the others—cleaner, better flowers. I'm a nut for quotations, and he liked the adages and proverbs I recited. He said, 'We'll talk again.' I didn't print anything of this. I knew he wasn't supposed to be talking to me.

"We met for lunch; I don't remember where. I was tall, slim, and fairly attractive. When I came in, he said, 'Oh my God, you're better-looking than your picture *on purpose,* so people will be surprised.' I said, 'One can't be a genius and beautiful.' He was wearing an open shirt, jeans, and horn-rimmed glasses. I said, 'Listen, Jimmy, you're no great prize, and if I saw you at a gas station and said, "Fill 'er up," I wouldn't look at you again.'

"He asked me flat out, 'How do I handle these reporters?' First, I told him, 'Don't trust anyone, even me. And you'll have to talk to Louella. Don't tell her to go fuck herself. *Don't* talk politics. When you talk to Harrison, tell him you've had a sprain or some other accident. He loves them.' I also told him about some of the duties he'd have, such as escorting starlets.

"He said he felt good about *Eden.* He referred to his director and costar as Mr. Kazan and Miss Harris.

---

1. The Warner Brothers commissary.

"We argued over who knew more four-letter words. But I don't remember his being vulgar again, only in that first conversation. He admired my ingenuity. We were on an even playing field. The reason I got along with him—and ended up getting more than others from him—is that I was trained. I wasn't a personality or out to promote myself. The big columnists were all starstruck; I was amused and bemused by Hollywood. There was a pecking order among them, and I would only get the crumbs. I would just observe; I would not get in the way."

It is difficult to identify a reporter whose first encounter with Dean was pleasant. With the exception of Rochlen, none had the panache to roll with his punches. The eminent Hedda Hopper recoiled in horror when she lunched at the Green Room and got her first glimpse of what she called the "dirty shirttail school of acting." "Against a wall," she fretted, "sat two boys—one slouched down on his coccyx. They balanced forks on water glasses, wiped the face of Keefe Braselle, whose picture hung above them, got extra chairs on which to rest their feet, and gave the appearance of a couple of Roman soldiers resting up from the wars."

Hopper muttered to herself that these two could only be Kazan imports from the Actors Studio; and surely enough, they were pointed out to her as Dean and Richard Davalos. She kept an eye on them as they "glanced about the room occasionally with brooding eyes" and failed to stand when a woman friend approached them to say hello. Eventually she suggested to a press agent that Dean be deported to New York. She condemned the incident in her column, deploring the obsolescence of glamour at Warner Brothers and concluding, "Well, that's show business—at least the 1954 couldn't-care-less kind."

When Hopper's uncomplimentary remarks appeared, Dick Clayton called her. "I explained that Jimmy wasn't the typical Hollywood actor who could just talk a blue streak to the press," he says. But Clayton's mediation was to no avail; Hopper had written Dean off and almost never mentioned his name in the next few months. Much later, chatting with him under more civil circumstances, Hopper reminded him that his behavior had been wretched. He agreed but confessed that he had "wanted to see if anybody in this town had guts enough to tell the truth."

Louella Parsons had the grace not to belabor Dean's keeping her waiting two hours for what would be their only interview. But, like her contemporary, Hopper, she missed the well-dressed and polite actors of yesteryear. Sheilah Graham's distaste for Dean became clear when, babbling that Pier Angeli insisted Dean was only a passing fancy, she snidely added, "I hope so."

Mike Connolly of the *Hollywood Reporter* seems also to have found Dean unpalatable, since he printed the wickedest item of all, an apparently deliberate botch of Dean's name: "James *Best* of Kazan's *East of Eden* company shouldn't start believing his publicity till he starts getting it."

Nonetheless, the press could not afford the luxury of sustaining a grudge against Dean, no matter how bilious his behavior, because its livelihood was contingent on inducing public curiosity about him. He had been too minor an actor in his earlier Hollywood incarnation for anyone to remember him, so when the announcement of his casting in *Eden* went out, he was referred to, for lack of a catchier handle, as a "legit actor" or "New York actor" or "from the stage." Now it was up to the Hollywood press to transform this unknown quantity into a star. Media expert Tysl said the devices most often used to accomplish this were linkage and repetition.

Within the space of a year, there would be three phases to Dean's publicity: linkage to Pier Angeli, linkage to Marlon Brando, and finally, freestanding items. Ordinarily, news items from a movie set would enhance the star-building process, but with Kazan's ban in effect the press had only what Warners agents fed them, which they might not choose to use.

Kendis Rochlen led the pack in linking Dean to Pier Angeli, reporting on June 22 that they had been together on Angeli's birthday, washing Cisco, his palomino. Only days later, Sidney Skolsky and Louella Parsons, ear to the ground, would take up the Dean-Angeli chase.

Rochlen followed the spirit if not the letter of Kazan's law by waiting until the *Eden* set shut down to print anything to betray her stolen conversations with Dean. On August 16, her column was the first to carry a Dean quotation and photo; again, it was about his relationship with Angeli. In fact, the only non-Angeli or non-*Eden* publicity that summer came from *Daily Variety*'s Army Archerd, who divulged that

Dean had been a parking lot attendant three years before. To spice up the item, Archerd speculated that the dents in Dean's MG might relate to that fact.

The Angeli summer fling was a gold mine of publicity for Dean during the three months it lasted. But as it petered out—and as the *Eden* embargo ended, enabling the press to see and hear Dean for themselves—journalists began using Dean's and Brando's names in the same sentence with increasing frequency. Comparisons with Brando were certainly not new. "People were telling me I behaved like Brando before I knew who Brando was!" Dean said in the *Los Angeles Times*. James Sheldon, David Diamond, Frank Corsaro, and other New Yorkers had remarked on the similarity long before Dean left for Hollywood. But now it seemed that to associate the two names conveyed a sense of hipness in the messenger. The Warners publicity department, of course, did all it could to encourage the association.

One of the earliest quips in this vein came from Army Archerd, who said, "James Dean, brought out here by WB for *East of Eden,* may be another Brando—wears leather jacket, blue jeans, and may even have a motorcycle." Soon after that, Kendis Rochlen wrote, "To put it mildly, he's the most offbeat character to hit the movie lots since the days of 'early Brando.' " Fan magazines jumped on board in the fall. *Motion Picture* suggested Dean was "as tough to handle as Brando," and *Modern Screen* touted him as "a Brando type."

For a time, the columnists would get a kick out of playing up a supposed rivalry between the two nonconformists. "Jimmy Dean can play all the conga drums he pleases," laughed Connolly. "Smirks Brando, 'That was last year's publicity.' " Connolly also alleged that Dean was seeing Brando's psychiatrist.[2] Archerd disclosed that Brando could do a "terrific" imitation of Dean. But Skolsky's scoop was that Dean gave "really excellent impressions" of Brando doing Chaplin and of Chaplin doing Brando. Graham and Archerd called Dean "the poor man's Marlon Brando." Parsons scoffed, "Now come on, young Mr. Dean, how about forgetting the Brando bit?" One article professed to

2. This was probably meant as a joke. There is no evidence that Dean ever consulted Dr. Bela Mittelmann in New York.

explain "Why Dean Can Never Be Like Brando."

Everyone knew Dean idolized Brando, Kazan said, because he spoke about him in a "cathedral hush." In New York, Dean had pestered Christine White to tell him every detail about her encounters with Brando; and Arthur Storch, who once dated Brando's secretary Susan Slade, says Dean was constantly after Slade to tell him details of the eminent actor's personal life.

But Dean wanted his Brando worship to remain private, and he considered public comparison to be an unfriendly gesture. Terry Moore recalled that when she introduced him to her speech coach, Marie Stoddard, "Jimmy decided he would shock little old Marie. He warned her, 'Don't give me any of this shit that I remind you of Marlon Brando.' "

To Philip Scheuer of the *Los Angeles Times,* Dean professed to have no interest in imitating Brando. He admitted he and Brando were identified with the "same school," but felt his personal modes of expression were as valid as the older actor's. "It's true I am constantly reminding people of him," Dean admitted. "They discover resemblances—we are both from farms, dress as we please, ride motorcycles, and work for Elia Kazan." Dean said he was neither disturbed nor flattered by the comparison.

Dean and Brando were indeed a lot alike. Both had mothers who encouraged creative pursuits; both had been exceptional in high school dramatics. In Brando's earlier days, his behavior at parties was much like Dean's was now: silent and withdrawn. Complaints about the two from fellow actors were identical: they never did the same business twice; they couldn't be relied on for cues. One significant difference was Brando's disdain of bullfights; his innate compassion for animals would not allow him to relish such a sport.

Both Dean and Brando felt revulsion at the press, although Brando's stemmed from the relentless publicity that afflicted him after *A Streetcar Named Desire,* whereas Dean's, absent any previous picture, was innate. Brando's first encounter with Hedda Hopper, in fact, was as much a farce as Dean's. First, Brando refused to go to her home, so Hopper grudgingly agreed to come to his set. She spoke without interruption for twenty minutes, during which Brando appeared to be dozing. Hopper snapped her fingers and asked him if he had been listening. He said he had. "Do you care to answer my questions?" she asked. "I don't believe so," came the reply. Incensed, Hopper rebuked Brando with the assertion that she had come, against her will, only as a favor to his producer. "Thanks for nothing, and good day," she said as she retreated in a huff.

Linkage of Dean with Brando was a marketing tool and would persist until *Eden* was out in the theaters. But Dean had already begun standing on his own in the gossip columns (admittedly a dubious distinction) before that; the turning point came with sneak previews of *Eden* in December 1954, when columnists and the public finally saw his work. Dean could still make two trips to New York in anonymity after *Eden* was wrapped up, but right after the sneak previews, his third trip was picked up by the *Hollywood Reporter*'s "Travel-Log" column. Word of his comings and goings in Gotham would henceforth be dispatched back to the movie capital.

Some reporters thought Dean was so good, once they had seen *East of Eden,* that they forgave his earlier sins. After Hedda Hopper's disastrous July encounter with Dean, "Nobody could have dragged me," she said, to an *Eden* preview. But Clifton Webb, who did attend a preview, discreetly went to bat for Dean. He told Hopper he had just seen an extraordinary performance and that regardless of her justifiable distaste for Dean she should exercise her clout and arrange a private screening. On December 9, Kazan had the picture screened for her in a projection room at Warner Brothers.

Dean's performance had "such power, so many facets of expression, and so much sheer invention," Hopper said, that her tune changed on the spot. Only four days later, she knighted him "the brightest new star in town" and predicted that with the right parts he could be the top actor in the industry within a year. Then she phoned Jack Warner himself to ask if Dean would be interviewed at her home. Dean consented and ended up spending two hours with her.

Connolly, arguably the most talented and mirthful of the gossips, rushed over to Dean's camp for the same reason as Hopper: the appeal of Dean's acting. He, too, waxed rhapsodic immediately upon having seen *East of Eden.* After the Encino sneak preview, Connolly unabashedly called Dean "Hollywood's brightest new star" and said the performance "puts him at the very top with the all-time greats." As if to balance such lavish praise, Connolly followed up by observing that those who could compare Dean's two Broadway shows to *Eden* insisted his performances never varied. Then he elevated Dean to his roster of "quotable" stars by attributing to him a bromide about the advantages of bachelorhood: being able to get into bed from either side. He avidly chronicled Dean from then on and conducted the last full-fledged in-depth interview with him.

While Connolly was whooping Dean up, Sheilah Graham, the most persistent of the Brando linkers, managed to keep Brando out of her item on Dean's new Porsche Speedster, which she alleged was purchased "because the girls won't ride tandem on his motorcycle." Graham dubbed him "Hollywood's newest odd man out" and claimed he would be throwing a party at New York's 21 Club with the theme of rags to riches. Army Archerd noted that Dean's satisfaction with agent Dick Clayton led him to urge his New York friends to employ Clayton, too.[3]

When *East of Eden* opened in Hollywood, the press fell over itself passing on tidbits about Dean's amazement at his celebrity. He was spotted lunching at Musso's as crowds lined up across the street for the opening, or else driving down Hollywood Boulevard "nightly" to watch fans waiting to get in, or even standing (wearing glasses, unrecognized) outside the Egyptian Theater to keep an eye on ticket sales.

After less than a year, *Dean* was now a name for others to be linked to. Archerd said photographer Dennis Stock was to Dean what photographer Milton Greene was to Marilyn Monroe. Connolly quipped, "James Dean is to Googie's what Shelley Winters is to McDaniels' market."

The increased coverage and its favorable nature, however, did little to change Dean's intrinsic wariness and dislike of reporters. Philip Scheuer of the *Los Angeles Times,* the first journalist to score a major interview with Dean, wrote that the Hollywood press felt ignored and insulted by Dean, for whom small talk was an unpleasant burden.

One of Dean's most memorable tantrums occurred in New York, where he had gone not to assist Warner Brothers in promoting the world premiere of *Eden* but to be photographed by Dennis Stock for

---

3. Clayton said this would have referred to Richard Davalos.

Life magazine. On February 11, 1955, Larry Golob, eastern publicity director for Warners, cabled publicity chief Mort Blumenstock in Hollywood, fit to be tied over Dean's barbarous behavior during attempts to introduce him to the press. Golob complained that Dean initially refused to be interviewed by an impressive array of journalists. The office finally got him to change his mind, but that was a mistake. "He fouled himself up and got one magazine writer sore as blazes," Golob fumed. In desperation, Golob begged Kazan to weigh in and knock some sense into Dean, but Kazan didn't want any more involvement with the monster he had created.[4]

Golob sent the telegram just as Dean left New York for Indiana, where the *Life* photo sessions would continue; Dean's contempt for the Fourth Estate carried over to his native heath. "When contacted at his aunt's home, Dean said he did not have time to grant interviews," the Sunday *Marion Leader-Tribune* apologized. Here was a paradox. Until now, Dean resented the press because of excessive publicity. But in Indiana, he was nursing a grudge against the *Leader-Tribune* because he felt it had given him insufficient coverage while he was on his way up.[5] To make his point, he invited local sportscaster Bill Fowler to dinner at the Winslows'. Fowler, he felt, was the only local reporter who had promoted him before he was famous. "It's a cinch I'm not lettin' that goddam paper in my home," he growled to Fowler. He had told the *Leader-Tribune* he might talk to them later in the week, knowing full well he would be back in New York by then.

These attitudes never really abated. Right before Dean's death, both Rochlen and Graham reported that as he was leaving the Green Room, he spied a photo of himself on display. He shouted, "I told them I don't want my picture up with all these phonies!" (it was hanging between portraits of Anita Ekberg and Tab Hunter, Graham noted), then ripped the photo off the wall and tore it up.

In spite of all this misanthropy, Dean nonetheless dispensed numerous quips to inquiring scribes during the eighteen months of his life

---

4. Both Golob and Blumenstock died suddenly the following year at fifty-two and fifty-four, respectively. Their job was fraught with stress.
5. For starters, the paper had not noted any of Dean's movie bit parts when they played in Grant County in 1952.

as a star. He never spelled out his criteria in deciding whom he would favor, but he did tell Bob Thomas, Hollywood correspondent for the Associated Press, "I don't care what people write about me. I'll talk to the ones I like; the others can print whatever they please."

The full-length, autobiographical interviews Dean gave could be counted on one hand; of these, only two were printed during his lifetime. There were a number of "second-tier" (not of significant length) interviews: perhaps a few interesting quotes, but scant introspective or biographical information. These were sometimes the work of reporters whose papers could give them only limited space. Other columnists might catch an occasional quotable comment for use in an article not exclusively devoted to Dean. Gossip columns, in turn, trafficked in short, pithy, kaleidoscopic paragraphs.

Erskine Johnson of *Motion Picture* and the *Los Angeles Mirror-News,* who preferred writing about actresses, carried very little about Dean until interviewing him just as *Rebel Without a Cause* was ending. Johnson extricated enough material for five Dean items throughout June 1955. Dean, who seemed to speak pleasantly, said he was interested not in winning an Oscar but only in "learning the tools of my trade as an actor." He also spoke in defense of himself, Brando, and Clift: "They may call us cocky and maybe even difficult. But they never say about us, 'He doesn't know what he's doing.' "

The *New York Herald-Tribune*'s Hollywood correspondent, Joe Hyams, was introduced to Dean through insurance agent Lew Bracker, a mutual friend, in mid-1954. Despite his usual suspicion of reporters, Dean liked Hyams and immediately began trusting him with private information, not the least of which was his secret meetings with Angeli. Hyams was so pleased to be the confidant of a movie star that he wrote scarcely a word about Dean while he was alive; the one time he devoted his column to him was to describe a visit during which Dean, rather than Hyams, asked all the questions. Not a morsel of interesting data leaked out. (New York–based gossips—Dorothy Kilgallen, Louis Sobol, Walter Winchell, Earl Wilson, Radie Harris—understandably had less to say about Dean as long as his activities were centered in Hollywood.)

Louella Parsons never took the same shine to Dean as Hopper did. She printed occasional paragraphs about him but was far too preoccupied with Debbie Reynolds and Eddie Fisher in 1954 and 1955 to give Dean or anyone else much attention. She did note, when Dean was about to return to Hollywood on the verge of the *Eden* premiere, that he had thirteen fan magazine interviews waiting for him, even though he hadn't yet been seen by the public but "only by us critics."

The columnist who seemed genuinely to dislike Dean was Sheilah Graham. She grudgingly mentioned him a few times in 1955, usually in a variation on the Brando-Dean cliché. While many columnists were applying the term "female Marlon Brando" to actresses such as Vampira and Ursula Andress, Graham may have been the only one to use "female James Dean" (she affixed it to Terry Moore). Graham wrote several volumes of memoirs but never mentioned Dean.

Neither did Sidney Skolsky include Dean in his one volume of memoirs, *Don't Get Me Wrong—I Love Hollywood,* even though he was always a fan and friend. Skolsky's philosophy as a columnist was to plug newcomers and unknowns as frequently as possible, and he went the extra mile where Dean was concerned. He would print letters from girls wanting to form Dean fan clubs and asking how to go about it.

Kendis Rochlen, as noted, was the first to publish quotations from Dean (including his famous reference to Pier Angeli as "Miss Pizza"), most of which were recycled in the fan magazines. Although she saw Dean through the Angeli saga and then maintained an affectionate bond with him until his death, her column's format could not accommodate a long interview.

"Both of us had the same type of drive," she said, "so we understood each other. What we had, no one else had, an unerring sense between the bogus and the real. He knew I was doing it on my own, a rebel in my own way. I told him, 'I've never written a line, or a sentence, that I like, but I still try to write over my head.' He said, 'That's what I'm trying to do with my acting.' He wrote me a note that said, 'I'm interested in the craft, not the crap.'

"I shared with him Elinor Wylie's poem, 'Let No Charitable Hope.' He liked it and even said he wanted to live by it. I said, 'Jimmy, let's not let any years escape our smile.' He copied it down. I also quoted T. S. Eliot's *The Waste Land* to him: 'April is the cruellest month . . .' So he bought that and read it to me over the phone. He thanked me for it.

"I think Jimmy came to Hollywood with the hope of doing a good

In *Rebel Without a Cause,* Plato (Sal Mineo) and Jim (Dean) spot trouble brewing at Griffith Planetarium. *(Photofest)*

Director Nicholas Ray *(left)*, boxing coach Mushy Callahan, and Dean on the *Rebel* set. *(Photofest)*

Buzz (Corey Allen) and Jim square off in the knife fight sequence in *Rebel*. *(Photofest)*

A moment of unfeigned chaos in the *Rebel* knife fight sequence. *(Photofest)*

Mrs. Stark (Ann Doran) is horrified as Jim roughs up Mr. Stark (Jim Backus) in *Rebel. (Photofest)*

Jim and Judy (Natalie Wood) kindle a romance in *Rebel. (Photofest)*

Friends Jack Simmons and Dean on the *Rebel* set. *(Photofest)*

Hollywood publicity still of Dean. *(Photofest)*

Elizabeth Taylor and son
confer with an aging Jett Rink
(Dean) on the *Giant* set.
(Photofest)

George Stevens, Jr., Taylor, Dean, and *Giant* director George Stevens survey the
Texas landscape. *(Photofest)*

During what ought to be his most triumphant moment in *Giant*, Jett Rink (Dean) passes out from intoxication while dedicating his luxury hotel. *(Photofest)*

Giant author Edna Ferber, in Hollywood to review her troops, inhales Dean's smoke. *(Photofest)*

Dean and date Ursula
Andress attend an August
14, 1955, bon voyage party,
hosted by Frank Sinatra
(right), for Patsy D'Amore
(cutting cake), owner of
the Villa Capri restaurant.
(Neal Peters Collection)

Actress Jeanne Baird, Miss
Sports Car Race 1954,
presents Dean with racing
trophies. *(Archive Photos)*

The remains of Dean's Porsche Spyder after the fatal September 30, 1955, collision near Cholame, California. *(Archive Photos)*

Dean's headstone in Fairmount, Indiana. Contrary to many accounts, he was not buried next to his mother; she had been laid to rest in Marion, ten miles to the north. *(Author's Collection)*

job at what he loved doing, what he found worth doing. He wanted to be a star in the sense that it meant he was good at what he did. I think he identified with misfits and loners. He wasn't a misfit, but he was a loner, and he wanted very much to please himself with his work. He was young and vulnerable and shy, not sullen (even though I used the phrase 'dirty shirt' about him). He called himself a hick.

"He knew he would eventually have to play Hollywood's game. He would learn their rules and then bend them to his own rules.

"When he was lovesick over Pier, I told him to read a sonnet by Edna St. Vincent Millay, 'The heart once broken is a heart no more.' He asked me how I knew all this poetry. I told him it was a great use of time when stuck in traffic, especially Millay. Later he called me and said he'd been browsing in Pickwick on Hollywood Boulevard and had bought me a book that contained the sonnet. He left the price tag in it! He never wrapped anything. He wasn't playing to me.

"Once I wrote in my column that lots of girls were dying for dates with him, but if he were unknown, he'd probably be labeled a bore. He called me and said, 'Well, you got that right.' I could talk with him like that.

"I went to a special press screening of *East of Eden* and called him the next day to congratulate him. He asked, 'What did you think?' I replied, 'I cried and I cared.' He said, 'There you go, being alliterative again.' "

Dean was featured in one of Sidney Skolsky's weekly celebrity profiles ("Tintypes") on June 16, 1955, but it was not an interview. Most of Dean's quotes were lifted either from his studio biography or from other writers' previously published pieces. Skolsky's few original observations were made from his longtime vantage points at Schwab's counter or a table at Googie's: "He still pouts like a child when not getting enough attention" or "He must win at everything he does." Certain Skolsky hallmarks—the subject's favorite foods and what kind of bed and pajamas he or she slept in—were trotted out (in Dean's case, conventional-size bed, conservative pajamas).

Dean would give only four major interviews. The first was to Philip Scheuer, appearing on November 7, 1954, in the *Los Angeles Times;* the second was to Howard Thompson of *The New York Times* and published just after the world premiere of *East of Eden*. Both of these would be widely plagiarized by all varieties of gossipmongers in the months to come.

Hedda Hopper's interview, conducted at her home, probably in early December 1954, was extensive, but she waited a few months to publish it. Then, owing to syndication and different cut-and-paste jobs by editors all across America, its innumerable incarnations differed in varying degrees from one another, making it difficult to know exactly what Dean said. The interview was never printed in its entirety until Hopper's 1963 autobiography, and by then it had been heavily altered.

Finally, in August 1955, Mike Connolly spent several hours chatting with Dean at the latter's rented Sherman Oaks home. The resulting piece came out posthumously in *Modern Screen* in December 1955.

Although these four substantial interviews contain stretches of the truth, by and large Dean seemed to speak with thoughtfulness and candor. To Scheuer, he made his famous remark that "I'm a serious-minded and intense little devil, terribly gauche . . . and so tense I don't see how people stay in the same room with me. I know I wouldn't tolerate myself!"

In the same interview, Dean made an uncharacteristic political remark—a momentary lapse in his heeding of Rochlen's advice not to talk politics: He denounced communism as "the most limiting factor of all." The context for the statement was Dean's avowed hatred of anything that limits progress and growth, whether a school of thought, a school of acting, or an institutional policy.

The interview with Howard Thompson was the least honest Dean ever gave. First, he made his notorious but untruthful claim that in high school he had begun his winning rendition of "A Madman's Manuscript" with a scream. He allowed Thompson to propagate the myth that he had won the Donaldson and Perry awards for his role in *The Immoralist*. Then, by lionizing Lee Strasberg as "an incredible man, a walking encyclopedia, with fantastic insight," he left the false impression that he had flourished at the Actors Studio.[6]

---

6. Similar comments Dean made to *Esquire* writer Frederic Morton at this same time show that he wanted to be perceived as an active Studio member even though he did almost no work there. He said, "No, of course I don't feel I've graduated from the Studio. I may or I may not make two hundred thousand dollars next year, but I won't

But the Thompson interview contained some good statements on Dean's approach to acting. The most interesting was his analysis of stage versus screen. "The cinema," he mused, "is a very truthful medium because the camera doesn't let you get away with anything. On stage, you can even loaf a little, if you're so inclined. Technique, on the other hand, is more important. My aim, my real goal, is to achieve something I call camera-functioning on stage."

Dean twice lamely denied being a Hollywood-basher, reeling off some of his favorite movies to prove it. He conceded that if one looked hard enough, one could find human beings in Hollywood who were "sensitive to fertility."

In the Hopper interview, Dean made a rare public utterance about his mother. "When I was four or five, my mother had me playing violin. . . . My family came to California and before it was over my mother had me tap-dancing." (He called himself a child prodigy.) "My mother died when I was eight—and the violin was buried, too. Then I left California. I was anemic. . . ." Hopper noted Dean's hesitation at this point, and his next crack may have been to fight back tears: "What this story needs is a background of music."

Dean's ramblings to Hopper ranged from the sublime to the ridiculous. The latter came in the false assertion that he had won the Indiana state championship in pole vaulting. But there was something ineffable in his response to Hopper's query as to how someone as young as he could know, as shown in his *East of Eden* performance, so much about character and people. "This gift astonishes me," he confessed.

At their session's conclusion, Hopper said she wanted to be his

---

be able to afford graduating. In Hollywood the emphasis is on externals. What angles are best for your profile and how you should stand to appear taller and what path to use for walking from here to there and all that stuff. But the Studio makes you develop motivation. It makes you work from the inside out. It's just laziness if an actor tells you that pictures don't let him work truly. You've got to make personal sacrifices in Hollywood, publicity tours and all that stuff, but you don't have to compromise professionally. They'll permit you to be a good actor, especially if you work under a great guy like Gadge as I did in *East of Eden,* but you really have to *want* to be one. And that desire I get from the Studio. And if that sounds stuffy, don't quote me."

Dean's real opinion of Strasberg, says Jonathan Gilmore, usually involved naming an object the great teacher could "shove up his ass."

friend if he ever encountered trouble. "I'd like you to be," he responded. She gave him her phone number, telling him he could call at any time of day or night. "You mean that?" he asked. "I don't say things I don't mean," she assured him. According to Joe Hyams, Dean didn't like Hopper but found her useful as an advocate, so he did what he had to do to secure her favor.

Mike Connolly conducted his interview in the first week of August 1955. Dean was docile and charming, offering his guest freshly brewed coffee and raisin bread with cream cheese. He may have been impressed by Connolly's eminence at the *Hollywood Reporter;* or he may have known, instinctively or through the grapevine, that Connolly was homosexual. In any case, Dean wanted to demonstrate his hi-fi equipment, which was state of the art. He played several of his favorite opera records; judging from the tone of the ensuing discussion of favorite divas, either man could have held his own among opera buffs. Here Dean reflected the influence of both Leonard Rosenman and Frank Corsaro as he dropped comments about vocal modulation and the soundness of atonal music.

By the end of the interview, Dean had Connolly eating out of his hand. The journalist had noticed all the doors and windows open as he approached the house; later, when four neighborhood children dropped by, Dean welcomed them in and invited them to look around the house and backyard. "And this is the James Dean they've been calling a hermit!" Connolly fawned. When Dean sensed Connolly was pumping him about women (or "girls," as Connolly and everyone else talked in the Fifties), he merely grinned and recounted how three gossip columnists propagated three versions of his being out with three different women on the same night, when "all the time I was sitting in the Villa Capri with my insurance agent!" Had the same probing been done by a less luminous reporter, Dean might not have tolerated it.

In response to Connolly's asking whether he had lost anything after *East of Eden* made him famous, Dean was positively angelic. "I fought it for a long time," he admitted. "But after a while I think I started learning what so many actors have learned—about that certain communicative power we have that so few people are privileged to have. We find that we can reach not only the people with whom we work on the soundstages here in Hollywood but people all over the world! And then we start thinking, 'I'm famous, all right, and I guess this is what I wanted, so now how do I face it?' And then the responsibilities come. And you have to fight against becoming egotistical."

All in all, the Connolly interview is the most remarkable Dean ever gave. Dean's facility with highbrow topics demonstrated that his lifelong campaign to soak up human experience like a sponge and to sap the knowledge of learned friends had paid off. After the interview, according to Connolly's researcher, Joe Russell, Dean sent Connolly an autographed photo with the inscription, "I know, Mike, we all march to a different drumbeat."

The Symptoms of Fame

Kazan had witnessed the effect of success on many an unknown actor, and was almost voyeuristically alert to the phenomenon. "I don't expect it to be honorable," he warned. In Dean's case, Hollywood was saying he was a big star even before *Eden* filming ended, and Kazan saw it go to his head as he began to be rude to the wardrobe man and to complain about scenes he was expected to do. The great director said he knew Dean would "quickly spoil rotten."

While Kazan was merely resigned to the phenomenon, Lee Strasberg was terrified by it. "As soon as you grow up as actors," he preached at a Studio session shortly after Dean died, "now that you've really made it . . . what the hell happens with it? The senseless waste, the hopping around from one thing to the next, the waste of the talent, the waste of your lives, the strange kind of behavior that not just Jimmy had, but that a lot of [actors] have."

Not everyone believed that fame had affected Dean. Christine White, a leading exponent of the view that it did not, remembers his first visit to New York after *Eden,* when he tracked her down at her friend Barbara Dalton's apartment. "We heard a loud thump-thump on the stairs. I opened the door and there stood Lenny Rosenman, who announced, 'Mr. Dean is walking up the stairs backwards.' When Jimmy came into view he looked different. I asked, 'Have you gotten taller, or is that fame?' He said, 'It can't be fame because I'm not aware of it.'

"I sat down in a chair, but he grabbed my arm and pulled me up out of it, saying, '*I'm* sitting in this chair.' But then he pulled me back down into his lap. That was his way of giving an affectionate hello. His eyes fixed on the ash from his cigarette, and he asked, 'Now what am I gonna do with this?' He wanted to put it in my pocket, but Barbara brought over an ashtray—which he wanted to put on my head! I was then working twelve hours a day in a soap opera, and he said, 'I'm too crazy to do a soap.'

"He never thought of himself as a star, only as someone with big lucky breaks coming. He was always a little quick, a little distant. But he never acted the star, even after *Eden*. It was like it was in one ear and fell out because he didn't really receive it unto himself."

Dizzy Sheridan agreed with White. Back from St. Thomas, she had a happy reunion with Dean at a friend's party. "He was leaping and jumping all around like a clown, which he did very often when he was happy," Sheridan reminisced. "Wherever I went at that party, if I would go into the kitchen to get food, he would follow me out there and stand and talk. Never anything about Hollywood or what he was doing but what *I* was doing, or how was the old gang."

Sadly, some of Dean's New York friends did find him tainted by the Hollywood experience. Alec Wilder, formerly one of his most enthusiastic mentors, was horrified. "When Jimmy came back to New York," wrote Wilder, "he didn't go to the Iroquois. Oh, no. He came to the Algonquin. I'll never forget the sight of him. His glasses were dirty, his sweater was dirtier, he looked like a lost messenger boy. But, of course, that was all carefully calculated. And no longer was he an old friend of the bellmen with whom he had spent so many idle hours. I remember he took from his filthy windbreaker a copy of some spooked-up badly written paperback on religion."

But the last straw for Wilder was Dean's repudiation of Rogers Brackett. Brackett had recently fallen on hard times and was between advertising jobs; over a drink, he asked Dean to lend him some money. Dean not only refused but informed Brackett that he had outgrown him. When Wilder heard of this, he went looking for Dean and confronted him.

"I read him the riot act," Wilder wrote, "about his dreadful behavior towards Rogers. For nowhere in all his publicity had Rogers's name been mentioned. I told him he was morally bound to write Rogers a letter of apology. He claimed that he couldn't do it, so I wrote a letter as Jimmy might have. Then I forced him to rewrite it so that it could be mailed in his handwriting. Thank God, that did a little to mend the cracks. For the following evening Rogers came by, and the three of us had a very pleasant, giddy evening. But the damage had been done, and, as far as I know, they never met again."

According to Arnold Sundgaard, while Wilder was scolding Dean, he ranted that Brackett ought to sue him for repayment of past assistance. Dean replied, "I didn't know it was the whore who paid; I thought it was the other way around." Sundgaard was "surprised he had the intellect to make so shrewd an observation."

Dean had purchased two recordings of Wilder's music in March 1954, just before making *East of Eden,* a probable indication that he still held the composer (and his circle of friends) in esteem. His views on Brackett, Wilder, and their world changed over the summer, and Wilder attributed this to fear of having Brackett's role in his life exposed.

With Frank Corsaro, Dean shared a meal at the Capri on West Fifty-second Street. "He was extremely nervous when he came back," recalls Corsaro, "drinking brandy and swirling it around in the snifter, behaving as if he were on edge. He was telling me how he had 'handled' Kazan. I felt he had started believing his own publicity—and he was not equipped to deal with it. He reflected a proclivity for declivity."

Corsaro felt Dean's difficulties with Hollywood stemmed from his androgyny, which was and is a problematic concept for an essentially puritanical American public. "Jimmy's is a highly sexualized image," mused Corsaro. "He's a younger version of what someone said of Brando, the 'brute with girl's eyes.' Jimmy, Brando, and Clift knew how to play the field; how to project a unique mixture of 'delicate macho'— 'Save me, but don't come too close.' Jimmy lived a complex, shady existence. Emotionally, he was a male hustler.

"Jimmy couldn't help the androgyny; he was glorified for it while being told at the same time to stamp it out. His cruelty arose out of that conflict."

Dean had returned to New York principally to work in "Run Like a Thief," a *Philco Television Playhouse* drama that aired on September 5, 1954. He played Rob, a busboy and protégé of a headwaiter (Kurt Kasznar) in a swank hotel. The waiter finds a bracelet belonging to the hotel's owner but rather than return it gives it to his wife (Gusti Huber). For a time Rob is the chief suspect in the theft.

The director, Jeffrey Hayden, reminisced. "Jimmy was different, in the sense that he didn't want to learn his lines. Kurt Kasznar and Gusti Huber, on the other hand, were very mature, experienced, wonderful actors from the Viennese school. They knew all their lines before the first rehearsal and wanted to start in on the staging immediately, while Jimmy wanted to feel his way into the part. I kept trying to reconcile the two.

"On the day before camera blocking I saw Gusti sitting in a corner and her shoulders were heaving—I knew she was weeping. I asked her what was the matter. She said, 'I'm frightened and embarrassed! It's so late and we haven't set the business! Jimmy mumbles and I feel lost.' Now, Jimmy was my friend from the Actors Studio. But at that moment I was angry. I turned around from Gusti and I let him have it. Things blew up. I took a long walk around a long block. I came back and said, 'Let's go to work.' And Jimmy did things letter-perfect. He didn't hold back at all." *Variety* hailed Dean's acting as "beyond reproach."

Dean's other business in New York was to audition to replace David Wayne (last performance, September 18) as Sakini, male lead and master of ceremonies in *The Teahouse of the August Moon*. (Whether he auditioned in ignorance or defiance of his Warners contract, which allowed a Broadway play only after his third picture, is unknown.) Director Robert Lewis wrote that Dean was "paralyzed with fear" at the prospect of assuming a convincing Japanese attitude and accent. Lewis gave him a pep talk, but when Dean came out on stage, he uttered two lines and then started laughing uncontrollably. Lewis encouraged him to try again, but on his second attempt he got out even fewer words before getting the giggles. This time he ran out of the theater and kept on going.

What really captivated and diverted him on this trip was the pursuit of photography, both still and moving. He brought Roy Schatt to Leonard Rosenman's thirtieth birthday party, an intimate gathering of *East of Eden* alumni, where the two of them delighted in photographing composer Rosenman and cast members Jo Van Fleet and Barbara Baxley. He also dragged Schatt to a camera shop to supervise his purchase of a Bolex 16mm movie camera and accessories. A Hollywood cameraman had befriended him and "showed me a lot of things," he told Schatt, and now he was set to launch his career as a filmmaker.

For several days Dean barked orders at Schatt, Martin Landau, Bill Gunn, and Bob Heller as they hauled—despite a colossal heat wave—lights, wires, and props around Schatt's small studio and even smaller backyard. They were not only the actors but also the lighting crew and prop men in his experimental film, for which "there was no script, unless it was in his head," Schatt grumbled. Despite their long-suffering assistance, none of them ever saw the finished product.

Bidding New York good-bye, Dean flew back to Hollywood for his Lake Arrowhead date with Pier Angeli and to meet with Batjac, John Wayne's movie company, to discuss a project close to his heart: a bullfighting movie based on *Matador,* the novel that had inspired his first Actors Studio scene. (The movie would never materialize, and the relationship with Angeli was, of course, on its last leg.) In California, he was still squatting on the Warners lot in the star dressing room Kazan had arranged for him during the *Eden* filming. This had been tolerated while Jack Warner had been away on his annual August holiday in Cap d'Antibes, but now Warner was back and, for insurance reasons, wanted Dean out. Dick Clayton managed to stall Warner temporarily while trying to find Dean a new place, but Dean seemed in no hurry to leave. Finally Warner ordered that his belongings be removed from the dressing room.

In the face of this crisis, Clayton simply turned his own apartment, at 1741 Sunset Plaza Drive, over to Dean. Meanwhile, according to Nicholas Ray, Dean avenged Warner's affront by removing the name and number plates from all the office doors on the lot and hanging them from ceilings or any unusual place. "Then," claimed Ray, "he rode away on his motorcycle, vowing never to make a film there again . . . regardless of contract."

Although the dressing room incident was highly offensive to Dean, it did not appear to have been regarded gravely by Warner Brothers. In late September, the studio was considering loaning Dean to M-G-M for the movie *The Cobweb,* in the role of an artistic young mental patient, but balked when M-G-M wouldn't pay what they were asking for him. Then on October 7, Warners exercised its option under the *Eden* contract to tap Dean for a second picture *(Rebel Without a Cause)*—certainly not the course of action an aggrieved studio would take.

Further, Dean was needed on the lot throughout the fall for post-recording and filming of added scenes for *East of Eden,* and the studio seemed willing to overlook almost any behavior, no matter how bizarre, in view of the incredible product they were getting from him.[1] That product was already apparent, even in the picture's still-primitive state. On October 1, Kazan ran a rough cut of it for Dean, Christopher Isherwood, and Don Bachardy. "It didn't even have music yet," Bachardy recalls. "Jimmy came in after the lights went out, and sat down."

Isherwood and Bachardy still harbored lingering skepticism about Dean's star potential. "Suddenly, in the screening room, we were blown away," Bachardy continues. "As soon as it was over, Jimmy left through the same door he'd come in. A great shaft of light flooded the room. Chris ran after him to tell him how wonderful he thought his performance was. He ran a whole block to catch up with him. When he got back, I asked, 'What did he say?' Chris said, 'Nothing—he just got the biggest smile on his face.' "

Nicholas Ray had moved into a Warners office (next to Kazan) in the last week of September to set up production on *Rebel Without a Cause.* One day Dean came in and questioned him about his project; two days later he returned with his actor friend Perry Lopez, who came from a tough New York neighborhood, and told Ray that perhaps Lopez could offer some insights into juvenile delinquency. "After a few more incidents like that," Ray wrote, "I decided he had to play Jim Stark [the male lead in *Rebel* who confronts and surmounts gang violence and paternal weakness]."

As a matter of fact, Dean had secured his upcoming role in *Giant* as the surly ranch hand-*cum*-oil tycoon Jett Rink by the same method,

---

1. Biographer Venable Herndon felt Dean was "exploited in the same way Mozart was." Daniel Mann's wife, Sheri, observed, "People like Jimmy were exploited for their strangeness in this town. Studios didn't care about helping them to be better persons."

even before he met Ray; he simply began hanging out in director George Stevens's office, which had a *Giant* logo and map of Texas on the door. Stevens, whose first choice for Jett Rink had been Alan Ladd, later compared casting Dean to "going to Des Moines to get a big league pitcher." But, he said, "I let him decide. I gave him the part to read. He read it, and came back glowing. 'That's me,' he said. 'I want that part. What do we do, make a test or something?' I told him no test was necessary—the part was his. There is a lot in this character that Jimmy Dean presumed himself to be."

Even though he required no test, Stevens did ask CBS in New York to airmail a kinescope of "The Killing of Jesse James." Of all Dean's television roles, his portrayal of Robert Ford, James's killer, was the closest in genre to Jett Rink. Stevens viewed the kinescope on September 28. However, the point at which he made up his mind to cast Dean is uncertain. The press would hint as early as December 24 that Dean seemed likely for Rink, but Warners would not announce it officially until March 16, 1955.

When he was not adding finishing touches to *Eden* or hustling his next movie role at the studio, Dean began to fill the void left by Pier Angeli with new friends: Maila Nurmi a.k.a. Vampira, Jack Simmons, Keenan Wynn, and Arthur Loew, Jr. Nurmi had mesmerized Los Angeles as hostess of a horror movie program, dressed and made up as the Charles Addams cartoon character Morticia. She attended the *Sabrina* premiere specifically to cruise for new friends, and as if out of a police line-up, selected Jack Simmons, an aspiring actor, and James Dean as her targets. Wasting no time, she cornered Simmons, but Dean, who escorted Terry Moore, got away. However, the next day, as Nurmi and Simmons were lunching at Googie's, an all-night hamburger joint, he came in.

"It was a very weird thing," Simmons recalls. "Three different people who knew both Jimmy and me—a Broadway producer, a rodeo rider, and my friend Connie Lawrence—all had told me I reminded them of Jimmy Dean. So, when Jimmy came into Googie's, I went up to him and said, 'We don't look a thing alike.' He asked, 'Well, are we supposed to?' We talked for a good forty minutes. In fact, he was there with Connie Lawrence. I brought him over to meet Vampira."

Once that momentous introduction had been made, "We were

never again separated," joked Nurmi. "Oh, I occasionally went home to my husband." The routine was always the same—meeting at Schwab's drugstore at Sunset and Crescent Heights, drinking coffee until it closed at midnight, then moving next door to Googie's. "When we first met," said Nurmi, "I was the famous one that people were crowding around. Jimmy would be pushed aside and he'd call to me over the heads, 'Asses and elbows!' meaning that's what he had in his face. Later when he became famous, I was on the outer fringes, yelling 'Asses and elbows' to him! I had him on my show once.

"He was fast and reckless. Jack had an antique hearse, and one night we were going up Sunset Plaza Drive, Jimmy on his motorcycle in front of us, with our spotlights on him. He held his hands over his head and his hips were swaying from side to side, so that the motorcycle was almost lying on its side. Any car coming the other way wouldn't have seen him and he would've been killed instantly. I was yelling at him to stop, but the only way to get him to stop was to pull over and turn our lights off so he no longer had the stage and audience."

Motorcycles were the basis of Dean's friendship with the actor Keenan Wynn. Although Wynn was a working actor and a fixture in Hollywood society, his real ambition, according to his son, was to have his own motorcycle shop and ride, ride, ride. Wynn was an early Dean pal and taught him motorcycle hill climbing. He also brought Dean for the first time to Arthur Loew's house.

Arthur Loew, Jr., a producer at M-G-M, was the scion of film industry royalty on both his paternal and maternal sides. Sometime that fall, Wynn and Rod Steiger stopped by Loew's house at 1372 Miller Drive, above Sunset Boulevard, telling him they had a new star out in the car who was extremely touchy and moody if provoked. But instead of heeding the warning, Loew began ribbing Dean when he came in. To Wynn's and Steiger's surprise, Dean started laughing and relaxing; he and Loew had hit it off.

"Jimmy had a terrific personality, kind of cuckoo. I only knew vaguely that he had been a New York actor," Loew remarks. "It was very informal at my house. I was a bachelor then and didn't have a regular running home. Lots of people were often there, and they were off-the-wall and fun. It was not a stiff, cocktail party atmosphere; it was more like a club.

"Once Robert Mitchum, Errol Flynn, Artie Shaw, and Jimmy were all there, and a policeman came to the door for directions. I asked him to come back in the house and hold my arm as if I were under arrest, to get a rise out of the others. The cop stayed for about an hour, caught up in conversation with all of them. Then his car radio went off, and he told us he had to investigate a burglary in progress. 'Why bother with that?' I asked him. 'You could bust Mitchum for dope, Flynn for having a thirteen-year-old girl upstairs in the bedroom, Dean for speeding'—Jimmy would be up to seventy-five by the time he was out of my driveway—'and Shaw for bigamy, and you'd be promoted to captain tomorrow!' He loved it."

A year earlier, Dean's close friend Eartha Kitt had begun an intense romance with Loew that ultimately collapsed in the face of heavy pressure from Loew's family. Kitt felt she had been shut out abruptly and was devastated; in the fall of 1954, while in New York rehearsing for the Broadway play *Mrs. Patterson,* she occasionally phoned Loew's home, and often Dean would answer. Dean, she said, would reassure her that Loew loved her and was trying to be strong in the face of familial coercion. Unfortunately, the romance would not be salvaged.

On any given night, Dean was likely to be with one or more of these new friends. With Nurmi and Simmons in tow, he once showed up at Nicholas Ray's bungalow at the Chateau Marmont. Dean made his entrance by doing a backwards roll and then trained his gaze on Ray. "Are you middle-aged?" he asked.

Ray, who was then forty-three, admitted that he was. Dean then interrogated him about a 1952 fire that destroyed an old Sunset Strip casino next door to Ray's former home. He wanted to know if Ray had actually cut his bare feet while carrying a puppy to safety. Ray confirmed all these details. "Vampira had told him the story," Ray wrote. "He had come to find out if it were true. He seemed to approve." Ray would indulge any eccentric behavior of Dean's to encourage him to play Jim Stark in *Rebel.*

In between all these Hollywood diversions, Dean made a quick trip to New York for another television commitment, this time an episode of *Danger* called "Padlock," on November 9. The two-character drama featured Dean as a gunman on the lam and Mildred Dunnock as an eccentric old woman from whom the fugitive steals everything. Dunnock remembered his arriving for rehearsals "like something shot out of a cannon" with "enough momentum to walk up the wall."

No sooner had Dean completed "Padlock" than another television job, the November 14 presentation of *General Electric Theater,* brought him back to the coast. In an adaptation of the Sherwood Anderson short story, "I'm a Fool," he would play a racetrack stableboy who believes new clothes and an assumed name will help him rise in status. He meets an elegant city girl (Natalie Wood) who falls for his false identity and promises to write him when she gets home, but her train comes before he can muster the courage to tell her the truth. The *Hollywood Reporter* billed this as his "live West Coast TV debut" (the claim was technically correct, since his minor 1951 television appearances had been filmed).

"Natalie was young and her concentration wasn't the best," recalls Don Medford, who directed "I'm a Fool." "At the end, just before she boarded her train, Jimmy was relating to her and she turned her head away instead of being eye to eye with him as the moment required. So he grasped her face and turned it toward him!"

Both trade papers praised Dean's acting. To the *Hollywood Reporter,* he came across as a "broodingly powerful young actor with a definite career before him." *Daily Variety* noted his "sensitive and moving performance" and singled him out for "excellent thespic work."

"I'm a Fool" had been rehearsed in a remote hall in East Los Angeles, says Medford. "We all lived in Beverly Hills or West Hollywood, so we had to come home on the freeway. I remember being on the freeway when suddenly, whooshing out of nowhere, Jimmy came zigzagging in and out of the lanes in front of me on his motorcycle, hands in the air as if to balance himself. It scared the shit out of me. At the next morning's rehearsal I pinned him up against the wall and said, 'Don't play with your life like that!' He just smiled at me."

Similar recollections of anxiety over Dean's motorized swashbuckling come from Arthur Loew, Jr. "There were nights I'd be driving home on Sunset Boulevard at two or three A.M.," Loew says, "and suddenly there would be Jimmy, passing me on his motorcycle doing about one hundred. Then, in what seemed just a few seconds later, he'd be coming back from the opposite direction. This could go on three or four more times. I would lecture him, 'That's not safe!' Everyone at my place was always telling him to be careful. But Keenan Wynn would tell me Jimmy knew how to handle the bike and was really adept."

At Nicholas Ray's invitation, Dean began to attend the Sunday salons at Ray's Chateau Marmont bungalow, where there was music and singing (starting with bop at one P.M. and ending with Bach at one A.M., according to *Daily Variety*) and always lots of movie industry talk. Many scenes of *Rebel* were conceived at these gatherings. "It was exploratory on both sides," Ray said. "Was he going to like my friends, would he find their climate encouraging? Both of us had to know." Dean met many notables at these events, including *Life* photographer Dennis Stock.

Screenwriter Andrew Solt remembered meeting Dean at Ray's one Sunday afternoon, and was as unimpressed as Christopher Isherwood and Don Bachardy had earlier been. "There sat in the corner a little boy, emaciated, the whole thing could have been one hundred and twenty-five pounds," recalled Solt, "a little effeminate, dark, the only thing that made him a little interesting was that he had a cat on his shoulder. Then Nick came out, positive and beaming, and he said, 'I want you to meet my new star, Jimmy Dean.' We talked, I forget what about, and Ray said, 'What do you think of him?' I couldn't lie. I said, 'This, a star?' He said, 'He'll be the biggest star.' I said, 'Well, I wish you lots of luck,' but I couldn't see it. And, of course, he saw exactly what this boy would look and act like on the screen."

On December 1, the screenwriter Stewart Stern arrived in Los Angeles, with no thought of being drawn into any movie project, let alone *Rebel Without a Cause*. "I had a great apartment in New York," Stern says, "and I only intended to spend Christmas with my cousin Arthur Loew." Dean was already at Loew's when Stern arrived, and though initially distant and suspicious, the actor soon warmed up when he found Stern could match his prowess at imitating barnyard animals bleat for bleat.

As a fixture in the Loew house, Dean quickly came to know Stern. "He would often stand outside," recalls Stern, "looking into the dining room, scouting out if anyone was there who made him uncomfortable. If he approved, he'd just tap on the glass and come in and eat. If not, he'd leave. On other nights, we'd hear his motorcycle. He'd pull into the drive and check the cars. Too many made him leave. If he knew whose they were and he liked them, he'd come in."

By December, *East of Eden* had been edited and scored and was ready for public previews; Kazan had it run for a select audience, including Christopher Isherwood, Don Bachardy, Tennessee Williams, and Joshua Logan, on December 4. The *Hollywood Reporter* divulged that a woman at the screening fawned out loud ("Who *is* that wonderful boy?") over Dean in nearly every scene until he could stand no more and walked out of the projection room.

There were two public sneak previews in local theaters, the first on December 6 in Huntington Park. A bewildered Kazan recalled that the women in the audience began screaming as soon as Dean appeared on the screen; he had no idea of what prompted this sudden and unexpected hysteria, and he had a point. Certainly the industry itself was becoming familiar with Dean's name, but only a modest amount of publicity (and one or two photos of him with Pier Angeli in the fan magazines) had reached the general public. Perhaps the recent television show with Natalie Wood had impressed the women at Huntington Park in the same way *Hill Number One* had moved the Immaculate Heart student body nearly four years before.

Dick Clayton accompanied Dean to this first preview and remembers it as "spellbinding. I couldn't believe that the guy on screen was the same guy I knew, and I'd even been on the set watching the filming. The camera was magic." Also in the Huntington Park audience was the editor of *Motorcyclist* magazine, who wrote immediately to Jack Warner that Dean was sensational. Keenan Wynn had told the editor about Dean several weeks before, but now he saw for himself that Wynn's enthusiasm was justified.

The second sneak preview ran later that week at Encino's La Reina Theater, and the audience "went crazy," wrote Mike Connolly. Dean had asked Loew and Stern to attend with him, but did not brief his guests on what movie they were about to see. Stern says Dean hadn't even mentioned that he was in the picture. "The theater was jammed," Stern relates, "and suddenly Jimmy pulled us after him over the rope into a reserved VIP section. I thought an executive would kick us out. I prayed for the lights to go down before we were discovered as impostors. When Jimmy's name came on, I asked, 'Is that you?' He nodded and laughed. I said something brilliant, like, 'You're kidding.' After the film he asked me what I thought of the picture, and I said it was wonderful. He followed with 'And what about me?' and I said it was one of the most sensitive and talented performances I'd ever seen in my life."

Loew recalls, "This was the first time I'd ever been with anyone who had walked into a preview as a nobody and come out a star. When we walked into the theater, no one paid him more attention than they paid to Stewart and me. At the end, I recall, it was really quiet, since people were stunned."

At week's end, Dean was behaving like someone who had arrived, showing up at the Crescendo nightclub in a foursome with Lili Kardell, Tennessee Williams, and Anna Magnani. Kardell, a nineteen-year-old Swedish actress, had been signed the month before by Universal to a seven-year contract and would be Dean's date often in the coming months. "Lili was slightly bovine and quite beautiful," says Jack Simmons. "Jimmy and I called her the Cat Lady."

Dean appeared again on *General Electric Theater* on December 12 in "The Dark, Dark Hour"; the cast included Ronald Reagan and Dean's friends Constance Ford (of *See the Jaguar*) and Jack Simmons. Dean played a "hepcat" hoodlum whose friend Peewee (Simmons) had been seriously wounded in a gun battle. He breaks into the home of a doctor (Reagan), whom he forces at gunpoint to operate on Peewee. Donald Medford directed; it was his fourth television show with Dean.

"The original script, as was our habit, was sent to the sponsor [General Electric] for approval," Medford recounts. "They rejected it because they didn't want to show sympathy with juvenile delinquents. Mort Abrahams, the producer, and I were disappointed, because it was a labor of love for us. So I had an idea: 'Let's get Jimmy Dean to play it—let's have the writer take out the controversial dialogue and let Jimmy fill it in.' So the script was resubmitted after the names and title had been changed, and it was accepted!

"As part of his deal with G.E. as its weekly host, Ronald Reagan could choose to play in up to six shows per season. To our horror, he chose this one. He was delighted to be in it. Jimmy was a smashing success. We got telegrams and raves from other directors, which *never* happens.

"Well, the next day, Mort Abrahams and I were fired. G.E. realized the script had been a ruse. And Reagan called a press conference. He stated that he hated the role and had been coerced into playing it, and all juvenile delinquents were bastards who deserved what they got.

"But Jimmy was fabulous. He did things on the air that rocked us in the control room. Peewee was lying on the doctor's table, terribly scared. The doctor left the room, and in an effort to calm Peewee, Jimmy turned the radio up and took his hand and pretended to jitterbug with him. That was original! Another thing he did was to tap on the lens of Peewee's glasses and ask, 'Are you home, Peewee?'

"Jack Simmons was just a person at Googie's, really. Jimmy would sit at Googie's and study people by the hour. That was his key to people, I felt. He was delighted that we cast Jack. But I'm afraid we did Jack a terrible disservice by casting him, because after that he thought he was an actor!"

Daily Variety didn't like "The Dark, Dark Hour" and thought Dean was "called upon to overact." The *Hollywood Reporter* carried no review, but its television columnist wrote, "We heard many good words for James Dean's performance on Sunday night's *G.E. Theater,* with high praise for the gangster lingo."

As if to recuperate from this incredibly full week of sneak previews, celebrity sightings, and television work, Dean once again escaped to New York. When he arrived on December 19, several show business people were waiting to meet with him, including Frank Corsaro, who would soon direct *A Hatful of Rain* and was interested in him for one of the junkies; and William Inge and Harold Clurman, writer and director of *Bus Stop.* He didn't go with either project, but offers of Broadway plays were now a regular occurrence in his life.

Flying to New York right on Dean's heels was Nicholas Ray, ostensibly to do casting for *Rebel Without a Cause* but really to bolster Dean's likely participation in the picture. They dined together every evening of Ray's visit, and by the time he was ready to leave, he felt he had earned Dean's confidence. This was borne out by Dean's asking Ray for advice on how to cure a case of crabs; Ray took the younger man to a drugstore to find a remedy. "I want to do your film," said Dean as a parting shot to Ray, "but don't let them [Warners] know it."

Dean spent both Christmas and New Year's Eve with Roy Schatt. On Christmas morning, they were joined by Martin Landau and roamed Manhattan, taking pictures. Later Dean was the Landau family's guest for Christmas dinner. After dinner, Dean offered to read to

Landau's three small nephews. He didn't patronize them; he read one of his own favorite selections, Federico García Lorca's "Ode to Walt Whitman." Even though such a poem was beyond the small boys' comprehension, they were enthralled by Dean's expressiveness.

On January 4, 1955, Dean was in "The Thief" (*The U.S. Steel Hour,* then on ABC), playing Fernand Legarde, the strange younger son of a wealthy French family, suspected—wrongly, in the end—of stealing his parents' money. (It was a role in which his lack of interest in time and place was painfully obvious.) Although this broadcast had been Dean's main reason for being in New York, he was in no hurry to leave the city, and spent much of the next two weeks in the company of Ray's son Tony, who was minding his father's business: the director wished specifically to see Dean through the eyes of the younger generation and had assigned Tony to tail him.

Tony Ray would give an interesting report. Dean's crowd was always the same: Barbara Glenn, Bob Heller, Bill Gunn, Martin Landau, and Roy Schatt, and they congregated either at Dean's Sixty-eighth Street digs or Schatt's. At any given moment, Dean was likely to be banging his bongo drums, Gunn dancing as if he were Gene Kelly, and everyone talking about the theater, or philosophy, or reading plays out loud. No one ever seemed to go home.

Through his own experience and what his son told him, Nicholas Ray would also observe what was perhaps the most shocking of all the strange attitudes Dean exhibited after becoming conscious of his fame: convincing himself that he had had no help in getting where he got and that he owed nothing to anyone. That he had been fed and befriended by many generous friends in his years of struggle seemed not to matter to him anymore; the same boy who had mooched meals from UCLA football players was now accusing his pals of freeloading at his expense. An old friend wanted to buy a secondhand camera for twenty-five dollars and asked Dean to split the cost. "Why should I go and buy a secondhand camera with you?" Dean reportedly snorted. "I can get all the new stuff I want now."

Later in the month, just before catching a plane to Hollywood to work in "The Unlighted Road," a *Schlitz Playhouse of Stars* drama, he was killing time in his apartment, chatting with Bill Gunn. "He was always afraid of flying," Gunn said. "He had to take a late-night plane to the coast for a TV show. I wondered why he wanted to keep on talking and talking until just before plane time. 'So I'll conk out on the plane,' he told me, 'and wake up on the coast. These planes—they'll fall out of the air.' " Gunn told him he was being morbid. Instead of responding, Dean walked over to his closet, took out his old blue suit, and gave it to Gunn.

Dean would spend a very full nine days in Hollywood before ricocheting back to New York. For *Schlitz Playhouse of Stars* he portrayed a drifting Korean War veteran who finds a job at a roadside diner and unwittingly becomes a pawn in a racketeering scheme. The female love interest was played by actress Pat Hardy. "Jimmy was determined to make this role very realistic," Hardy explained. "He even had a pebble in his shoe. I asked him why and he said, 'This guy's just back from Korea and he's been wounded in the leg.' The pebble was to make him limp just right. But I reminded him of what he was always telling me— 'Think'—make the limp in your mind. I believe he did away with the pebble altogether." The show was filmed, eventually airing on May 6.

One evening at Googie's, Dean met a young woman, a singer named Toni Lee, who had lost a leg in a motorcycle accident. According to Bill Bast, who chatted with her one evening in Googie's, Lee was impressed that Dean, alone among all the regular customers, had the nerve to inquire about her missing limb.

Knowing Dean's admiration of Brando, Lee informed him of an artist's studio on Melrose Avenue that displayed a bust of Brando in its window. In fact, Dean had seen the bust and was delighted that Lee knew its sculptor, Kenneth Kendall. On January 22, Lee called Kendall and brought Dean over, in the same manner that Arlene Sachs had presented Dean to Roy Schatt in New York.

"I had terrible stage fright—I don't know why," remembers Kendall. "I knew only that he was hailed as Brando's rival, but I had no idea of his talent. He inspected the Brando head in the front window. This led into my showing them my painting of Brando as Marc Antony, holding a scroll inscribed in Latin: 'Did you wonder who was the greatest actor of our time? This is the man; this is Brando.' Toni Lee interjected, 'Jimmy's going to be the biggest actor in this town!' No doubt he told her that.

"Jimmy could hardly get out, 'Would you consider sculpting me?'

It hadn't been discussed in advance that that's what he wanted. I told him my fees; he said he was leaving for New York in four days and would bring me a folio of his photos to look over regarding the sculpture project. But I never saw him again. Unfortunately, I gave away six James Dean cigarette butts, a few days after his visit, to someone who had prepared a very elaborate horoscope which I was supposed to give to Jimmy. Believe it or not, September thirtieth was to be one of his good days!"[2]

After the session at Kendall's studio, writes Lee in her autobiography, she and Dean went to Googie's for coffee. While seated in a booth, they overheard some nearby actors planning to take dates to a movie premiere. One actor suggested Lee as a date, to which another replied, "Do you think I want to be seen with a one-legged girl?" Lee was so hurt that she fled the booth and drove away, leaving Dean behind.

At four o'clock in the morning, Lee heard her doorbell ring and found Dean wanting to see her. Lee reports that after Dean entered, he asked her to "do something" for him—to take off her clothes—and that trusting him, she undressed. "Kneeling on the floor in front of me," she wrote, "he ran his fingers over the scars on the stump . . . he went over them one by one. When he finished he very gently kissed the leg. 'It's beautiful,' he said, 'and you're beautiful. And don't let anyone convince you otherwise. Now get dressed.'"

Whenever she saw Dean after that, Lee wrote, he would tell her "over and over again" that she was special and ought not to let herself be smothered by Hollywood's ugliness. "There was never any romance between us," she reported; "there was friendship."

Dean spent some of his few January evenings in Hollywood at Ciro's, where Sammy Davis, Jr., was performing. Dean was a frequent ringsider with Ella Logan, a Scottish songstress best known for her role in the Broadway musical *Finian's Rainbow.* Logan was a friend of Kazan and had met Dean on the *Eden* set—and was "everybody's earth

---

2. Kendall did sculpt Dean many times in the ensuing years, eventually memorializing him with the handsome bronze bust that was installed on the grounds of Griffith Planetarium in 1988.

mother," according to Jack Larson. While Davis dazzled the multitude, Dean doodled on the paper tablecloth—but now that he was famous, customers spying what he left behind asked the management if they could buy it as a souvenir.

Davis's final show at Ciro's, on January 26, was a grand night in Hollywood. Logan and Dean were there, and *Daily Variety*'s Army Archerd, on hand to record the comings and goings of the glitterati, observed "socialite" Spencer Martin heckling Dean over his black shirt and unkempt hair. Dean simply ignored Martin. Later Archerd watched Dean drive away on his new motorcycle, a Triumph that frightened everyone but its owner.

Later that night Dean arrived at Logan's Brentwood home, where a party in Davis's honor was in full swing. Dean's journalist friends, Kendis Rochlen and Sidney Skolsky, worked the crowd in search of good copy, and Marlon Brando showed up in an elegantly cut gray suit and narrow black tie. The revelry would persist until six in the morning. Davis manned the bongo drums for several hours, while Logan and Nat Cole sang. The merrymaking peaked with Davis and Logan spoofing the scene in *A Star Is Born* in which James Mason slaps Judy Garland. But in Skolsky's opinion, the night's real entertainment was "watching James Dean watch Marlon Brando, who was casing Jimmy Dean."

A few days earlier, Dean had bruised his left leg in a fall from the Triumph. Perhaps the way he roared up to the party was the last straw for Logan, who begged Brando to have a word with Dean about safe driving. Brando obliged. "If you get in an accident," the august actor cautioned, "you're liable to slide off and lose half your face. That's okay if you're in some other business, but as an actor you'll have trouble getting by without it." Going beyond the call of duty, Brando also urged Dean to see a psychiatrist.

While Dean had been in New York, Stewart Stern slaved away at the screenplay for *Rebel Without a Cause*. Largely on the basis of enthusiastic recommendations from Dean and Leonard Rosenman, Stern had been hired by Ray, beginning his work on New Year's Day. Now temporarily reunited in Hollywood, he and Dean stopped at Googie's one night with Dennis Stock. Dean's admiration for Stern was such that he wanted Stern to come to New York with him and Stock and write the text of the *Life* photo essay Stock would be shooting; he also envisioned Stern as the writer of his life story.

"Anyway, Dennis left," says Stern. "Jimmy and I started talking very personally. A couple of times before this I had seen him be cold or abrupt with people—but these things always ended in something causing pain for him. He was always putting people through a series of circus hoops before letting them get close. He was like Marlon: he ate people—consumed all they knew, their mannerisms, all he could use as an artist. Everyone was a source for his creativity. He really wanted to be a participant in life. But he was constantly fucking himself over by behavior designed to alienate people.

"This kid had no experience! He'd come off the farm into the big city, where he was manhandled by people way beyond him in worldliness. He was trying to construct for himself, out of all they could teach him, and in a very short time, the equipment to live in this world—to prepare not only for his roles but for his life.

"At the core of this, I sensed a terrible, yawning feeling of inadequacy and emptiness and yearning, and I told him that. As much as he wanted and needed friends, he often drove them away. The time at Googie's was the closest I ever felt to him, and the closest he ever felt to me. People wanted to sit down with us, but he would indicate that he didn't want to be interrupted."

The following night, accompanied by Dennis Stock (but not by Stern, who was shackled to the *Rebel* screenplay), he flew back to New York. Pat Hardy drove Dean to the airport, later recalling the same characteristic Bill Gunn had observed: Dean's fear of flying. "This may sound stupid," he told her, "but if anything happens to me, please deliver this message to [Hardy declined to identify the friend]."

Stock would follow Dean to many of his favorite hangouts, all within a small radius of Times Square. Dean particularly wanted to be photographed at the Actors Studio, an occasion recalled by Arnold Sundgaard: "I was a member of the playwrights unit at the Actors Studio. Jimmy had by now achieved his Hollywood fame. At one of the sessions, Jimmy, now the young star, appeared. He was wearing a dark, rather shabby coat, and he hunched down in a seat up front and turned up the collar of his coat. He seemed to know that he was being scrutinized as someone who had made it, and used the collar to shield himself from burning eyes. All it served to do was to make him the most prominent character in the room. Or so I thought. At one moment, the collar fell into place on his shoulders, but he quickly adjusted it to its original casual position. No question he sensed his dilemma—how not to preen while enjoying his moment in that galaxy of established professionals. It was a lesson in bravura self-effacement. At the same time it showed the charismatic qualities that made him what he was on film."

From New York, Dean and Stock flew to Indiana for five days of exploring Dean's roots. Sue Hill, Dean's former debate partner, remembers, "Jim came in the Dairy Bar where I worked. It was the meeting place of Fairmount then. The men who came in for breakfast and coffee breaks gave him a hard time about his lack of military service—small-town humor barbed with cracks about how he liked New York instead of Korea. He joked back, 'At least C-rations are edible—very little of the food in New York is.'"

Dean's new policy of forgetting his old friends carried over to Fairmount. He had never failed on previous visits to look up Adeline Brookshire at the high school, but this time he made no move to see her, even though he did go to the school, when no one was there, to pose in the auditorium, in a classroom, and on a stairwell for Stock. Brookshire knew he was in town and finally tracked him down at his grandparents' home. His conversation with her amounted to a torrent of complaints about the "bunch of leeches" who followed him around. She was quite hurt by the experience.

On the other hand, Dean's boyhood friend Bob Middleton recalled of the same visit, "He hadn't changed towards me—but he *was* changed. You can't travel with that Hollywood crowd and not change." On February 17, Middleton drove Dean and Stock to the Indianapolis airport. He remembers that they ate lunch together at a downtown restaurant. "Jim loved to chew on wheat grains, and before leaving the Winslows' place, he'd stuffed his pockets full of wheat," said Middleton. "At the restaurant, we sat in a booth by the window with a planter. Jim made a furrow in the dirt with his finger, planted a few grains of wheat, and covered them over. He thought it was really something."

Back in New York, preparations for the March 9 world premiere of *East of Eden* at New York's Astor Theater were by now in full swing, and Warner Brothers had mounted a high-profile campaign to introduce their new star. Miles White—who had had no contact with Dean since 1951 and still didn't know his real name—was sitting at the Algonquin Hotel's bar one day when Dean came in and spotted him. " 'Hamlet' came up and said hello," says White. "I didn't even recognize him at first. It amused him that I introduced him as Hamlet to my friends. He left. Then someone came over to me and asked, 'Do you know who that was?' Right then, *East of Eden* was about to open and Dean's name was plastered all over Broadway. People were even wearing buttons that said, JAMES DEAN MUST BE SEEN. I was astonished that he and Hamlet were one and the same."

When Dean called Barbara Glenn, she told him she had met a man she was planning to marry. Although the betrothal she had announced the previous summer had fallen through, this time Dean correctly inferred that it was the real thing, and he was taken aback. He asked to meet Glenn's fiancé, and at first she was leery of the antisocial behavior she knew he was capable of. But when the three of them met for dinner, Dean was a model of good humor. Then he called and asked to see her alone. Once again she hesitated, but he did one of two things he had never done before with her; he begged. So she went to his apartment.

For Barbara Glenn, who had possibly meant more to him than anyone since his mother, Dean had reserved the most bizarre behavior of his life. When Glenn entered his apartment, she noticed an open suitcase on the bed, full of cash. Dean told her to take it. She was confused, but since she had frequently loaned him money over the years, she asked if he was trying to pay her back. He replied, "You can't leave me, Barbara. You can't go. We can't end like this." Glenn retorted that she was getting married and that was final. Bidding him good-bye, she started down the stairs. Then Dean, who had argued with her countless times but never raised his voice, began to scream. Flinging fistfuls of the money down the stairwell, he railed, "And when I die, it'll be your fault."

On the night of the *Eden* premiere, which was a benefit for the Actors Studio, Kazan, John Steinbeck, and Jack Warner were in attendance, resembling a minor-league Holy Trinity. Representing the cast were Jo Van Fleet, Raymond Massey, and Richard Davalos. Dean, however, knew that if he had hated the *Sabrina* premiere, he would have found the *Eden* benefit even more unpalatable, so he returned to California the weekend before. Ironically, *Daily Variety* announced he had come back "to help the *Eden* campaign." Although he did agree to a television interview at the beginning of *Lux Video Theatre* on March 10, Dean was, in truth, much less interested in publicizing his movie debut than preparing for *Rebel Without a Cause,* which would roll at the end of the month.

During March, Dean had a series of consultations with actor Frank Mazzola, who would play gang member Crunch in *Rebel.* Mazzola had been involved with gangs in real life and advised Dean on "delinquent" personalities, speech, and mode of dress. Twice Mazzola took Dean to gang hangouts and even a club meeting. Sometimes the two would meet with Ray to go over the script, working until the wee hours.

Stewart Stern had rented a basement apartment just off Laurel Canyon Boulevard, and Dean enjoyed coming by on his way to the studio. "He'd gun his motorcycle outside, early in the morning, and I'd come out and he'd lead me to the studio, and we'd have coffee," says Stern. "He'd show off on the motorcycle, doing 'no hands' over Mulholland Drive, down to the canyon where Highland runs through, and my heart would stop."

When *Rebel* filming began on March 30, Dean would work without a vacation until just before his death; he had seen New York and Indiana for the last time. The most recent impressions he had left in those places were what would forever linger in the minds of his friends and colleagues. Those who felt *East of Eden* had not changed him were right. Hadn't he always been reckless, moody, and contemptuous of authority, and hadn't he always been magnetic, entertaining, and a pal just the same? But those who thought he *had* changed were right, too, because all of his self-destructive tendencies were now greatly magnified. And Hollywood had made him rich enough to afford the tools to finish the job.

Finish Line

Dean's propensity toward self-destruction can be traced to his days as an adolescent on a Whizzer motorized bicycle (if not earlier). Where others might look at a motorcycle and see a zesty mode of transportation, he saw a means of executing daredevil stunts. "Sometimes Jimmy'd do funny things," recalled a hometown friend, "like getting people on the back of his motorcycle and trying to scare the hell out of them." As he grew older and more prosperous, smaller two-wheelers were incessantly traded in for ever more powerful models, and his reputation as a hellion on wheels grew proportionately. "James Dean calls his motorcycle his murdercycle," noted the *Hollywood Reporter* in late 1954.[1]

While in high school, Dean added bullfighting to his roster of dangerous passions, an obsession that lasted a good five years. Although he apparently never got into the ring, he showed a consistent disregard for safety while playing matador with Manhattan taxis and buses. Bull-fighting, however, fell quietly by the wayside once Hollywood enabled him to afford cars that could hold their own on the racetrack. He had

---

1. Early one morning in March 1955, noted Hollywood photographer Phil Stern was driving west on Sunset Boulevard when a motorcyclist came roaring down Laurel Canyon and ran a red light, missing a serious collision with Stern by the narrowest of margins. The photographer shouted obscenities at the rider until he saw it was James Dean.

been incapable of frugality where motorcycles were concerned, and now his acquisition of race cars would be profligate: within seventeen months, an MG, two Porsches—a Speedster and a Spyder—and a Lotus IX on order.

Three years earlier, Beverly Wills had observed, "No matter how depressed he was, if Jimmy had a chance to get behind something that had terrific speed, he would laugh and come alive again." Besides finding exhilaration in his encounters with speed, Dean was also tapping into sensations of power and sex. Announcing the acquisition of his MG to Barbara Glenn, he dubbed himself "H-Bomb Dean" and wrote libidinously that he was channeling his sex drive into fast curves and broadslides. In fact, he added, he and the sleek red roadster were "mak[ing] it together."

Initially, he raced the MG and then the Speedster over the Hollywood Hills, up Laurel Canyon and Cahuenga Pass, and on Mulholland Drive, but his craving for speed could not be confined to the public highways. On the last weekend of March 1955, just before he went into *Rebel Without a Cause,* he entered himself and the Speedster in the California Racing Club's Palm Springs airport course meet. To the amazement of everyone, he won first place in the novice race and second place in the main event. "Everybody figured it was just a publicity stunt," said one veteran sports car enthusiast. "But Dean went crazy. He went out front and left everybody. He was blasting—going like a bomb."

Heavy restrictions on what and where Dean could drive were imposed by both Elia Kazan and George Stevens during the making of their respective pictures, but in a sense, Hollywood was only taking away with one hand what it gave back with the other. After Dean's last day of work in *Giant,* September 17, 1955, he couldn't get to the races fast enough—and, thanks to six months of steady film work, he had the finances to get himself there. On September 21, he impulsively traded in his Speedster toward a sixty-nine-hundred-dollar Porsche Spyder, all the better to enter an upcoming meet in Salinas. It was while he was en route to Salinas that he was killed, perhaps the most famous highway fatality of all time. How excessive his speed was at the time of the collision is, even today, a matter of dispute. Two hours before the accident, however, just south of Bakersfield, he had been ticketed for speeding.

The hours and minutes leading up to that fatal September 30 accident have been painstakingly and obsessively reconstructed by fans and car-racing aficionados, but the various accounts are highly speculative and give no insights into Dean's life. The only relevant issue presented by the catastrophe, in fact, is whether it was really an accident. Dean's death has been called "suicide by inadvertence," and suppositions that he harbored a death wish have abounded. Certainly some of his friends said they remembered his remarking that he wouldn't live past thirty, or that he had to do things fast because he wouldn't be around long. After two other newcomers to Hollywood, Robert Francis and Suzan Ball, died tragically on July 31 and August 5, respectively, he predicted, "I'm next." In addition, there were Dennis Stock's macabre photos of him reclining in a coffin in a Fairmount funeral parlor and Sanford Roth's lugubrious shots of him standing with his neck in a hangman's noose.

But for every death-wish declaration he allegedly made, a countervailing statement reflecting the hope of a longer life can be found. To Gene Owen, Dean said he might play Hamlet "in about eight years," and he told Mike Connolly, "I've got five more years to look" for a spouse before reaching the marriageable age of thirty. Philip Scheuer recorded Dean's projection that "I'll have a few years to develop my own style." Inspired by Sanford Roth's photos of Paris, Picasso, and Cocteau, he said he couldn't wait to broaden his existence and tour the cultural capitals of Europe. If nothing else, he wanted to live to race, publicly expressing hopes of doing the circuit of the most prestigious international meets in the coming years.

Virtually all of his close friends urged him to seek help from a psychiatrist. Correspondence from two Los Angeles practitioners Dean had consulted—Carel van der Heide and Judd Marmor, an authority on homosexuality—was reviewed by biographer Joe Hyams, but it was nothing more than bills and confirmations of appointments. Any files on Dean, of course, have remained confidential, and thus whatever feelings he may have expressed to therapists about his own death are unknown.

Fortunately, there is no uncertainty about the seriousness with which Dean took his acting in the two movies he was about to make. Although he publicly said very little about his approach to *Rebel Without a Cause,* his performance as the confused, undernurtured teenager Jim Stark would prompt the reviewer for *Sight and Sound* to exult that "only a superb interpretation could have given [the unhealthy parent-son relationship] the texture of a deeply corrosive, psychic disorder, and James Dean magnificently achieved it." Of his work in *Giant,* Dean would say, "An actor should thoroughly understand the character he is portraying and there is no better way than trying to be that person in the hours away from the camera. I developed a program of understanding Jett [Rink] and of doing the things he'd be likely to do. I didn't want any jarring notes in my characterization."

Rebel Without a Cause, unlike Dean's other movies, was an original story, not an adaptation. That he was able to make the picture at all was due to a rarefied environment, seldom possible in Hollywood, enabled by extraordinary relationships with his director, Nicholas Ray, and his screenwriter, Stewart Stern.

Ray's perceptive and empathic gifts had enabled him quickly to zero in on the core of Dean's psyche. "To work with him," Ray observed, "meant exploring his nature, trying to understand it; without this, his powers of expression were frozen." Although Dean was generally perceived as being tough, Ray saw that he had "no hard professional shell" and was unable to shrug off lack of sympathy or understanding from a director. As a result, "there were probably very few directors with whom Jimmy could ever have worked."

The original story of *Rebel Without a Cause* was Ray's, but he had great difficulty articulating that story. Before discovering Stewart Stern, he dismissed two other screenwriters who could not flesh out his ideas adequately. His one strong conviction, as Stern recalled later, was that "there was a big misconception that so-called juvenile delinquency was a product of economic deprivation. He felt that it was emotional deprivation."

Before Stern rescued the project, screenwriters Leon Uris and Irving Shulman grappled in vain with Ray's nebulous concept. Uris began working in mid-October 1954 and would last less than a month. Although there is no record of Uris and Dean meeting, there is reason to believe they conferred. Uris's main character, already called Jim, invites his friends to his home where he develops photos in a darkroom. "This hobby," notes Ray's biographer, "and the classical records (Mahler, Beethoven) already suggest the influence on the character of James Dean."

Ray hired Irving Shulman in early November, in part because he thought Shulman and Dean would find common ground in sports cars. But despite the shared passion, Shulman and Dean didn't hit it off at all. Shulman made several contributions to the story line, but to Ray, they did not reach "the *heart* of the story," which, as he was now beginning to see it, was about becoming a man.

When it was clear that Shulman wouldn't work out, Ray began to feel desperate. He later learned there had been talk in the Warners front office about abandoning the project. At some point during these anxious days, Ray sought help from someone he hoped would have insights into Dean—Isabel Draesemer.

"Nick Ray called me up," Draesemer remembers, "and asked, 'Did you have Jimmy Dean as a client?' He wanted some consultation on the script from someone who knew the industry and knew what he was trying to do. I went to the studio to meet with him at least six or eight times.

"Ray would read me lines from the script. He'd ask, 'Is that Jimmy?' Most of the time, I'd say, 'No. It's too straight. Jimmy doesn't just hit the ball back to you; he bounces all over.' Later, when I saw the movie, just as soon as I saw Jimmy's drunken business with the toy monkey at the beginning, I thought, 'Ray's caught it—that's the essence of Jimmy!' I think my only pay for those consultations was a run-of-the-picture contract for my client Jack Grinnage [who played gang member Chick]. I didn't ask; Ray didn't offer."

Once Stewart Stern took over as screenwriter, his major contribution, as suggested by Ray's biographer, may have been to grasp that juvenile delinquency was only "an alibi" for making the film; it was really "a unique opportunity to say something about the nature of loneliness and love."

Jim Stark, hero of *Rebel Without a Cause,* encounters a unique series of challenges within a twenty-four–hour period, ultimately overcoming familial dysfunction and peer rejection to find himself as an adult. Arrested for public drunkenness the night before his first day at a new school, he meets two other teens at the police station who will become his good friends: Judy, who was picked up while wandering the streets at one A.M., and Plato, brought in for shooting puppies. The next day, on a school trip to Griffith Planetarium, Jim tries to ingratiate himself with a tough, leather-jacketed gang, but they taunt him and goad him into a knife fight with Buzz, their leader. After Jim surprises Buzz by disarming him, Buzz proposes continuing the duel later that night with a "chickie run"—a form of amusement in which contenders drive at high speed toward a cliff, with the first one to leap from his car before reaching the edge being designated chicken. Buzz drives to his death and Jim inherits his girl—Judy. For the rest of the film, Jim, Judy, and Plato evade the remaining gang members, who don't want them to go to the police. The chase concludes back at Griffith Planetarium, where the police misguidedly shoot Plato because he is armed and, they think, dangerous. Finally, Jim reconciles with his father, who promises henceforth to be a role model for him.

Dean's tacit approval of the *Rebel* project can be inferred from his efforts to get his friends into key roles. When Ray had been scouting in New York, Dean presented Christine White to him in hopes of having her play Judy. Later he tried to do the same for Ruda Michelle (*nee* Podemski), the young actress who had earlier tested with him for *Battle Cry*. "In March 1955 I was visiting friends in Malibu," says Podemski, "and one day I was out lying on the beach in a bikini with my eyes closed. Suddenly, I felt a body fall on me, and I heard those familiar words, 'My Podemski.' It was Jimmy, of course, and he was dressed in blue jeans and was walking along with two girls. He asked, 'What are you doing here?' He asked if I had talked to Warner Brothers about the Judy role. I said no and that I was sure Warners would use contract players. He said, 'Come with me *right now.*' He made me go with him—he just dumped the two girls and I wrapped a towel or something around myself—and we drove to Warners in his convertible car. He took me to an office and introduced me by saying, 'This is who I want for Judy.' I can't remember who I talked to." (The role, of course, went to Natalie Wood.)

Dean also envisioned the role of Plato, the lonely boy befriended by Jim Stark, being played by Jack Simmons. Together they made a test of a scene in which they had to laugh hysterically in reaction to a friend's shocking and fatal accident. When Simmons was uncertain about being able to summon such laughter, Dean went into an impromptu comedy routine calculated to give him the giggles. Since the test was being made on the old *Streetcar Named Desire* set, Dean ran up the staircase bellowing, "Stella-a-a-a!" à la Brando. Then he led Simmons behind the set, where they had a urinating contest, seeing if either could make his stream go over the set and into the camera. Dean's maneuvers produced the desired hysterics, but Simmons was not chosen and had to be content with the role of Moose, a minor gang member.

Production of *Rebel Without a Cause* got under way on Wednesday, March 30, at Griffith Planetarium, kicking off with the knife fight between Jim Stark and Buzz (Corey Allen). Both actors wore chest protectors, but their knives were real. During one take, Allen nicked Dean behind the ear, and when blood ran, a first-aid man was summoned. As Dean rested in a chair, wiping sweat from his forehead, a reporter approached, asking, "Isn't this pushing realism a bit?" Dean replied, "In motion pictures, you can't fool the camera. If we were doing this on stage, we'd probably be able to gimmick it up—but not in a picture. Film fans are too critical these days."

Dean and Corey Allen were trained for the knife fight by Mushy Callahan, a former welterweight boxing champion now working as a prop man for Warners.[2] But Dean was also getting some pointers from Roger Donoghue, a young boxer and all-purpose assistant to Nicholas Ray, who always seemed to be at the Chateau Marmont and on the *Rebel* set. "Jimmy and I would be in the Marmont's pool," Donoghue recounts, "up to our waists, and I was teaching him to box—left jab, hook off a jab, right upper cut, and all the combinations. I'd also take him to fights at the [American] Legion."

The picture had been set to be filmed in black and white, and the footage from its first four days was in fact without color. But after word got around Warners (thanks to the cameramen) that Ray's project was the finest on the lot, top brass decided *Rebel* would henceforth be filmed in WarnerColor. Eventually all four days' scenes had to be retaken.

Dean came down with laryngitis for three days in mid-April, and the company had to shoot around him. "Lili Kardell and Vampira have been taking turns bringing him hot soup and making hot tea," wrote Sidney Skolsky. Then, just after the laryngitis subsided, a self-inflicted ailment afflicted him. During the scene at the police station in which

---

2. In his capacity as adviser to all fight scenes in all Warner films, Callahan had also coached Dean in fisticuffs for his brawl with Richard Davalos in *East of Eden*.

Jim Stark is interviewed by a juvenile officer, he is encouraged to take out his frustrations on the officer's desk with his fists. Subsequent Hollywood mythology had Dean hitting the desk so hard that he broke a bone in his right hand and was taken to Riverside Drive Hospital. The actual damage, however, was a bad bruise, and he was transported no farther than the Warners first aid office.

To prepare for such an intense scene, Dean reportedly holed up in his dressing room drinking red wine and listening to Wagner's *Ride of the Valkyries,* keeping the *Rebel* company waiting for an hour. (Earlier in the police station sequence, in fact, Dean is heard humming the *Valkyries* theme.) The scheme of psyching himself up by listening to heroic classical music may have been part of a trend pervading Hollywood just then: an item in the *Hollywood Reporter* two weeks earlier noted actor Jack Palance's playing a Richard Strauss composition to arrive at the right mood for a scene.

Sidney Skolsky, whose daughter, Steffi, was playing a gang member, visited the set one day and had a good look at Dean's modus operandi as a film actor. "He talks to few people on the set," reported Skolsky. "When he does get into a conversation, he listens with the same intensity he puts into his acting. He usually wanders away and has to be summoned to play a scene. Generally, he comes running to do the scene. Or he will stand to the side of the camera, jumping and waving his arms. Sometimes he will box a little with his stand-in, former champ fighter Mushy Callahan."

On May 6, The *Los Angeles Herald-Express*'s Harrison Carroll visited the set, finding Dean, with Jim Backus and Ann Doran (Mr. and Mrs. Stark), enacting the scene in which Jim Stark arrives home, mentally and physically drained, from the chickie run. Jim wants to report Buzz's death to the police, and when his mother vehemently opposes this action, he demands that his father stand up to her. When his father makes no move, Jim angrily grabs the lapels of his bathrobe, picks him up, lugs him down the stairs as if he were a sack of potatoes, and starts to choke him. Backus, according to Carroll, was nervous about going into the scene.

"We did the master shot yesterday," Backus said, "and Dean was so carried away once that he grabbed the [stair] railing and broke part of it. We went over a couch and knocked over a table. I thought I was a goner. I might have been, but this boy is as strong as a bull. Even while he was flinging me around, he held onto me so that I wouldn't fall."

Carroll watched the scene and then spoke to Dean, looking for a quote. "You had Backus jittery," the reporter admonished. "Yes, I know," Dean replied, "but I have never hurt another actor in my life." Another reporter suggested that the scene's violence could goad the censors into action. Dean responded, "They'll be doing the country an injustice. . . . Since juvenile delinquency is based on violence, it is justified violence. We picture a very real situation that exists in this country; something that should be stamped out."

Backus, recovering from the scene's intensity with typical good humor, quipped, "Welcome to the Elia Kazan Hour." Later, Backus developed a standard response to those who asked him what it was like to work with Dean: "Let me put it this way—he's a far cry from Victor Mature."

Dean became fond of Ann Doran and started referring to her as "Mom" off the set. Doran admired his dedication and hard work. "He liked to rehearse," she remembered, "at any time—one, two, or three o'clock in the morning. Rather than disturb my family, he would come to my house during the night, and we might discuss characterizations. He would drink gallons of coffee and even smoked marijuana until I told him it was making me sick. Sometimes he complained about people who tried to intrude in his life or hoped to get someplace on his coattails. Though I'm a great talker, I did a lot of listening. He widened my life."

Late in May, Sidney Skolsky was back on the *Rebel* set and heard an insistent call coming over the loudspeaker: "James Dean, please . . . James Dean, please—report on set!" Skolsky was amused to watch Dean emerge from a portable dressing room and grumble, "Yeah, I heard you—James Dean, that's my name." The soundstage portions of the chickie run sequence were being filmed that day, and Dean was supposed to leap from a stolen car just before it plummets over a cliff. A prop man was installing a mattress under the soundstage's green grass to soften Dean's fall, but Dean told him to take it away. "People will say Dean can't even do his own stunts—he has to have a mattress," he objected. The prop man reluctantly obliged, sighing, "All right, but it's Errol Flynn's mattress."

Dean's Hollywood social life had become of great public interest by the time *Rebel Without a Cause* rolled. He had ceased going to Googie's, adopting in its place the small but high-profile Villa Capri on McCadden Place. As with Jerry's Bar back in New York, the Villa Capri was an Italian restaurant where he was on a very friendly basis with the owner and waiters, and could come in the back door and eat in the kitchen if he wished. But the Villa Capri catered to a higher social stratum than Jerry's, and was *au courant* enough to warrant a klieglighted party in celebration of the mere opening of two new restrooms. The press often noted Dean's comings and goings at the popular eatery. For example, with Lili Kardell on his arm, he was a main attraction at the powder room fête. On a subsequent evening, at the same restaurant, Frank Sinatra and Humphrey Bogart amused themselves by razzing Dean, ordering milk and crackers for him and telling him to comb his hair with a comb instead of a wet rag.

Lili Kardell, Dean's most frequent escort during these months, made such an impression on Kendis Rochlen that the columnist would exclaim, "Wait until you gander Jimmy Dean's date at the [Oscar awards] tonight." But Dean's name was linked with other starlets as well, more than he could possibly have juggled successfully: Lori Nelson, a blond actress who was also a Dick Clayton client; Julie Robinson, a dancer with the Katherine Dunham troupe and supposedly his "mambo instructress"; Dana (pronounced "Donna") Wynter, a newly arrived British starlet with whom he was said to be "an item"; Lucy Marlow, a minor actress (*A Star Is Born*) to whom he sent flowers; and April Channing, a "New York show girl" he was keeping in touch with.

The heightened publicity made Dean even more guarded about his privacy, and for a time he was determined to go beyond merely avoiding Googie's to maintain it. On March 23, Rochlen reported, "James Dean, who's tried to keep his phone number and address a big secret, has decided that his Sunset Plaza apartment isn't remote enough for his I-want-to-be-alone routine." Rochlen's information was irrefutable; Dean had taken her with him to inspect a house that seemed to be the ultimate in isolation. Situated at the top of Laurel Canyon, it could be reached only after a steep hike. The owner showed them the bedroom with its king-size bed and told them Lana Turner had slept there.

Satisfied that there were no nearby neighbors who would complain if he played his bongos, Dean shelled out six months' advance rent. But word of his plans leaked out, and curious fans began driving to the site and exploring it. In the end, he was more willing to forfeit his deposit than his privacy, and stayed on Sunset Plaza Drive for a few more months.

Jonathan Gilmore, Dean's good friend in New York, was now back in Hollywood and often visited Dean on various *Rebel* sets. "It was while he was finishing *Rebel,*" says Gilmore, "that we compared names of male hotshots—directors, producers—that had put the make on both of us." Gilmore would spend hours at Dean's Sunset Plaza Drive apartment, which he recalled was "littered with paper cups and takeout orders from Googie's, plus stacks of papers and spools of recording tape and his clothes, thrown carelessly into the closet." In retrospect, it was hero worship, says Gilmore. "I did whatever Jimmy asked and would lie awake most of the night listening to him on the phone, not letting on that I was bored."

Despite their closeness, avers Gilmore, "It was apparent that Jack Simmons was Jimmy's closest friend for a time. There arose a certain kind of pecking order." Simmons explains that he and Dean "had a love like a brotherhood."

Simmons describes Dean as "a man of few words. Once Bill Bast came up to me in Googie's and said, 'Oh, Jack, will you please give Jimmy a message?' I brought Jimmy the message and the only thing he said was half of a tsk-tsk. Or when he and I were coming out of the La Reina Theater after the sneak preview of *East of Eden* and I asked him what he thought of Jo Van Fleet's performance. He answered with only one word: 'Flawless.' "

Sadly, Dean's friendship with Maila Nurmi was fading away. They had resumed meeting at Googie's early in March, after he fled New York and the *East of Eden* world premiere, but within days he had initiated his boycott of Googie's. Kendis Rochlen queried Nurmi about Dean in late March and found her keeping a stiff upper lip. "Oh, Jimmy doesn't go for me," Nurmi said. "He's in love with my duenna! I'm just helping him get a little polish. For instance, the other day I gave him a Japanese ear picker so he won't keep using those awful toothpicks." Nurmi explained that although she saw Dean several times per week, what they had amounted to nothing beyond friendship. "You might say that I like him but he doesn't like me," she deadpanned.

Trouble was rumored early in April when *Daily Variety* noted, "Vampira's steaming mad at four fan magazines who wanted to make a deal with her—promised to shoot layout of her if she'd produce pal James Dean." In their separate ways, each was feeling exploited. (The following year, after Liberace signed Vampira for his nightclub act, she would tell him, "You're the only one who's been nice to me since Jimmy Dean died.") Jack Simmons notes, "After months of palling around with Vampira, Jimmy just ignored her. I asked him, 'Is there any reason you're shuffling her out of your life?' He answered, 'She's too infantile.' "

Interestingly, the issue of the draft seems to have reared its head once again for Dean in the spring of 1955 (although his surviving Selective Service records say nothing about it). In early May, word went over the wire services that he "had just received his draft notice." *Daily Variety,* on May 12, prattled that he had worked into the wee hours on *Rebel* the previous night, "then reported five hours later for his Army physical." The only reportage on the physical came four days later, when *D. V.* cracked that no one there had recognized him—"must've been the wardrobe." But the same day, the *Hollywood Reporter* warned that Nick Adams (gang member Cookie in *Rebel*) would play Jett Rink in *Giant* if Dean were drafted. Finally, columnist Sheilah Graham put things at ease by reporting that Dean's draft call had been for reclassification only. "He won't be called into the Army for about two years. If the Army knows what it's getting into, they'll let Jimmy alone," Graham snickered.

During the making of *Rebel,* Nicholas Ray—unlike Kazan and Stevens—encouraged Dean in the pursuit of competitive racing, betting that it enhanced the creative juices. Thus graced with his director's imprimatur, Dean entered another race, this time at Bakersfield's Minter Field, on Sunday, May 1. When he crossed the finish line of the nineteen-mile, six-lap event, he had come in third overall and first in his class of car. He had now won three trophies for his first three races, making it clear that he had an amazing natural aptitude for the sport.

Rebel production, after a few days of retakes, finally ended on May 26. Roger Donoghue recalled that it was after midnight, and Dean, his friend Perry Lopez (not in the film), Ray, Natalie Wood, and others were standing around in the daze that comes when such a consuming project is finally over. Ray proposed going to Googie's—Dean apparently saw no harm in it—so everyone piled into Ray's old Cadillac except for Dean, who climbed on his Triumph and led the party there. "As we got four or five blocks from Googie's," said Donoghue, "Jimmy put his legs up over the back of the machine and rode like that. Nick turned round and said, 'That should be the end of the film!' Anyway, we all ended up at Googie's, and it was like all the kids didn't want it to end, and Nick didn't want it to end."

The *Rebel* shooting schedule overlapped with the herculean preparations going on elsewhere at Warners for *Giant,* and mild turf wars broke out between the respective personnel over Dean's availability; being caught in the middle irked him, and it showed. He refused to do wardrobe and makeup tests for *Giant* on April 30, a rare day off from *Rebel,* citing as his excuse the laryngitis from which he had already recovered.

On May 18, he arrived late at a press luncheon celebrating the start of *Giant* production. When a photographer asked him if he would kindly remove his glasses for a picture, Dean gave no sign that he had heard. The photographer importuned, and Dean remained silent but clipped on his dark lenses over his glasses. He was, it seemed, prone to incivility that afternoon. When director George Stevens introduced each member of the cast, Dean was the only one not to bow or even stand when his name was announced. Then, during lunch, Joe Russell recalls, "Jimmy put his elbows on the table and slouched in his chair. Kendis Rochlen, who was sitting next to him, said, 'For God's sake, Jimmy, sit up and act like a gentleman!' "

Later, trying to quell widespread displeasure over his performance at the luncheon, Dean claimed to have come directly to it from the *Rebel* set, feeling very concerned about being photographed unshaven and with bags under his eyes. Daily production logs, however, show that he finished working the night before at 10:30.

Because *Rebel* had ended eleven days behind schedule, Dean was forced to forgo a planned trip to Fairmount and the Indy 500 and had to go immediately into his preparatory work for *Giant.* Before catching his train for location in Marfa, Texas, on the evening of June 3, he would spend virtually all his time either in postrecording for *Rebel* or in wardrobe and makeup tests for *Giant.*[3] According to columnist Erskine Johnson, Dean would not be using wrinkle makeup as he aged twenty years in *Giant*—only "graying temples, a receded hairline, and a few forehead lines will mark young Dean's forty-fifth birthday as Jett Rink. It's still a two-and-a-half hour makeup job and might have been longer except that Dean rebelled: 'Look,' he argued—and won—'a man of forty-five shows his age in thoughts and actions, not in wrinkles.' "

His only day off before journeying to Texas was Memorial Day, and the holiday offered him one last, cherished chance to race before George Stevens's prohibition on life- (i.e., picture-) threatening activities went into effect. This time it was a Santa Barbara event. From an unlucky starting position, he maneuvered his Speedster up to fourth place by the start of the final lap, and was working hard to move into third when he overrevved the car's engine and burned a piston, coasting to a halt at the edge of the track. According to Sidney Skolsky, "his face was a mask of dejection." From then until mid-September, the Speedster would be in the garage, having its engine rebuilt.

Even from the beginning of Dean's experience in *Giant,* the dominant theme was the friction between him and George Stevens. Three months earlier, Dean had told *The New York Times* that Stevens was "so real, unassuming . . . the greatest of them all." But their initial collegiality dissipated once Stevens became intensely preoccupied with the project. Dean grew wary—as Ray had perceived, he had "no hard professional shell"—and asked his trusted agent, Dick Clayton, to come to Marfa. "I went down to Texas and spent a night or two on the *Giant* set, because Jimmy had asked me to go," says Clayton. "He was apprehensive about George Stevens, who he said had already been standoffish and giving him orders." The *Hollywood Reporter* caught wind of the situation and on June 6 noted, "They say George Stevens told James Dean he is not a railroad lantern and must not wag his head once in *Giant.* And no hopscotch—just walking." Stevens was apparently trying to nip any of Dean's "Brandoisms" in the bud.

---

3. Dean literally had no time between the two films. Warner Brothers records show that he was post-recording on *Rebel* until 6:30 P.M. on June 3, then caught his train to Texas at 7:00 P.M.

In *Giant,* the cowhand Jett Rink is jealous of cattle baron Bick Benedict's wealth and beautiful wife, Leslie. Bick's sister, Luz, dies and leaves a parcel of oil-rich land to Jett, initiating the ascent of Jett's fortune. Eventually, when none of Bick's three children is interested in taking over the gargantuan family ranch, Bick sells it to Jett. To the horror of Bick and Leslie, their daughter, Luz II, has a brief romance with Jett, but gets over him after seeing him collapse in an alcoholic stupor while delivering a speech at the opening of his new luxury hotel.

All of the premonitions of trouble with Stevens came true. Over the hundred-plus days of filming, there would be at least three very public confrontations between director and actor. The first of these happened in Marfa, according to Carroll Baker (the actress who played the nubile Luz Benedict II). Baker's autobiography explains that, despite the stifling Texas heat, Stevens expected the entire cast, stars included, to stand by on the set in full makeup and costume at all times. After Dean stood around like this for three days without being filmed, Baker wrote, he rebelled and refused to report on the fourth day; consequently Stevens dressed him down on the fifth, accusing him of costing the company an entire day of lost production.[4] Word of the fracas leaked to *Daily Variety,* which revealed that Dean had been told "in no uncertain terms" that Stevens was directing *Giant.* "Who told him?" *D. V.* asked. "Stevens!" On July 1, Sidney Skolsky, noting that the *Giant* company ought to be back in Hollywood in another week or so,[5] added that "Stevens appears to have Dean behaving after [their] initial beef."

Stevens's show of authority back in Marfa, however, seemed not to have impressed or intimidated Dean, for on Saturday, July 23, he failed to report for work, despite being given a makeup call the previous evening. The assistant directors were aware that he wanted to spend Saturday afternoon moving from Sunset Plaza Drive to new quarters in

---

4. Warner records show that Dean and Baker were, in fact, "held" on location for three consecutive days, June 16, 17, and 18, 1955. However, the fourth day, June 19, was a Sunday, and the company did not work. On the fifth day, June 20, Dean worked from 9:00 A.M. to 7:15 P.M.
5. Most of the *Giant* company left Texas for Hollywood on July 9, but Dean stayed on an extra three days for scenes of Jett Rink on his newly inherited property. He flew back to Hollywood on July 12.

Sherman Oaks, and had told him he would most likely finish his scenes by noon. But ultimately that was not enough to persuade him to come to work. They spent the bulk of the day scrambling to find him, relaying several messages through his answering service in the morning and finally, as noon approached, deputizing Dick Clayton to take up the chase. Both the service and Clayton assured the studio that Dean would be right there.

Arthur Loew, Jr., remembers this incident because Dean came to Loew's Miller Drive house while the Warners posse was combing the lower half of California for him. "Jimmy said, 'They made me wait, so I'll make them wait,' " Loew recalls. "I told him, 'You can't do that! If you're having problems, you've got to resolve them.' Henry Ginsberg [coproducer of *Giant*] was a friend of mine [Loew was a movie producer himself]; he knew and liked Jimmy. I called Henry, who was an older, wiser, and mature man. He talked to Jimmy, not like a producer but in a fatherly fashion. He got it worked out."

Dean finally did speak personally to an assistant director late in the afternoon; he said he would not be in at all—even though studio equipment had been left in place since the morning in case he materialized—and that he had been "too tired to work" when his wakeup calls had come in. Once again, *Daily Variety* reported the incident, which, as luck would have it, occurred right after they had printed his remark that he wanted to take all of the coming year off from acting. "Guess he wasn't kidding us when he said he was tired," chuckled *D. V.,* adding clairvoyantly that despite Henry Ginsberg's assurances that all was well, it expected to hear more of this ongoing saga.

Stevens had pretty much reached the end of his rope with Dean and asked a Warners factotum to compile a list of delays in filming attributable either to Dean's tardiness or outright absences. Aside from the troublesome July 23 no-show, the memorandum, dated August 1, listed twelve delays on eight different days, some as short as three minutes. (The list did not note any full day of missed shooting in Marfa as claimed by Carroll Baker, although some grievance during those weeks had provoked Stevens to berate Dean publicly.)

How Stevens intended to use this list is unknown, but an unfortunate incident the day after its compilation made its existence somewhat moot. What happened was simply that Dean arrived late on the set, but his infraction's gravity was exacerbated by a display of professionalism from actress Mercedes McCambridge (Luz Benedict in the film). Only a few hours before morning call, McCambridge had fallen in her bathroom, hitting her head on a brandy snifter. Even though she had, according to *Daily Variety,* been "stitched from head to foot," she still managed to arrive on time. When Dean sauntered onto the set, offering no apology or excuse, Stevens blew up, vowing never to direct another film with him in it. Then he walked off the set, leaving the direction to an assistant.

Dick Clayton, one of Hollywood's great peacemakers, went into action with a proposed truce. "Jimmy and I drove over to Steve Trilling's [executive assistant to Jack Warner] home in Beverly Hills to ask if Jimmy could get his calls at home, since he lived only fifteen minutes from the studio. Jimmy said, 'Maybe Liz Taylor and Rock Hudson can be chatting on the set all day and then go right into a scene, but I can't. I have to be able to concentrate.' Trilling approved the scheme, says Clayton."

Dean's difficulties with Stevens differed significantly from those he had had with Daniel Mann in *The Immoralist,* in that Stevens's exasperation was based solely on professional, not personal, considerations. Throughout filming, and then afterward until *Giant* was released, Stevens frequently praised Dean's acting in print. "The boy's so preoccupied," he said only days after the last and worst confrontation. "He's the kind that can be late even if he's right there on the set. He gets himself all wound up before going into a scene. But his work is wonderful. Everything went fine Wednesday [August 3, the day after the McCambridge accident] and Jimmy even showed up for his makeup call fifteen minutes early."[6]

The most specific compliment Stevens would pay Dean was that the actor "could mold psychological impediments into his speech and into his movements. This was his finest art. Instinctively he seemed to understand all the impediments people have when they try to communi-

---

6. If Dean's disposition on the *Giant* set seemed improved, he may simply have transferred his obstinacy back to *Rebel.* On Saturday, August 6, he refused to report for post-recording of dialogue on *Rebel,* despite a 9:00 A.M. call. To be fair, he may have been suffering from a bad wisdom tooth, which would be pulled on August 12.

cate." Stevens also admitted that he sometimes underestimated Dean, but "sometimes [Dean] overestimated the effects he thought he was getting—then he might change his approach, do it quick, and if that didn't work, we'd effect a compromise. All in all, it was a hell of a headache to work with him. . . . He had developed this cultivated, designed irresponsibility. 'It's tough on you,' he'd seem to imply, 'but I've just got to do it this way.' "

For all the accounts of discord, there had been times when director and actor worked well together. A reporter who watched the scene of Jett Rink pacing off his inherited property said Stevens took time to explain its significance and mood to Dean, then rehearsed him in it. Dean nailed it on the first take, after which Stevens beamed, "That's just swell, Jimmy." Rock Hudson told an interviewer that it was a common sight to see Stevens and Dean taking long walks together. Although Hudson could never hear what was said, sometimes he could see one or both of them gesticulating as if in heated discussion. The business Stevens needed to take up with Dean was usually done privately, said Hudson, never involving the rest of the cast.

The eventual review of *Giant* in *Sight and Sound* examined the Dean-Stevens relationship in critical terms: "In the later scenes [i.e., when Dean had cosmetically aged to forty-five], Dean for the first time in his tragically short career had to go beyond the characterization of the young rebel, and his technical resources fail to see him through. His relative failure throws some incidental light on Stevens's direction of his players. . . . Putting it very approximately, one might say that Kazan works through his actors, while Stevens prefers his actors to work through him."

Edna Ferber, author of the novel *Giant,* had visited Warners in the last week of July to inspect the film's progress. Dean liked and charmed Ferber, trying to teach her some of the rope tricks he had mastered. She called him a "genius" and shrugged off his troubles with Stevens as "success poisoning," a syndrome she said she knew very well from the days when she had simultaneous hit shows on Broadway. Later she wrote him a letter outlining her conception of Jett Rink's character, explaining that a cruel man can fool the average person by affecting a superficial layer of gentleness—but that she and Dean wouldn't be fooled because they happened to be above average.

Dean's social life during *Giant* filming was no less high-profile than during *Rebel.* Although he still saw Lili Kardell, she was openly seeing other men throughout the summer. His most frequent date, once he was back from Texas, was Ursula Andress, a Swiss actress recently put under contract by Paramount. Their names were first linked in the columns in late July after an evening at the Villa Capri. In August they made two especially memorable appearances, the first at a bon voyage party for Patsy D'Amore, the Villa Capri's owner. "Dean surprised regulars," wrote Sidney Skolsky, "by coming all dressed up: blue suit, white shirt, and tie. Also, Jimmy didn't make his usual entrance through the kitchen, but through the front door, with lovely Ursula Andress."

The pair also went to an August 29 dinner at Ciro's sponsored by the Thalians, a charitable organization composed of young actors and actresses. "Even James Dean wore a tux," reported one trade paper. "Ursula Andress and James Dean departed huffily immediately after dinner, before the show started," noted another. Later, Andress explained that Dean had wanted to go club-hopping to show off his tuxedo.

Andress accompanied Dean to an intimate dinner in honor of pianist Walter Gieseking, who was in Los Angeles to give two concerts at the Hollywood Bowl. Gieseking was a friend of Kira Appel, Hollywood correspondent for *France-Soir,* who had befriended Dean on the *Giant* set. With remarkable nerve, Dean asked Appel to invite him to her home to meet Gieseking. Although the great musician had never heard of Dean, he approved. Where most admirers would shrink even from asking Gieseking for an autograph, Dean wanted to play duets with the master on Appel's out-of-tune upright piano, a request Gieseking graciously humored.

Dean told one reporter that he and Andress fought "like cats and dogs—no, on second thought, like two monsters. I guess it's because we're both so egotistical." But he said he admired her, and credited her with inspiring him to want to see Europe. Their romance, however, was relatively short-lived, because by early September Andress had discovered and moved on to actor John Derek, whom she would soon marry. Perhaps that is why, when Dean was spotted in mid-September at the Tallyho Club, he was once again in the company of friend Toni Lee.

The day after completing his work on *Giant,* Dean went with James Sheldon, who was now directing on the West Coast, to a dress rehearsal of *Our Town,* starring Frank Sinatra, at NBC. "Jimmy was scheduled to do Hemingway's *The Battler* on the same show [Producers Showcase] the next month," says Sheldon. "He wanted to check it out. I knew the producer and that's why Jimmy wanted me to go with him. He was supposed to tease *Battler* at the end of *Our Town,* but it wasn't done."

Many other projects were waiting in the wings for Dean, including a property called *Gun for a Coward* that Warners had purchased with him in mind; the *Hollywood Reporter* said it was "about a sissy-britches who becomes a hero through stress." In the realm of legitimate theater, playwright John Van Druten's new work, *Dancing in the Chequered Shade,* was a spoof on Brando-and-Dean–type actors, and Van Druten was said to have followed Dean to Marfa, Texas, to sign him for it. Dean's most imminent commitment was to television for "The Corn Is Green," but the biggest news of his future was his pending loanout to M-G-M (in exchange for their loaning Elizabeth Taylor to Warners for *Giant*) for *Somebody Up There Likes Me,* a biopic of boxer Rocky Graziano.

But because he had been forbidden to race during *Giant,* Dean was far less focused on acting than on getting back to the track. "In those final days," said his stunt driver friend Bill Hickman, "racing was what he cared about most. I had been teaching him things like how to put a car in four-wheel drift, but he had plenty of skill of his own."

On Labor Day, Dean returned to Santa Barbara to watch his insurance agent and friend Lew Bracker compete in his first car race. At the Talk of the Town restaurant that evening, friends said, he was crestfallen still to be under George Stevens's orders not to race. It was Bracker who, later in the month, alerted Dean that Competition Motors on Vine Street in Hollywood was displaying a new Porsche Spyder in its showroom window. When Dean saw the Spyder, it was love at first sight. Racing it around Warners, Dean was, according to Sheilah Graham, "chased by the cops who told him to drive slowly or get off the lot."

On September 16, Harrison Carroll reported, "In case Warners doesn't know it, James Dean has big racing plans after he finishes *Giant*. 'I want to enter at Salinas, Willow Springs, Palm Springs, all the other places,' Dean tells me. 'Of course, I'll miss some of them because I have to do ["The Corn Is Green"] in New York. But maybe I can catch a race back there.' " Asked by Carroll whether Warners would approve, Dean replied, "When a man goes home at night, the studio can't tell him not to do what he wants to do."

Dean asked almost every friend in his address book to ride with him to Salinas, but by the day of the journey, September 30, only Hickman and *Giant* still photographer Sanford Roth had committed to go. The other member of the party would be Rolf Weutherich, Dean's favorite mechanic at Competition Motors, whose services as pit crew in Dean's future races were part of the sales agreement. At about 2:30 P.M., with Dean at the wheel of the Spyder and Weutherich beside him, Hickman and Roth following in another car, the party left Hollywood and headed for Salinas, first cruising north on Highway 99 (now Interstate 5), then, north of Bakersfield, turning west onto Highway 466 (now Route 46) toward Paso Robles.

Just over three hours later, the Spyder was way out in front of Hickman and Roth, descending into San Luis Obispo County's Cholame Valley. In the senseless, banal way of most traffic accidents, Dean had a head-on collision with a Ford making a left-hand turn onto Route 41. Although Dean's actual speed was never ascertained, the time of day—5:45 in the evening, just before dusk—made it difficult for the Ford's driver to detect the approach of the small, low Spyder with its dull, gray color. The other driver, in fact, claimed not to have seen the Spyder. Weutherich was thrown from the car, but survived with a broken jaw, a broken leg, and severe cuts and bruises. Dean, in the driver's seat, had virtually no chance to survive; the impact broke his neck, and he died almost immediately. "When I first got to him," said Bill Hickman, who had been too far behind the Spyder to witness the accident, "I thought he was alive, because there seemed to be air coming from his nostrils. They told me later he had died instantly. His forehead was caved in and so was his chest." At the age of twenty-four years, seven months, and twenty-two days, Dean was gone.

Back in Hollywood, two gala events, the WAIF Whisper Ball and the Makeup Artists Ball, were getting under way. When news of Dean's death arrived, there were faintings, shrieks, collapses, and many tears. Guests at the Makeup Artists Ball were startled to note that one of the ads in the souvenir program featured cutouts of Dean's eyes with the caption, "Thanks, Hank." It was a salute to Dean's makeup man at Warner Brothers.

Throughout the next week, as Warners flew its flags at half-mast, Hollywood's shock deepened as word spread of Dean's recent making of a highway safety commercial. It was filmed on July 29 on the *Giant* set, with actor Gig Young, himself a racing devotee, querying Dean about his feelings on competitive racing versus speeding on public roads. Dean said racing was much safer than driving on the highways, because "half the time you don't know what this guy's going to do, or that one." When Young asked him how he might advise teenagers who drive, Dean provocatively responded, "Take it easy driving—the life you save *may be mine.*"

In New York, some who had known Dean were able to accept the news calmly because, they say, they sensed the calamity was inevitable. Frank Corsaro stoically asked, "How did he do it?" Barbara Glenn grieved, saying, "I knew it was imminent. I knew some day he was never coming back." Lee Strasberg simply commented, "It somehow was what I expected." When Elia Kazan got the news from his neighbor John Steinbeck, he sighed, "That figures."

Still other New Yorkers felt it was their duty to tidy up Dean's reputation for posterity. "The night after Jimmy died," says Dane Knell, his understudy in *See the Jaguar,* "Bobby Heller, Billy James, Bill Gunn, and I had been drinking and decided to break into his apartment. There had been rumors that he'd been ignoring draft notices, and we wanted to protect his memory and keep such a story out of the press. We went in through the window; there's a balcony outside of it. I don't remember how we got onto the balcony. I took a photo that showed Jimmy on a motorcycle. But we didn't find any draft papers."

The fact that Dean left behind two unreleased movies tended to soften the finality of his death. *Rebel Without a Cause,* with which he would be most closely identified, was released less than a month after the accident. Although Dean did not live to see the extraordinary public reaction to it—which, paradoxically, could have amounted to much less, had he been alive—he had seen the finished product at a September 17 sneak preview at Westwood Village Theater in Los Angeles. Another year would pass before the release of *Giant,* but in December, *Daily Variety* disclosed that one of Dean's last wishes had been that Nicholas Ray be the first "outsider" to see *Giant*'s Jett Rink scenes. Screening the scenes for Ray, George Stevens let it be known that he hated to cut Dean's footage and edited it last.

Immediate speculation on what direction Dean's career might have taken showed cautious respect for the dead, focusing only on which movie roles would have been perfect for him. What was not discussed publicly was whether the aggressive disrespect and defiance he had shown to a succession of directors, most recently George Stevens, and to his studio, could have been sustained in Hollywood. Even Brando, after backing out of a contractual obligation to appear in *The Egyptian,* had been brought to his knees when Twentieth Century–Fox's arsenal of legal talent squared off with him. Being fired, or sued, might not have stopped Dean from working immediately, but a cumulative record of difficulty would eventually have harmed his career, and the alternatives were sparse—a degree of self-exile from the industry, as with Brando, or death, as with Monroe and Garland. Dean often stated that he longed to direct, and he might have abandoned acting for directing as soon as possible, but this would not have assured harmonious working relationships with studios and distributors.

Commenting on the tragic combination of characteristics that composed James Dean, Leonard Rosenman eloquently reflected, "Jimmy's main attraction (and the singularly important element in his public attractiveness) was his almost pathological vulnerability to hurt and rejection. This required enormous defenses on his part simply to cover it up, even on the most superficial level. Hence the leather-garbed motorcycle rider, the tough kid having to reassure himself at every turn of the way by subjecting himself to superhuman tests of survival, the last of which he failed." Unwittingly, Rosenman was echoing Frank Corsaro's insight that Dean was glorified for precisely those aspects of his personality he had been told to stamp out.

In truth, said Rosenman, Dean actually hated the attention-getting facets of his personality—"the not-caring attitude, the daredevil exploits on motorcycles and in race cars, and his seeming independence from society." Rosenman suggested that Dean's chronic impatience with formal learning had subverted both his natural intelligence and his potential to achieve the respect as an intellectual that he sought.

When *Giant* was finally released, a variety of reviewers praised the last acting job that would ever be seen from Dean. "He has caught the Texas accent to nasal perfection," said *Time*, "and has mastered the lock-hipped, high-heeled stagger of the wrangler, and the wry little jerks and smirks, tics and twitches, grunts and giggles, that make up most of the language of a man who talks to himself a good deal more than he does to anyone else . . . [he] clearly shows for the first and fatefully the last time what his admirers always said he had: a streak of genius."

Of all the commentary on Dean's performance in *Rebel Without a Cause*, none, in the end, was as perceptive as that of the director himself. The secret to Dean's "fine, intense perception" of the Jim Stark role, wrote Nicholas Ray, was that both he and the character were "jealously seeking an answer, an escape from the surrounding world." In the end, both character and actor found that escape, but Dean, in so doing, breached the point of no return. What he had really hoped for, asserted Ray, was the escape achieved by Jim Stark—"a full, complete realization of himself."

Early death suffuses our young heroes—artists, religious martyrs, athletes, politicians—with legendary status all out of proportion to their actual contribution and achievement, but certainly James Dean's demise deprived the public of a larger body of intriguing cinematic work. A gentler psychological makeup might have facilitated a longer life, but the dramas that compose Dean's earthly record were achieved because of—not in spite of—his self-destructiveness, insecurity, and vulnerability. The gift of artistry can be a curse as well as a blessing; it is, as John Updike writes, "a current from beyond that burns out the wire."

Television, Stage, and Film Credits

Television

"Hill Number One," *Family Theatre* (Easter special, broadcast on all stations nationwide), 25 March 1951. Cast: James Dean as John the Beloved; also Regis Toomey, Gene Lockhart, Joan Leslie, Ruth Hussey. Director: Arthur Pierson. Producer: Father Patrick Peyton. Writer: James D. Roche.

"T.K.O.", *Bigelow Theatre* (Dumont), 29 October 1951. Cast: James Dean, Martin Milner, Jack Bernardi, Carey Loftin. Director and Producer: Frank Woodruff. Writer: Ted Thomas.

"Into the Valley," *CBS Television Workshop* (CBS), 27 January 1952. Cast: James Dean as a G.I.; also George Tyne, Robert Baines, Michael Higgins, John Compton. Director: Curt Conway. Producer: Norris Houghton. Story: John Hersey. Adaptation: Mel Goldberg.

"Sleeping Dogs," *The Web* (CBS), 20 February 1952. Cast: James Dean as a boy trying to solve his brother's murder; also Anne Jackson, E. G. Marshall, Robert Simon, Nancy Cushman. Director: Lela Swift. Producer: Franklin Heller. Writer: Marie Baumer.

"Ten Thousand Horses Singing," *Studio One* (CBS), 3 March 1952. Cast: James Dean as a bellhop; also John Forsythe, Catherine McLeod, Vaughn Taylor, Joe Morass. Director: Paul Nickell. Producer: Worthington Minor. Writer: Karl Tunberg.

"The Foggy, Foggy Dew," *Lux Video Theatre* (CBS), 17 March 1952. Cast: James Dean as Kyle McCallum; also James Barton, Muriel Kirkland, Richard Bishop. Director and Producer: Richard Goode. Writer: J. Albert Hirsch.

"Abraham Lincoln," *Studio One* (CBS), 26 May 1952. Cast: James Dean as court-martialed soldier William Scott; also Robert Pastene. Director: Paul Nickell. Producer: Donald Davis. Story: John Drinkwater. Adaptation: David Shaw.

"The Forgotten Children," *Hallmark Hall of Fame* (NBC), 22 June 1952. Cast: James Dean as Bradford; also Cloris Leachman, Nancy Malone, Don McHenry, Lee Lindsey. Director and Producer: William Corrigan. Writer: Agnes Eckhardt.

"The Hound of Heaven," short dramatic presentation on *The Kate Smith Hour* (NBC), 15 January 1953. Cast: James Dean as an angelic messenger; also John Carradine, Edgar Stehli. Director: Alan Neuman. Producer unknown. Writer: Earl Hamner, Jr.

"The Case of the Watchful Dog," *Treasury Men in Action* (NBC), 29 January 1953. Cast: James Dean as Randy Meeker; also Crahan Denton, Dorothy Elder, Thom Carney, John Fecher, Biff Elliot. Director: Daniel Petrie. Producer: Robert Sloane. Writer: Albert Aley.

"The Killing of Jesse James," *You Are There* (CBS), 8 February 1953. Cast: James Dean as Bob Ford; also Walter Cronkite, John Kerr, Helen Warnow, Addison Powell, James Westerfield, Carl Frank. Director: Sidney Lumet. Producer: Charles W. Russell. Writer: Leslie Slate.

"No Room," *Danger* (CBS), 14 April 1953. Cast: James Dean, Martin Kingsley, Irene Vernon, Kate Smith. Director and Producer unknown. Writer: Mary Stern.

"The Case of the Sawed-Off Shotgun," *Treasury Men in Action* (NBC), 16 April 1953. Cast: James Dean as Arbie Ferris; also Joseph Downing, Anita Anton, Coe Norton, Humphrey Davis, Ben Gazzara. Director: David Pressman. Producer: Everett Rosenthal. Writer: Albert Aley.

"The Evil Within," *Tales of Tomorrow* (ABC), 1 May 1953. Cast: James Dean as lab assistant Ralph; also Rod Steiger, Margaret Phillips. Director: Don Medford. Producer: Mort Abrahams. Writer: Manya Starr.

"Something for an Empty Briefcase," *Campbell Soundstage* (NBC), 17 July 1953. Cast: James Dean as ex-convict Joe Adams; also Susan Douglas, Frank Maxwell, Robert Middleton, Don Hamner. Director: Don Medford. Producer: Martin Horrell. Writer: S. Lee Pogostin.

"Sentence of Death," *Summer Studio One* (CBS), 17 August 1953. Cast: James Dean as death row prisoner Joe Palica; also Betsy Palmer, Gene Lyons, Ralph Dunn, Virginia Vincent, Barnet Biro. Director: Matthew Harlib. Producer: John Haggott. Story: Thomas Walsh. Adaptation: Adrian Spies.

"Death Is My Neighbor," *Danger* (CBS), 25 August 1953. Cast: James Dean as psychotic janitor JB; also Walter Hampden, Betsy Palmer, Frank Marth, Andrew Duggan. Director: John Peyser. Producer: Franklin Heller. Writer: Frank Gregory.

"Rex Newman," *The Big Story* (NBC), 11 September 1953. Cast: James Dean, John Kerr, Carl Frank, Wendy Drew, Donald McKee, Ken Walken. Director: Stuart Rosenberg. Producer: Robert Lewis Shayon. Writer: Alvin Boretz.

"Glory in Flower," *Omnibus* (CBS), 4 October 1953. Cast: James Dean as Bronco Evans; also Hume Cronyn, Jessica Tandy, Mark Rydell, Ed Binns, Frank McHugh. Director: Andrew McCullough. Producer: Fred Rickey. Writer: William Inge.

"Keep Our Honor Bright," *Kraft Television Theatre* (NBC), 14 October 1953. Cast: James Dean as Jim; also Joan Potter, Michael Higgins, Larry Fletcher, Addison Richards, Bradford Dillman. Director and Producer: Maury Holland. Writer: George Roy Hill.

"Life Sentence," *Campbell Soundstage* (NBC), 16 October 1953. Cast: James Dean as imprisoned felon Hank Bradon; also Georgann Johnson, Nicholas Saunders, Matt Crowley, Charles Mendick. Director: Garry Simpson. Producer: Martin Horrell. Story: Margaret Kleckner. Adaptation: S. Lee Pogostin.

"A Long Time Till Dawn," *Kraft Television Theatre* (NBC), 11 November 1953. Cast: James Dean as Joe Harris; also Naomi Riordan, Ted Osborn, Robert Simon, Rudolph Weiss. Director and Producer: Richard Dunlap. Writer: Rod Serling.

"The Bells of Cockaigne," *Armstrong Circle Theatre* (NBC), 17 November 1953. Cast: James Dean as stevedore Joey Frasier; also Gene Lockhart, Donalee Marans, Vaughn Taylor, Karl Lucas. Director: James Sheldon. Producer: Hudson Faussett. Writer: George Lowther.

"Harvest," *Robert Montgomery Presents* (NBC), 23 November 1953. Cast: James Dean as Paul Zelenka; also Dorothy Gish, Ed Begley, Reba Tassell, Vaughn Taylor, John Dennis, John Connell. Director: James Sheldon. Producer: Robert Montgomery. Writer: Sandra Michael.

"The Little Woman," *Danger* (CBS), 30 March 1954. Cast: James Dean as Augie, a counterfeiter on the lam; also Lydia Reed, Frank Maxwell, Albert Salmi, Lee Bergere. Director and Producer: Andrew McCullough. Writer: Joe Scully.

"Run Like a Thief," *Philco Television Playhouse* (NBC), 5 September 1954. Cast: James Dean as Rob; also Kurt Kasznar, Gusti Huber, Ward Costello, Barbara O'Neill. Director: Jeffrey Hayden. Producer: Gordon Duff. Writer: Sam Hall.

"Padlock," *Danger* (CBS), 9 November 1954. Cast: James Dean as an escaped felon; also Mildred Dunnock, David Hardison, Ken Konopha. Director and Producer unknown. Writer: Louis Peterson.

"I'm a Fool," *General Electric Theatre* (CBS), 14 November 1954. Cast: James Dean as a racetrack stableboy; also Eddie Albert, Natalie Wood, Roy Glenn. Director: Don Medford. Producer: Mort Abrahams. Story: Sherwood Anderson. Adaptation: Arnold Shulman.

"The Dark, Dark Hour," *General Electric Theatre* (CBS), 12 December 1954. Cast: James Dean as a "hepcat" killer; also Ronald Reagan, Constance Ford, Jack Simmons. Director: Don Medford. Producer: Mort Abrahams. Writer: Arthur Steuer.

"The Thief," *U.S. Steel Hour* (ABC), 4 January 1955. Cast: James Dean as Fernand Legarde; also Mary Astor, Paul Lukas, Diana Lynn, Patric Knowles, Nehemiah Persoff. Director: Vincent J. Donehue. Producer: The Theatre Guild. Story: Henri Bernstein. Adaptation: Arthur Arent.

"The Unlighted Road," *Schlitz Playhouse of Stars* (CBS), 6 May 1955. Cast: James Dean as Korean War veteran Jeff Latham; also Pat Hardy, Mervyn Vye, Edgar Stehli. Director: Justus Addis. Producer: William Self. Writer: Walter C. Brown.

☆　☆　☆

Because of the haphazard and incomplete nature of record-keeping in the "Golden Age of Television," a definitive James Dean videography may never be achieved. Other television appearances by Dean, mostly minor, for which only incomplete documentation exists, are as follows:

"Jackie Knows All," *The Trouble with Father,* 1951. Cast: James Dean, Martin Milner.

Various episodes, *Mama* (CBS), circa January 1952. Cast: James Dean as Nels's friend (and possibly Nels in one episode); also Dick Van Patten, Rosemary Rice, Peggy Wood, Judson Laire.

Unknown episode, *Suspense* (CBS), 1952. Director: Robert Stevens.

Interview to promote *East of Eden,* preceding "Life of Emile Zola," *Lux Video Theatre* (NBC), 10 March 1955.

☆　☆　☆

Dean made at least two television commercials, the first produced by Ben Alcock of the Milton Biow Agency for Pepsi, in the winter of 1950–51. The other was a highway safety spot with Gig Young, filmed 29 July 1955 on the *Giant* set.

Dean also worked "backstage" in at least two television programs: *Beat the Clock* (CBS) as a stunt tester in early 1952, and subsequently *Hallmark Hall of Fame* (NBC).

Stage (Broadway)

See the Jaguar by N. Richard Nash; opened 3 December 1952, Cort Theater. Cast: James Dean as Wally Wilkins; also Arthur Kennedy, Constance Ford, Phillip Pine, Arthur Batanides, Dane Knell, Margaret Barker, Roy Fant, Florence Sundstrom. Director: Michael Gordon. Producers: Lemuel Ayers and Florence Jacobson. Incidental music: Alec Wilder.

The Immoralist, adapted from the novel by André Gide by Ruth and Augustus Goetz; opened 8 February 1954, Royale Theater. Cast: James Dean as Bachir; also Geraldine Page, Louis Jourdan, David J. Stewart, Charles Dingle, Adelaide Klein, Bill Gunn, Vivian Matalon (Philadelphia only). Director: Daniel Mann. Producer: Billy Rose.

Stage (Off-Broadway, etc.)

End As a Man by Calder Willingham; workshop performances 10 and 17 May and 11 June 1953, Actors Studio. Cast: James Dean in a nonspeaking role as a scribe; also Ben Gazzara, Arthur Storch, William Smithers, Albert Salmi, Anthony Franciosa, Peter Mark Richman. Director: Jack Garfein.

The Scarecrow by Percy Mackaye; opened 16 June 1953, Theatre de Lys. Cast: James Dean as the Scarecrow's mirror image; also Patricia Neal, Douglas Watson, Eli Wallach, Anne Jackson, Bradford Dillman. Director: Frank Corsaro. Producer: Terese Hayden. (Dean did not participate in the two-week reprise of *The Scarecrow* beginning 7 July 1953.)

The Fell Swoop by Jonathan Bates; rehearsed reading 23 June 1953, Palm Garden. Cast: James Dean; remainder unknown. Director: Sherwood Arthur. Producer: New Dramatists Workshop.

Trachiniae (Women of Trachis) by Sophocles and translated by Ezra Pound; rehearsed reading 14 February 1954, New School of Social Research. Cast: James Dean as Herakles' son; also Anne Jackson, Eli Wallach, Adelaide Klein, Earle Montgomery, Joseph Sullivan. Director unknown.

☆ ☆ ☆

Dean, especially during his New York years, participated in other workshop productions and readings for which no records have been found.

Film

East of Eden, Warner Brothers, released March 1955. Cast: James Dean as Cal Trask; also Julie Harris, Richard Davalos, Raymond Massey, Jo Van Fleet, Burl Ives, Lois Smith, Albert Dekker, Lonny Chapman, Timothy Carey, Betty

Treadville, Harold Gordon. Director and Producer: Elia Kazan. Screenplay: Paul Osborn, based on the novel by John Steinbeck. Music: Leonard Rosenman. Photography: Ted McCord.

Rebel Without a Cause, Warner Brothers, released October 1955. Cast: James Dean as Jim Stark; also Natalie Wood, Sal Mineo, Jim Backus, Ann Doran, Edward Platt, Marietta Canty, Jack Simmons, Corey Allen, Dennis Hopper, Jack Grinnage, Frank Mazzola, Nick Adams, Beverly Long, Steffi Sidney, Virginia Brissac, William Hopper, Rochelle Hudson. Director: Nicholas Ray. Producer: David Weisbart. Screenplay: Stewart Stern. Adaptation: Irving Shulman from a story by Nicholas Ray. Music: Leonard Rosenman. Photography: Ernest Haller.

Giant, Warner Brothers, released October 1956. Cast: James Dean as Jett Rink; also Rock Hudson, Elizabeth Taylor, Mercedes McCambridge, Jane Withers, Chill Wills, Carroll Baker, Dennis Hopper, Sal Mineo, Victor Millan. Director: George Stevens. Producers: George Stevens and Henry Ginsberg. Screenplay: Fred Guiol and Ivan Moffatt, based on the novel by Edna Ferber. Music: Dmitri Tiomkin. Photography: William C. Mellor.

Film (Cameo Roles)

Fixed Bayonets, 20th Century–Fox, released November 1951. James Dean uncredited as a G.I. Cast: Richard Basehart, Gene Evans, Michael O'Shea, Bill Hickman, Tony Kent. Director: Samuel Fuller. Producer: Jules Buck. Screenplay: Samuel Fuller, suggested by a novel by John Brophy. Music: Roy Webb. Photography: Lucien Ballard.

Sailor Beware, Paramount, released January 1952. James Dean uncredited as a boxer's second. Cast: Jerry Lewis, Dean Martin, Corinne Calvert, Marion Marshall, Leif Erickson. Director: Hal Walker. Producer: Hal Wallis. Screenplay: Martin Rackin and James Allardice, from a play by Kenyon Nicholson and Charles Robinson. Music: Joseph Lilley. Photography: Daniel L. Fapp.

Has Anybody Seen My Gal?, Universal, released July 1952. James Dean uncredited as a malt-drinking college student. Cast: Piper Laurie, Rock Hudson, Charles Coburn, Gigi Perreau, Rod Barkley (uncredited). Director: Douglas Sirk. Producer: Ted Richmond. Screenplay: Joseph Hoffman, based on a story by Eleanor H. Porter. Music: Joseph Gershenson. Photography: Clifford Stine.

Acknowledgments

The author wishes to single out for special thanks individuals who made unique and unforgettable contributions to this book: Adeline Nall, for countless discussions of the family trees of Grant County, Indiana, over morning coffee; Christine White, for cheerfully giving a walking tour on a drizzly November day of her and Dean's old New York haunts; Harvey Phillips, for presenting (through his foundation) annual concerts featuring the great music of Alec Wilder; Cordelia Hamilton and Tom Golden, for a tour of Stony Point, New York, and the former Lemuel Ayers home; Phillip and Madelyn Pine and Art Batanides, for a side-splitting, thigh-slapping discussion of the Broadway of 1952–54; and Marshall Barer, for a complimentary ticket to his performance of his own impossibly witty lyrics at New York's Don't Tell Mama cabaret.

To encounter a source who kept and then preserved diaries, engagement calendars, or other precise records of yesteryear is always a godsend to a biographer. Joyce John Hood, Adeline Nall, Miles White, David Diamond, and John Michael Hayes were such sources for this book. Charlotte Freedland Green saved the day by providing access to her own archives of UCLA memorabilia after research at UCLA itself proved fruitless. The author is particularly grateful to Don Bachardy for sharing vital information and dates from Christopher Isherwood's diaries.

Permission to quote from Alec Wilder's unpublished manuscripts, *The Search* and *The Elegant Refuge,* was granted by Thomas Hampson, executor of Wilder's estate, and in the case of the latter, by co-author James T. Maher as well. Wilder's biographer, Desmond Stone, graciously provided entree to all of Wilder's friends and to many of Rogers Brackett's friends interviewed for this book.

For hospitality in Indiana: Barbara and Don Jordan, Gerald Ness, J. Kent Calder, Dr. Jan Shipps, Tom Alvarez and Wayne Kreuscher, and Adeline Nall. In New York: Jim Hoover and John Aubry, John Bennett, John Wolf, John Willis, Carrie Carmichael, and Jan-Gijs and Inez Schouten. In Los Angeles: Sue Bergin and Albert Brecht. In Madison, Wisconsin: Mike Bemis.

For constructive criticism of portions of the manuscript: Gus Nasmith, Allison Wielobob, James T. Maher, John Gilmore, Barbara Glenn Gordon, Desmond Stone, Lou Cutell, Charlotte Freedland Green, and David Diamond; and for painstaking review of successive drafts of the proposal, Wyn Craig Wade.

Many archivists were extravagantly generous with their time and assistance: Daniel Einstein and Lou Ellen Kramer of the UCLA Film, Television & Radio Archives; Ned Comstock and Stewart Ng of the Doheny Library, University of Southern California; Leith Adams of Warner Brothers Archives; Sam Gill and Howard Prouty of the Margaret Herrick Library, Academy of Motion Picture Arts and Sciences, Beverly Hills; David Loehr of the James Dean Gallery, Fairmount, Indiana; Ellen Gartrell and Ian Lekus of the J. Walter Thompson Archives, Duke University; Bill Barry of the Motion Picture, Broadcasting, and Recorded Sound Division, Library of Congress; Jana Jevnikar of New Playwrights, New York; and Brian Quinn and Jennifer Lewis of the Museum of Television and Radio, New York.

Finally, for superlative competence and grace under pressure, the author wishes to thank: Charles Spicer, editor, and Tory Foran, Lauren Sarat, and Katerina Christopoulos, editorial assistants at St. Martin's Press; and literary agent Nina Graybill.

The following persons gave interviews, wrote letters, or both: Corey Allen, Harriett Bette McPherson Allen, Dick Altman, Marjorie Armstrong, Don Bachardy, Alice Backes, Marshall Barer, Arthur Batanides, Orson Bean, Warren Newton Beath, Jill Corn Beck, Judy Bell,

James Bellah, Harve Bennett, Jack Bernardi, Rod Bladel, Patricia Bosworth, Jack Bradford, Kip Brown, Rex Buller, Jackie Cain, Hugh Caughell, Sarah Ayers Christian, Tony Cichielo, Dick Clayton, Karolyn Cleveland, Joel Climenhaga, Anna Lee Cloud, Harvey Cocks, Douglas Colby, Frank Corsaro, Ward Costello, Rex Couch, M.D., Denton Cox, M.D., Walter Cronkite, Mart Crowley, Robert Custer, Lou Cutell, Ruda (Michelle) Podemski Dauphin, Joe Della Sorte, Richard DeNeut, David Diamond, Bradford Dillman, Roger Donoghue, Margaret Ann Curran Duncan, William Engvick, Ahmet Ertegun, Richard Eshleman, Geraldine Fitzgerald, Louis Fontana, Shirley Hill Foss, Bill Fowler, Gerold Frank, Dudley Frasier, June Ericson Gardner, David Garfield, Hank Garson, Jim Gavin, Mike Gazzo, Richard Gearin, John Gilmore, Allen Ginsberg, Ruth Goodman Goetz, Tom Golden, Mrs. Manuel Gonzalez, Brad Gooch, Barbara Glenn Gordon, Michael Gordon, Bruce Graham, Dulcie Gray, Charlotte Freedland Green, Morris Green, Donna Jean Morris Grubbs, Cordelia Hamilton, Diane Hanville, James Harelson, Julie Harris, Kay Smith Harris, Radie Harris, Xen Harvey, Jeffrey Hayden, Terese Hayden, John Michael Hayes, Gordon Hein, Bob Heller, Franklin Heller, Venable Herndon, Addie Barkdull Hite, John Holden, Joyce John Hood, Dwight Hoover, Norris Houghton, Burl Ives, Anne Jackson, Dorothy Jeakins, Tamara Jiva, Lamont Johnson, Phil Jones, Kenneth Kendall, John Kerr, Marjorie Kientz, Eleanor Kilgallen, Archer King, Wright King, Jerry Kinser, James Klain, Dane Knell, Gail Kobe, Roy Kral, Karen Sharpe Kramer, Garth Lambrecht, Jack Larson, Joan Leslie, Beverly Linet, Arthur Loew, Jr., Perry Lopez, Salem Ludwig, James T. Maher, Karl Malden, Daniel Mann, Sheri Mann, Vivian Matalon, Pat McGilligan, Nina Skolsky Marsh, Don Martin, Robert Dale Martin, Joe Masteroff, Don Medford, Robert Middleton, Fran Miller, Mitch Miller, Martin Milner, Joanne Mock, Terry Moore, Sue Hill Moreland, Kendis Rochlen Moss, Madison Musser (pseudonym), Adeline (Brookshire) Nall, N. Richard Nash, Vivian Nathan, Lola Small Nelson, Lori Nelson, Bill Nichols, James O'Rear, Betsy Palmer, Carolyn Parks, Bill Payne, Nehemiah Persoff, John Peyser, DeVier Pierson, Madelyn Pine, Phillip Pine, Paul Pogue, Robert Pulley, Doris Quinlan, Rosemary Rice, Peter Mark Richman, Ralph Riley, Monte Roberts, Pat Roberts, Leonard Rosenman, William Matson Roth, Marion Rothman, Maxine Rowland, Betty Todd

Rubien, Martin Russ, Joe Russell, Sally Sadowsky, Terry Sanders, Elaine Schatt, Roy Schatt, Dick Schenk, Richard Scott, Victor Allen Selby, Eileen Shanahan, Theodore Shank, Shirley Sharp, Artie Shaw, James Sheldon, Vern Sheldon, Elizabeth Sheridan, Arnold Shulman, Jack Simmons, Margaret Webster Sisson, Barbara Whiting Smith, Donald Spoto, Elaine Steinbeck, Stewart Stern, Beverly Stockert, Desmond Stone, Arthur Storch, Susan Strasberg, Arnold Sundgaard, David Swift, Lela Swift, Larry Swindell, Selma Tamber, Isabel Draesemer Terry, Bob Thomas, Dick Van Patten, James Wasson, Dirk Wales, Eli Wallach, Pat Wayne, Christine White, Kay Mock White, Miles White, Calder Willingham, John Willis, Marcus Winslow, Jr., William Zavatsky, Phil Ziegler.

The following persons declined to participate: Bill Bast, Elia Kazan, Eartha Kitt, Russ Meyer, Paul Newman, Stuart Rosenberg, Toni Lee Scott, Lois Smith, James Whitmore, Joanne Woodward.

The following persons did not respond to letters or phone calls: Anna Maria Alberghetti, Ursula Andress, Sid Avery, Carroll Baker, Lew Bracker, Marlon Brando, Paul Burke, Lonny Chapman, Jeff Corey, Vic Damone, Richard Davalos, Marion Dougherty, Ben Gazzara, Pat Hardy, Maggie Henderson, Georgann Johnson, Louis Jourdan, Martin Landau, Cloris Leachman, Martin Manulis, Andrew McCullough, Victor Millan, Elizabeth Montgomery, Donald O'Connor, Gene Owen, Marisa Pavan, Debbie Reynolds, Mark Rydell, Arlene Sachs, William Smithers, Ruth Stegemoller, Rod Steiger, Jo Van Fleet, Jane Withers.

Notes

In cases where the source of information is evident, no citation is provided here.

Abbreviations

AM Aljean Meltsir, "James Dean, His Life and Loves," *Motion Picture,* Sept. 1956.

AMPAS Academy of Motion Picture Arts and Sciences, Margaret Herrick Library, Beverly Hills, California.

AN Adeline Nall as told to Val Holley, "Grant County's Own," *Traces of Indiana and Midwestern History,* Fall 1989.

AW Alec Wilder, "The Elegant Refuge," unpublished manuscript, Sibley Library, Eastman School of Music, Rochester, New York.

BB Bill Bast, *James Dean: A Biography* (New York: Ballantine, 1956).

BE Bernard Eisenschitz, *Nicholas Ray: An American Journey* (New York: Faber & Faber, 1990).

BW Beverly Wills, "I Almost Married Jimmy Dean," *Modern Screen,* March 1957.

CA Cindy Adams, *Lee Strasberg, The Imperfect Genius of the Actors Studio* (New York: Doubleday, 1980).

CB Carroll Baker, *Baby Doll* (New York: Dell, 1985).

DD David Dalton, *James Dean: The Mutant King* (New York: St. Martin's, 1983).

DK Dorothy Kilgallen

DS Dizzy Sheridan, "In Memory of Jimmy," *Photoplay,* Oct. 1957.

DV *Daily Variety*

EJ   Erskine Johnson

EK   Elia Kazan, *Elia Kazan: A Life* (New York: Knopf, 1988).

HC   Harrison Carroll

HCN   *Hollywood Citizen News*

HH   Hedda Hopper

HR   *Hollywood Reporter*

HT   Howard Thompson, "Another Dean Hits the Big League," *New York Times,* March 13, 1955.

JD   James Dean

JG   John Gilmore, *The Real James Dean* (New York: Pyramid, 1975).

LAMN   *Los Angeles Mirror-News*

LAT   *Los Angeles Times*

LOP   Louella O. Parsons

NR   Nicholas Ray, "Rebel—the Life Story of a Film," *Daily Variety,* Oct. 31, 1956; reprinted in Allen Rivkin and Laura Kerr, eds., *Hello, Hollywood!,* Doubleday, 1962.

NYJA   *New York Journal-American*

NYP   *New York Post*

PH   Paul Hendrickson, "Remembering James Dean Back in Indiana," *Los Angeles Times Calendar,* July 22, 1973, p. 22.

PS   Philip Scheuer, "Jimmy Dean Says He Isn't Flattered by Being Labeled 'Another Brando,' " *Los Angeles Times,* Nov. 7, 1954, Pt. IV, p. 3.

RM   Ronald Martinetti, *The James Dean Story* (New York: Pinnacle, 1975).

RWT   Robert Wayne Tysl, *Continuity and Evolution in a Public Symbol: An Investigation into the Creation and Communication of the James Dean Image in Mid-Century America* (East Lansing: Michigan State University, 1965).

SG   Sheilah Graham

SS   Sidney Skolsky

VH   Venable Herndon, *James Dean: A Short Life* (New York: Doubleday, 1974).

WB   Warner Brothers Archives, University of Southern California, Los Angeles, California.

1: *A James Dean Primer*

PAGE

1   That summer, network: HR, Aug. 2, 1951, p. 2.

1   "Several boys worked": RWT, p. 29.

2   "And sometimes, for": Ibid.

2   "The man had": RWT, p. 30.

3   "Dean must have": James T. Maher to author.

4   Radio in Hollywood: HR, Aug. 2, 1951, p. 2.

4   Brackett's mother discovered: VH, p. 99.

PAGE

5 Gossip columnist Hedda: HH, *The Whole Truth and Nothing But* (New York: Doubleday, 1963), p. 174.

5 Similar statements were: LOP, "James Dean, New Face with Future," *Cosmopolitan,* Mar. 1955, p. 44.

5 "It was really": RWT, pp. 29–30.

6 "The guy we": Larry Swindell to author.

6 "It's my belief": AW.

7 "The stories Hollywood": Evelyn Washburn Nielsen, "The Truth About James Dean," *Chicago Sunday Tribune Magazine,* Sept. 9, 1956, p. 22; Evelyn Washburn Nielsen, "Secrets from Jimmy Dean's Past," *Movie Stars Parade,* July 1956, p. 46.

7 "Hell, I've said": PH.

7 "The late Jimmy": Walter Winchell column (fragment).

7 Daniel Mann, who: AM.

7 Dean himself would: RWT, pp. 106–107; DD, p. 147.

8 Recent biographical efforts: See Paul Alexander, *Boulevard of Broken Dreams: The Life, Times, and Legend of James Dean,* (New York: Viking, 1994).

9 While living in: DD, p. 151.

10 The Actors Studio's: Frank Corsaro, *Maverick* (New York: Vanguard, 1978), p. 16.

10 "Dean had no": EK, p. 538.

11 Meeting Dean for: VH, p. 99.

11 In New York: David Garfield, *A Player's Place* (New York: Macmillan, 1980), pp. 95–96.

12 "No, I didn't": HT.

12 But while costar: WB.

2: The Recovering Hoosier

14 While living in: DD, p. 85.

14 Although Indianapolis: Jane and Michael Stern, "Cafeteria," *The New Yorker* (on early years of automobile industry), Aug. 1, 1988, p. 44.

15 During the widespread: Gerald W. Johnson, "The Ku-Kluxer," *The American Mercury,* Feb. 1924, p. 209.

15 Issues of the: See, for example, "Klansmen Show Marion Something," *Fairmount News,* Nov. 28, 1922; "Klan Pays Visit to King's Chapel," *Fairmount News,* Dec. 5, 1922; "Great Revival Comes to Close," *Fairmount News,* Dec. 12, 1922; "Fairmount Has a Real Fourth," *Fairmount News,* July 6, 1923.

15 Nicholas Ray, his: NR.

15 One such adoptee: Larry Lee Smith to Adeline Nall, Jan. 24, 1956.

P<small>AGE</small>

16 His parents, Winton: Application for Marriage License, July 26, 1930, in James Dean files, Special Collections, Marion (Indiana) Public Library.

17 Zina Gladys Pitsor: *LaPorte* (Indiana) *Herald-Argus,* Sept. 26, 1992.

17 Mildred Dean's cousin: Lottie Wilson Patterson to Adeline Nall, undated.

17 Sources close to: Evelyn Washburn Nielsen, "Secrets from Jimmy Dean's Past," p. 59.

17 "His arms and": AM.

17 In the summer: Fairmount High School *Breeze,* Oct. 29, 1948.

17 The family first: Santa Monica telephone directories of the period, Los Angeles Public Library.

17 Mildred was said: Nielsen, op. cit.

18 (The only thing: HT.

18 A friend from: AM.

18 As a high: JD, "My Case Study," courtesy of Adeline Nall.

18 Barbara Glenn, a: DD, pp. 7–8.

18 Marietta Canty, an: Wayne Jones, "Interview with Marietta Canty," *We Remember Dean International* (newsletter), July 1986.

19 "Jimmy was never": AM.

19 Middleton remembered Dean: *Screen Stories,* Nov. 1956, p. 86.

20 Dean captured two: Awards ceremony program in scrapbook of Joyce John Hood.

20 Early in the: Fairmount High School *Breeze,* op. cit.

21 An article on: *Muncie Star,* Nov. 29, 1948.

21 During a home: Fairmount High School *Breeze,* Feb. 11, 1949.

21 Having attained this: Selective Service records.

21 A magical transformation: Ken Hill, "Hill-Side Views," *Marion Chronicle-Tribune,* Aug. 13, 1970, p. 22.

22 During the regular: Earl L. Conn, "Coach Remembers Jimmy as a Pretty Fair Athlete," *Muncie Star,* Sept. 28, 1975.

22 At the program's: Adeline Nall to author.

24 At season's end: Hill, op. cit.

24 But Dean continued: AN.

25 Forty years later: Vern Sheldon to author.

25 Finally he repaired: Adeline Nall to author.

25 His reputation as: Fairmount High School annual (not paginated), 1947, entry on Hi-Y club.

25 As a chaplain: "Rev. James DeWeerd Heads Kletzing College," *Fairmount News,* June 23, 1949.

26 Much later an: *The Indiana Freemason,* July 1969, p. 20.

26 "To really understand": Evelyn Washburn Nielsen, "What Jimmy Dean's Home Town Can Now Reveal," *Movie Stars Parade,* Aug. 1956, p. 62.

PAGE

26 DeWeerd later explained: AM.

28 Biographer Joe Hyams: Joe Hyams, *James Dean: Little Boy Lost* (New York: Warner, 1992), p. 20.

28 When DeWeerd allegedly: "Cadle Tabernacle Will Observe Anniversaries," *Indianapolis Star,* Oct. 11, 1952, p. 10; "Dr. DeWeerd to Lead Revival," *Fairmount News,* Feb. 11, 1954, p. 1.

29 McPherson, who died: Marjorie Armstrong to author.

30 Graduation came the: AM.

30 At a farewell: "James Dean Was Honored at Farewell Party Monday Night," *Fairmount News,* June 2, 1949; *Marion Leader-Tribune,* June 1949.

3: *Byron James*

31 Writing to his: "James Dean Joins Theatre Group at Santa Monica, Cal.," *Fairmount News,* June 30, 1949.

32 In high school: Beverly Linet, "The Secret Happiness of Jimmy Dean," *Movie Life,* Aug. 1956, p. 66.

33 The melodrama opened: *"Scarlet Gulch* Opening for Third Season," *Santa Monica Evening Outlook,* Aug. 10, 1949, p. 13.

34 After *Scarlet Gulch:* AM.

35 The 1949 festivities: "Sixty Attend Annual Fairmount Picnic," *Fairmount News,* Oct. 13, 1949, p. 1.

37 Practice sessions began: *The Corsair,* Oct. 5, 19, 26; Nov. 2, 1949.

38 At the time: Gene Owen, "An Unforgettable Day with Jimmy Dean," *Movieland,* Feb. 1957; Gene Owen, "The Man Who Would Be 50: A Memory of James Dean," *Los Angeles Times Calendar,* Feb. 8, 1981, p. 5.

39 Dean apparently relished: JG, pp. 43–44. ("Pat Henchie" was a pseudonym for Dianne Hixon.)

39 A chance encounter: Fremont Power, "Visit Proved Ingenuity of James Dean," *Indianapolis News,* Oct. 10, 1967.

41 A ten-day series: *Pasadena Star-News,* Jan. 21, 1950, p. 7; Jan. 28, 1950, p. 7; *Los Angeles Times,* Jan. 21, 1950, Pt. II, p. 2.

41 Dean dropped by: "Fairmount Buries James Dean's Body," *Fairmount News,* Oct. 13, 1955, p. 1.

41 Almost immediately he: *The Corsair,* Feb. 22; Mar. 1, 1950.

41 Dean chalked up: "Bucks Run Over Harbor, 74–48," *The Corsair,* Feb. 22, 1950; "Corsair Melonmen End Season with 68–59 Win Over San Diego," *The Corsair,* Mar. 8, 1950.

42 Wrapping up the: *The Corsair,* Mar. 22, 1950, p. 2.

42 However, a three-week: *Marion Leader-Tribune,* July 9, 1950, p. 2; *Fairmount News,* July 13, 1950, p. 4.

43 Dean told Brookshire: AN.

P<small>AGE</small>

43   Jennie Andrews Lee: Adeline Nall to author.

44   He once mentioned: VH, p. 70.

4: *The Reluctant Bruin*

45   "There are no": Lou Cutell to author.

45   When he registered: "The Enigma of James Dean," *Delta,* Summer 1962.

46   The first letter: AM.

47   He squired her: The photo was published in Bill Bast, "There Was a Boy," *Photoplay,* Sept. 1956, p. 40.

48   Dean, meanwhile, had: AM.

49   If Dean felt: *UCLA Daily Bruin,* Dec. 1, 1950.

49   Harve Bennett, the: *Campus Theater Spotlight,* Dec. 1950.

49   To the Winslows: AM.

52   Oddly, the *Spotlight: Campus Theater Spotlight,* Dec. 1950.

54   At that time: See "Film Actors Back Guild in Election," *New York Times,* July 3, 1951, p. 15; "Actors Ask Easing of Union Provision," *New York Times,* Aug. 27, 1951, p. 15.

55   As revealed a: "The Enigma of James Dean," op. cit.

56   Gonzalez, inspecting Dean's: AM.

56   Another holds that: BB, p. 12.

57   Dean pouted and: Dick Altman to author.

58   Dean was somewhat: Adeline Nall to author.

58   Billed by the: HR, Feb. 21, 1951, p. 16.

58   Finding himself on: BB, pp. 10–12.

59   A month later: BB, p. 30.

59   "Whitmore said he": RWT, p. 28.

60   Larry Swindell, who: Larry Swindell, "Campus One-Acts Premiered," *UCLA Daily Bruin,* Mar. 22, 1951, p. 3.

60   "The school said": Mike Connolly, "This Was My Friend Jimmy Dean," *Modern Screen,* Dec. 1955.

60   To Howard Thompson: HT.

60   When Hedda Hopper: HH, op. cit., p. 173.

5: *Heads or Tails?*

61   According to the: Dan Jenkins, HR, Mar. 22, 1951, p. 7.

61   *The New York: "Hill Number One* Seen," *New York Times,* Mar. 26, 1951, p. 30.

61   The *Hollywood Reporter:* HR, Mar. 26, 1951, p. 7.

63   Whitmore believed that: RWT, p. 28.

63   Her account of: BW.

64   So high were: *TV-Radio Life,* June 8, 1951, p. 34.

64   Despite an April: DV, Apr. 27, 1951, p. 11.

PAGE

65 Jonathan Gilmore, a: JG, p. 49.

65 "He even called": RWT, p. 30.

66 He was fired: BB, p. 34.

67 Elsewhere, Ted Avery: BB, p. 48.

67 The *Bigelow Theatre:* DV, Oct. 30, 1951.

67 Filming began on: DV, June 19, 1951, p. 6.; Jack Bernardi to author.

67 Dean was paid: Pay stub displayed at Fairmount Museum.

67 Since April 1951: Review, *TV-Radio Life,* June 15, 1951, p. 20.

67 "My first memory": Alec Wilder, "The Search," unpublished manuscript, Sibley Library, Eastman School of Music, Rochester, New York.

68 But Lurene Tuttle: "Foundation Is Formed to Honor James Dean," *New York World-Telegram and Sun,* July 11, 1956.

68 However, a soprano: June Ericson Gardner to author.

68 His pay stub from: Displayed at the Fairmount Museum.

69 now it was Bast's: BB, p. 44.

69 His pay stub (net: Displayed at the Fairmount Museum.

69 The only comment: *Variety,* Nov. 21, 1951.

69 The trade press: HR, Aug. 8, 1951, p. 2.

69 The first to: "Hickman Breaks Ankle," HR, July 26, 1951, p. 6.

69 Other casualties included: "4th 'Bayonets' Casualty," HR, Aug. 2, 1951, p. 3.

70 There is no: SS, NYP, Oct. 20, 1954.

71 "No doubt two": NR.

72 Brackett and Dean: BB, p. 50; RM, p. 46.

72 Once, Dean took: RM, p. 46.

72 When Brackett and: Kenneth Kendall to author.

72 Once, between sets: Martin Russ to author.

74 Beverly Wills had: BW.

74 His old nemesis: "The Enigma of James Dean," op. cit.

74 Early in August: DV, Aug. 9, 1951, p. 2.

75 Brackett kept up: RM, pp. 47–48.

75 With the trade: DV, May 14, 1951, p. 1.

76 *Sailor Beware* was: HR, Oct. 4, 1951, p. 8.

76 It may also: *Sailor Beware* daily logs, AMPAS.

77 As soon as: Receipt for transmission job displayed at Fairmount Museum.

78 Coburn, who was: Maurice Zolotow, *Shooting Star* (New York: Simon & Schuster, 1974; biography of John Wayne), p. 297.

78 However, Brackett later: RM, p. 46.

79 Dean may have: *Fairmount News,* Oct. 25, 1951, p. 6.

79 Whether he and: James Harelson, David Swift to author.

79 Beverly Wills said: BW.

79 After taking a: RM, p. 50.

79 His company also: James Harelson to author.

PAGE

79 Three days before: "FHS Grad in Movies," Fairmount High School *Breeze,* Oct. 12, 1951.

80 They remember that: Jill Corn Beck, Sue Hill Moreland to author.

80 A few basketball: Bill Payne to author; Bernie Lehman to Adeline Nall.

81 At the conclusion: *Fairmount News,* Oct. 25, 1951, p. 6.

81 Without specifying the: AM.

6: *Manhattan 101*

84 Dean devised: BB, p. 65.

84 "He ate a large": VH, p. 99.

84 A perennial recipient: Whitney Balliett, *The New Yorker,* Dec. 28, 1987, p. 91.

85 Wilder found Dean: AW.

86 Within his first: JD to James DeWeerd, undated, courtesy of Stewart Stern.

86 When Beverly Wills: BW.

88 This happened to be: *Indianapolis Star,* Jan. 19, 1952, p. 11.

88 On January 27: Norris Houghton, *Entrances and Exits* (New York: Limelight, 1991), p. 197.

89 One day while: DS.

91 Kilgallen's warning was: Max Wilk, *The Golden Age of Television* (New York: Delacorte, 1976), p. 110.

93 Muriel Kirkland recalled: JG, p. 68.

95 The stunts were: Wilk, *The Golden Age,* p. 110.

96 Frank Wayne echoed: DD, p. 84.

97 Those who knew: William Engvick, James T. Maher, Jackie Cain, Dudley Frasier to author.

98 Churchill held: RM, p. 60.

100 When they met: *Variety,* Aug. 20, 1952.

100 Bill Bast relocated: BB, p. 55.

101 Sheridan said he: DD, p. 103.

101 During May: Shirley Hill Foss to author.

101 Jane Addams Reed: AM; also *Berne Witness* (Indiana newspaper article on Adams Central High senior trip to New York), May 7, 1952, p. 1.

102 "New York is": HT.

7: *The Unbearable Lightness of Acting*

111 Actress June Havoc: CA, p. 205.

111 A very young: Joanne Kaufman, "Studio System," *Vanity Fair,* Nov. 1992, p. 238.

112 The panel's decision: EK, p. 476.

PAGE

114 In a 1959: "Future Stars Often Hard to Recognize," *Chicago Sunday Tribune,* May 31, 1959.

114 "The way he": JG, p. 80.

114 Redfield described: Derek Marlowe, "Soliloquy on James Dean's Forty-fifth Birthday," *New York,* Nov. 8, 1976, p. 42.

115 Legend has it: Kaufman, op. cit.; CA, p. 205.

117 When his brief: RM, p. 67.

117 Kazan has been: Clarke Taylor, "Elia Kazan Ponders the Dean Image," *Los Angeles Times,* Sept. 30, 1985.

117 The Actors Studio: RWT, p. 36.

117 The sessions were: EK, p. 439.

117 The worst thing: Kaufman, op. cit.

117 Strasberg explained: Seymour Peck, "The Temple of 'The Method,' " *New York Times Magazine,* May 6, 1956, p. 27.

119 Dean "listened impassively": Garfield, *A Player's Place,* p. 95.

119 Frank Corsaro later: Frank Corsaro, *Maverick* (New York: Vanguard, 1978), p. 16.

120 He told David: Garfield, *A Player's Place,* p. 94.

120 When Dean died: Robert Hethmon, *Strasberg at the Actors Studio* (New York: Viking, 1966), pp. 27–30.

120 When a reporter: Jim Cook, "Hollywood Tragedies: James Dean," *New York Post,* Nov. 28, 1955.

121 "The most important": Erskine Johnson, "N.Y. Drama Schools 'Protect' Hopefuls Against Hollywood," *Los Angeles Mirror-News,* June 23, 1955.

8: *Pleasing the Skipper*

122 Fans hold that: Walter Kerr, *New York Herald-Tribune,* Dec. 4, 1952.

123 Ayers took over: Bert McCord, "Ayers Buys *Jaguar,*" *New York Times,* Apr. 17, 1952.

125 The yacht trip: RM, p. 68.

125 The yacht was: Leah Salisbury to Therese Brandes, Sept. 23, 1969 (in Ruth and Augustus Goetz papers, University of Wisconsin, Madison, Wisconsin).

125 Rogers Brackett later: RM, p. 68.

126 "For some strange": DS.

127 Relief came in: DS.

127 He was a: "Barnstorming Bonanza Burning Out," *The Sporting News,* Oct. 22, 1952, p. 17; "Stars Nip Indees," *Dubuque Telegraph-Herald,* Oct. 12, 1952.

130 Alec Wilder wrote: AW.

130 Shirley Ayers may: William Engvick to author.

PAGE

131   Alan Brock, the: *Classic Film Collector,* Summer 1975.

132   By now, Ayers: Elliot Norton, *Boston Post,* undated clipping in *See the Jaguar* file at New York Public Library for the Performing Arts (Lincoln Center), New York City, New York.

132   (They had not: Lemuel Ayers to ANTA members, Nov. 21, 1952.

132   "He seemed completely": DS; DD, p. 83.

132   Much later, Wilder: AW.

133   Paltry funding made: Michael Gordon to author.

133   One critic would: R. E. P. Sensenderfer, *Philadelphia Evening Bulletin,* Nov. 19, 1952.

133   "He could sing": "Jimmy Dean and His Four Closest Pals," reprinted in David Dalton, ed., *James Dean Revealed!* (New York: Dell, 1991), p. 77.

134   In August, Dorothy: DK, NYJA, Aug. 14, 1952.

135   "The curling toes": RWT, pp. 38–39.

135   Elsewhere in the: RWT, p. 220.

135   "Certain aspects of": RWT, p. ii.

135   Margaret Barker, cast: Fred Fehl, *On Broadway* (Austin: University of Texas, 1978), p. 221.

136   They complained that: Evans Clinchy, *Hartford Times,* Nov. 14, 1952.

138   Back in New: Jack Shafer, "What Jimmy Dean Believed," *Modern Screen,* Oct. 1957.

9: *Lonely Shepherd of the Iroquois*

147   At that time: Charles Higham, *Brando* (New York: New American Library, 1987), p. 115.

148   Dizzy Sheridan's one: DS.

149   Bast said they: BB, p. 89.

10: *Barbara, Betsy, and Bates*

156   His screen test: Fred Zinnemann, *A Life in the Movies* (New York: Scribner's, 1992), p. 143; "Indiana Funeral for Actor Dean," *Chicago Sun-Times,* Oct. 2, 1955, p. 4.

157   She could see: DD, p. 115.

158   Dizzy Sheridan would: DS.

160   One of Dean's: The pay stub is displayed at the Fairmount Museum.

162   Spring commencement exercises: Kay Smith Harris to author.

163   Latin phrases infested: BB, p. 92.

163   Bates was a: *London Daily Telegraph,* Nov. 16, 1959; Jack Garner, "James Dean's Jeans to Be Sold by WXXI," *Rochester* (New York) *Democrat and Chronicle,* Apr. 20, 1988; obituary, *Variety,* Aug. 9, 1967.

164   The director, Jack: Garfield, *A Player's Place,* p. 95.

164   The play was: Milton Bracker, "Slow Route to Big Time," *New York Times,* Jan. 10, 1954.

PAGE

164   *End As a:* Robert Wahls, "Our Newest Producer Is a Hula Expert, Too,"
       New York Daily News, Oct. 11, 1953.

165   "The night of": DD, p. 141.

165   One of Dean's: DD, p. 79.

167   This was Jonathan: Joe Masteroff to author: résumé of director
       Sherwood Arthur at New York Public Library for the Performing Arts
       (Lincoln Center).

168   Soon after "Briefcase": John Howlett, *James Dean: A Biography* (New
       York: Simon & Schuster, 1975), pp. 55–56; DD, p. 127.

169   Martin Landau reports: DD, p. 107.

169   Wendy Sanford, a: *Chicago Sun-Times,* June 19, 1959, p. 30.

173   Patty Magda, a: Patty Magda to Hedda Hopper, Oct. 1955, in Hedda
       Hopper collection, AMPAS.

174   There were seven: VH, p. 123.

174   Dean's difficulty with: Walter Goodman, "How Some Famous Actors
       Learned to Be Who They Are," *New York Times,* Nov. 9, 1988.

11: *From Bachir to Cal*

177   Unfortunately, there was: Selected Billy Rose correspondence at New
       York Public Library for the Performing Arts (Lincoln Center).

177   The "three African": Walter Kerr, *New York Herald-Tribune,* Feb. 9,
       1954; *Variety,* Feb. 10, 1954.

179   Once Dean had: DD, p. 94.

179   While on the: Howlett, *James Dean,* p. 56.

179   Dean's return trip: Phil Ziegler to author.

180   Dean's understudy would: Hildegarde Johnson, "It's Time to Tell the
       Truth About Jimmy Dean," *Movie Parade,* Nov. 1956, p. 17.

181   Athman and other: David Diamond to author; André Gide, *Journals,*
       Vol. I (New York: Knopf, 1947), p. 348.

181   The dance that: Maurice Zolotow, "The Season On and Off Broadway,"
       Theatre Arts, Nov. 1954, p. 87.

182   In the afternoon: *"East of Eden* Star Praised by Teacher," *Marion
       Leader-Tribune,* Apr. 6, 1955, p. 1.

183   "He decided to": Kaier Curtin, *We Can Always Call Them Bulgarians*
       (Boston: Alyson, 1987), p. 312.

183   A month earlier: HR, Nov. 27, 1953, p. 2.

184   However, Mann once: Sheri Mann to author.

184   Whatever their source: RWT, p. 43.

185   Jourdan was not: Phillip Pine to author.

185   "Getting the right": Beverly Linet, "The Secret Happiness of Jimmy
       Dean, *Movie Life,* Aug. 1956.

185   "He was supposed": RWT, p. 40.

PAGE

185 A review the: Henry T. Murdock, *Philadelphia Inquirer,* Jan. 12, 1954.

186 Geraldine Page remembered: RWT, p. 41.

186 She, Dean, and: Vivian Matalon to author.

186 What struck her: RWT, p. 41.

187 Ortense and Marcus: Barbara Glenn Gordon to author.

187 At the curtain: Linet, op. cit.

189 At the end: Radie Harris, HR, May 25, 1954.

189 Schatt had never: Roy Schatt, *James Dean: A Portrait* (New York: Delilah, 1982), p. 27.

189 Another milestone was: Louis Sheaffer, "Sophocles Turns Slangy in Ezra Pound's Free Version," *Brooklyn Daily Eagle,* Feb. 17, 1954.

190 He alerted Kazan: EK, p. 534.

191 Only three days: Kazan correspondence in *East of Eden* files, WB.

191 Elsewhere, Kazan revealed: Frederic Morton, "Gadge," *Esquire,* Feb. 1957, p. 49.

192 The previous year: Zinnemann, *A Life in the Movies,* p. 143.

192 Warners executive William: HR Dec. 8, 1953, p. 2; Orr correspondence in *Battle Cry* files, WB.

192 Kazan was informed: Leith Adams and Keith Burns, eds., *James Dean: Behind the Scenes* (New York: Birch Lane, 1990), p. 18.

193 On March 5: Harry Mayer memo, Mar. 5, 1954, in Jack L. Warner Collection, WB.

193 To reassure Jack: Adams and Burns, *James Dean: Behind the Scenes,* p. 16.

194 He sat in: *New York Times,* Feb. 17, 19, 28, 1954.

194 The report most: RM, p. 84.

194 Once Schatt and: Schatt, *James Dean: A Portrait,* p. 32.

195 Actor William Redfield: Marlowe, *New York,* Nov. 8, 1976, p. 42.

195 Webb's only known: Hopper, *The Whole Truth,* p. 169.

196 Although author Joe: Susan Bluttman, "Rediscovering James Dean: The TV Legacy," *Emmy,* Oct. 1990, p. 54.

196 The director was: EK, p. 534.

12: Every Eden Has Its Eve

198 That very week: SS, NYP, Apr. 15, 1954.

198 Director Nicholas Ray: NR.

199 According to Bill: BB, p. 99.

199 Stopping by Clayton's: Terry Moore, *The Beauty and the Billionaire* (New York: Pocket, 1984), p. 282.

199 Moore was an: See, for example, Michael Case, "The Plot Against Terry Moore," *Motion Picture,* Mar. 1955, pp. 60–61.

PAGE

200 Dean looked up: Gene Owen, "An Unforgettable Day with Jimmy Dean," *Movieland,* Feb. 1957.

202 The *East of: East of Eden* files, WB.

202 Kazan initially hoped: EK to Paul Osborn, Apr. 19, 1954, Osborn papers, University of Wisconsin, Madison, Wisconsin.

202 In fact, Kazan: EK, p. 535.

202 In shooting Massey's: Raymond Massey, *A Hundred Different Lives* (Boston: Little, Brown, 1979), p. 377.

203 "She says that": Alice Hoffman, "Change of Heart," *Modern Screen,* Dec. 1954.

203 Angeli's romantic pride: Debbie Reynolds, *My Life* (New York: Morrow, 1988), p. 126.

203 Doubly devastated, Angeli: Hoffman, op. cit.

204 Hollywood commentators felt: EJ, *Motion Picture,* Oct. 1954, p. 4.

204 June 14 was: *Silver Chalice* files, WB.

204 That Saturday was: Cal York, *Photoplay,* Nov. 1954, p. 26.

204 On Sunday she: KR, LAMN, June 22, 1954.

204 When Dean had: Lee Ferrero to Ned Moss, *Silver Chalice* files, WB.

204 Being attracted to: Helen Weller, "I'm on My Own Now," *Motion Picture,* Dec. 1954, p. 68.

204 "Pier talked about": Kirk Douglas, *The Ragman's Son* (New York: Simon & Schuster, 1988), p. 194.

204 "Everything about Pier": KR, LAMN, Aug. 16 & 30, 1954.

205 One Sunday afternoon: Owen, op. cit.

205 In late June: SS, HCN, June 28 & July 6, 1954.

205 Just after Skolsky: LOP, NYJA, July 11, 1954; LOP, *Chicago American,* July 16, 1954.

206 "Reason James Dean's": DV, July 9, 1954.

206 "I was anxious": "Interview with Elia Kazan," *American Film,* March 1976; EK, p. 537.

206 Julie Harris remembers: VH, p. 146.

207 For the sake: EK, p. 537.

207 Kazan had the: News releases in *East of Eden* files, WB.

207 Press accounts of: EK, p. 538.

208 The next day: Peter Manso, *Brando: The Biography* (New York: Hyperion, 1994), p. 291.

208 "Along came Jimmy": VH, p. 151; Dick Clayton to author.

209 Mike Connolly of: HR, Aug. 25, 1954.

209 Erskine Johnson claimed: EJ, LAMN, July 30, 1954.

209 Louella Parsons wrote: LOP, NYJA, Aug. 28, 1954.

209 "I drove him": Hoffman, op. cit.

209 Dean and Reynolds: NYJA, Aug. 27, 1954, p. 1.

PAGE

210 Two nights after: HR, Aug. 30, 1954, p. 2; SG, "Christmas Dreams," *Photoplay,* Dec. 1954.

210 She and Dean: HR, Sept. 7, 1954, p. 2.

210 She even turned: HR, Sept. 14, 1954, p. 2; SG, HCN, Sept. 28, 1954; SS, NYP, Sept. 21, 1954; HR, Sept. 23, 1954, p. 2; HH, LAT, Sept. 25, 1954.

211 In the wake: HR, Sept. 24, 1954, p. 2; SS, NYP, Sept. 27, 1954; Case, op. cit.

211 Having seen Dean: KR, LAMN, Sept. 24, 1954.

211 Kazan was now: EK to Paul Osborn, undated, Osborn papers, University of Wisconsin.

212 On the day: DV, Sept. 22 & 24, 1954.

212 Angeli went to: DV, Sept. 29, 1954, p. 1; Bob Thomas, "She Accepted!" *Motion Picture,* Jan. 1955; Alice Hoffman, "All of a Sudden, My Heart Sings," *Modern Screen,* Jan. 1955.

212 Damone had told: SS, NYP, July 4, 1954.

213 In July he: DV, July 27 & 30, 1954.

213 Then, less than: SS, NYP, Sept. 28, 1954.

213 When Angeli was: Thomas, op. cit.; DK, NYJA, June 1 & July 3, 1952; DV, July 2 & 3, 1952.

213 Despite the startling: "Death of Dean in Auto Crash Stuns Hollywood," *New York Post,* Oct. 2, 1955.

213 "She broke the": KR, LAMN, Nov. 2, 1954.

214 Invitations were a: HR, Dec. 9, 1954, p. 2.

214 Various scribes reported: SS, NYP, Dec. 1, 1954; HR, Dec. 7, 1954.

214 "I hate to": SG, HCN, Nov. 3, 1954.

214 "Pier Angeli and": HR, Dec. 1, 1954, p. 2.

214 "Check with the": SS, NYP, Dec. 24, 1954.

214 The baby, a: LOP, *Modern Screen,* Nov. 1955, p. 10.

215 Although Dean had: HR, June 22 & 23, 1954.

216 Leonard Rosenman said: VH, p. 158; DD, p. 198.

216 "We've got to": KR, LAMN, Aug. 16 & 30, 1954.

216 During the days: HR, July 26, 1954, p. 2.

216 Shortly after Dean: "Hollywood Tragedies," *New York Post,* Nov. 28, 1955, p. 4.

13: *Meet the Press*

217 Hollywood was then: John Francis Kreidl, *Nicholas Ray* (New York: Twayne, 1977), p. 63.

218 "The replacement chosen": RWT, p. 52.

218 Although Dean cooperated: Hopper, *The Whole Truth,* p. 171.

220 "Against a wall": HH, LAT, July 7, 1954.

220 Much later, chatting: Hopper, *The Whole Truth,* p. 170.

PAGE

220 Louella Parsons had: LOP, *Cosmopolitan,* Mar. 1955, p. 44.

221 Sheilah Graham's distaste: SG, HCN, Aug. 17, 1954.

221 Mike Connolly of: HR, July 7, 1954, p. 2.

222 To spice up: DV, July 27, 1954, p. 2.

222 "People were telling": PS.

222 One of the: DV, Apr. 22, 1954, p. 2.

222 Soon after that: KR, LAMN, Aug. 16, 1954.

222 For a time: HR, Feb. 1 & Mar. 14, 1955; DV, Mar. 7, 1955; SS, HCN, June 16, 1955; SG, HCN, Aug. 12, 1954; LOP, *Modern Screen,* Mar. 1955, p. 12; *Movie Secrets,* Dec. 1955 (cover).

223 Everyone knew Dean: EK, p. 538.

223 Terry Moore recalled: Terry Moore, *The Beauty and the Billionaire,* p. 284.

223 **To Philip Scheuer: PS.**

223 One significant difference: SG, HCN, Nov. 3, 1954.

223 Brando's first encounter: Bob Thomas, *Marlon: Portrait of the Rebel as an Artist* (New York: Random House, 1973), p. 62.

224 Dean could still: HR, Dec. 17, 1954, p. 4.

224 After Hedda Hopper's: Hopper, *The Whole Truth,* p. 169.

224 On December 9: Hendricks to Jack Warner, Dec. 9, 1954, WB.

224 Connolly, arguably the: HR, Dec. 10, 1954; Feb. 4, 24, and 25, 1955.

225 While Connolly was: SG, HCN, Jan. 20 and Feb. 18, 1955; DV, Feb. 25, 1955.

225 When *East of:* HR, Mar. 16, 21, 1955; SS, NYP, Mar. 21, 1955.

225 After less than: DV, Mar. 31, 1955; HR, Mar. 25, 1955.

225 The increased coverage: PS.

226 On February 11: Adams and Burns, *James Dean: Behind the Scenes,* p. 69.

226 "When contacted at": *Marion Leader-Tribune,* Feb. 15, 1955, p. 12.

226 Right Before Dean's: KR, LAMN, Sept. 2, 1955; SG, HCN, Sept. 15, 1955.

227 He never spelled: Bob Thomas, Associated Press dispatch, May 1955 (fragment).

227 Erskine Johnson of: EJ, LAMN, June 3, 28, 1955.

227 Hyams was so: Joe Hyams, *New York Herald-Tribune,* June 30, 1955, p.19.

228 She did note: LOP, NYJA, Mar. 3, 1955.

228 While many columnists: SG, HCN, Mar. 22, 1955.

230 To Scheuer, he: PS.

230 The interview with: HT.

231 In the Hopper: Hopper, *The Whole Truth,* p. 172.

232 Mike Connolly conducted: Mike Connolly, "This Was My Friend, Jimmy Dean," *Modern Screen,* Dec. 1955.

PAGE

14: *The Symptoms of Fame*

234 Kazan had witnessed: EK, p. 535.

234 While Kazan was: Hethmon, *Strasberg at the Actors Studio,* pp. 27–28.

235 "When Jimmy came": AW.

235 Brackett had recently: RM, p. 113.

236 Dean had purchased: Receipt displayed at Fairmount Museum.

237 Dean's other business: Robert Lewis, *Slings and Arrows* (Briarcliff Manor, N.Y.: Stein and Day, 1984), pp. 230–231.

237 He brought Roy: Schatt, *James Dean: A Portrait,* pp. 38, 112–115.

238 Bidding New York: HR, Sept. 7, 1954, p. 2; LOP, NYJA, Sept. 13, 1954.

238 This had been: HR, Aug. 9 & Sept. 9, 1954; DD, p. 199.

238 In the face: Clayton to author.

238 Meanwhile, according to: NR.

239 Then on October: R. J. Obringer to JD, Apr. 2, 1955, WB.

239 Nicholas Ray had: HH, LAT, Sept. 27, 1954; HR, Sept. 27, 1954.

239 One day Dean: NR.

239 As a matter: DV, July 1, 1954, p. 2; Harold Hutchings, "Stevens Gives His Appraisal of Dean," *Chicago Sunday Tribune,* Oct. 21, 1956.

240 Stevens, whose first: Ibid.

240 Even though he: Warners internal memoranda, George Stevens papers, AMPAS.

240 The press would: HR, Dec. 24, 1954, Mar. 17, 1955.

240 She attended the: VH, p. 177.

241 Although Wynn was: Ned Wynn, *We Will Always Live in Beverly Hills* (New York: Morrow, 1990), p. 92.

241 Although Wynn was: SG, HCN, Apr. 4, 1955.

241 He also brought: VH, p. 153.

242 A year earlier: DV, Apr. 8, July 26, 1954; HR, June 14, Aug. 5, 1954; SG, HCN, Aug. 6, 1954; Eartha Kitt, *Confessions of a Sex Kitten* (New York: Barricade, 1989), pp. 137–141.

242 With Nurmi and: NR.

243 Dunnock remembered his: VH, p. 123.

243 The *Hollywood Reporter:* HR, Nov. 11, 1954, p. 10.

243 Both trade papers: HR, Nov. 16, 1954, p. 10; DV, Nov. 15, 1954.

244 At Nicholas Ray's: DV, Nov. 23, 1954, p. 2.

244 Many scenes of: BE, p. 236.

244 "It was exploratory": NR.

244 Dean met many: Dennis Stock, *James Dean Revisited* (New York: Penguin, 1978), p. 14.

244 Screenwriter Andrew Solt: BE, pp. 526–527.

244 On December 1: SS, HCN, Mar. 25, 1955.

PAGE

245 By December, *East:* Don Bachardy to author.

245 The *Hollywood Reporter:* HR, Dec. 8, 1954, p. 2.

245 There were two: W. Bagnall to Jack Warner, Dec. 7, 1954, WB.

245 A bewildered Kazan: EK, p. 538.

245 Also in the: Bagnall to Warner.

245 The second sneak: HR, Dec. 10, 1954, p. 2.

246 At week's end: HR, Dec. 14, 1954, p. 2.

247 *Daily Variety* didn't: DV, Dec. 14, 1954; HR, Dec. 14, 1954, p. 14.

247 When he arrived: Jane Deacy to JD, displayed at Fairmount Museum.

247 Flying to New: BE, p. 237.

247 They dined together: NR.

247 Dean spent both: Schatt, *James Dean: A Portrait,* pp. 87, 107.

247 Later Dean was: Hildegarde Johnson, "It's Time to Tell the Truth About Jimmy Dean," *Movie Parade,* Nov. 1956, p. 51.

248 Although this broadcast: NR.

248 Later in the: Hildegarde Johnson, op. cit., pp. 50–51.

249 "Jimmy was determined": Evelyn Bigsby, "He Had a Little Boy Lost Quality," *TV-Radio Life,* May 1956.

249 One evening at: "Singer Sues for Loss of Leg," *New York Herald-Tribune,* Jan. 30, 1954, p. 7.

249 According to Bill: BB, p. 127.

250 After the session: Toni Lee Scott, *A Kind of Loving* (New York: World Publishing, 1970), pp. 77–81.

250 Dean spent some: DV, Jan. 27, 28, 31, 1955.

251 Later that night: KR, LAMN, Jan. 29, 1955; SS, NYP, Feb. 2, 1955.

251 A few days: HR, Jan. 26, 1955, p. 2.

251 "If you get": KR, LAMN, Jan. 29, 1955.

251 Largely on the: BE, p. 238.

252 Pat Hardy drove: Evelyn Bigsby, op. cit.

253 Dean's new policy: AN.

253 "He hadn't changed": *Screen Stories,* Nov. 1956, p. 86.

254 When Dean called: DD, pp. 210–211.

255 Ironically, *Daily Variety:* DV, Mar. 3, 1955, p. 2.

255 Although he did: Randall Riese, *The Unabridged James Dean* (Chicago: Contemporary, 1991), p. 524.

255 During March, Dean: WB.

15: *Finish Line*

256 "Sometimes Jimmy'd do": PH.

256 "James Dean calls": HR, Nov. 24, 1954, p. 2.

257 Three years earlier: BW.

257 Announcing the acquisition: DD, p. 192.

PAGE

257   "Everybody figured it": "His Love Destroyed Him," *Modern Screen,* Feb. 1957.

257   On September 21: Lee Raskin, *We Remember Dean International* (newsletter), Apr. 1988.

258   Certainly some of: Roy Schatt, *James Dean: A Portrait,* p. 31; Warren Newton Beath, *The Death of James Dean* (London: Sidgwick & Jackson, 1986), p. 25.

258   To Gene Owen: Gene Owen, "An Unforgettable Day with Jimmy Dean," *Movieland,* Feb. 1957, p. 75; Mike Connolly, "This Was My Friend, Jimmy Dean," *Modern Screen,* Dec. 1955, p. 80; Sanford Roth, "The Assignment I'll Never Forget," *Popular Photography,* July 1962, p. 71; PS; "His Love Destroyed Him," op. cit., pp. 65–66.

258   Virtually all of: Leonard Rosenman, "Jimmy Dean: Giant Legend, Cult Rebel," *Los Angeles Times Calendar,* Dec. 18, 1977, p. 70; Frank Corsaro to author; Stewart Stern to author.

258   Correspondence from two: Joe Hyams, *James Dean: Little Boy Lost,* pp. 179, 215.

258   Although he publicly: Derek Prouse, *Sight and Sound,* Winter 1955, p. 61.

259   Of his work: RWT, p. 242.

259   "To work with": NR.

259   His one strong: Patrick McGilligan, ed., *Backstory II: Interviews with Screenwriters of the 1940s and 1950s* (Berkeley: University of California Press, 1991), p. 287.

259   Uris began working: BE, p. 234.

259   Ray hired Irving: BE, p. 237.

260   When it was: Nicholas Ray, "Story into Script," *Sight and Sound,* Autumn 1956, p. 74.

260   Once Stewart Stern: BE, p. 239.

261   When Ray had: Christine White to author.

261   Since the test: DV, Mar. 24, 1955, p. 2.

261   Then he led: RWT, p. 106.

262   As Dean rested: DD, p. 246.

262   The picture had: BE, p. 244.

262   "Lili Kardell and": SS, HCN, Apr. 18, 1955.

263   The actual damage: Adams and Burns, *James Dean: Behind the Scenes,* p. 94.

263   To prepare for: Jim Backus, *Rocks on the Roof* (New York: Putnam, 1958), p. 155.

263   The scheme of: HR, Apr. 5, 1955, p. 2.

263   "He talks to": SS, NYP, June 19, 1955.

263   "We did the": HC, "Dean Terrorizes Film Set," *Los Angeles Herald Express,* May 21, 1955.

PAGE

264   Another reporter suggested: EJ, LAMN, June 10, 1955.

264   Backus, recovering from: DV, May 2, 1955, p. 2.

264   Dean became fond: Hank Klibanoff, "James Dean, Rebel," *Washington Post,* Sept. 30, 1955; Doran speech in Marion, Indiana, Sept. 29, 1985.

264   Late in May: SS, HCN, May 25, 1955.

265   He had ceased: HR, Apr. 18, 1955, p. 2.

265   For example, with: DV, Apr. 8, 1955, p. 2.

265   On a subsequent: HR, May 11, 1955, p. 2.

265   Lili Kardell, Dean's: KR, LAMN, Mar. 30, 1955.

265   But Dean's name: Lori Nelson, "The Dean I've Dated," *Motion Picture,* Sept. 1955; HR, Apr. 4, July 15, 1955, p. 2; HR, Apr. 26, 1955, p. 2; DV, Apr. 29, 1955, p. 2; SS, HCN, May 23, 1955.

265   The owner showed: SS, "Demon Dean," *Photoplay,* July 1955.

266   Gilmore would spend: JG, pp. 94, 118.

266   They had resumed: SS, HCN, Mar. 22, 1955.

266   Kendis Rochlen queried: KR, LAMN, Mar. 28, 1955.

267   Trouble was rumored: DV, Apr. 8, 1955, p. 2.

267   The following year: Mike Connolly, *Screen Stories,* Aug. 1956, p. 8.

267   In early May: *Akron Beacon Journal,* May 3, 1955, p. 14.

267   Finally, columnist Sheilah: SG, HCN, June 2, 1955.

267   Roger Donoghue recalled: BE, p. 252.

268   He refused to: DV, May 2, 1955, p. 2.

268   On May 18: DV, May 19, 1955, p. 2.

268   Because *Rebel* had: DV, Apr. 25, 1955, p. 2.

269   According to columnist: EJ, LAMN, June 6, 1955.

269   From an unlucky: Gus Vignolle, "Career Closes After Three Races," *Motoracing,* Mar. 9–16, 1956, p. 8.

269   According to Sidney: SS, NYP, June 19, 1955.

269   Three months earlier: HT.

270   The first of: CB, p. 124.

270   Word of the: DV, June 27, 1955, p. 2.

270   Stevens's show of: Adams and Burns, *James Dean: Behind the Scenes,* p. 136.

271   Once again, *Daily:* DV, July 25 & 26, 1955.

271   Stevens had pretty: Memorandum in George Stevens papers, AMPAS.

272   Only a few: KR, LAMN, Aug. 5, 1955.

272   Even though she: DV, Aug. 4, 1955, p. 2.

272   "The boy's so": KR, LAMN, Aug. 5, 1955.

272   The most specific: *Screen Stories,* Nov. 1956, p. 84.

273   Stevens also admitted: Hollis Alpert, "It's Dean, Dean, Dean," *Saturday Review,* Oct. 13, 1956, pp. 28–29.

273   A reporter who: John Bustin, *Austin Statesman,* June 28, 1955.

PAGE

273   Rock Hudson told: Interview transcript in George Stevens papers, AMPAS.

273   The eventual review: Penelope Huston, *Sight and Sound,* Winter 1956, p. 48.

273   She called him: DV, Aug. 1, 1955, p. 2.

273   Later she wrote: Ferber to JD, letter displayed in Fairmount Museum.

274   Although he still: HR, July 19, Aug. 3, 1955.

274   Their names: DV, July 28, 1955, p. 2.

274   "Dean surprised regulars": SS, NYP, Aug. 18, 1955.

274   "Even James Dean": DV, Aug. 31, 1955, p. 2; HR, Aug. 31, 1955, p. 2.

274   Later, Andress explained: Vi Swisher, "Thanks for Everything," *Movieland,* May 1956.

274   Andress accompanied Dean: Ibid.

274   Dean told one: Mike Connolly, "This Was My Friend, Jimmy Dean," *Modern Screen,* Dec. 1955.

274   Their romance, however: HR, Sept. 9 & 29, 1955.

274   Perhaps that is: HC, *Los Angeles Herald Express,* Sept. 14, 1955.

275   Many other projects: HR, May 26, Aug. 12, 1955; HR, June 22 & 28, 1955; SS, NYP, Sept. 26, 1955; LOP, NYJA, Apr. 14, 1955.

275   "In those final": PH.

275   At the Talk: "His Love Destroyed Him," op. cit.

275   Racing it around: SG, HCN, Sept. 21, 1955.

276   Just over three: AM.

276   "When I first": PH.

276   Back in Hollywood: DV, Oct. 3, 1955, p. 2; HR, Oct. 3, 1955, p. 2.

277   Throughout the next: DV, Oct. 5, 1955, p. 2.

277   It was filmed: HR, Aug. 1, 1955, p. 2.

277   When Elia Kazan: Elaine Steinbeck to author.

278   Another year would: DV, Dec. 9, 1955, p. 2.

278   Even Brando, after: Manso, *Brando,* pp. 381–386.

278   Commenting on the: Leonard Rosenman, op. cit.

279   When *Giant* was: *Time,* Oct. 22, 1956, pp. 108–110.

279   Of all the: NR.

279   "a current from": John Updike, "This Side of Coherence," *The New Yorker,* June 27, 1994, p. 194.

Bibliography

Books

Backus, Jim. *Rocks on the Roof*. New York: Putnam, 1958.

Baker, Carroll. *Baby Doll*. New York: Dell, 1985.

Berle, Milton. *Milton Berle: An Autobiography*. New York: Delacorte, 1978.

Bosworth, Patricia. *Montgomery Clift*. New York: Harcourt, 1978.

Brando, Marlon. *Songs My Mother Taught Me*. New York: Random House, 1994.

Collins, Joan. *Past Imperfect*. New York: Simon & Schuster, 1984.

Corsaro, Frank. *Maverick*. New York: Vanguard, 1978.

Curtin, Kaier. *We Can Always Call Them Bulgarians*. Boston: Alyson, 1987.

Curtis, Tony, and Barry Paris. *Tony Curtis: The Autobiography*. New York: Morrow, 1993.

Cronyn, Hume. *A Terrible Liar*. New York: Morrow, 1991.

Dalton, David. *James Dean: American Icon*. New York: St. Martin's, 1984.

Davis, Sammy Jr. *Yes I Can*. New York: Farrar, Straus, 1965.

Douglas, Kirk. *The Ragman's Son*. New York: Simon & Schuster, 1988.

Gooch, Brad. *City Poet: The Life and Times of Frank O'Hara*. New York: Knopf, 1993.

Gottlieb, Polly Rose. *The Nine Lives of Billy Rose*. New York: Crown, 1968.

Guinness, Alec. *Blessings in Disguise*. New York: Knopf, 1986.

Higham, Charles. *Brando: The Unauthorized Biography*. New York: New American Library, 1987.

Houghton, Norris. *Entrances and Exits: A Life In and Out of the Theatre*. New York: Limelight, 1991.

Kitt, Eartha. *Confessions of a Sex Kitten*. New York: Barricade, 1989.

Kreidl, John Francis. *Nicholas Ray*. New York: Twayne, 1977.

Levant, Oscar. *The Unimportance of Being Oscar*. New York: Putnam, 1968.

Lewis, Robert. *Slings and Arrows.* Briarcliff Manor, N.Y.: Stein and Day, 1984.

McGilligan, Patrick. *Jack's Life: A Biography of Jack Nicholson.* New York: Norton, 1994.

Manso, Peter. *Brando: The Biography.* New York: Hyperion, 1994.

Massey, Raymond. *A Hundred Different Lives.* Boston: Little, Brown, 1979.

Minnelli, Vincente. *I Remember It Well.* New York: Doubleday, 1974.

Moore, Leonard J. *Citizen Klansmen: The Ku Klux Klan in Indiana, 1921–1928.* Chapel Hill: University of North Carolina Press, 1991.

Moore, Terry. *The Beauty and the Billionaire.* New York: Pocket, 1984.

Neal, Patricia. *As I Am.* New York: Simon & Schuster, 1988.

Reynolds, Debbie. *My Life.* New York: Morrow, 1988.

Riese, Randall. *The Unabridged James Dean: His Life and Legacy from A to Z.* Chicago: Contemporary, 1991.

Schary, Dore. *Heyday: An Autobiography.* Boston: Little, Brown, 1979.

Scott, Toni Lee. *A Kind of Loving.* New York: World Publishing, 1970.

Stern, Phil. *Phil Stern's Hollywood.* New York: Knopf, 1993.

Strasberg, Susan. *Bittersweet.* New York: Putnam, 1980.

Thomas, Bob. *Marlon, Portrait of the Rebel as an Artist.* New York: Random House, 1973.

Torme, Mel. *It Wasn't All Velvet.* New York: Viking, 1988.

Tynan, Kenneth. *Bull Fever.* New York: Atheneum, 1966.

Van Doren, Mamie. *Playing the Field.* New York: Putnam, 1987.

Wade, Wyn Craig. *The Fiery Cross.* New York: Simon & Schuster, 1987.

Wakefield, Dan. *New York in the Fifties.* Boston: Houghton, 1992.

Wilk, Max, ed., *The Golden Age of Television.* New York: Delacorte, 1976.

Williams, Tennessee. *Five O'Clock Angel: Letters of Tennessee Williams to Maria St. Just.* New York: Knopf, 1990.

Winters, Shelley. *Shelley II.* New York: Simon & Schuster, 1989.

Wynn, Ned. *We Will Always Live in Beverly Hills.* New York: Morrow, 1990.

Zinnemann, Fred. *A Life in the Movies.* New York: Scribner's, 1992.

Articles

Acocella, Joan. "Perfectly Frank" (review of Brad Gooch's *City Poet: The Life and Times of Frank O'Hara*). *The New Yorker,* July 19, 1993, pp. 71–78.

Bluttman, Susan. "Rediscovering James Dean: The TV Legacy." *Emmy,* Oct. 1990, p. 50.

Bracker, Milton. "Slow Route to Big Time" (on *End As a Man*). *New York Times,* Jan. 10, 1954, Sec. II, p. 3.

"The Enigma of James Dean." *Delta,* Summer 1962.

Hendrickson, Paul. "Remembering James Dean Back Home in Indiana." *Los Angeles Times Calendar,* July 22, 1973, p. 22.

Holley, Val. "H. L. Mencken and the Indiana Genii." *Traces of Indiana and Midwestern History,* Winter 1991.

Hoover, Dwight. "Daisy Douglas Barr: From Quaker to Klan 'Kluckeress.' " *Indiana Magazine of History,* June 1991, pp. 171–195.

Hutchings, Harold. "The Woman Behind James Dean." *Chicago Sunday Tribune Magazine,* Mar. 3, 1957, p. 20.

"Interview with Elia Kazan." *American Film,* March 1976.

Jennings, Tom. "Santa Monica College Celebrates Sixty Wild Years." *Santa Monica Outlook,* Nov. 10, 1989.

Klibanoff, Hank. "James Dean, Rebel." *Washington Post,* Sept. 30, 1985.

Kozinn, Allan. "Moondog Returns from the Hippie Years." *The New York Times,* Nov. 16, 1989.

Lehman, David. "A Poet in the Heart of Noise" (review of Brad Gooch's *City Poet: The Life and Times of Frank O'Hara*). *New York Times Book Review,* June 20, 1993, p. 18.

Menand, Louis. "The Last Emperor" (review of Sally Bedell Smith's *In All His Glory* [biography of William S. Paley], Simon & Schuster, 1990). *The New Yorker,* Feb. 18, 1991.

Morton, Frederic. "Actors' Studio." *Esquire,* Dec. 1955.

Poling, James. "Programs Packaged to Go" ("Beat the Clock"). *Collier's,* May 24, 1952, p. 22.

Ray, Nicholas. "Story into Script." *Sight and Sound,* Autumn 1956.

Roth, Sanford. "The Assignment I'll Never Forget: Jimmy Dean." *Popular Photography,* July 1962.

Sheaffer, Louis. "Sophocles Turns Slangy in Ezra Pound's Free Version." *Brooklyn Daily Eagle,* Feb. 17, 1954.

"Shurr's Deacy to Open Own Talent Agency." *Variety,* Aug. 20, 1952.

Sragow, Michael. "The Method of 'The Method' " (review of Steven Vineberg's *Method Actors: Three Generations of an American Acting Style,* Schirmer, 1991). *The New Yorker,* Jan. 20, 1992.

Stern, Jane and Michael, "Cafeteria." *The New Yorker,* Aug. 1, 1988.

Swisher, Vi. "Thanks for Everything." *Movieland,* May 1956.

Tomkins, Calvin. "A Touch for the Now." *The New Yorker,* July 29, 1991, p. 40.

Wahls, Robert. "Our Newest Producer Is a Hula Expert, Too" (profile of Claire Heller). *New York Daily News,* Oct. 11, 1953.

Wilson, William. "Wally Berman, Semina Figure." *Los Angeles Times,* June 5, 1992.

Zolotow, Maurice. "The Season On and Off Broadway." *Theatre Arts,* Nov. 1954, p. 87.

Index

3592